Bl[...]

D0648477

WAI-WAI

NICHOLAS GUPPY

WAI-WAI

THROUGH THE FORESTS
NORTH OF THE AMAZON

John Murray

FIFTY ALBEMARLE STREET LONDON

Printed in Great Britain by
Butler & Tanner Ltd, Frome and London
and published by John Murray (Publishers) Ltd

To

DR. BASSETT MAGUIRE

and

THE NEW YORK BOTANICAL GARDEN

in admiration of their work

in the Botanical Exploration of

northern South America

Contents

CONTENTS

Part Three

FROG INDIAN COUNTRY

Part Four

OUT OF THE FOREST

Illustrations

From photographs by the author

ILLUSTRATIONS

Acknowledgements

The author wishes to thank many colleagues and friends for their help: in particular Dr. Bassett Maguire and Dr. Richard Cowan of the New York Botanical Garden, and Dr. Alston of the British Museum, for their identifications of plants; Miss Jacqueline Engert and Mrs. Osyth Leeston for their reading of the manuscript; Miss Belinda Brooks and Miss Deirdre O'Connor for their heroic typing; Mr. Peter Denman, Lord Doune, Mr. and Mrs. Max Pearson, his aunt, Mrs. H. B. Hill, and Mr. and Mrs. L. V. Williamson of Burningford Hall Hotel, Dunsfold, Surrey, for providing havens where much of the work was done; and his publisher for his patience. Above all he wishes to thank his mother for great encouragement.

"To what purpose, we say, is a bird placed in the woods of Cayenne with a bill a yard long, making a noise like a puppy dog, and laying eggs in hollow trees? The toucan, to be sure, might retort, to what purpose were gentlemen in Bond Street created? To what purpose were certain foolish, prating Members of Parliament created, pestering the House of Commons with their ignorance and folly, and impeding the business of the country? There is no end to such questions."

—Sidney Smith: review of Waterton's
Wanderings in South America
in the *Edinburgh Review,* 1826

PART ONE

Land of the Wai-Wais

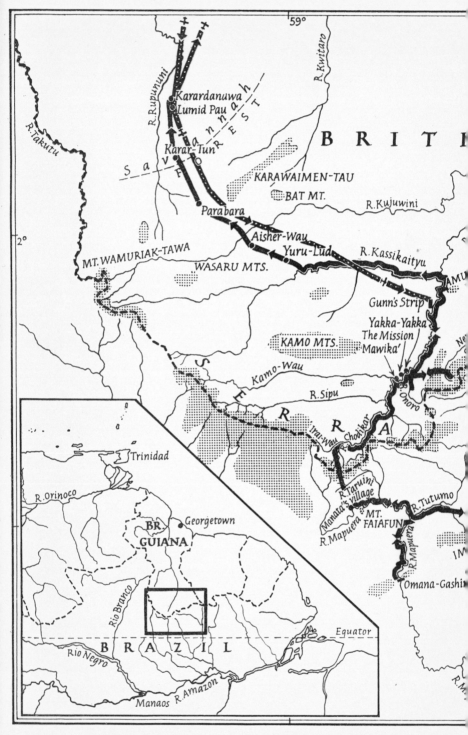

SKETCH MAP OF

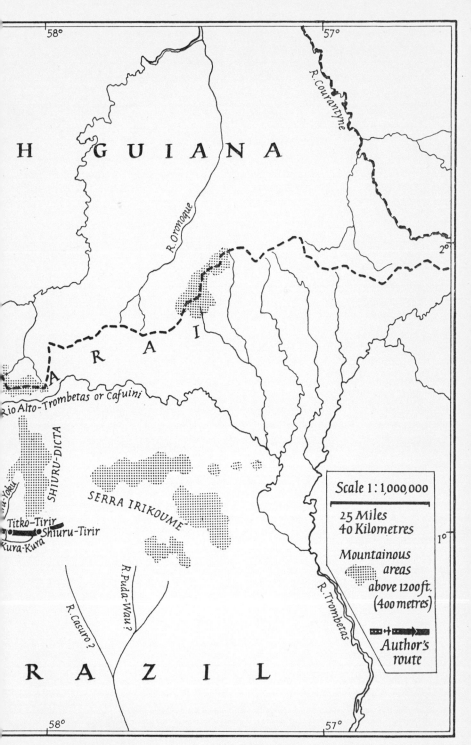

ACARAI REGION

I

The Flight

It was the weather that worried me. For nearly a month we had had constant sunshine in Georgetown, the capital of British Guiana, but where I was going, on the borders of Brazil, the rainy season was not yet quite over. And it was most important for my plans that it should be—for we intended to try to bring the plane down in the middle of the vast forests that stretch from the savannahs south to the Amazon, in a tiny patch of swampy grassland, called Gunn's Strip, which during the war had been cleared of bushes as a possible emergency landing-ground.

It was flooded for half the year, and of the very few flights that had been made there the last had been nearly disastrous: it had taken three weeks to dig the Dakota out of the soft ground and drain the strip sufficiently for it to get off again. Colonel Williams, chief of British Guiana Airways, and a great pioneer of forest flying, who would be my pilot, was a little doubtful if we could land there at all in mid-September. If we had to turn back, the flight would have been a most expensive waste of time—and it would mean weeks of overland trekking and canoe travel, burdened with heavy equipment and supplies.

It was therefore very anxiously that each morning I drove from my office—the Forest Department headquarters—to the flying-boat station a few miles up the Demerara River to tune in to an American missionary who for three years had been living among the Wai-Wai Indians near Gunn's Strip. With his mission as base my plan was to explore southwards into the almost unknown jungles of the upper Essequebo River region, along the Brazilian border, and in Brazil itself. Seated in the radio room overlooking the mile-wide chocolate-coloured river, on which floated bauxite ships, strange rafts of timber

3

with little palm-thatched houses on them, canoes, amphibian
flying-boats, I would listen through the crackling of static and
interference from stronger stations to his faint voice telling me
that there had been no rain, that during the night an inch had
fallen in a storm, that the sun was shining, or the sky overcast.
But now for several days the weather had been smiling: and at
last, three days before our tentative flight date, came the news
that the strip was firm.

Three years before, my friend Dr. Cennyd Jones had returned
from a two weeks' visit to the villages of the Wai-Wais. His
photographs were astonishing. They showed that there still
existed in the far south of the colony a tribe untouched by
civilization, marvellous in the beauty of their painted bodies
and feather ornaments.

The Wai-Wais were said to be the legendary White Indians,
and many fabulous tales were told about their land—of villages
of women, of aquatic people, of a city of Indians deep in the
jungle. Jones himself had seen, living among them, men of two
tribes whose names I could not find in any of the literature
on South American Indians—the Mawayáns and Fishkalienas.
The great unmapped forests between the savannahs and the
Amazon had still many secrets to yield—but why should the
government send me to a region to which few men had ever
been, almost inaccessible, and unlikely to be developed for
generations?

My work as a botanist in the Forest Department took me far
into the interior of British Guiana. I travelled across savannahs,
up great rivers, into mountains, surveying the forests and collecting their plants. Scarcely anywhere was the whole immense
territory even inhabited, nowhere adequately mapped—and the
least known part of it lay in the extreme south, in the country
of the wild and beautiful Wai-Wais. I longed to go there and
see them—and how many unknown plants, how many new and
strange things awaited discovery there, in the mountains along
the Brazilian border—the mysterious Serra Acarai, a rugged,
densely-forested range rising between the waters of Guiana and
those of the Amazon!

Only once had a botanist visited the Serra Acarai, and then
only for a short while on the British side—and the whole area

4

south of them was quite unknown. But it was not only to see the Wai-Wais and collect new species that I wanted to go there —it was to examine the nature of the forests themselves. From all that was known there had never been more than a few hundred inhabitants in the region, and east of Wai-Wai land, round the New River, there might never have been any at all. Forests so completely virgin were almost unique upon earth, and it was important that they should be studied while they were still undisturbed—especially as they were also likely to be extremely ancient in type, for the Acarai Mountains were thought to have remained above a shallow sea that covered the greater part of Guiana between 25,000 and a million years ago, during the great Ice Ages of Pleistocene or late Tertiary times: in which case their flora must be directly descended from that which survived then.

I was trying to develop a theory to account for the distribution of the different vegetation types in Guiana, and it was most important from my point of view, therefore, to examine these forests; but such work alone, interesting though its results might be, was for a long while held to be of insufficient urgency to justify an expedition. Then, unexpectedly, the New York Botanical Garden gave the Forest Department a sum to use for plant-collecting, which once accepted had to be used—and missionaries moved into Wai-Wai territory and reopened Gunn's Strip. This gave me my chance: several forest products were already being flown to the coast from various parts of the interior—why not also from Gunn's Strip? I thought of as many commercial possibilities as I could with which to tempt my chief: I might find new forests of balata trees, from which came a rubber-like gum used in manufacturing submarine cables, machine belts, and golf balls; I might find stands of wild rubber, Brazil nuts, oil plants, or new medicinal plants used by the Indians—extracts of curare arrow-poison had already become important in abdominal surgery, and the Wai-Wais might have new kinds or modes of preparation; or I might find being used by them or neighbouring tribes something like the remarkable contraceptives, apparently oral, by means of which the women of one tribe were reported to be able to stop their menstrual periods for years at a time without ill effect—during

5

which time, of course, they could not conceive. Even the rock specimens I brought back might lead to mineral discoveries. In any case, I argued, now that it was becoming more accessible, we ought to know something about such a region.

To my delight my chief, Dennys Fanshawe, was as enthusiastic as I, and the expedition soon had official approval. And because our objectives were largely scientific the Government of the State of Para granted me permission to enter Brazil: I had *carte blanche* to wander as widely as I could—indeed, the further I went the better.

But I knew that in such a land, smothered in 120-foot-high forest, with only a compass and vague, conflicting maps to guide me, where I should get to and what I should see would be very much a matter of luck.

For more than a month now I had been organizing the trip: calculating the amount of work to be done and the number of men I should need for cutting trails, felling trees, carrying the equipment; purchasing rations, finding, borrowing or buying camp, surveying and scientific equipment, medical and photographic supplies, and much else; and packing all this into cases so that each weighed sixty to eighty pounds, a moderate load for a man. (One hundred pounds was usually held to be a standard load, but it seemed likely that the going would be a little rough.)

Much thought had to be given to the trade goods needed for paying the men. For the semi-civilized Wapisiana Indians who would form the nucleus of the party I bought penknives, mouth-organs, shirts, trousers, canvas boots, colourful belts and hats. But for the Wai-Wais I had to be more careful, for I was determined to buy nothing which would alter their way of life, and eventually I fixed on a few simple things: red, white and blue beads, fish-hooks, knives, scissors, combs, axes, cooking-pots, cutlasses, needles, safety-pins . . . and, as *pièce de résistance*, a large and clumsy umbrella which I pictured myself presenting to some particularly puissant chief.

Who should I take with me? First, and most definitely, I decided upon Jonah Boyan, an Arawak Indian who had been on most of my previous expeditions. He was small, yellow-skinned and gnome-like, with large round glasses and a wide, toothy grin—a cartoonist's Japanese; he was old, and perhaps a little crotchety, yet, because he was such an expert field naturalist by far the most useful person in exploring new territory. He knew practically all the trees of the colony by sight: a remarkable feat—for not only are there many hundreds of them, but in the forests they have to be recognized by their bark alone, the flowers, and even the leaves, being nearly always far out of sight in the dense canopy of intermingled tree-tops. If Jonah did not know a tree it was certainly rare, and quite likely a new species.

Then there was Andrew Macdonald: half-Scot, half-Macusi Indian, he had lived among the Wai-Wais and spoke their language as well as English and Wapisiana, and in 1938 he had been on the Terry-Holden Expedition, the only expedition to cross the Acarai Mountains and descend the Mapuera River, on their far side, to the Amazon. No one would make a better interpreter and guide: by perseverance I at last succeeded in getting him released from his duties as a Government ranger on the far interior savannahs and I arranged for our plane to land near his ranch to pick him up.

I needed also a general handyman, a dependable person who could act as foreman, a good bushman, able to cut a trail by compass through the forest, and a good bowman in a boat, familiar with rapids and rough water. Such men are hard to find, but one day when I arrived at my office there was a man of inscrutable countenance awaiting me, leaning against a post with one leg curled around it. He was short, tremendously broad and deep-chested, and obviously of gigantic strength. From his face, which was very handsome, rather like that of an Egyptian Pharaoh, and impenetrably black, I guessed that he was half Arawak, half East Indian. He was dressed in khaki, and wore an Australian bushranger's hat with a curled-up brim. This he swept off, and, approaching me, introduced himself as George Gouveia, a man of many years' experience in the bush. Most important, he also had already been to the Serra Acarai, some eighteen years before, working with the Boundary Commission. He had the highest reference: the Commissioner of the Interior.

"Take him along," said the Commissioner when I rang him up. "He's an excellent fellow—in fact, he once saved my life when a jaguar knocked me down. It sprang on me from behind, and was standing over me, cogitating, when George rushed up and chased it away. He might do the same for you!"

And I needed yet another man, to operate a tiny four-horse-power British-Seagull outboard motor, which I had bought as an experiment, thinking that as it weighed only forty-five pounds we should be able to carry it with us over the mountains into Brazil—for with it we could travel much faster than by paddling, and even more important in a devitalizing climate, would not be exhausted at the end of each day. But it takes skill to operate an outboard motor on rivers choked with vege-tation and full of submerged rocks, and it was only after much deliberation that I selected one of the boat hands of the Forest Department, a slim, quiet-seeming young negro. He had other qualities: he was a good cook, and would be able to look after me, as a sort of batman; but I had one or two doubts about him:

"Tanner," I said, "no making-baby with those Wai-Wai girls, d'you see?"

His face became exceedingly solemn. . . .

"If you do, the men are going to kill you and eat you—so watch out: they're wild people."

. . . then of a sudden, uncontrollably, it expanded into a terrific grin, revealing a set of teeth that would have shamed a shark.

Many problems appeared only at the last minute: I found that safety regulations forbade our carrying ordinary gasoline in drums with us on the plane; nor would our little engine ordinarily run on 100-octane aviation fuel. But a little experi-menting showed that a mixture of this with kerosene and lubricating oil in the proportions of 6 : 2 : 1 worked perfectly, and Colonel Williams agreed to let me take empty drums, and drain some aviation fuel from his Dakota's tanks when we arrived at Gunn's Strip.

Then, when all was ready, I found that we were over weight for the flight, and that there was nothing that could be elimin-ated. So, two days before the expedition set off I sent the black

8

pharaohic George Gouveia ahead with 1,500 pounds of equipment. He was flown three-quarters of the way to Gunn's Strip, to the airstrip of Lumid Pau, on the South Rupununi Savannah —a vast grassland in the south of the colony—and left there to await my arrival: for, by the time we reached him, the plane would have burnt enough weight of petrol to be able to take on the extra load.

At last, early in the morning of September 18th 1952, Jonah, Tanner and I set off from Georgetown, through the sleeping streets of white houses and beautiful gardens, past the teeming market-places, gay with fruit and fish and coloured faces, past green miles of sugar plantations; then through forest, until, twenty-five miles from the capital, we reached the airfield.

Our Dakota, standing beside the over-arching forest trees, gleamed in the sunlight like a huge silver dragon-fly. Around her loitered groups of men, apparently idle: nothing seemed to be happening.

Then of a sudden we were aboard, and with us a trained nurse who was going to the mission station. The sun poured down upon the thin aluminium fuselage until we could hardly endure the heat inside. Sweat streamed from our faces and bodies as we sat jammed uncomfortably together on metal bucket-seats along the sides of the aircraft, amidst a welter of cordage holding the baggage secure.

Half an hour later our breaths were steaming, our teeth chattering as we cruised southward at 4,000 feet. Below us the Demerara River and its low-lying forests moved slowly past. A tiny lozenge on the wrinkled brown surface was a canoe; thin yellow lines in the dark green were timber extraction paths; patches of white, charcoal kilns. Sometimes, far to the right, between dazzling cloud banks, we glimpsed the broad grey ribbon of the Essequebo River, hundreds of miles up which lay our destination. The foam masses of the Great Fall of the Demerara appeared for an instant—creamy, toppling gently down a smooth incline—then unbroken forests beneath the cloud rifts. Cloud towers, standing above the white rolling masses, indicated mountains. What continents of whiteness!

On our right we passed a range unmarked on any map: three

years before I had come as far, after a week of travel through the falls and rapids of the Essequebo.

I relaxed a little: at least the packing was over. But there was still much to be done even on our way to Gunn's Strip: we had to collect Andrew Macdonald; and at Lumid Pau, during the fleeting hour or two we should spend there, sort out the baggage sent on with George, load the plane with all that it could take of it, and find six Wapisiana Indians to form the nucleus of the expedition's working force (for the Wai-Wais might not want to work) and to carry all that was left overland and by canoe to the mission.

It was a great deal to hope to accomplish in the time—it would be very much a matter of luck: yet there was no alternative, for Lumid Pau was almost completely isolated, and there was no way of communicating with it rapidly. A month before I had sent a message saying I would be landing on September 18th for two hours, and needed men, and all those—if any— who wanted work would have assembled at the airstrip. Already George would have started trying to find suitable ones—he might even have found them. But until I had actually seen them and reached agreement with them I was in suspense.

Already we had been aloft for an hour, flying over the magnificent sweeping landscapes of northern South America. In its westward swing the Essequebo passed beneath us, an expanse of angular islands, white rapids, and black water. Then the canyons and mesas of the Pakaraimas, until, where the Rupununi River poured its yellow-brown flood into the Essequebo, we inclined down to land on a strip hewn out of the forest— Apoteri.

Jagged blue mountains, Indian huts, a cluster of dugout canoes flashed past and we jolted to a standstill. Here we picked up a balata buyer who wanted a lift to our next stop (which it would otherwise have taken him a week to reach), and as we flew on I talked over my plans with him.

The country-side was changing rapidly: first there was the level flood-plain of the Rupununi, densely forested, gleaming with small mirror lakes, ox-bows cut off from the river, in which the *Victoria regia* spread its giant leaves. Then tongues and patches of yellow grassland appeared, consolidating until the forest formed only a series of islands in the plain, full of the citron-coloured powder-puffs of a tree in flower. In the grasslands dark expanses of water showed; and in the forests sometimes only the very crowns of the trees could be seen, isolated above the black floods of the abating rainy season.

Then there was nothing but grassland, a level yellow carpet stretching away to the uttermost horizon—the North Rupununi Savannah. At Karanambo, beside the Rupununi River, we landed on a stretch of dry, sparse grass to deposit, taxi-like, our balata buyer, and pick up Andrew Macdonald.

A scarlet jeep was waiting a few yards off beside a thatched hut. Around it lolled a cluster of dark, desperate-looking men with wide-brimmed straw hats, rifles, and knives stuck in their belts. Presently two of them came forward: in front a tall rangy man who approached the plane with the keen eyes and cautious eagerness of a hunter stalking his quarry—Tiny McTurk, a wild man if there ever was one, in love with the life of hunting and fishing, bushranging and cattle-ranching, and famous in all these parts; and behind him, carrying two bulging sacks and a long curved knife, a huge bear-like shambling fellow with bloodshot eyes and pointed eye-teeth showing at the corners of his mouth: my interpreter, Andrew Macdonald.

"I've got everything you want in these sacks," he said, with a curiously gentle smile. "Forty pounds of farine, and forty-eight pounds of tasso [dried and compressed meat]. I slaughter one of my own cows as soon as I hear you want it."

He extended an enormous soft hand, which I shook, then clambered up into the plane.

In the meantime the missionary nurse, a hefty wench, was distributing leaflets to some Indian women, drab squaws in the frowzy sacks of semi-civilization. McTurk edged up to me and shook my hand impulsively. Speaking rapidly, with his eyes darting in all directions as if he might have to make a break for it, he wished me luck.

A moment later we were off, above the trim thatched houses of Andrew's ranch, the expanse of yellow grass bejewelled with islands of flowering trees, and the meandering Rupununi. Karanambo ranch and Yupukari, a large village of Macusi Indians, slid by. An expanse of flooded savannah to the west was Lake Amuku, beside which legend had once placed the Golden City of Manoa, El Dorado's capital. Clouds appeared *en masse* in front, and rain forced its way in a fine spray into the pilot's cabin. The Colonel and I kept up a conversation by shouts.

Suddenly dark blue mountain-peaks showed to right and left, towering above us—the Kanuku Mountains. Following the river, we flew steadily south between them. Scarlet trees shone here and there on their lower slopes, and then, in a while, patchy Indian fields, like moth holes in the jungle. As we left the gorge there spread out before us one of the world's most beautiful sights—the glorious South Savannah of the Rupununi, a shimmering expanse of gold with solitary peaks and chains of ice-blue mountains rising into the clouds. This was the land of the Wapisiana Indians, and these were their sacred mountains, the scenes of the creation of their race. Straight ahead was Mount Shiriri, upon which the Ark of their legend came to rest after the Flood, rising from the plain like a tall castellated berg, concealing on its upper slopes legendary groves of wild bananas; while, a low knob on the horizon, was the stump of the Tree of Life.

Below us, caught in a spider's web of paths, were the tiny huts of Sand Creek Village, the northernmost village of the tribe; then a couple of ranches: Wichabai Pau, and Dadanawa ("The Hill of the Monster"), the headquarters of the world's largest ranch—2,800 square miles of open range.

Now we were over the satanic country-side of the South Savannah. Lines of black rocks shattered the rolling reddish hills, or formed gigantic piles on their summits. In the hollows and valleys palms waved above tussocky green bogs. Much of the lower ground was still under water, but in a month's time everything would be parched and burning.

In all this lonely expanse I saw only a solitary Indian hut, two small corrals, and half a dozen cows—the rest, no doubt, lying where they could find shade, for the full heat of the day was upon us.

Behind us the blue piles of the savannah mountains slowly faded from view, while more and more greenery showed on the ground below. Suddenly, at an angle ahead, I saw the airstrip of Lumid Pau, and as the plane tilted towards it, on a low hill the numerous thatched houses of Karardanawa, the southern-most Wapisiana village. This was the last outpost of semi-civilization.

George was there, beside our pile of baggage. The whole village had turned out to see us—people travelling to the mysterious country further south.

A small, finely-formed, smiling man came up to me. He would like to come with me, he said, and he knew of five other good men who wanted work.

I studied him closely: he was Basil Griffiths, an Arawak who had settled on the savannahs, and whom I had heard was a reliable man and capable at organizing. Luck seemed to be with me.

"Right," I said at last. "I want you to be at the mission two weeks from today, with everything that we have to leave behind——"

"That means seven hundred pounds for you, Basil," called out the Colonel, who had been sitting in the shade under a wing, computing the weight of gasoline burnt and the extra load we could manage.

Hastily we set to work dividing the pile on the ground—eight hundred pounds of urgently needed rations, gasoline drums, and trade goods, and seven hundred pounds of stuff for which we could wait.

"You'll have to feed yourself on the way in," I told Basil, "and when you reach the mission I may not be there, because while I'm waiting for you I want to try to cut across to the New River. But I'll leave you some rations and a note telling you what to do next. You can have one of the tarpaulins to take with you."

"Be careful of one thing, Mr. Guppy," warned Basil. "When you reach the mission you will find seven Wapisianas already there. They want work, and as soon as they hear you are coming they gone in ahead to meet you. But three of them are bad men, wanted by the police. Hire Charlie, and James, and Albert and Gabriel. But don't take the rest. They will cause you trouble."

With this briefest of exchanges we parted.

As we climbed aboard the Colonel looked at the molten blue sky:

"Fine weather, eh, Nick?" he said. "Looks as if we might make it. But I don't trust the weather down south."

Floating away to the south-east, we soon left the yellow stony wastes behind. Islands and promontories of forest appeared, and then we were over the solid jungle. From here on to the Amazon, save for Gunn's Strip, there was nothing but forest, unmapped, almost unvisited. Somewhere ahead the Serra Acarai pushed skyward.

Dense, dark blue-green, almost black, unrelieved by any flowering trees, the melancholy forests rolled below. The sun shone fiercely on our wings; we floated in the centre of a bubble of iridescence, azure above, slaty blue beneath.

The Colonel was in good humour with life and the weather. He pointed out to the co-pilot various landmarks of the route, which he alone knew. To the left the blue hulks of three mountains—Bat Mountain, Karawaimen-tau, Maroudi Mountain. The Kujuwini, or River of the White-headed Maroudi Bird, sprawled undulating below, green with algae. We passed over a thousand-foot cone of grey granite rising above the greenery, a vast bicuspid.

Then, within a few minutes, an amethystine tinge appeared below, and ahead we saw a dark world of black clouds. From them hung sheets of rain. Far away to the right the Kamo Mountains, "Mountains of the Sun", showed as a chain of black humps—beyond, pale grey, the vague forms of the Acarai.

The rain was straight ahead. White blobs low down on the forest were clouds on the tree-tops, indicating the heaviness of the downpour. Gunn's Strip might be a morass: a single day's rain could ruin it. We held our breaths.

A dark cold curtain swept around us, enclosing us, hiding the ground from view. The Colonel cursed: the rain was everywhere, splattering on the glass of the cabin, raging past the wings, whirling about inside the fuselage. Then the forest appeared again, with the faint line of the Kassikaityu, the "River of the Dead", an angular glint of water between the trees. Towering black clouds were hanging in a yellowish sky.

In the sodden black forest a tiny patch of savannah appeared,

14

unaccountably striped down the middle, like a zebra, with a white herring-bone pattern—Gunn's Strip.

Through thin rain and mist we swung round and round.

"Drains," said the Colonel, pointing to the stripes. "We dug them when we got stuck last time. We're going down. Unload as fast as you can. Throw everything out before she sinks in."

Banking, circling, swinging—all sense of direction was lost. Sometimes the earth appeared below through a window as I scrambled back to my seat over the roped luggage, sometimes the blank livid sky: then the horizon with fantastic serrated mountains, the Acarai, the Kamo, and others I knew not where. One I remembered, over-arching like a horse's head. Steep pointed ranges—and the forest rose, and they sank behind, and with a great bumping we were on the ground, running the length of the strip on to higher cleared land.

The doors were opened, and the Colonel and I jumped down. We bent over, examining the earth.

"It's firm, all right," he said. "I'm going to walk along for a bit and run her nearer the river if it's okay there. It'll save you carrying the stuff about three-quarters of a mile—Look out, Nicky! Here they come—watch out for the arrows!"

Approaching through the rain were a dozen almost naked vermilion-painted men, carrying immense bows and arrows.

2

Darkness on the Essequebo

Although the rain had bedraggled the Indians' feather head-dresses, armlets and earrings, and streaked their paint, they glowed like lanterns against the sombre background of trees. But they were friendly enough and full of smiles as they surrounded us. While shaking hands, I glimpsed the approach of another astoundingly clad group—the missionaries, two men and one wife, in vivid jitterbug shirts, accompanied by the women of the tribe.

They too were friendly, and together we walked towards the river end of the airstrip, with the plane taxi-ing behind us, a terrifying monster as it rushed from side to side to avoid soft patches of ground. It was a muddy, churned-up, depressing place, with every few yards a shallow gurgling drain piled full of brushwood and covered with white sand.

The ground was flooded at the lower end, so as fast as possible we drained off our 80 gallons of fuel and unloaded the plane. Then with a goodbye wave from the cockpit the Colonel swung her around and away she went, rising low over the forest into the blank white sky. I felt suddenly a little lost.

One missionary and his wife had returned to Georgetown, and the other, Mr. Leavitt, now invited us to spend the night at his station. Leaving most of the luggage under two tarpaulins, we set off along a little winding path.

Steady rain began to pour as we entered the forest. It was so cold that it was hard to believe that we were near the Equator and only a few hundred feet above sea-level. For a couple of hours we floundered along, chilled to the marrow, in the thick sodden undergrowth. The path was skating-rink slippery, and full of the knife-like spikes of newly cutlassed saplings and branches. At every step we risked disembowelment. There were

16

frequent mires of black peat through which we had to wade knee-deep, and high clay banks up which we pulled ourselves, hand over hand.

Two more depressing hours I have seldom spent, and my admiration grew for Miss Riedle, the nurse, who was a few yards ahead. I decided I had misjudged her: she had never before been in a tropical forest and, sustained by her religion, was far more cheerful during this first encounter than I should have been.

At last we arrived at a high levee which sloped steeply down to the gloomy black waters of the Essequebo. There were four canoes below, and as a chain of men formed to load them, the missionary, the nurse and I sat down to watch.

A small brick-coloured crab walked on a root, laved by the olive water; a few yards out, floating like a thick crow-bar out of the depths, rose an electric eel. It touched the surface with its snout, then subsided as slowly, leaving a spreading ring. The dark trees dripped. It was a melancholy place.

It was amazing to see how readily, after three years, the Wai-Wais were doing the missionary's work for him; but as yet they had none of the sullenness of the tribes, longer missionized, who had come to realize their inferiority to the white man in everything except muscle.

In contrast with their bland, humorous faces were the sharp, toothbrush-moustached, Spanish-looking Wapisianas whom Basil had told me about. They exuded a distrustful, foxy air; they could not look one in the eye. I had been among them before, and knew that they were nice enough, but that it would be impossible to deal with them man to man except after a long period of confidence-winning. The missionaries had taught them that all their old customs and beliefs were not only wrong but wicked, their legendary past that of savages living in darkness; the ranchers had driven them off their old lands, and the traders had shown them the superiority of manufactured goods to their own products. They had lost their self-confidence and pride in their own achievements; they had turned inwards and now led secret lives, among themselves, with an outward show to deceive their conquerors. They no longer wanted to cultivate their fields; they wanted to eat flour and tinned milk

17

and other shop-bought food. They were discontented, for ever on the look-out for odd jobs with which to earn a little cash. Their clothing symbolized their degradation: ragged dirty shorts and ragged dirty khaki shirts; canvas yachting boots and battered felt hats. Withal I was very glad that they were there, for I had a hold over them: they wanted money, and they knew I would pay them well.

However, I should still have to treat them very carefully, for like all the Guiana Indians they were very proud: they had never been slaves, their tribal society was classless, and they had no tradition of servitude. They might have glimpsed civilization and learned the necessity of working, but they were still fully conscious of how recently they had been self-sufficient, and resented the idea of compulsion. They would desert in an instant if offended—the history of the interior of Guiana is full of desertions, strikes and murders. But with tact we should soon be friends, and they would work well for their pay.

Over the Wai-Wais, on the other hand, I had no hold: their wants had not yet been increased enough. They would only work if they wanted to, or if they liked me personally.

"They are very difficult," said the missionary; "completely untrustworthy, like children."

They were laughing and joking among themselves as they hustled to and fro. There was a great magnificence about their free-moving bodies—graceful, smooth, in the Greek tradition, not over-developed, knotted, hideous, like a modern muscleman's. At ease they stood tall and proud, like guardsmen of an outlandish eighteenth-century regiment—an effect enhanced by their peruke-like hairstyle. Their hair, almost bluish black, was parted from ear to ear across the top, smoothly combed forwards and backwards, cut to an even, bowl-like fringe in front, and plaited behind into a waist-long pigtail, the end of which was usually thrust into a tube of bamboo, plain, or covered in elaborate beadwork and hung with bunches of feathers or even the complete skins of birds—toucans, humming-birds, cotingas, parrots—forming a bunch that sometimes must have weighed at least half a pound.

The men wore small red loin-cloths or laps, fringed with feathers, bands of white beads round their biceps, and of blue

FONYUWÉ

"Two scarlet macaw feathers . . . swept, like gigantic moustaches,
from below his nose" (*p. 40*)

THE SEA OF LEAVES

THE MISSION

beads, with a single strand of white, above their calves. They had mother-of-pearly earrings of freshwater mussel-shell fringed with scarlet and yellow toucan feathers, and sometimes bead-and-featherwork flaps on their hips, and bandoliers of beads across their chests.

The women wore aprons of heavy and beautifully-patterned beadwork, edged with sprigs of red or yellow feathers, arm and leg bands of beads or red cloth, and shell-and-feather earrings. Their hair was cut shoulder-length behind, but left loose, and was a little longer than the men's in front. Some were quite pretty, if a trifle thick-waisted, and they managed their very simple aprons with great modesty, kneeling down and sitting back on their legs, instead of squatting like the men.

"A shameful lot," said the missionary, "especially the women. The sight of their nakedness is bound to make the lusts of the flesh rise in a man. The first part of our work is naturally concentrated upon making them wear proper clothes. We hope that within two or three years there won't be a woman exposing her breasts in the tribe."

"You will have them clothed like the Wapisianas?" I enquired.

"Yes. Naturally. We will concentrate upon the women, for they are the cause of all the sin. However, they are weak vessels, perpetually vain, and by appealing to their vanity it should be easy to make them wear decent clothes. That is one reason why we spare no expense to establish a comfortable station—you will be surprised how comfortable we are—we already have an electric washing machine and we hope soon to have a refrigerator—so that our wives can live with us and set an example of Christian dress and modesty, which the native women will want to imitate. Once a few articles such as guns for the men, or clothing for the women, have become necessary for them, we can really get down to catechizing, for they will have to earn money and in consequence will have to live round the station where we can control and guide them into better ways. There is plenty for them to do—housework, cutting wood, clearing and planting and tending the mission fields. And the more they do, the more time we in turn will have for our devotions."

B 19

"But how can you pay for all of that?"

"Oh, to begin with we will have to rely on outside help—money from abroad. Back in the States our Mission is always campaigning and raising money. Later, we may be able to make ourselves self-supporting. We'll set the Indians to work bleeding balata, or gathering Brazil nuts, or making basket work which can be sold at the coast. We hope eventually to be able to afford two charter flights a year into Gunn's Strip. After all, our life is a lonely and self-sacrificing one, and it would make it very much easier if no one had to spend more than six months at a time in the interior unless it was absolutely necessary. And then we have to think of our children, as they grow up, and of the women."

"How many missionaries have you now got?"

"At present we have a staff of five—two men and their wives, and now Miss Riedle, who is a trained nurse. Later we may have one or two more workers in this field."

"Good heavens!" I exclaimed. "I had no idea there were so many of you! But is such a large establishment really necessary when there are so few Indians? I understand from Dr. Jones that there are only thirty-three adult Wai-Wais in British Guiana. Why, there are huge areas elsewhere in the colony, for example in the gold and diamond-mining districts like the Mazaruni, where there are hundreds, even thousands, of people living in appalling conditions without either medical or religious care. They *really* need help. Wouldn't the labours of five people, and the money spent on supporting a remote and almost inaccessible station, do more good in such places?"

"That is not the point," said Mr. Leavitt. "There are probably another two hundred Indians across the border in Brazil, and it is they in whom we are really interested. The Guiana Wai-Wais will act as seeds, spreading the Word to them—that is why we must make concentrated efforts to convert them first of all. In the meantime we are trying to get the Brazilian Indians to leave their villages and come and settle over here. We are offering them beads, knives, mirrors—everything they love. We have sent messengers across telling them that they will be much better off here. And some have come."

"Why did you not establish your station in Brazil in the first place?"

"The Brazilian Government has refused us permission. One of our missionaries was killed by the Indians over there, and the government has made a lot of difficulties ever since. However, the brother of the missionary who went back on the plane is down there trying to persuade them to change their minds. As soon as we get permission we will move across and establish a new station. We are going to go across ourselves next year and try to locate the best site. And then we plan to bring in a light airplane so that the Indians can be tracked down to their remotest villages in the wilderness. None will be able to remain hidden."

"But even so . . . I still don't understand why you should spend such enormous sums of money on so few people, and pass by thousands who are far worse off. So far as I can see, these Indians lead happy, simple lives according to their old customs. Besides, I'm quite sure that there is far more sin to be tackled in New York, or London, or Georgetown, or even out on the savannahs. These people are living in a sort of Garden-of-Eden stage."

The missionary was losing his patience with me:

"My friend, you miss the point completely. In New York and Georgetown the people have been baptized; here, their souls are in danger, and we must save their souls for Christ. Our mission is concerned solely with work among wild tribes who have never heard the Gospel before—that is why it is called the Unevangelized Fields Mission. It is inter-denominational. We work with all the churches, except the Catholics, and we would like to work with them. Besides, this is no Eden. There is a terrible lot of sin here, unbelievable. Why, at times the Indians brew up a lot of their beer and have dances which may go on all night. They get drunk, and—ugh!—they are quite disgusting. They do things that are too horrible to talk about. Do you know that sometimes they may go off with a woman who is not even their own wife? We intend to stamp out all drinking and dancing, and we have already managed to stop a good deal of smoking. They still grow their own tobacco round the villages, but I doubt if you'll find them smoking round the mission."

21

I was silenced for a moment. But I had one final question: "Tell me," I said, "do you respect these Indians as people?" The answer was conclusive:

"That is completely beside the point. We *love* them—we love them in Christ. Our object is to save souls. Nothing else matters."

I had no wish to antagonize Mr. Leavitt, so I dropped the subject. Argument would be unmannerly, for I was his guest, at least as long as I used the Mission as my headquarters. Besides, there was much that I could learn from him about the Indians, and probably much upon which we could agree.

The missionary's canoe was loaded: a large, rather unstable dugout, about twenty feet long, with a powerful Archimedes outboard motor. A cheerful, brightly-striped youth came to point out the channel, and we started off upstream.

The river was full of rocks—broad shelving banks and protuberant granite boulders, which we had to change course constantly to avoid. It was about one hundred yards wide, very winding, the forests along the sides mostly a tangled growth sixty to seventy feet high, dark dull green, relieved at times by a wisp of purple-flowered vine. Sometimes down a stretch we glimpsed a low hill, a swelling mass of tree-crowns.

Occasionally there were shallow bays lined with swamp acacias—feathery trees with spreading umbrella crowns from which flapped snakebirds, gawky, antediluvian-looking monsters. On a spray overhanging the water sat a green basilisk, an iguana which plunged precipitately as we passed.

Darkness fell swiftly: the high forested banks drew closer, and soon we were steering only by a dim ribbon of light overhead, and by our ears, listening for the sound of water washing and breaking on the rocks. Sometimes we passed close to rocks, floating ghosts, huge and dim; and once, in the midst of a loud-rushing line of rapids, hovered for several moments beside a hump as large as a wallowing elephant, until, by paddling to assist the engine, we succeeded in moving forward. A single touch of a rock in such a place, or engine failure, might have upset us.

As the hours passed I grew sleepy. The rain had stopped, but we were drenched and shivering. It seemed that we should for ever be afloat in this bitterly cold cavern of blackness, brushing against nameless things, our engine pounding and shuddering.

Then Miss Riedle came to the rescue and produced a torch, and a woollen cardigan each. At once life became more bearable. I awoke from my comatose state. Soon we saw a waving light, and then, miraculously, we were ashore, being led in to an excellent dinner prepared by the missionary's wife.

It was a cheerful sight—roast chicken, okras, plantains, creamed yams—all set on a checkered tablecloth in the midst of an attractive kitchen-dining room with a wood-burning stove at one end, and with chintz curtains and gay china plates as decorations. The walls were of baked mud, the floor of palm-strips, but it was luxury compared with what I had anticipated.

As we sat down, utterly weary, there was a moment's silence. Calvin, the missionaries' small son, was restrained from an act of destruction; then Mr. Leavitt said:

"Proverbs 3, 5 and 6"—and he and his wife and Miss Riedle chanted what was obviously a cornerstone of their faith, and perhaps also a mild reproof to the intellectual arrogance of a visiting scientist:

"Trust in the Lord with all thine heart, and lean not unto thine own understanding. In all thy ways acknowledge Him, and He shall direct thy paths."

Through the open door a couple of Wai-Wais gaped at the white man's mysteries.

"Let's sing a song," said Mr. Leavitt. "What shall we sing? O.K. Florence, you choose."

"Let HIM clear your skies,
When clouds are grey,
Only remember
That HE's there night and day."

After this, his face serious above the writhing orchids of his shirt, he leaned upon his elbow and prayed, concluding:

". . . and Lord, we thank You for bringing Mr. Guppy here. Guide him in this unknown land, and help him and all his men in their work, to accomplish the purpose of their expedition. Amen."

I was deeply touched. No welcome could have been kinder.

And then Mr. Leavitt suggested that, as there was a spare kitchen, like the one we were in but without any furnishings, I could have it as a storeroom. There was a padlock—and it would be as well if I used it.

"The Wai-Wais are terrible thieves," he said. "Warn the men never to leave anything unwatched, or they'll lose it. It's lucky that you have a few Wapisianas, for they are a bit more reliable. Don't trust the Wai-Wais an inch. Never be dependent on them, or they'll desert you and leave you stranded as soon as they become bored with working for you."

I accepted his offer gratefully: if we could leave some of our baggage behind until we needed it, instead of having to carry everything wherever we went, we should be much more mobile and far more could be accomplished.

"And tonight there's a bed for you," he added. "While you are getting things organized you must let us help you. You must have all your meals with us. And later, when you want to supplement your diet, don't hesitate to go into our field and dig up all the yams you need. We have more than enough."

I still remember the excellence of Mrs. Leavitt's cooking—particularly her fried okras, and her beautifully creamed yams. But that night I was almost too tired to think. It had been a long day, full of strain, and of a multitude of impressions. However, with four men and most of my supplies, I was installed safely at my base. During the two weeks before the rest arrived and the main task of the expedition—the crossing into Brazil—began, a lot of interesting things could be done. There was a feeling of success in the air.

As I went off to bed I asked the missionary:

"What is the name of this station?"

"Kanasenay," he replied, "which means, 'God Loves You'. There is no 'd' in Wai-Wai, and 'n' is the nearest equivalent, so 'God' becomes 'Gon'—which in our system we spell 'Kan'."

3

Travellers' Tales

Just before dawn I awoke and strolled around the mission. Within a wooden stockade which enclosed about an acre were four palm-thatched houses. Two of these, built of wooden slats and raised on piles, were dwelling-houses; the others, at ground-level, were mud-and-wattle kitchen-dining rooms, of which one was to be my storeroom. There was a small enclosed garden with newly-dug earth, and there were two flower-beds raised on trestles as a protection against ants. A few young fruit trees and a trellised pea-vine completed a very attractive picture.

The settlement was on a low hill, newly cleared of forest, with the prostrate trunks of trees lying in confusion down the slope and tumbling into the water. The Essequebo swung inwards from the right and curved smoothly away to the left, black and shiny as a snakeskin. Beyond it, behind, and all around rose the enclosing green battlements of the forest, only the tangled hill-slope and the long reach of river giving any sense of space.

Behind the stockade was a large cleared space with a few scattered sheds—one housing an electric generator, another a group of sleepy-eyed goats who scrambled forward at sight of me, the rest chickens and turkeys. To one side a winding path led to a privy, and at the back, sheltered by a line of bushes at the base of the sheer one hundred and twenty foot forest wall, were three small conical thatched houses with roofs that swept to the ground.

A fire was alight in one of these, and from it stepped very daintily a big, genial-looking old man. With tight-closed lips the corners of his mouth lifted in a curving smile, and his eyes twinkled behind half-closed lids; he shook hands, and remained standing, smiling and scrutinizing me, very handsome

25

and dignified. Then he turned and disappeared into the house again, while I resumed my wanderings.

Never before in my travels in Guiana had I seen so large and comfortable an establishment. It represented an altogether different approach to missionary work from that of the Anglican and Jesuit priests whom I had known, who to a great extent shared the lives and poverty of their flocks.

The sun was up when the Leavitts rose: the chickens were released in a rush from their coops, the goats were milked, and I was invited across to breakfast.

The day's chief work was to bring the men and goods from Gunn's Strip.

A quarter of a mile below the mission we found ourselves in a whirlwind of yellow butterflies—they were pouring over the eastern forest wall and spreading across the river, fluttering in our faces and gyrating wildly round our heads. The two main streams headed down-river on either side, while a number of subsidiary counter-trickles climbed again over the opposite forest roof, or jigged about above particular trees or shrubs. The air was so filled with their wings that sometimes it was impossible to see more than a dozen feet ahead; then there would be a lull, with only a few hundred in sight.

After about five miles we came out of the swarm, and the river again lay limp between its drab banks. As we went I tried to memorize the channel, the water-swirls indicating concealed rocks, the steering-points through turbulent rapids. One point in particular I noticed: two tall tower-like trees that Mr. Leavitt pointed out as marking the almost completely vegetation-smothered mouth of the Onoro River, from which I intended to cut eastwards towards the New River.

By midday all the luggage was at the riverside and several canoes had gone ahead paddled by the Indians, so heavily laden that they seemed likely to sink at any moment. The boat that the missionary had lent me for the duration of the expedition, a fifteen-foot dugout, with a transome to which I attached my little motor, had itself only about two inches of freeboard, and swerved, rolled, and wallowed so dangerously whenever the water was at all rough that I had to go at half-speed.

By nightfall, however, everything was at the mission: the

Wai-Wais had come *en masse* to stay at the three small conical houses in order to inspect me and receive payment for their work, and I settled down with the missionary and Andrew to find out all they knew about the region.

Reared on the Brazilian-dominated savannahs, Andrew was a strange mixture of reticence and braggadocio. There was something flamboyant about his enormous shambling figure and broad hat—yet his face, with its pointed eye-teeth, was that of a puzzled teddy-bear.

With powerful gestures he told the story of the Terry-Holden Expedition and its descent of the Mapuera River (on the far side of the Serra Acarai) to the Amazon.

"Mr. Guppy, I don't know how to tell you what a terrible river that Mapuera is! You been in the rapids in the Essequebo? Crab Falls? Below Rockstone? Right! That ain't nothing to the Mapuera. There you will see the Gran'daddy of river-falls. There is rapids on that river five and eight kilometres long. *Three times* we have to build boats.

"Where we first reach it it is a very tiny small river, scarcely enough to float in. We build a corial [canoe] and push it downstream for three days, with our baggage in, before there was enough water to embark. Lower down the Indians have cut out all the wood good for boats, so you *must* build up topside.

"One week down we meet Indians, and we trade our boat for theirs. Don't ask me why! They got a bad boat, I'm telling you. But from then it was trouble. The river sinks into a deep winding ravine, with sides so steep they would be impossible to climb. Then you come out into a really strange place with big, big, bare rocks rising right up out of the water above the trees. From the top you can see for great distances.

"What's that? No, there was no savannah, nothing but dense forest.

"Once we leave the canoes and walk inland for ten or twelve miles to see some Indians. All the way we had heard about this 'Big Village' which is suppose to be somewhere around there. But when we arrive we find a village just like the others. The young boys were being initiated for manhood. They were dressed completely in Ité palm leaves, so you could only see their feet, and they were dancing in a circle and blowing small whistles.

"The sun was setting when we start back. It was lucky Dr. Holden insist we go back, for heavy rain start to fall. It was so dark we could not see our own hands, and we had to feel with our feet. We reach the landing about two o'clock in the morning, and the river had rise up so much the boats was beginning to float off the rocks where we had pulled them. Another fifteen minutes and everything would have gone.

"Three times that night we had to shift to prevent getting swept away. The river rose twelve feet, and at last we was all afloat hanging on to the trees. Then for three days rain fell steady and we were never dry. We paddled down river all the time."

"What a terrible time—but did you have any trouble from the Indians?"

"At first it was O.K.—all the Indians high up are friends of the Wai-Wais. They are, the Barokoto—we met a few, but we never saw a village—they are just like the Wai-Wais. Then Shilliau, then Kalawian. These are a very tall people. The men carry a long staff, with a fork at the top, and from each half of the fork they have a long macaw feather. They like to stand on one leg, and they rest their chins in the fork and look out through this 'V' of feathers.

"Below this there are the Katawians, who are very fierce. They tell us if we had come from below they would have killed us. But nobody bad comes from upstream, so we were O.K. The reason is because of the Brazilian rubber hunters and nut collectors and prospectors being so trigger-happy in the old days. So the Indians are now savage—and now it's the Brazilians who are trying to make friends again.

"Well, below the Katawians the Wai-Wais and the other Indians would not go. All below were enemies. So the six of us went on alone. The next Indians were a very short, dwarf set of people, called Areka, A-ika, or some such name. Then we met with the Powisian, and that is where we have our worst escape.

"We was running short of food, and we see a path coming down to the river. So we walk up, and in a short way we come to a village—but when I see there was nothing but women I was badly frightened.

" 'Let's go,' I tell Dr. Holden. 'There would be at least one old man if this was peace. But all the men are gone. They must be going to attack us. Or maybe they are raiding some other village.' But the doctor say no, we need food. So we put out some beads and knives on the ground, and point to our mouths, and presently the women bring us cassava and yams. They were very frightened, and they were completely naked. They didn't even wear a small apron.

" 'Come,' I say to the doctor, 'the men will be back any minute, we got no time to lose.' So we went back to the boat, and sure enough, just round the bend downstream we saw all the men standing in a mass on a bank of rocks. They was all in warpaint, and the doctor insist that we go right up to talk with them. But when we see how wild-looking they was, we steer off again. At that they let out a terrible shout, and loose off arrows into the air."

"Good heavens! Andrew, I hope we don't encounter them!" I exclaimed.

"Oh, no chance of that," he replied. "We won't even get so *far* as the Mapuera. It's a terrible long way, and *we* had real equipment. That expedition was a big affair, properly organized, with plenty of people. We had *wireless*. It was only when we *get* to the Mapuera that the rest turn back. Then Dr. Holden, Mr. Melville, and I, and three others, continue on. Besides, how are you going to look after our health? Remember, Dr. Holden was a great doctor. He knew everything about how to fix wounds."

"Don't you worry, Andrew," I said. "We'll get there. And as for wounds, I have fixed plenty. This is not my first expedition. I have very good medical equipment, and as much drugs as we shall ever need. But let us know about the rest of the trip."

"A few days later we were again near to starving. And then we strike lucky. We turn a bend, and there is a large camp! It was the highest camp of the Brazilian Boundary Commission, situated exactly on the Equator. From then onwards life was simple. We get food, and we continue down the river in their boat. It was a wonderful trip, that expedition. But it finish me.

From then I have seen everything. I don't want to travel no more. I want to settle with my wife and live quiet. I'm an old man. Leastways, I feel old. I don't like these forests—I didn't want to come on this trip and leave my ranch, but my boss say, 'You must go and help Mr. Guppy,' so I come. But I don't *want* to come. I got only *one* life."

"Oh, come!" I exclaimed, startled by his sudden vehemence, "you're not as old as all that! I hope you'll like the Mapuera better this time."

He made no answer at first, and a look of stubbornness came over his face. Then very meekly he replied:

"Well, sir, I tell my boss Mr. Angoy I will come and help you only on condition this is my last trip. So if it must be, I will go."

"Anyway, Andrew, you won't be going over much of the same country as you've seen before, because I don't want to go down the Mapuera at all. It is the Acarai Mountains that I am interested in, and the country south of them. So when we reach the Mapuera I'm going to try to strike east, along their southern edge."

His interest revived:

"You will never reach there. No one has been there. It is there that the Mawayán Indians are supposed to live."

He paused. "But I still don't want to go unless I has to. And if that's where you want to go, I am no use at all, because I know nothing about that part."

"You are our only interpreter, Andrew. I'm afraid we'll still need you. Anyhow, I hope you begin to feel better about it. Meanwhile there are two weeks before Basil comes, so I'm going to send George Gouveia ahead clearing a trail and see if we can reach the New River. Its head should only be about sixteen miles east of here. And that way I should be able to look at the northern side of the mountains as well."

He opened his mouth—at that moment there was an uncanny scream from the darkness outside the kitchen.

Up leaped Andrew at once, seizing his knife and torch, and rushed out, with us following. A hysterical cacophony of chicken cries came from beyond the stockade: dimly we saw a pale form leap away through the bushes behind the coops. Pointing to a place where the grasses were flattened, Andrew showed us where the "tiger"—jaguar or ocelot—had lain.

Mr. Hawkins, the missionary who had returned to George-town on the plane, and his brother had also crossed to the Mapuera, three years before. When we returned to the kitchen I asked Mr. Leavitt if he knew anything about what they had seen.

"They went for about six weeks," he said, "and visited all but the furthest village of the Wai-Wais: but the people from it came to see them when they heard of their visit. It is said to be the biggest village. But there is also said to be a 'Big Village' somewhere there, which Andrew mentioned, and which they tried to reach. It is called Kashima, and in it there are supposed to be people from several different tribes living in harmony. There are said to be many large houses and hundreds, perhaps even thousands, of Indians living there. But I think it is just a legend.

"Hunger and hardship forced them back. They suffered a great deal when crossing the Acarai ridge. One day they prayed and prayed that they might find something to eat. And the Lord sent an old, old parrot, and they shot it as it sat in the crown of a tall tree. It was very tough, but they blessed the Lord for providing for them, as He always does."

"Do you know if they saw any tribes apart from the Wai-Wais? Or even heard of any?"

"I don't really know, but I have only heard of two—the Mawayáns, whom Andrew mentioned, who live very far away on another river, and of whom one or two have visited us; and the Fishkalienas, who are supposed to be very dangerous, who live below the Wai-Wais on the Mapuera."

It was puzzling: the names of the different tribes did not fit together or make sense—they must have moved around con-siderably, or perhaps be known by many different names.

After saying goodnight I wandered to the river to brush my teeth. I was worried about Andrew. He had once been notorious for his riotous life, and for that very reason, as unlikely to be influenced by the missionaries, he had been selected to accom-pany them for a few months when they first went among the Wai-Wais—to make sure that they stuck strictly to the terms upon which they had been admitted: to do medical work and give religious instruction, but not to interfere with the diet or customs of the Indians. It was said that after several months he had emerged a pious, reformed character—which he denied, of course. But he seemed to have lost his enthusiasm for life.

It was a black night, the sky scarcely luminous as I stumbled along the path between tangles of debris. Insects rustled in the dried leaves, and when I stood out on a long branch overhanging the water, with the torch fixed in a fork while I washed, a large fish suddenly scared me by jumping and flapping almost under my feet.

A high wind blew out of the east, smelling of damp leaves and strange flowers, and excitement mounted within me as I thought of the adventures ahead, and that at last I was in the land of the Wai-Wais.

Of the rare occasions on which this region had been visited before the arrival of the missionaries, by far the most interesting was the first, when in 1837 one of the greatest but least known of nineteenth-century explorers, Robert Schomburgk, ascended the Essequebo to mark the southern boundary of British territory: "after three days' painful march [from his canoes] we arrived this afternoon at one of the sources of the Essequebo at a spot surrounded by high trees interwoven with lianes, so much so that we could not get sight of sun or stars; . . . we hoisted the British Ensign, which we secured firmly to one of the trees, there to remain till time destroys it, and after drinking Her Majesty's health in the unadulterated waters of the Essequebo, the only beverage within our reach, we returned towards our corials." [1]

Schomburgk came also to investigate a rumour that had first reached the coast some thirty years before: that at the head-waters of the Essequebo there lived amphibious Indians who dwelt like otters in under-water caves. Instead he rediscovered a tribe with a romantic history—the Tarumas, long considered extinct. They had originally lived at the mouth of the Rio Negro, and in 1668 had helped build Fortalezza da Barra, where now stands the city of Manáos. They had been converted to Christianity, and soon after were wiped out in a series of

[1] Canoes.

epidemics. What Schomburgk had found were the descendants of the very few who had refused to give up their independence, and had wandered for four hundred miles through the wilderness until in the upper reaches of the Essequebo they had made a new home.

They received him with the greatest, most devoted hospitality he had ever encountered among the Indians, and he found them an interesting people, famous among the interior tribes as manufacturers of apron belts and cassava graters, and as trainers of hunting dogs; however, he remarked, the women "especially distinguished themselves by their ugliness and their indescribable filth". Altogether there were about five hundred of them, but when, only six years later, Schomburgk paid them a second visit, only about one hundred and fifty remained; while of two neighbouring tribes, the Atorads and Daurais, who had numbered two hundred or more in 1837, he found only nine adults and a few children. The first wave of the diseases of civilization had reached them.

If syphilis came from the New World, we have repaid the score a hundred times over, for it seems that of the vast populations of Indians who once lived in South America, described in all the early travellers' accounts, the greater part were exterminated less by enslavement or Spanish tortures than by epidemics of the common diseases of civilization—the less serious like chicken-pox, the common cold, measles, mumps, scarlet fever, whooping-cough, as much as pneumonia, tuberculosis, smallpox, dysentery—all of which were unknown to them, and to none of which they had (or even today, in remote places, have) immunity. In many places nine-tenths, in others even the entire population, was wiped out.

At a once populated village, now apparently deserted, Schomburgk turned aside:

"I quietly betook myself to one of the houses to have a look inside—and what a shock I got on seeing some small-pox cases looking at me from out of just as many hammocks! One of the unfortunates who had got over the terrible disease, that had now spread so far inland, was already up and about once more. The scars that had been left gave the poor devil a still more revolting appearance, while the larger pits had taken on in general a dark black colour ... small-pox is undoubtedly the most devastating and probably also the last scourge to seal the doomed extinction of the Guiana aborigines. Shocked and affected by the gruesome sight I hurried back to our camp."

Bitterly he cried, " . . . one might almost assume that all these people are ordained by Providence only to live upon earth for a limited period."

About thirty years later a geologist, Barrington Brown, briefly visited the Tarumas:

"We found four men, a woman, and a girl, all in the greatest state of perturbation. None of them had ever seen a white man before, or people wearing clothes, consequently they looked upon us as supernatural visitors at first. They all trembled with fright and quivered like leaves." Soon, as they gathered courage, more appeared. "When the men approached us their wives walked close behind them, and though wishing to see our boat, they were too timid to come near. When, therefore, a man came to examine it, his wife abandoned him and took refuge behind a relative or neighbour; but if he stood up at a distance, she stood close behind him, with her hands clasped round his neck; and it was quite touching to see a row of first rank husbands and rear rank wives squatting in this apparently loving condition."

By 1925 there were only seventeen adults and three children alive; and the following year influenza completed their destruction.

Soon after they became extinct another tribe, the Wai-Wais, moved northwards and took over their territory. They also had been discovered by Schomburgk on his first journey, further south, up a tributary of the Essequebo called the Caneruau—about one hundred and fifty of them, paler-skinned than the Tarumas:

"The Wayawais are great hunters, and famed for their dogs: they are filthily dirty . . . even more so than the Wacawais, who are notorious throughout Guyana. This tribe particularly traps the *Harpyia destructor* [harpy eagle] for its ostrich-like feathers . . ."

Leaving his canoes, he continued southwards on foot over the Serra Acarai. One evening he saw, about twenty-five miles away to the east-north-east, a rugged mountain peak called Pirikitu. Two days later, having crossed the watershed into the Amazon basin, he came upon a village of Barokoto Indians: "The men were stout and well made, with high foreheads; the heads were adorned with caps made from the feathers of the breast of the eagle, the crest of the egret, the macaw, and the parrot. They carried bows 6½ feet long." From them he learned that the mountains continued westward for twenty days' march, through country inhabited by the Harakutyabo, a savage tribe which would allow no strangers to enter its territory; and that to the east were the Maopityans, or *Frog* Indians.

From there he returned to the Essequebo, without, apparently, having reached the Mapuera.

On his second visit to the Tarumas, when he found that tribe so very much reduced, he had been anxious to travel not southwards but to the east, to extend the British frontier to the Courantyne River, the boundary with Dutch Guiana. By great good fortune he had found his old friend the chief of the Barokotos visiting them, and by prophesying a partial eclipse of the sun Schomburgk had so impressed him that the chief promised to take him to these Frog Indians, who might help him on his way.

Messengers were sent to them, so that they could come and carry his loads over the mountains to their country; and when at last they appeared he saw that they "differed essentially both in build of body and in attire from all other Indians that [I] had become acquainted with during the course of [my] travels . . . their figures if more slender were nevertheless more bony than that of the Taruma . . . and their facial expression, on account of the lustrous eyes, brighter. Their head was compressed laterally . . . their faces are unusually long, with the result that the whole head simultaneously becomes much smaller circumferentially than among the remaining Indians. The back of the head appeared among the men to be almost vertical towards the top. The frontal bone was but small, the cheek bones on the other hand sharp and projecting, while the great distance from ear to ear was especially striking . . ."

Examining a new-born child he convinced himself that this peculiar shape of head was not produced artificially.

Walking east-south-east from a tributary of the Essequebo called the Urana, he and the Indians crossed the Onoro River near a 100-foot waterfall, climbed several mountains with picturesque names—Zibingaatzacho, Honicuri-Yiatzo, Kabaio-kitza—descended, through valleys filled with a wonderful variety of palms, over the Acarai watershed to a tributary of the River Caphuiwin [now called the Alto-Trombetas], and came at last to the Frog Indian village," which consisted of two large bee-hive houses; on the top of these there rose a second smaller bee-hive roof from which hung several flat pieces of wood shaped into all kinds of figures that were swayed backwards and forwards by the wind . . . the larger, . . . with a height of 100 feet and a diameter of 86."

These two buildings contained the remnants of the "once powerful" tribe of the Maopityans or Frog Indians. Evidently *they* were not the otter people, if such a tribe existed.

Schomburgk completed his journey by paddling down the Alto-Trombetas, up one of its tributaries, recrossing the Serra Acarai, and descending the Courantyne to the sea—a phenomenal journey that has never been repeated.

Barrington Brown, the second visitor to this part of the world, also saw a few Frog Indians—three who were visiting the Tarumas. He learned that their form of head was a manufactured one, "being produced by the application of two flat pieces of wood to the sides of the infant Maopityan immediately after its birth. There the wood is tightly bound, until the head becomes flattened at the sides, and of course heightened at the top."

Even if the Frog Indians did not live under water, he found rumours of such a tribe still current: "another tribe of Indians, called Toonahyannas, or Water People, are said to live more to the south, near the headwaters of the Trombetas, who have ponds of water encircled by stockades, to which they retire for the night, sleeping with their bodies submerged."

Some Toonahyannas, or Tonayenas, were actually seen in 1914 by the American anthropologist William Curtis Farabee, the second man to visit the Frog Indian country, and the only man to make a journey comparable with Schomburgk's in this region: "At Miñai Ulud on the Apiniwau [Alto-Trombetas] we

36

found a young man with his wife and baby who had come from the region east of the Honawau River a long time ago. He had forgotten his former language which he said was entirely unlike Parukutu. His peculiar appearance led to our inquiries about him. He had a very flat upper face, broad nose, thick lips, and projecting face—all Negro characteristics, yet he was not negroid in colour or appearance. His wife had a very narrow lower face"—and that is the last that has been heard of them, though they are still rumoured to exist.

With four Wapisiana Indians Farabee and his Scots companion John Ogilvie crossed the mountains, descended the Mapuera River, ascended its tributary the Buna-wau, and travelled overland eastwards to the Trombetas, encountering Indians of the Wai-Wai, Parukutu (Barokoto), Mapidian (Maopityan), Waiwĕ, Chikena, Katawian, Tonayena, and Diau tribes, before finally following Schomburgk down the Courantyne. For four and a half months they were among tribes who had never seen a white man before. "None had ever seen matches or guns or clothing. All had beads or knives; all wanted fish-hooks and many got their first from us."

Like Schomburgk, they lived off the country. Farabee lost 48 lb. "I had beri-beri according to the diagnosis of the natives. They pressed their fingers into my swollen feet and legs, making deep dimples which would remain for a long time ... eight months afterwards I was able to lace my shoes again."

Between 1933 and 1938 a joint Anglo-Brazilian Boundary Commission surveyed the watershed of the Acarai Mountains. Many lives were lost from beri-beri (a vitamin deficiency disease) and the work was held up for long periods due to the difficulties of the country. Of the Indians, the Brazilians found that those on their side of the border were affable, even solicitous, though often engaging in bloody fights among themselves. On the Mapuera and its tributaries they contacted the Parukutus (Barokotos), among whom they found that there were about three times as many women as men, and some villages almost entirely of women; and on a branch of the Alto-Trombetas, the Pianocotos. Their report mentions "Mauaianas" as living on the River Eito, a tributary of the Urucurina, itself a tributary of the Mapuera, but so vaguely, without any description, that it seems probable that this information was derived from other Indians; while as for the Frog Indians, it states: "Nothing is known about the Maopityans (Frog Indians) found by Schomburgk about 100 years ago in the valley of the Cafuini (Alto-Trombetas). It can be presumed that this tribe is extinct."

Except along the actual border no maps were made, and by a curious omission no scientists accompanied the survey, so that the whole region still remained almost unexplored. Dr. Holden's expedition of 1938 and the missionaries' foray added little to our knowledge, and away from the rivers there were still huge unvisited areas, the tribes were still mysterious, and Schomburgk and Farabee remained the best sources of information.

4

Discoveries

From the Wai-Wai encampment behind the mission came the sound of wild flutings and the barking of dogs. Dawn was at hand: life was stirring. The flute wove its silver arabesques in the air: Arcadian ripplings of rising and falling scales, a warbling pastorale, then a savage, irresponsible burst or a clear, delicate, wavering note sustained for several seconds: music of great beauty, played with masterly lightness of touch.

It was hard to analyse: I was entranced—I had heard nothing like it before. The scale was unfamiliar—it was certainly not pentatonic, more like a mode; and the time was free, with an irregular rhythm suggesting derivation from speech. Rather Gregorian, perhaps, but gay and often highly embellished, and not in the least austere.

A pale flush of pink came through the window. I had slung my hammock in the kitchen so that the men could use both tarpaulins in their camp by the river, and all around me were the massive shapes of crates and cartons, piled there the previous evening.

The barking rose to a crescendo: presumably the dogs were being fed. The fluting ceased, and then began again, much nearer.

Presently two noses were pressed against the wire-meshed window, and a soft voice called:

"Meeshterguffin!"

It was Kirifakka, the slender youth who had been our river pilot two days before; and with him a short, very muscular man (whom he pointed to as "Fonyuwé"), whose face was illuminated by an enormous smile. Both were bright red all over, with their chests striped a darker shade. Their cheeks were covered with delicate patterns—swastikas, crosses, zigzags—of red and black grease-paint and their hair was glossy with palm oil, and stuck all over in front with little fluffs of white down.

Realizing that this was at least partly for my benefit, I sprang from my hammock and greeted them. Fonyuwé glowed with pleasure as I examined his stylish pigtail-tube, hung not only with bird skins but the tail of a monkey, his necklaces and bandoliers of beads and seeds, and his elaborate bead and feather garters and belt. Most impressive of all were two scarlet macaw feathers which swept, like gigantic moustaches, from below his nose, their quills stuck through his nasal septum. Each was decorated along the shaft with tiny blue iridescences from a humming-bird's breast, and at the tip with a pendant tuft of toucan feathers: artistically, executionally, decoratively —they were masterpieces. He stood quite still as I inspected them, then seized my hand and said, "Oh, Meeshterguffin!"— all the English he knew, but enough to show how much he appreciated my admiration.

Kirifakka, meanwhile, was leaning in a graceful curve against a post, tootling gently, with solemn, concentrated face, at his flute: a bamboo tube about fifteen inches long, with four holes, and a semicircular notch at one end; and played in a most peculiar way—held under his lower lip so that he blew down upon the notch, with much nodding of his head up and down to alter the quality of the breath.

Suddenly he caught my eye and burst into laughter; then handed the flute to me. His soft brown eyes sparkled with fun when all my efforts failed to produce a sound. Next, Fonyuwé took it and instantly blew out a stream of notes: obviously the virtuoso who had awakened me.

As I breakfasted—alone, for Tanner had now organized my cooking—more and more Indians gathered in festive costume. Some were even more elaborately dressed than Fonyuwé, with tiaras and crowns of golden and scarlet feathers, yard-long macaw tail-feathers rising from their shoulders, and masses of black, white and scarlet feathers pendant from their wrists— like vast, brilliantly-plumaged birds, their finely-proportioned figures making them look much taller than they were (seldom above five feet four inches).

The women were thick-set by classical standards, and their breasts a little full, but even among the middle-aged and elderly ones there was much beauty. They were less elaborately dressed than the men, and inclined to overpaint carelessly, with stripes of colour splashed all over them; but with their patterned bead aprons, graceful carriage, and gentle ways, they were full of charm, and the babies they carried—clad chiefly in bead necklaces and feather earrings—were exceedingly pretty. Some had already been given names—but most were addressed simply as "*Yimshigeri*", meaning baby.

Among the crowd were several older men, including my dignified friend of the previous morning, his remarkable, shrewd face conspicuous, and with him his wife, a sweet-smiling marmoset-like old lady. Noticing the friendly respect with which he was treated I was not surprised to learn that he was Moiwa, the chief, or *tushau* of the tribe: an elective, semi-honorary post, carrying little personal power but much weight in conference.

Like all the older people, he wore no make-up; but even beneath it it was possible to see how pale in complexion these Indians were. Their name "Wai-Wai" is the Wapisiana for tapioca, and the Brazilians call them "Indios do Tapioc", and regard them as the "White Indians". But their name for themselves is "Wéwé", or wood, and means people who live in the forest.

What most impressed me as the day passed and I worked, checking and sorting equipment and supplies, was the excellence of their manners: the room was filled with Indians, bursting with curiosity, but they sat quietly, watching what I was doing, and waiting patiently before interrupting me if they saw I was busy.

Whenever a particular treasure or novelty came into view a gasp of delight would be heard—the first thing that won such universal approval being my hammock, swathed in its green cocoon-like mosquito net:

"*Kiriwanhi!*" came the loud concerted hiss: "Wonderful, marvellous!" as Mr. Leavitt explained.

It was an ordeal being watched so closely, but for fear of offending their good feelings I pretended not to mind. Not one of them seemed in the least likely to be a thief, yet Mr. Leavitt's warning had been justified: the previous evening, while Andrew, Jonah and I had been dining with him, half of our tasso and three-quarters of our farine had been stolen—a severe loss. Fortunately there was a woman working for the missionary who could make us more farine, but the dried meat was irreplaceable. Tanner and I were continually vigilant, feeling that the thief or thieves might be in the storeroom with us. Gradually, however, from their open ways, we were reassured, and our suspicions began to fall on the Wapisianas as we became more and more friendly with the Wai-Wais.

One or two of the children were very engaging, in particular a slender little girl who was very shy and would skip away whenever I looked at her, and a small boy called Machanowra, a shrimpish creature with enormous pop-eyes, a huge dirty belly, and stick-like legs. Every now and then I would point at him with arm extended and utter his name slowly, to his unceasing delight: he would hide his head in confusion, and then slip his hand into mine.

It was wonderful to discover how, with only two or three words—*kiriwanhi* (good), *chichibé* (bad), *atchi* (what is that?)—signs, smiles, and goodwill, one could make oneself understood and carry on even quite elaborate conversations.

By mid-afternoon I had paid off all the men, Wai-Wai or Wapisiana, who had helped bring the luggage from Gunn's Strip. The three untrustworthy Wapisianas I dismissed; the remaining four, under George Gouveia, I sent off with two weeks' rations, a tarpaulin to sleep under, a compass and a new cutlass each to cut eastwards from the Onoro mouth towards the mysterious New River.

This, a tributary of the Courantyne, is one of the largest rivers in British Guiana, yet probably the least known. Its mouth is about six miles wide—yet so obscured by rapids and islands that Schomburgk sailed past without seeing it. It was discovered, quite by chance, by Barrington Brown: "I went on with one boat, intending to explore the main Courantyne; but taking channels along the western side of the river, amongst a confusing array of islands of all sizes, discovered a river hitherto unknown." He went up it for about three weeks, until stopped by a barrier of large granite rocks; whereupon leaving his boat, he cut westwards "... to the Essequebo and back through the densest forest I ever traversed".

The region round the New River was uniquely interesting to me, a botanist searching for truly virgin forest, for, so far as is known, it has never been inhabited; indeed, not only in Schomburgk's time (when the Frog Indians took him within a few miles of its source) but today the Indians did not seem to be aware of its existence—there was much Wai-Wai laughter when we told them that George was going to look for a big river!

According to my calculations the extreme upper part of the New River could only be about sixteen miles away: if George and his men had five days' start (for they would probably make two or three miles a day, clearing a path along which the rest of us could follow carrying equipment), it would give me time to look at the forests round the mission; then, following them, I should be able to spend a few days exploring before returning to meet Basil, his five men, and the baggage from Lumid Pau.

When they arrived the main expedition would begin: over the Serra Acarai to the Mapuera, then eastwards, somehow, towards the Mawayán Indian country—though if we found anything of outstanding interest by the New River—Indians, or an easy way across the mountains into Brazil—I might divert the whole expedition in that direction.

Twenty minutes downriver with the outboard motor, and just above the Onoro mouth, was Yakka-Yakka, the nearest of the four Wai-Wai villages in British Guiana, and there I went as soon as my work was finished.

A dugout canoe tied to a tree indicated the landing, and from it a short path led through the forest to an enormous clearing of about sixty acres, where the forest had been felled and planted with cassava, sugar-canes, yams, bananas, and much else.

Straight ahead, framed by the trees of the path, and nestling among the silvery green arrows of the sugar-cane, stood the village, a single conical house thatched with pale yellow palm straw; about twenty-five feet high, with, above it, borne by the projecting centre-pole, a second miniature cone of thatch to protect the smoke-hole; while below the eaves its low wall curved in gracefully to form sheltered doorways on two opposite sides. It was of a singular perfection of form: it had, one felt, architecture and dignity far beyond its pretensions.

To one side were two or three small shelters in the shade of one of which sat a woman hammering upon a board, a little boy tugging at her breast, a tame toucan hopping and shuffling beside her. As we approached she disappeared into the house, and two men came out bearing stools. We shook hands and sat down outside the entrance, while the woman brought out a basin of drink, a few flat discs of cassava bread, and a small pot of meat stewed in pepper sauce. The large bowl, containing a gallon or more of liquid, circulated two or three times, and we drank deeply of the refreshing, slightly acid cassava beer. Then we broke off fragments of the bread and dipped them in the stew.

We explained that we had come merely on a social visit, and would like to see the house. Then very courteously we were invited to enter. At once from all sides there rose a savage uproar of barkings and snarlings. In the dim light from the two doorways I could see that all round the inside wall there were shelves about four feet from the ground, on which stood packs of raging, bristling hounds, rearing and tugging at their leads in violent efforts to break loose and get at us. Suddenly a figure leaped up from a hammock and darted about brandishing a stick and smacking their noses with his hand. They instantly quailed, and contented themselves with deep internal rumblings of discontent, so that despite an occasional drawn-back lip I was able to look closely at them.

These were the famous Wai-Wai hunting dogs, one of which may be a man's most valued possession. They seemed to form a fairly homogeneous breed, short-haired, with long curling tails, rather like small, slender foxhounds, with the same irregular blotching of black or brown on white. Like the dogs of all American Indians, their origin is mysterious: they may be indigenous—but perhaps they were originally Portuguese dogs, brought first into this region by the extinct Tarumas?

Our rescuer was Chekemá, the haughtiest and most supercilious of the braves who had come to see me in the morning, and the only one who had seemed disagreeable. He had puffed-out cheeks, pouting lips, a foppish air—but now he was very pleasant, and brought out several things for us to examine: first a bow of spotted snakewood, elegantly curved, triangular in section, and nearly eight feet long. Near the centre it was decorated with bunches of crimson and black feathers and a wide band of intricately patterned string work, the thread-like string of which, slowly increasing in diameter, wound spirally to one end of the bow where it was secured with a clove-hitch, and from there, forming a stout bowstring of even thickness, hung loose, to preserve the tension of the wood.

Placing his knee against the centre, Chekemá bent and strung the bow and offered it to me, but I could barely pull it. Then, selecting an arrow from a cluster (stuck, with many other bundles and packages, in the thatch) he in turn took the bow, and with his left hand at arm's length drew the string back to his cheek.

Never before had I seen so powerful a bow, nor arrows so long—between five and seven feet—and beautiful. They were made of the strong slender flowering stem of the arrow-grass (*Gynerium sagittatum*) and flighted with the black, brown, and white mottled vanes of the harpy eagle, or black curassow's feathers, or the blue and red primaries of a macaw, bound to the shaft with neat and variously patterned and painted string-work. Above and below the vanes, which were twisted to make the arrows revolve in flight, and above the point, were decorative tufts of orange, scarlet, or blue feathers. The notch was an inserted plug of wood, and the points were very various: slotted, for the insertion of poisoned wooden tips, carried in a separate quiver; blades, of bamboo or steel (fashioned from knives) for big game; with a hand-like spread of short points for small flying birds; or long, narrow and saw-toothed, of hard wood, for large birds and fish.

Each must have taken several hours to make, and each might be damaged beyond repair at its first use; but each was a perfectly balanced, true-flying weapon which might mean the difference between food and hunger for its owner.

The interior of the house was circular, about thirty feet across, with a beautifully swept clean earthen floor, and the

45

air sweet with the incense-smell of the Indian's body-paint. Each of the four families living here had its own fireplace—consisting of a few large stones and a circular griddle-disc of metal or clay—round which, between subsidiary roof-uprights, were slung their hammocks: in tiers, the wife's lowest (for it is her duty to stoke the fire at night to warm the family and keep away mosquitoes), the children at the top.

In the centre of the house was the main upright, with, at the top of it, in the apex of the roof, a platform of sticks used as a loft for storing large cooking-pots, bunches of bananas, and sheaves of arrows. Hanging from it and from different ceiling rafters, on cords fifteen or twenty feet long, were trays on which were more pots, packages wrapped in palm leaves and joints of smoked meat out of reach of the dogs; stuck in the thatch of the roof, or hanging on individual strings, were many other objects—while beneath the peripheral dog-shelves were faggots of firewood : the whole interior forming a masterly essay in the use of space. Conveniently placed were all the objects which four families—some fifteen people—needed: kitchen, hunting, and sleeping equipment, as well as private possessions; and there was still a feeling of roominess.

Most of the people were away cutting a new field, and it was getting late, so I decided to return. Outside, however, there was one activity which interested me: the woman, hammering away at her board. She was making one of the cassava graters for which, since the earliest times, her tribe had been famous. Following rough black guide lines painted by her husband, who had fashioned the rectangular board of soft wood, she hammered tiny chips of stone—five or six thousand to each grater—into its surface, each into a previously punched crack. When she had finished, the grater would be painted by her husband with vermilion paint mixed with latex to hold the chips in, and decorated with a design in black: the ends and back with stylized zigzag patterns, the centre of the front with a simpler, more carefully executed motif, perhaps of an alligator, a monkey, a cross, or a collection of dots.

These graters are to the Wai-Wais what oil is to Venezuela—their chief export and source of wealth. As far back as we know they have been carried from tribe to tribe—the great traders and travellers of the region being the Wapisianas—and today when they reach the savannah they fetch between $5.00 and $10.00 each, or the equivalent in trade-goods, while the few that trickle through to the coastlands bring up to $15.00. There is a steady demand for them because grating is an essential stage in the preparation of cassava, the root-vegetable which is the staple food of all the Indians, and because they are not merely the most efficient graters for this purpose, but easy on the hands of the Indian women.

From their sale come most of the beads, knives and other manufactured articles which the Wai-Wais possess, the rest being derived from a few other exports—bows and arrows, curare arrow poison (which they do not make themselves, but buy from even remoter tribes), trained hunting dogs, and special palm stems used for making the outer tubes of blowpipes.

That evening I heard tremendously fast drumming from the Wai-Wai camp behind the mission. Churumá, one of the braves, was beating his "*Samahora*", a small drum covered with a monkey-skin, held between his knees as he crouched on the ground. Facing him in the darkness I could just distinguish, rapt, motionless, a semicircle of little children.

As he drummed, he kept up a low muttering-chanting, occasionally rising to a shout. He would pause, then his drumming would begin again with heavy, rhythmic thuds, slowly growing more rapid and accelerating to a smooth crescendo, until after four or five minutes a continuous stream of sound issued from his hands, which, even from a few feet away, were blurred to invisibility. Then there would be another abrupt silence, followed again by a slowly mounting climax. This was repeated over and over again. The songs (his physical effort not in the least apparent in his voice) were, I was told, each different, and were imitations of animals and birds.

The chief appeared, bringing a stool for me and a bowl of cassava drink. Through Mr. Leavitt I told him my plans, and how I intended to try to visit the Indians on the Mapuera. At once he was interested, and when I asked him whether he would perhaps come with me, smiled and said, if he could.

Meals were being prepared, and I could see behind him into the cavernous interior of the nearest house. Illuminated by the

47

firelight, it seemed to be filled with vast swinging sausages—hammocks, bulging with men and women.

The chief led me in—there was the usual outburst from the dogs, silenced by their mistresses—so that I could examine something which he brought down from a rafter: a little oblong basket-work box, from the corners of which hung bunches of feathers, black and gold, scarlet and white, with on its sides a complex woven design of two beasts like heraldic lions with tails curled over their backs, facing each other, separated by a vertical criss-crossing. The two halves slid apart, and I saw that it was a vanity-case, filled with his treasures.

First there was a delicate comb, with slender wooden teeth and a bone back tufted at each end with orange feathers; then a piece of beeswax, a fragment of mirror, a tiny leather bag which proved to be the inverted breast of a baby harpy eagle containing its down (tufts of which are used as a hair decoration), an aluminium spoon, three match-sized sticks of dark red wood shaped like minute paddles, and three black globular objects the size of walnuts—the dried fruits of a tree of the rose family—filled with red, orange, and black grease-paint, and plugged at the apex with cotton.

The miniature paddles were make-up applicators—the broad ends for thick lines, the pointed ends for details. Holding the chief's mirror, I painted a red and black bull's-eye on the tip of my nose. Mr. Leavitt was startled, but the chief was amused, and brought down a few more objects: a long bamboo flute, a gourd of palm oil, and a heavy lump of slightly adhesive red, incense-scented body paint, of the consistency of a well-kneaded clay, wrapped in a palm leaf to preserve its colour from sunlight and soot from the fires, which soon gave everything exposed a black, greasy coating.

The following morning the chief, Jonah, Andrew and I went for a walk in the forest behind the mission. No sooner did we plunge into its gloom than Jonah and I noticed a strangeness about everything: try as we might we could recognize few of the trees—nearly all were new to us, and some, probably, to science. For Jonah, the old Arawak naturalist, and for me, this was a most exciting moment.

"Never before did I see so many new species," said Jonah.

"Mr. Guppy, this is a wonderful place! Even with Dr. Maguire in the Pakaraima Mountains I seen nothing like this."

"Whatever else happens, Jonah, from this place alone we can collect enough to make the expedition worth while."

"I think so, Mr. Guppy."

A moment like that makes life worth living. And every year there are fewer places on the surface of the globe where such a feeling is possible.

On all sides of us the undergrowth was thick with small palms bearing bunches of bright red fruit. On the ground was an abundance of feathery ferns and selaginellas, and here and there around rose the columns of the larger trees, grooved, channelled, or rough according to species, and of many shades and mixtures of browns, greys, and reds. As we went along I asked the old chief the names of the different plants, and Jonah would give me their nearest Arawak equivalents, for the Indian names are precise and extremely useful:

"*Atchi?*" I would say, pointing to a trunk, and the chief might answer: "*Makwauru,*" to which Jonah would add: "*Haudan*"—meaning, in this case, *Eschweilera holcogyne*, for this was one tree which we recognized. Whenever a species was new to us we collected as representative a sample of its leaves, flowers and fruit as possible, for later examination and identification, and naming, if new to science (a process which might be relatively simple, or might require years of study and comparison of our specimen with others in collections all over the world); and so engrossed were we that in four hours we walked only a few hundred yards.

The path led straight up a hill and there forked, one trail leading away, I was told, to Gunn's Strip. Along the other we continued for a few yards, and then emerged into blazing sunlight, at the edge of a new field which the Indians had cut for the missionaries.

It was a scene of appalling devastation: a vast unearthly scrap dump of jumbled fallen trees lying fifteen feet deep in places, hideous under the vertical glare of the midday sun. The smaller branches had been gathered in piles and fired, rather unsuccessfully, so that golden dried leaves, charred twigs, and ashes formed a deep layer beneath the enormous silvery, reddish, or blackened trunks that undulated over the ground. The whole thing would have to be burnt again when it had dried out from the recent rains, and then two or three months hence planting would begin between the trunks which had not been consumed, or were too heavy to move.

As soon as our eyes had adjusted themselves we picked our way carefully along one log after another to the summit of the hill, never once setting foot on the ground. There, strain as I might, I could catch not a glimpse of anything over the surrounding forest: where were the mountains I had seen from the plane? That strange horse's head? How could I tell where to direct my explorations if I could see nothing, even from a hill-top? It was frustrating. I felt imprisoned by that high serene wall of vegetation.

Was there anywhere, I asked the chief through Andrew, where I could get a view? He thought. From his old village I might have seen far, but the forest had grown up again: there was nowhere now.

Against the brown of the tree-tops there were one or two golden or brownish smudges: flowers or buds, perhaps, of a tree or tangling liane, or, quite likely, young leaves. Noting carefully where they were—for from under the shade of the forest it was much harder to detect the presence of likely specimens in the canopy—we made our way to the nearest, and found that it was a *Protium*, about 100 feet tall, its bark and sap pungently aromatic. Even if the best tree-climber had ascended it (and the first branch was eighty feet above) he might have found nothing, for often only one branch of these forest trees is in flower at a time, and that may be hidden in a neighbouring crown. But in any case, hateful though it was to do so, we had to fell it, for it was part of our policy to secure specimens of the heartwood of all the larger trees for testing as possible timber, ply, or veneer woods, or as sources of various chemicals.

As the tree came crashing down it thrust aside many plants of the undergrowth, and revealed, close to where we stood, two beautiful milky-juiced shrubs, of the family Apocynaceae, very much alike, but one with pink, the other yellow, flowers; and, as a quadruple reward, in its crown we found not only

CHURUMÁ

YAKKA-YAKKA VILLAGE

WAI-WAI INTERIOR

GIANT TREE

delicate sprays of bursting buds but a vine with masses of egg-like dark brown fruit—a species of *Gnetum*, the only relative of the conifers which is a climber. For years I had heard of this fabulous gymnosperm, and here at last it was! It stands in a very isolated and anomalous group, quite unlike any other of its relatives with its opposite ovate leaves and dichotomizing lateral inflorescences.

It was time for lunch. I thanked the chief for his help and company, and offered him as a present a shaving-mirror, magnifying on one side, a handsome, well-made thing. He was delighted: his crow's-feet deepened, his eyes twinkled, and his mouth lifted in its curious half-moon smile.

On our next outing we followed the path to the right. For a while it skirted the newly cut field, clinging to an almost vertical hill-side; then descended into a narrow curving valley where an abundance of delicate grass-green palms[1] rose out of thick waterlogged peat, and where the trees were festooned with mosses. Wading, we soon came to a steep bank and then a slope bearing beautiful tall rain forest.

From a tree-top a caracara—a brightly-coloured vegetarian hawk—screamed at us with a noise like the sharpening of knives: Andrew snicked off a small palm leaf, and rubbing the cut end against his cutlass blade produced an exact imitation; then, altering the angle, a jaguar's roar. He laughed and shrugged his burly shoulders, and flung the leaf aside.

As we walked we looked all about us for flowers in the lower storeys, and examined the debris of the forest floor for the signs, often minute, of their presence overhead.

Suddenly I stopped and picked up a pale pink bud about a tenth of an inch long, scarcely visible where it lay just off the path. Searching, we came upon a patch of ground liberally sprinkled with small pink flowers; and eventually, by craning our necks and scrutinizing the tree-tops, sighted a flowering branch one hundred and twenty feet above, and traced it to a massive tree a few yards away. A slash at its bark, and white milk flowed abundantly: the only tree at all like it which Jonah or I knew had white flowers, so we set to work with the axe.

[1] *Euterpe edulis.*

After about half an hour it began to crack and groan. We had cut carefully so as to direct its fall in the one direction in which it was not closely surrounded by equally large trees, in which trunk and crown might gather enough momentum to break through: even so, I thought for a moment it would be held upright by its neighbours. Then came a long-drawn series of splinterings and swishings as it slid and forced its way down between and through them.

As soon as the shower of twigs and branches from above had ceased, leaving Andrew to cut off a specimen wood block, I ran along the trunk—and stopped abruptly: halfway up it was aswarm with *Neoponera* ants, the heavy tanks of the ant world, an inch and a half long, black and hairy, and capable of putting one to bed with a single sting; and now, alarmed by my approach, standing on their hind legs and hissing like snakes.

Hastily I jumped down, and worked my way round through the bushes to where Jonah was already gathering armfuls of the exquisite strawberry-ice pink flowers from the creaming masses at the branch ends.[1] With its roots firmly twined round one of the main branches, I found a small tree with glossy leaves like miniature table-tennis racquets, and flowers like big cherry-red magnolias. It was as large as a good-sized holly—yet it was an epiphyte, and had been growing in the sunshine far above the earth, to which, for water, it sent down special roots like slim dangling cables. It was a *Clusia* (*C. palmicida*), one of a group of plants of which I was especially interested in obtaining specimens.

On the way back I learned from Fonyuwé (who was naming the trees for us that morning) that the small, red-fruited *Yurua* palms[2] that grew in clumps in the undergrowth all around were the ones used in manufacturing blowpipes. Their crowns of fishtail leaves were removed and their gently-curving, many-jointed, fifteen-foot-long stems wiped to remove a fur of tiny spines (intolerably itchy if they got into one's hands), cut off close to the ground, dried and bundled, and sent over Indian trade routes to the Macusis, Patamonas, Acawoios, and Arecunas two or three hundred miles to the north. These tribes

[1] *Macoubea* sp.   [2] *Cuatrecasea Spruceana.*

then hollow them, straighten them, and insert into them the smooth, straight inner barrels which, by routes even more obscure, reach them from yet further north: from one place only, and that closely guarded—the mist-enshrouded summit of a single precipice-walled table mountain called Marahuaquita in the Pakaraima Range. Only twice has the extraordinary grass, forty to fifty feet tall,[1] of which the internodes are used, ever been seen growing by white men—once by Robert Schomburgk in 1839, and again in 1950 by Dr. Bassett Maguire of the New York Botanical Garden, who succeeded in getting himself safe-conducted through hostile Indian territory by the Machiritare tribe who alone harvest it.

Back at the mission Jonah and I began sorting our specimens—selecting the best bits of each from the enormous bundles we had collected, arranging them in folders between sheets of blotting-paper, and placing these, pressed in tightly strapped piles, with a corrugated sheet between each folder, to let the hot air through, over a stove to dry. As each plant was dealt with it was numbered, labelled, described, and entered in a log book—a time-consuming process.

After the initial jubilation, Jonah had seemed a little undemonstrative, and now as the day wore on I noticed a certain pursing of his lips. When he wished, he could be the gayest companion, at other times emanate gloom like the blackest thunder-cloud. Usually I found it effective to ignore these moods and give him a word or two of praise, for I knew that beneath them he was a fine old chap; and as my first guide in the forests I had a strong affection for him. But he was old, and far from all that was familiar, faced with a new flora which he was too old to learn, and with Indians who knew it better than he.

"Ah, Jonah," I said, "how glad I am that you're here! We are going to have a tremendous amount to do, and I couldn't tackle it without your help."

He smiled briefly. "Yes, Mr. Guppy, that's right. But we must organize things in a certain way. When I was with Dr. Maguire we start very early in the morning and we collect:

[1] *Arundinaria Schomburgkii.*

then in the afternoon we press, so that we finish by four o'clock."

"Well, we'll try to do that, as far as we can. But with all these new plants I think that I shall be working late some nights, and I shall expect you to help me when it's necessary."

"Sir, the trouble is cooking. With Dr. Maguire one man used to cook all we dinners. Every evening we have corn-beef hash. If we could do things that way it would be best."

"Well, we haven't enough corned beef, or anything else to do that. But on all the other trips you've seemed to manage very well. . . . If I remember you and some of the others got together and took it in turns to do the cooking—couldn't you do that now?"

"Well, there's nobody I could go in with now. They all like different food."

"Perhaps as time goes by you'll get to know them better? Anyway, I'll try not to make things too bad."

Half-way through the afternoon the missionary came running to summon me to his kitchen. There, to my surprise, on a chair, his mouth and chest streaming with blood, was Fonyuwé.

He had toothache, and in trying to extract, the nurse and missionary had crushed the tooth with the pliers. His face was crumpled with agony.

I had never pulled out a tooth but I had seen it done—an inwards twist was necessary, to free the roots: a minute later it was out, followed by a gush of blood, and Fonyuwé relaxed.

But an hour later I was summoned again—he was still bleeding—what could be done to stop it? They had brought his hammock from the Wai-Wai camp, slung it under one of the houses and were clustered around. Pale, weak with fright, he lay there, convinced by all this that he must be dying.

"You don't realize how important this is to us," they said. "If anything goes wrong the Indians will never trust us again. It will put our work back years. The adrenaline is out of date— what *can* be done?"

"Try a mouthwash of strong potassium permanganate or salt solution," I suggested, rather alarmed at this dependence on my inexpert advice, "and perhaps the best thing of all would be to leave him alone so that he doesn't get into a panic."

However, late in the evening, long after the permanganate solution had stopped the bleeding, the agitated group still clung round, feeling Fonyuwé's pulse, brow, cheek, and reducing him to a semi-paralysis of fear. Stealing up behind them, I smiled at him, and flexed my arm to show that I thought he would soon be well. He caught my eye, nodded, and gave a rather cheerless twitch of the lips.

Every day Jonah, Andrew and I returned with our arms full of exciting new plants. As the chief had gone back to his village and Fonyuwé was still ill, we took with us as tree-namers other Wai-Wais, all pleased at the chance of earning a few beads or a knife: Wanawá, a gentle nonentity, gorgeously plumed with feathers; "Sam," whose real name was Gömöya, a scholarly, quiet, middle-aged man; Mawashá, the tall sly son of Chekemá; or Mingelli, a hard-working youth with a keen sense of humour, disliked for his independence by the missionaries, whose appearance intrigued me much—for he had strong Bourbon-Hapsburg features, crowned by a mop of wild hair, which made him look simultaneously like Alphonso XIII and John the Baptist.

On our third day I laid out the first of my sample plots—in the little boggy valley, filled with palms, behind the mission. An area of forest one hundred feet long and twenty-five feet wide was marked off with white cords, and a map made showing the exact location of every tree above fifteen feet in height. Then each tree was measured carefully: its diameter of stem, its height, the height of its first branch, and the height, width and shape of its crown; and, at the end of the day, a "profile" of the complete plot was drawn (p. 66 shows such a profile, but of Rain Forest, not Bog Forest).

Such profiles are like engineering diagrams: they show what the structure of the forest is, often more clearly than can be seen on the ground; and they enable an ecologist, in his study of plants in relation to their environment, to guess a great deal about it. Yet because no two bits of a forest are quite alike, they are only useful in as much as they are representative of the forest as a whole, which makes it very important how one selects where one lays out one's plot.

55

On this expedition I was testing a new and original way of doing this, based upon the simple theory that in an undisturbed area the natural vegetation of each site would be entirely typical of its topography and soil—hill, valley, river flood-plain, sand, clay, loam, whatever it was; and that by sampling many typical localities I could build up a picture of the region as a whole, and even trace the changes of the vegetation as topography changed, hills were worn away, sediment deposited, valleys choked and filled with waterlogged peat.

My belief was that not only could this be done, but that in future years, when aerial photographs of the country-side had been taken, mapping would thereby be simplified; for from the topography one would be able to guess what was in the forest, and if one could recognize a few of the trees on the photographs, one might be able to map the soils—and from such humble beginnings grow the great development schemes which will one day transform the tropics.

The next day—the day before we set off after George—I made two discoveries. I went, to pick bananas and dig yams, to the missionary's field of the previous year. It was a wild and beautiful place, its entrance festooned with globular, pendant, striped-skinned gourds, glossy, translucent in the sunlight, their yellow flowers hidden among tendrils; its banana patch a strange chapel of arched flapping leaves shedding and trans-mitting an intermittent green light, with underfoot an alter-nation of squelchiness from fallen stems and crunchiness from the charcoal of the original burn.

Digging in the yam patch, overrun by a network of passion-flower vines, I found a curious black loam, rich and moist, and full of broken pottery—of which, in a few minutes, I had collected a large pile. Most of the pieces were plain, evidently the remains of bowls of various sizes, without any trace of colour or painting, though some rim-fragments had simple designs of ridges or incisions. Judging from the forest around this field (for tropical rain forest, once disturbed, does not re-grow to its former state for several hundred years, during which time it passes through all sorts of secondary and inter-mediate stages), this must have been the site of a village abandoned at least fifty or seventy years before—a Taruma village, almost certainly.

Then, returning, I found two visitors awaiting me. One was an old man with a magnificent greying leonine head, whom I had occasionally seen pottering about the mission, as much as his lame right foot allowed; the other a man of about thirty, unpainted and very simply dressed—his sole ornament a necklace of black and white seeds—a meditative, rather deliberate fellow, who walked with bent head and a kindly, inquiring expression on his face.

Sitting down, the old man pointed to his foot: as best I could I washed it, applied antiseptic and a little sulphathiazole powder to a cut, and bandaged it. Realizing that very soon as he walked the bandage would get wet, dirty and torn, I advised him to wrap a piece of soft bark round it as a sandal.

He nodded, then as soon as I had finished produced, from a number of palm-leaf packages, two lovely men's vanity-boxes, like the one the chief had shown me, a bone comb, and some feather earrings, all of which I bought, paying him with a few fish-hooks, a file, a mirror, two small knives and some beads. Wrapping these up, he rose, and without another word or look hobbled away.

The younger man had been watching, and now I saw that he too had gone.

"That old man may look sweet and kind," said Andrew, "but watch out for him. He is the worst sorcerer in the whole tribe and everybody is afraid of him—yet the missionaries like him. They calls him 'Georgie', but his real name is Manatá".

"Who was the other fellow?" I asked.

"That was Kilimtu—he is the last living Taruma in British Guiana."

"What!—and he's gone! You mean that some of them survived?"

"Yes, three survived when the influenza kill off the tribe, and he is the youngest. The chief adopt him, as he got no child of his own. The other two is old men, and they lives in Brazil, with the Mawayán Indians."

To find them became one of my objects.

5

The Sea of Leaves

Towards the New River

" . . . Unless you hear to the contrary from me," I wrote to Basil, "if I have not returned from the New River when you arrive, do not wait. Take the thirty-six gallons of fuel and the boxes of rations and trade goods, which I have put aside, up the Chodikar River and over to the Mapuera. Charlie, one of the Wapisianas you mentioned, knows the Indian trail across and I shall send him to guide you. When you reach the Mapuera start work at once building two boats with transomes, large enough to carry 1000 lbs. of cargo and ten men between them."

The time had come for us to follow George. I handed my note to the missionary, shook hands, and we pushed off in the boat: Andrew, Jonah, Tanner and myself, and four Wai-Wais, Mingelli and Mawashá, the haughty Chekemá, Mawashá's father, and a budding sorcerer called Eoka, all from the village down river—but even with them we were short of men and the loads would be very heavy:

"Mr. Guppy, we will not be able to move," said Andrew gloomily. "We going to be right at the waterside this time tomorrow. We can't . . ."

"Enough," I said. "We *will* move. The loads are heavy, but I have seen heavier carried. And I shall try to get more Indians."

Just inside the mouth of the Onoro we came upon the remains of George's camp in a low-lying place, soggy and dripping from heavy rain earlier in the day. There I left Jonah and the four Wai-Wais to make camp, and with Andrew and Tanner went on up the river towards where the Wai-Wais

58

were cutting a new field. It was narrow and dark, overarched with forest and full of fallen trees, some projecting above the surface, but mostly hidden and dangerous to our progress. Sometimes, when we saw it in time, we put on speed and skidded across a shallow-lying log. At one point, where a section of hill-side had stripped away and all its trees lay flung across the river, we had to chop a way for the boat through the tangled mass of crowns. Then the river grew shallow, with deep pools full of rocks over which the water poured so softly that even when they rose close to the surface not a ripple gave warning. Fearful of breaking the propeller, we cut down speed, peering ahead into the yellow depths.

I had begun to wonder whether we should ever reach our destination when we saw three canoes tied at the waterside. A steep, winding path led up to a small clearing with a powis-tail —a fan-shaped shelter of palm leaves—under which Wayama ("the Turtle")—one of the Indians I knew—lay in his hammock. Beyond, the undergrowth of a large area on either side of the path had been cut preliminary to felling the bigger trees, and then we came out on to a large clearing on a precipitous hill-side, with in the middle two strange elongated houses like open-ended thatched-roofed Nissen huts.

Amid the usual barking of dogs the occupants emerged, greetings were exchanged, and Andrew began to explain our needs and what we had to offer.

Why were we cutting east? they asked. They had never heard of any river in that direction: nobody ever went there.

There was a rather frozen silence while they looked at us.

A very pale and toothy lad, heavily painted with spots and bars, beamed at me and came and sat beside me, holding a baby in his arms. As soon as it caught sight of my beard it burst into a wild howl of terror: I tickled it under the chin—its screams redoubled.

Suddenly everyone laughed and the ice was broken. I had feared that no one would come, but now two young men, about fourteen or fifteen years old, stepped forward. It took them a moment to collect what they needed for a two weeks' trip—a net hammock, red from the paint of their bodies, a bow, a dozen arrows, a cooking-pot, a few white discs of cassava bread, and a kitchen knife each, stuck naked into their loin-cloth belts at the back.

The younger, Manaka, looked just like the nicest English prep school boy. His companion was very different—a self-possessed, sturdy little fellow married to a middle-aged, hugely pregnant woman with colossal swinging breasts, who presented him when they parted with a dried monkey's leg.

At camp the tarpaulins had been put up, the Wai-Wais had built themselves a powis-tail shelter, fires had been lighted, and everyone was settling down for the night. Birds were still calling, so I lent my shotgun to Mawashá, who said he knew how to use one, and just as it grew dark he returned with a powis (curassow) and two 20-lb. monkeys—a spider monkey and a red howler. In a flash they were skinned and their white forms flung prostrate across a babricot—a framework of sticks—over the fire. Before they were properly cooked the Wai-Wais began cutting off pieces and chewing away.

Soon lamps were lighted and comfortably clad, after a dip in the river, in a pair of flannels and an Aertex shirt, I was eating a dinner of fried powis breast and boiled rice.

"This New River is a bad place," Andrew was saying. "There is terrible disease there. The men of the Boundary Commission was dying there like flies—like flies I'm telling you."

Jonah here raised his voice in mournful tones. "That's quite right, Mr. Macdonald. Doctor tell me never eat cold food in this part, or you will get sick. Always stop work, make fire and cook food. If you can't do that because you is travelling, wait till night for eating. And it seems to me I never meet a place so cold. It is very damp and chilly here tonight."

"Well, you needn't be worried," I explained, "the men on the Boundary Commission died of beri-beri, which they got because they lived on nothing but salt beef, salt pork, salt fish and salt biscuits. As long as we have fresh meat and fresh vegetables and fruit every now and again we will never get it."

"That's true," said Andrew; "the Brazilians never had beri-beri: they took beans and sprouted them and ate that. But all the same we are heading for trouble. Why is no Indians living at the New River? Because it is a bad place—that's what I'm saying. *There is no food there.* Father Cuffe and Father Cary travel up Courantyne and New River in 1908, and they nearly starve. They found *nothing* to eat. Do you know what they had to eat? *Cayman!* Which they catch in Onoro. We are going to *starve!*"

"At a pinch we'll eat *you*, Andrew," I said. "But I think you will bring us food. We'll use you as bait. All the caymans and jaguars will be after a big, meaty man like you."

Andrew laughed: "O.K., sir, you win. But I going to get them first!"

As soon as we had eaten we retired to our hammocks, but sleep did not come quickly. There was much chatter and merriment round the fire at the Wai-Wai powis-tail. I dozed, then was awakened by wild yells of laughter: the Indians were clustered at the water's edge, carrying flambeaux of lighted resin. One had clambered out over the water on a tree and was holding his flare close to the surface. With a quick slash he decapitated a sizeable fish, and then chopped again and again, while the others manœuvred a canoe to collect the bodies.

Most of the night the Wai-Wais seemed to be up, eating, catching fish and broiling or smoking them over the fire. Once I heard the sound of paddles as Eoka set off to Yakka-Yakka with a side of monkey and a couple of smoked fish for his wife; then for a while all was quiet, until, about 4 a.m., they began playing their flutes.

At daybreak they gathered round complaining of hunger. We gave them some farine (cassava meal) and as soon as breakfast was over set to work packing up the camp.

Jonah, Andrew and Tanner packed their loads into *warishis* —strong basketwork rucksacks, which they had brought with them—while the Wai-Wais wove themselves carriers from the large soft leaves of the Turu palm (*Jessenia bataua*), bound with ropes made by stripping bark off a young monkey-pipe tree (*Eschweilera*) which grew beside the tent, fracturing the crusty outer layers, and twisting the softer bast into spirals.

Even for nine men there was a lot to carry: a tarpaulin, rations for two weeks, a herbarium press, cooking equipment, hammocks, lanterns, fuel oil, clothes, cutlasses—the heaviest things being left for the two young lads, Manaka and Yakotá, until I insisted on a more equitable distribution.

My own burden I kept to a minimum—that required for my

work along the way: two cameras (a Rolleiflex and a Rollei-
cord), close-up lenses, exposure meter, tripod, spare rolls of
film and a few other accessories, a penknife, a bar of chocolate
and my notebooks and pencils.

Thus equipped, we set off along the trail: a swathe some four
feet wide where the saplings and shrubs of the undergrowth had
been cut off close to the ground. It led up a low hill of red earth,
then down steeply to a tiny crystalline stream under a shrubbery
of small palms, where, between the giant tree-columns, the
sun's rays slanted like searchlights, scintillating on diamonds of
dew in the semi-darkness. It was extremely cool and humid
here in the early morning.

Beyond, there were more low steep hills. It was difficult to
keep a foothold on the damp clay, and to maintain speed over
the obstacles of the path—the roots, pot-holes, lianes and
stumps—one had to skip like a dancer, scrambling, when necessary, over or under logs and fallen trees.

Between the hills were bogs of waving, feathery palms, where
large patches of sky could be glimpsed between the sifting leaves,
but where one had to step cautiously to avoid sinking into the
peat. Mostly the water was little over ankle deep, but towards
mid-morning we crossed one bog where the peat was porridge
thin, and where, between firm footholds on logs and fallen palm
fans, we sank to the knees or waist. Water-lilies were flowering
all around, dying broad-leaved trees gave evidence that somewhere water was being held back—that the whole area was
becoming increasingly wet—and after a while the delicate star-
like *Euterpe* palms were replaced by two sorts of *Mauritia*—a
smaller, its stem thickly encrusted with prickles,[1] and a massive
species[2] whose shafts rose to a great burst of fan-leaves nearly a
hundred feet above the ground. Under their watery shade we
floundered and struggled, until, dead weary, we came to a wall
of dry land, and at a level place a little further sank down to rest
for a few minutes, slipping off our loads and reclining, panting
and streaming with sweat.

We were making good speed, considering the country—at
least one mile an hour, I estimated.

Then onwards again. I wondered how far George had got—

---

[1] *Mauritia aculeata.*   [2] *Mauritia flexuosa.*

whether, in fact, the New River was as close as I hoped. Then I heard loud hallooings and shouts from just ahead—unmistakably in his voice! An instant later I found him and his men chatting with Jonah and Tanner.

"Good morning, Mr. Guppy," said he, "I come back for instructions."

"Have you found the New River, George?"

"No, sir, that is what I am come to ask you about," he looked very guilty—"straight ahead we run into high mountains and we cannot pass. From where the path end you can look all around. Ahead there is nothing but rocks and high cliffs. Men carrying loads cannot pass—it would be too terrible work. It would take a month to cut through. But I see to the north that the land is lower an' the mountains end, and I already cut two miles that way to see if we can get round. So I come back to help carry the loads, and to ask if what I am doing is right. We will reach my next camp this afternoon."

I was disappointed, and a little suspicious that he and his men might have been taking things easily, but as we went onwards the country grew steadily rougher—the hills steeper, the bogs narrower and drier—and we were ascending all the time.

Everywhere the trees were tall and stately, crowded together, smothering us beneath their innumerable layers of green; while occasionally we passed giants whose immense columns soared clean through the forest and spread above, 150 to 200 feet up, in great wheels of branches. The air was vibrant with the piercing calls of greenheart birds, green cotingas about the size of a thrush. From one to another they sounded the alarm, heralding our advance—"Pi-pi-yo! Pi-pi-yo!" their cries rang and echoed through the aisles of the trees.

Then there came a most peculiar cry like the lowing of a cow, or the groan of a door, or a long drawn-out yawn—"Mwaar; nyaarrr; ughaaarow!" Heart-chilling, horrible, it made vocal all the melancholy of the lonely miles of jungle—I had never heard anything like it before. It was the call of another cotinga, the cow-bird,[1] found only in these southern regions.

The sky—such as we could see of it—became black and overcast, and soon so dark that the men ahead were barely visible;

[1] The bald-headed cotinga, *Calvifrons calvus*.

there arose a strange humming, seemingly miles away, like the swarming of a vast mass of bees: a sinful man had died, said the Indians, and wasps were barring his entry into Heaven. Then came a continuous rumbling and rolling, growing louder and louder until it was replaced by the crashing of twigs and branches as a savage wind rushed through the tree tops. The trees shook as if they were grasses, and dead branches fell all around with shattering thuds. The wind passed, and again there was silence. It was only three in the afternoon, but night seemed to be upon us. Now we could hear the roar of approaching rain and imagine the white barrage as it swept over the forest towards us. We hurried downhill towards George's camp and had already begun to put up our tarpaulins when, with great thunderings and lightnings, the avalanche of water descended. In a few minutes the ground became a brown running river.

One by one the remaining men staggered in with their burdens. Manaka and Yakotá were the last to arrive. They threw down their huge loads under the tent and then flung themselves on the ground, dead weary, but laughing and waving their legs in the air.

It rained all night, but in the morning green light filled the undergrowth as the sun came probing down. George and his men started off early for their forward camp to continue their attempt at working northwards round the mountains, and we began to improve the clearing. Trees were felled to let in sun and air to dry the ground. A large palm-thatched shelter was built for Jonah, Andrew and Tanner, and powis-tails put up for the Wai-Wais. The small stream which ran in front of my tarpaulin was cleared of debris and a number of small benches and working tables put up along its banks.

When all this was done I explored towards the east along George's discontinued line. After a mile and a half it was obvious that we really *were* ascending a mountain. Immense boulders of granite protruded from the earth, slippery with a thin film of moisture, often densely overgrown with aroids, ferns and mosses. I scrambled to the top of one, forty or fifty feet above the ground, but could obtain no view, for even on the downhill side the trees still rose far above.

We crossed a small stream, skirted a gully, and continued,

climbing ever more and more steeply, following a narrow winding ridge until, at the extreme summit, we came to a fairly level patch of ground where the path ended, and where the forest was noticeably much thinner than on the slopes, like a young copse with small stems close together; but even here it was impossible to see through the trees.

Hearing running water, we descended to a beautiful rivulet which poured over a bed of mottled rock. Its water was icy cold and full of the hovering forms of tiny shrimps with scarlet eyes. Further down the slope was a thunderous torrent, roaring steeply among boulders. Its direction was north-west, indicating that we had not reached the divide between the Essequebo and the New River. My respect for George's judgment grew—laden porters would have suffered badly on these crumpled slopes. But nowhere could I discover where he had obtained his view over the country-side.

On our way back I asked one of the Wai-Wais the names of all the larger trees (more than twelve inches in trunk diameter) that grew beside the path. This very simple procedure brought out the startling variety of the forest: in one mile we passed one hundred and thirty big trees—but they belonged to seventy-six species, fifty-seven of which we had seen only once, six twice, and thirteen more than twice. By comparison a British oak-wood would probably contain about seven species of large tree.

Small areas of forest as mixed as this were not unusual further north—but here they covered mile after mile, everywhere appearing unvarying and uniform, yet with no two patches alike. Only by casting one's net very wide could one hope to find all the tree species in such a forest—probably four or five hundred in all. Then there were the completely different forests of the river-flood plains, and of the peaty, waterlogged valleys; and when the larger trees had been studied there would still remain the smaller ones, the shrubs and herbs, the epiphytes and lianes, the ferns, mosses, liverworts, fungi, in endless abundance and diversity.

Such then were the true primeval forests: in the time at my disposal I would be able to learn only enough to tantalize me.

My first sample plot in this region was, like the one behind

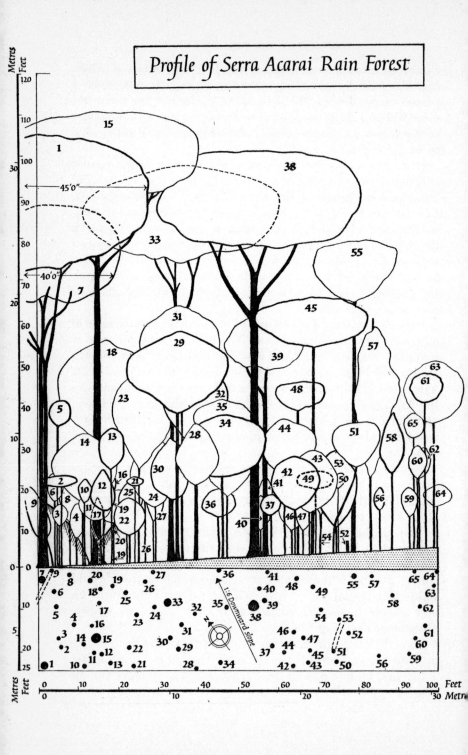

Profile of Serra Acarai Rain Forest

the mission, in a patch of bog forest, where for a day we wallowed under an ethereal canopy of quivering palm fronds. Next, constructing profiles for each, I studied a place where a small river was building up the level of the land by deposition, then moved to various types of hill slopes—steep, gentle, rocky—and finally to the summits, with their spindly copse-woodlands, or tangles of stilt-rooted *Clusias* growing on almost bare rock.

Gradually a picture began to emerge from the masses of detail—the picture of a whole landscape being moulded by water—driving rain-water, dripping leaf-water, percolating underground water, rushing hill-side torrents; of rock being weathered and changed to soil, of torrents digging their steep-sided gullies, and gradually washing away and levelling the hills; of the rivers of the lowlands building up their banks in times of flood with sediment from higher ground; and of these banks holding back the floodwaters so that in places the ground became permanently waterlogged and peat began to form—like the peat of northern moors, but bearing a giant forest and full of its leaves and branches.

Water, then, was the key to this country-side and to the green ocean that covered it; and with knowledge grew a sense of the wonderful beauty, the subtle detail, the changeability of these forests which I had at first thought monotonous.

Noon, Night and Morning in the Forest

After the first few days it seemed perfectly natural to be surrounded by necklaced and braceleted Indians, and I began to think of them as likeable human beings of great charm, and

PROFILE OF SERRA ACARAI RAIN FORREST

The forest is sometimes higher, and occasional large trees hold their crowns above the general level. Trees whose trunks are outside the profile area are not shown—hence the apparent thinness of the forest on the right of the profile, where in fact it was just as dense as elsewhere. Only trees above 15 feet in height and 4 inches in trunk diameter are shown.

with strong, distinctive personalities. *En masse* they smelt a little spicy or fishy, but it was only at times—when, for example, I saw one of them gnawing a half-raw monkey's head—that the sense of strangeness returned. And hard though we worked, the days were full of fun—wherever the Wai-Wais were there was always much laughter.

The only one whom I never quite trusted was the supercilious Chekemá. At first he was bored and peevish, using every excuse—fever or a supposedly sore foot—to avoid work. He lolled about the camp, highly painted and arrogant; and when he did come out was troublesome. The Wai-Wai language was very difficult to transcribe: pronunciation varied from person to person and the values of the consonants and vowels was different from our own. Most of the Indians were patient, but whenever I asked Chekemá to repeat a word he would become annoyed: he would lean his mouth close to my ear and suddenly shout, or would whisper almost inaudibly and then give a violent and unexpected puff of air—and smile broadly: a most exasperating brute.

Sometimes he would deliberately give me the wrong name for a plant, or let fly a stream of obscenities. I had almost given him up when I realized one day that he was becoming friendlier, and actually interested, in a mild sort of way, in our work, greeting each new and surprising request with a loud and emphatic "Ah . . . haaa!" and finding things to show me.

When most excited his voice rose to a shrieking, high-pitched staccato, like Hitler at a great moment—as, for example, one day when he rushed up and pulled at my elbow:

"Meeshterguffin, Meeshterguffin, Meeshterguffin, powisi, mm, mm, bang, bang, powisi, powisi!" pointing frantically into a tree.

I shook my head—Eoka had gone off with the gun. In an instant he darted away and returned with his bow and a very long wooden-pointed arrow. Cautiously he stalked forward, gazing transfixedly into the crown of a monkey-pipe tree. He was transformed: instead of hysterical, agitated, foppish, he had become unbelievably concentrated, his movements feline. Carefully he aimed, drawing his great eight-foot bow. Then, at the moment of release, his left arm fell, his right arched back in the semblance of a statue. I could only glimpse the shot, because of the thickness of the vegetation, but I saw the arrow fall with a bird at the end—a toucan, about the size of a small pullet, which he had picked off eighty or ninety feet above. Very carefully, so as not to disarrange the feathers, he skinned it; then with his heated cutlass blade singed the inner surface, and when it was dry attached this fresh trophy to his pigtail-tube.

The two young boys were like fawns, leaping and prancing, rolling about on the ground from sheer exuberance, or running up the trees like squirrels. With a twisted piece of liane between their feet to increase friction and steady their legs they could perform astonishing feats. They would shin up the smoothest trunk like looper caterpillars and high up swing from one tree to another and come slithering down yards away.

"Just like monkey," was Jonah's comment as he turned his back on one such exhibition.

Andrew was full of tricks which amused them. Once, when heavy rain caught us far from camp, we built a powis-tail for shelter and huddled under it while he imitated various creatures: he puffed out his cheeks, held his nose and said "Oomp! Oomp!" emphatically, deep in his throat, like a flock of trumpeter birds; he whistled through a piece of leaf like a tapir, snuffled like a wild pig, made a noise like a howler monkey; then, with a piece of leaf membrane against the roof of his mouth, emitted a piercing cry, made a pretence of cutting his throat, and sank to the ground, rolling his eyes up as if dead. A moment later he leaped up, growling, and began to show us puzzles made by folding and cutting leaves and stems—producing a chain, a row of figures and a double-barrelled gun.

Often the Wai-Wais tried to outstare me, particularly Mawashá, who would go solemn and owl-like for a moment, then burst into laughter. Once I crossed my eyes during such a staring match, and in a moment the whole group, astonished, had gathered round, saying "*Anoro*, Meeshterguffin!" begging me to do it again and again. My beard interested and horrified them, and as it grew denser they would reach up occasionally and fondle it, uttering loud exclamations of "Mmmmmmm!" or "Ahaaaaa!" or "*Chichibé!* CHICHIBÉ!"—"How awful!"

Torches and ordinary clocks they had seen at the mission,

but my self-winding wrist-watch, which went "Ping!" from time to time as I moved my hand, puzzled them—what could be in it?—and my fountain-pen they regarded as a great invention: Mawashá appeared one day covered with blue spots, which he showed me proudly as an example of what could be done with it.

The keenest hunter was Yakotá, who smelt animals constantly as he walked through the forest, his nostrils dilating, his ears and eyes alert for movement; the best shots with the gun were Eoka and Mawashá, but almost as much game was killed by the others with bows and arrows. In six days they brought in six trumpeter birds, one curassow, three toucans, and four monkeys—one of them a soft, pathetically human-looking ring-tailed capuchin. All were thrown at once on a babricot of sticks over the fire, and when they had been scorched and smoked a little the Wai-Wais would begin gorging themselves.

They never left anything for the next meal, so that despite all our efforts there was not enough meat to satisfy them; and each morning they complained of hunger until, to keep them happy, Jonah, Andrew, Tanner and I began giving them some of our own rations, thinking that once we reached the New River we should at least have plenty of fish.

The delay in getting there had begun to put a strain on our food supplies. We were not critically short, but we might become so, which was worrying. At a pinch I could send back to the mission for more, but our rations were carefully calculated for the whole trip, and we had few reserves because of the limited weight we had been able to carry on the plane.

All would have been well if the hunters had been more successful, but always the game seemed to be where the gun was not. They would see nothing while we, working at our plot, would surprise a deer, a herd of peccaries, or a flock of trumpeters.

After two such unsuccessful days the Wai-Wais decided to poison the streamlet which wound past my tent. They gathered lengths of the roots and stems of a fish-poison vine,[1] which grew in a great tangle nearby, and beat them to shreds, filling half a dozen baskets with the light yellow, unpleasant-smelling fragments.

[1] *Lonchocarpus.*

When these basketfuls were dipped and squeezed in the water a milky juice ran out, and soon the whole stream was opaque and whitish, and all the fish in it began swimming near the surface, jumping and splashing to avoid the asphyxiant— among them several small brilliantly coloured minnows—one scarlet-striped, another with a black and yellow sailfin, which caused my aquarist's heart to leap, for they were new to me. Many fish seemed to lose all control, and went round and round in circles, until at last they lay gasping and helpless on their sides; others beached themselves on the banks, under leaves or roots where they might be hidden.

As soon as they became stupefied the Wai-Wais, with yells of delight and excitement, jumped in and gathered them, chopping to kill the more active ones. But the catch was small—a few cichlids and three young haimara (a fish that grows to 40 lb.), and we had to wait several hours before we could drink again.

As fine weather continued the water-level of the creek fell rapidly, exposing the sandy bottom, until there was just a string of pools with shallow trickles in between.

One day I became aware of a disgusting smell: a little up-stream of the camp, caught among fallen twigs and branches, were floating gas-distended intestines and entrails which the Wai-Wais had flung into the water. To their dismay I made them gather up the rotting flesh, bury it, and clean the stream. They could not understand the need for this, and for a while were rather angry with me. However, I was adamant, for at the end of each day my first thought was to bathe, luxuriating on the sandy bottom and letting the water wash away my tiredness.

If we returned late, glowworms would be shining along the banks, and shrimps' eyes would flash red in the torchlight; my imagination would people the water with all sorts of monsters and I would hastily scramble out after my dip. Once dressed, the serious work of the evening would begin—sorting, pressing and describing the plants we had collected.

Jonah was in good humour these days, and as we worked through our bundles of specimens he would tell me tales— Indian legends or stories of his own life.

One night when we had lit the hissing, white-glaring lantern and were going through the last of a very large pile of plants,

I noticed the noise of a frog which always called just after dark
—"Wa; Wa; Wau; War; Er; Urk"—a loud, persistent, peculiarly laboured noise that sounded as if the animal were in pain.

"That is a big frog," said Jonah, "that lies alone in water
caught in the fork of a tree. It is called Adaba, and we have a
story about it: A long time ago there was a young man called
Haduri, who was stolen from his parents by the witch Adaba
who brought him up as her own son; but one day he meet with
some people and they tell him who his real parents were, so he
decided to escape. He thought a long time and he decided it was
best to go by water, because then she could not follow him; so
that is how the first corial [canoe] was invented.

"But Adaba caught him and brought him back. At this
Haduri became very angry, for he was a prisoner, and he
decided he must have vengeance. He knew that she loved honey
so he found a bees' nest in a tree and he split the tree and pulled
it apart. Then he told Adaba about the nest, and up she climbed
to search. As soon as she was inside, he released the tree and it
spring together and sealed her up; and so she is calling out for
pity now.

"But there is another interesting thing: in some way the old-
time Indians used this frog to prepare a charm for hunting,
which they said was irresistible. For many days before he went
out the hunter had to have nothing to do with women, or salt
or pepper; then he cut himself and rubbed this charm into his
body. After that animals would even come to him from far
off."

As we worked, or after dinner before we retired to our hammocks, our conversation would range over a wide variety of
topics. One day I asked the Wai-Wais the meanings of their
names. At first they were reticent; then Mawashá confessed
that he was named after that same large frog, Adaba, because it
went "Ma, Wa"; while Yakotá was named after another frog
which cried "Ko! Ko! Ko!"

Chekemá and Mingelli were apparently meaningless words,
"just names", though Andrew claimed that Mingelli was really
Miguel. Manaka was the name of the solitary *Euterpe* palm that
grows on dry land (*E. stenophylla*), while Eoka, our sorcerer's
name, meant blind.

How did people choose a name for a child? I asked.

For all sorts of reasons, said Eoka—for instance, his own little daughter Emau was so called in imitation of the noise she had made crying as a baby; and at Yakka-Yakka there were two people who had been named after times when only boys or girls were born—Wasumna, when there were no girls; Kwarumna, no boys.

Eoka went on to explain that really one should never utter a person's name loudly, because that might attract evil spirits. If one had to shout, it was best to confuse the spirits by describing the person instead of using his name—instead of "Eoka!" one should call "Emau-yin!"—Emau's father.

In contrast with these beautiful and somehow appropriate names were those of the Wapisianas with George, James, Albert, Charlie, Gabriel—which, linked with such surnames as Smith, Johnson or Mackintosh, seemed to reflect appallingly on the taste of their catechists.

Andrew was very fond of discoursing on the origin of place-names: Kassikaityu, he said, meant Paca (a large rodent, bigger than a hare) in the Taruma language, just like Urana in Wai-Wai. But this I knew to be wrong from reading Schomburgk and Farabee: "Kassi" meant "the dead" and "kityu" "river".

"Well, sir," said Andrew when I had told him this, "I guess that must be right, because there are other rivers with names ending 'kityu'. But do you know how the Essequebo gets its name? I have thought about this a long time, because it is a very strange word. My belief is this—the main part of that word is 'sipu', which is the Wapisiana name for the river. Now the Portuguese and the Spanish call it 'Rio Sipu', and what I say is, the Arawaks heard that and made up their own word which is 'Dissichipu'—from which the English gets 'Essequebo'."

The conversation turned to animals and I asked him if he had ever heard of a man being killed by a jaguar.

"Only once," he said, "but the jaguar is not so bad. Usually if it hear you coming it will go away. It is the deer tiger [puma] you have to watch out for. It like to jump on you from behind and knock you down. I know of many people that have had that—Mr. Bamford, the Commissioner of the Interior, is one;

and it was George Gouveia who rescue him. Another man was Father McKenna."

"How old is Father McKenna?" I inquired—he was a heavily bearded priest who lived on the savannah.

"I think he is about thirty, Mr. Guppy—but he look about fifty! Tell me, sir, what do you think about rejuvenation? Is it possible to make an old man young again by transplanting a young man's testicles?"

"I don't know. I think they've tried—but not very successfully—using monkey's glands."

"Well, sir," said Jonah, "I will tell you a very strange story that I know is true. One of my friends had a grandmother, a woman who was very old indeed—they said that she was well over a hundred years old. When she reached about 120 she recovered a set of teeth—small teeth like a baby's; she lost her wrinkles, her breasts became firm and she could walk upright and stand straight again. But soon after that she die."

"I will tell you of something like that that I read in the newspapers," said Andrew. "There was an old man in Berlin—a millionaire—who reach about eighty and decide he want to be young again. So he got hold of six girls—nursing girls you see—and he lie in bed and he feed from their breasts just like a baby. And for seven or eight months he live just like that, like a baby, and at the end of that time he have new teeth, and new hair, and he recovered his strength so that he could satisfy a woman. Well, what do you think of that?"

"Ha, that is very good," said Jonah, "I would like to be able to afford that."

"So would I," said I, "but I know of a case that is exactly opposite—of a very famous man in England who decided to miss middle-age altogether. So when he was thirty-five he went away for the week-end and returned as an old man—with his hair dyed white, walking slowly with the aid of a stick. From then onwards he behaved as if he was about eighty, and people treated him so."

There came a little chuckling cry from overhead, and something hit the canvas tarpaulin.

"Don't go outside, sir!" said Andrew, restraining me. He picked up his torch and, peeping out, shone it into the branches.

He could see nothing and presently came back. "That is a night monkey [kinkajou]. They are very bad animals. It heard us here, and it urinate upon the tent, hoping it would hit us. The Wapisianas say that if that happens you will waste away and die."

The night was full of noises; as the sounds of the day withdrew a finer web of vibrations presented itself, like that in a sea-shell held against the ear: tiny constant rustlings, cheepings, pipings, hissings, indicating the myriad small life of the forest—the insects and worms and frogs—the rare cries of night birds and animals, and the never-ceasing rain of solid particles—leaves, twigs, fruits, fragments of bark, petals; falling, drifting, sifting, precipitating down through the many layers of leaves to the floor of the jungle. Sometimes larger objects would drop with a startling thump nearby, or on my tarpaulin roof; sometimes some creature would move stealthily through the forest—never was the forest quiet, yet its sounds had about them the quality of silence.

As night drew on a chill stillness fell over everything. The air ceased to move: convection currents no longer carried water vapour from the transpiring plants upwards into drier regions; the temperature dropped and the humidity of the air increased steadily; beads of moisture condensed on every smooth surface; mosses, ferns and orchids absorbed their life-giving potions of liquid; and though the temperature might still be 70-75° F., the body lost warmth rapidly, for saturated air is an excellent conductor of heat. The Indians stirred in their sleep, rose and poked up their fires; and I, under two blankets, shivered and sweated violently, feeling as if the north wind were blowing down my spine, yet with my deceived body still perspiring in an effort to adjust itself to the temperature—a most unpleasant and uncomfortable state.

Clothes left overnight became damp, paper sodden, shoes moist and moulded, gun-barrels rusty: anything that might be damaged had to be put under shelter or packed away in tin trunks—despite which my cameras, whenever I took them out of their carrying cases, were always blue with mould, and films so damp-feeling that I began to wonder whether their emulsions would survive the journey. And my tarpaulin was as much a protection against falling dew as against rain or twigs; my mosquito net not only excluded insects but provided an additional sheath for my body—an outer insulating cocoon holding in the air which it had warmed.

Getting up one night, in the intense blackness, I went and sat with Jonah as he stirred a pot of soup over the fire.

"You know, Mr. Guppy, it is this cold and damp which is the worst things if you gets caught without shelter in the forest at night. A man can die of exposure."

"Have you ever got lost in the forest, Jonah?"

"No, that I never have done; it would be a most terrible experience. All we Indians fear that more than anything. It is very easy for a person who knows the bush well to get lost. There is a man at Bartica, living by the power station, who got lost only eight miles from the town. It was two weeks before some wood-cutters find him and during that time he lost his mind and all his hair turn white. He must have live on roots and insects, because mostly there is nothing else. Even now he is not right again; and he was wandering not far from a path."

"Apart from starvation, what about snakes and other animals —do you think there is any danger?"

"If you walks about at night there is bound to be danger, because that is when nearly every kind of creature is moving around. But if you build a shelter, and especially if you can make a fire, you will be all right. I think the worst thing of all is just being alone, which is why we Indians never go into the forest unless there is at least two of us."

Around 5.30 to 6 a.m. humidity was highest—usually at saturation-point. The air was like an icy breath, yet the water of the creek would be strangely warm as I took my morning dip. The mist banks of the night's moisture would be rising above the forest, dissipating their whiteness into a sky of deepening blue, against which the dewy twigs of the tree-tops would begin to sparkle in the sunlight as if encrusted with jewels.

Each morning as I drank my coffee and ate my farine porridge and the last of the bacon and eggs I had brought in, I felt wonderfully at peace with the world. The blue smoke of our fires would rise slowly amongst the moist, limp-hanging leaves

—some like huge pink rabbits' ears, others yellow, or of every shade of green from the palest lime to nearly black—until high up it suddenly caught the sunrays and incandesced into clouds of dazzling whiteness. Birds would sing in the undergrowth with remote hidden voices: a thrush, scuffling among the wild arrowroots of the stream banks, would call mechanically, a little speckled wren whistle a plaintive bubbling song. In the distance there was often the pale, silvery trilling of a tinamou, lost and desolate, or the yelping of a toucan. Everywhere, imperceptibly, the leaves would be slowly stiffening, assuming their different daytime positions, the moist forest drying, awakening, the bird songs changing.

Soon breezes would begin to stir in the undergrowth as the sun's warmth penetrated, and I would hear, suddenly, the irresponsible fluting-gurgling of a hangnest—like a stone being rattled in a tin can—or the piercing clarion call of the first greenheart bird: day had begun and with it our cycle of work, sweat and tiredness until once again we sank into our hammocks.

Hunger

Six days had passed while I waited for news from George—days of hard but rewarding work, walking through the forest, laying out plots, measuring and felling trees, collecting flowers and fruits and wood specimens.

How far had we got? Had I miscalculated in estimating that the New River was only sixteen miles from the Essequebo? It was twelve days since he had originally set off—it must be further! The tricky food situation made it imperative for us to move at once if we were going to move at all, so on the seventh morning I ordered packing to begin.

Just as we were ready, as if summoned by telepathy, George and three of his men arrived. They had found the New River at last, about eight miles ahead; but the going was so rough that George doubted if we could reach it in a day. He had an intermediate camp where we could spend a night, and one of the men, whose shoes had worn out, had remained there to guard the food supplies from animals—for the previous day a pot cover had been carried away by an ocelot and a jaguar had run off with a powis which Charlie had left on the path.

After a mile of level country the path forked, and, at George's suggestion, Jonah, Andrew and I turned aside for a while to follow the right branch to the look-out point, which we had hitherto failed to find, from which he had planned his final route.

Before long we were in low foothills; then commenced a steep, rocky climb. Spiny palms[1] filled the undergrowth, a stately monkey-pipe showered down its soft, strangely-shaped flowers, like little white kid gloves with yellow centres, fragrant of jasmine. The path seemed to hang from the tree-tops. Beneath an overhanging boulder there was a smooth spot—a jaguar's resting-place, said Andrew; then we were at the top, an undulating platform with the wind whistling through the trees, but yet no view.

George's path twisted on between the boulders into a woodland of small gnarled trees: *Clusias*,[2] poised on slender stilt-roots—like vegetable crab's legs which might at any moment begin to walk—myrtles, and others, all hung with orchids and mosses. Wild pineapples, silk-grass, more orchids, grew on the ground—then we burst through the last bush into the sunlight, on to a slope of rock with a great view stretching northwards over the illimitable expanse of tree-crowns.

Far ahead, a pale blue pimple above the smoky horizon, was the tooth of granite we had flown over. Fifty or sixty miles to its left were the north-western extremities of the Acarai Range, where it curled round to its anchoring points, the mountains of Wamuriak-tawa and Vindaua; in the middle distance the Wasaru Mountains—the Mountains of the Sun—rising perhaps to 3,000 feet; and to our right the high jumbled mountains we were attempting to skirt.

The *Clusias* grew right to the edge of the cliff, and their clustering roots supported a mat of leaf-mould, moss and litter through which a foot or stick occasionally and disconcertingly penetrated into the void, as we wandered, seeking fresh views. Below us yet more *Clusias*—a nodding, hummocky carpet of

[1] *Bactris* sp.   [2] *Clusia nemorosa* and *Oedematopus dodecandrus*.

small-leaved trees—stretched away smoothly, growing no doubt similarly on almost bare rock surfaces. In the branches of one of them, a few hundred yards down the slope, hung a brilliant orange globe—then it disappeared: a bird! There was only one bird it could be—the cock-of-the-rock, an almost mythically rare creature, seldom seen wild by civilized men. But it was gone, and we turned back to follow George.

By midday we had walked over several hills, crossed several bogs and streams, all drying up as the dry season advanced, and had glimpsed one more cock-of-the-rock: a vivid flash of orange, a whistling of wings, close by our heads. Then we caught a sound which grew steadily louder, like that of a stampede of wild animals, thundering over the ground, thrusting the bushes aside.

"That sound like a very big herd of pigs," said Jonah, "but I can't tell which way they going."

Sunlight shone between the trees ahead, and realization came as we walked to the brink of a steep slope. It was the sound of a waterfall. Peering downwards, I could see nothing for the trees, but a few yards further the path turned sharply east and there were glimpses of white water in a dark narrow gorge.

Beyond this river—most likely, from its direction of flow, the Urana or the Buna-wau, tributaries of the Essequebo which enter it below Gunn's Strip—began a terrific ascent of about 1,500 feet, which we took without pause. The forest here was superb, full of many kinds of monkey-pipe trees (so named from the shape of their fruits), the red earth was covered with delicate selaginellas, and the quiet was broken by the lowing of cow-birds. Then down we went again, up, and again down, descending to a dry saddle beyond which rose a mountain exceeding, in steepness and height, all those that had gone before.

The sun was low as with aching limbs I slowly climbed to the top. Andrew was already there, sitting with the gun in his lap.

"Golly, that was a steep hill," he said. "You need football boots to climb a thing like that."

He drew breath:

"Mr. Guppy, I got to speak with you. These Wai-Wais are giving plenty of trouble. You did not know it, but this morning they practically refuse to come. It is only I that persuade them, and Mingelli, who is the best out of the lot, and who likes you. Chekemá and Mawashá was telling the rest to refuse to do any work. They say the work is too hard and the food is not enough. But it is their fault because they will eat up everything all at once and then start complaining. It is to watch them that I walk ahead—I was afraid they might be stealing food from the loads. And I find them on top of this very hill, ten minutes ago, trying to open your own ration box. They laugh when they see me and pick up the loads and move off. But I was too weary, so I rest awhile."

"That is very bad, Andrew. If they can't control their eating, we will have to keep all the game shot, even by them, and issue a little each day."

"It is the only way, sir. But they won't like it." He looked worried; then as if suddenly remembering: "Did you see them cock-of-the-rocks, sir? That is the most wonderful thing I ever see. There was hundreds of them in that small dry valley before the Urana Creek. When I arrive they was in the trees and on the ground and several of them was dancing—jumping up and down and rolling over in little places they had cleared. I was watching when some of the boys came up and Mawashá fire the gun at them to get the feathers, and they all fly off."

This was mortifying news: no white man except Schomburgk had ever seen them dance. Had I walked ahead as I usually did I would have seen this wonderful sight, instead of merely glimpsing a couple of birds. Whatever the cost, I must try to see them on the way back.

Rising, our muscles aching, our bodies stiff, we commenced the long descent of the hill. Several hundred feet down there was a basin of palm bog, and then another downward slope with a river babbling somewhere to one side: a wide shallow stream, when we came to it, running over rocks and sand, its water glinting red in the light of the dying sun. It was flowing east: we had crossed the divide.

Beside a wide sweep stood the camp with all our baggage flung down under the tarpaulin, and a pot of tea waiting for me on a log. I blessed Tanner for his thoughtfulness and sank down beside it.

George approached with solemn face:

"Mr. Guppy, James was out collecting firewood when the Wai-Wais arrive, and when he come back he find all the food sacks open up, and half a gallon of rice gone, and a lot more. He see them washing the rice, but he didn't dare speak because they was looking very ugly, and they might desert. We men alone could never carry all this load out without several journeys. It is very serious."

Gabriel, Charlie's son, spoke up very slowly: "Lucky storehouse at mission have lock—else everything gone when you reach back. It was Manatá, the ol' man with the bad foot, who steal the tasso and farine from Andrew. I catch him where he hid them cover up with leaves, and I tell him he is a bad man, but I could not do anything or he stir up the Indians. Mr. Leavitt lose plenty. The Indians carrying his goods from Gunn's Strip open up everything and help themselves. An' if he speak to them they say shut up or we kill you. They don't like him at all —they just put up with him because they get goods from him."

"Good God!—what a situation for him."

"It is better that we turn back now," said Andrew, "because the further we go the more risks we run and the Indians think we are in their power: there is no saying what they might do. We are running bad risks, I'm telling you, sir."

"That is quite right, sir; it would be wise to start back tomorrow," agreed Jonah.

"Nonsense," I said. "We have about five days' food. We must keep it in one place and watch it carefully and make sure no more is stolen. Tanner, you are always in camp. Keep a sharp eye out. As for the danger, I think you are exaggerating. I'm certainly not going to spend twelve days getting to the New River and then turn back three miles away without seeing it. We will have to be careful, that is all."

There were other matters to be decided rapidly. Basil would soon be at the mission, and it was useless to continue forward at the rate of about a mile a day for the whole party. Undoubtedly we were within eight or ten miles of the watershed with Amazonia, but we might go on wandering for months without striking a large river on that side, finding Indians, or even being able to locate ourselves. It was better to do all that was needed in the New River neighbourhood as rapidly as possible, and then return and go with Basil to the Mapuera—to which there was the path over the Acarai used by the Wai-Wais, which Charlie knew.

It was a risk, with the Wai-Wais in their present mood, but I decided to send Charlie back to guide Basil, and with him James and Albert, two of George's men. If they left all their rations except the minimum needed for the return to the mission, the rest of us could stay a few days more. The other party, meanwhile, might be able to make the crossing of the Acarai with most of our stores and equipment and start constructing boats for descending the Mapuera in (Charlie was an expert boat-builder), before returning to meet us at the top of the Chodikar River, where the trail to the Mapuera began—and where, I calculated, we should be able to arrive in a further two weeks' time—to help with the loads that we should be bringing.

Gabriel translated my instructions into Wapisiana to make sure that his father understood. Charlie nodded, asked for twelve cartridges for his gun, and shambled off to his hammock prepared for an early start.

Because of his knowledge and skill, Charlie was quite one of the most important members of the expedition. In the old tradition of his tribe he was a great traveller and trader, and had spent more than half his life among the forest Indians on both the Essequebo and the Mapuera. He knew a little of their languages, and had even married into them, for one of his two wives was a Wai-Wai (the other being a Wapisiana, living on the savannah), for which reason he was often called Charlie Wai-Wai. He was silent, shy, annoyingly slow and forgetful— yet somehow lovable. I trusted him, though I hardly knew him, and he spoke so little English that our communication was chiefly by smiles and nods.

After dinner, I strolled in an amiable way through the supposedly mutinous Wai-Wais, bathed and retired to sleep. In the morning they seemed perfectly content. They picked up their burdens and moved off along the steep hill-side in single file. Charlie, James and Albert shook hands and took their departure, and Jonah, Andrew, Eoka and I walked back a little way to lay a plot in the small palm bog above the camp—a place of

FISH-POISONING

"A milky juice ran out, and soon the whole stream was opaque and whitish" (*p. 71*)

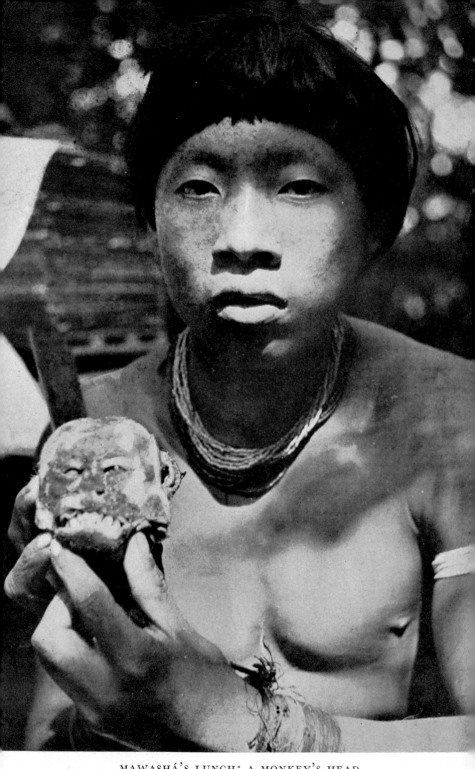

MAWASHÁ'S LUNCH: A MONKEY'S HEAD

wind-rustled young palms rising shoulder high from a particularly soupy black peat, crusted in leaves, through which we floundered heavily.

At lunch we sat on a group of boulders protruding above the surface of a sandy water-washed stretch of bare ground beside the river. The sun shone full upon us, and flies and insects buzzed around us. As my clothes dried my spirits revived. Looking at Eoka eating I began to take a more optimistic view of things. Andrew, Jonah and George were too gloomy: as long as the relationship of good manners between the Wai-Wais and myself was unbroken I felt sure they would not desert. I decided to reserve judgment on their thefts and to continue as if nothing had happened.

Black, carmine-spotted Papilio butterflies hovered over the cinnabar spikes and spirals of *Heliconias* and *Costuses*, lush herbs which grew in banks round the clearing, their banana-like leaves fluttering in the breezes. A large bluebottle, sunning itself on a stone, was suddenly pounced upon by a long-tailed brown skipper, and carried off over the bushes. I tried to see what happened next—but both had disappeared. It was an extraordinary occurrence: it looked suspiciously as if the skipper were a carnivorous butterfly, or at least a bloodsucker—for some moths, after all, have toothed tongues with which they scrape away the skin of a fruit before imbibing its juices.

Continuing eastwards, I got Eoka to name the trees on each side of the path. Despite his load, he was patient and persevering. He did not give the off-hand answers I had come to expect from Chekemá, but examined each tree carefully—going up to it, cutting it to see the colour of the slash, searching for its fallen leaves, leaning back to examine the crown—before replying.

We were in the heart of the mountains now: the slopes were overwhelmingly, backbreakingly steep, the path usually level only when we were skirting a precipitous descent, clinging to saplings and roots to prevent ourselves slipping sideways.

There seemed to be more than before of the vast tree-giants, with their far-flung lesser firmaments of branches. Strange epiphytes grew everywhere: an orchid[1] like a green centipede with miniature pineapple fruit crawled up the side of the trees:

[1] *Diocloea muricata.*

another species with blood-red flowers grew low, just above a hollow log from which a protruding waxy teapot-spout warned of a nest of stinging bees within. There were numerous signs of game: the bogs were full of the trampled footprints of herds of wild pigs—the spoor of a jaguar nearby: tinamous and toucans called, and many packs of monkeys passed above, running along the branches, swinging, drifting through the tree-tops.

The last two hills were the most breath-stealing; then for a quarter of a mile we walked along an undulating summit before descending sharply, with a glimpse of a mountain-wall on the opposite side of the valley, to the green tarpaulins pitched beside the New River.

The New River at last! Its clear yellow waters speckled with sunshine, coiling between steep banks of clay, criss-crossed by fallen logs. Quite small here (we must have been within half a dozen miles of its source), a mere forty feet wide, yet no torrent or mountain stream, but a real river, flowing in its own narrow flood plain, with an air of authority as befitted one that would grow to several miles in width. I had thought that we might make a bark canoe and paddle down it for a few hours or even days. But it was too choked.

Since reaching it, George and his men had spent much of their time fishing, and now they reported that there were no fish in it over six inches in length, which meant that somewhere below there were big falls that prevented their upward passage. It also meant that we could no longer hope to supplement our rations with fish.

The next morning I spent quietly, working at the collections made during our two days' walk. George and his men I sent to cut towards a waterfall whose vibrations filled the air, and beyond it if possible, up the steep mountain we had glimpsed in our descent, in search of a look-out point; Eoka and Andrew went out hunting, one with bow and arrows, the other taking the gun; Tanner busied himself washing my clothes; Jonah lay in his hammock, ill from the strain of the journey.

No sooner had the hunters left than a flock of trumpeters began to pass on the opposite bank of the river, picking their way delicately over the leaves, probing and searching for insects and uttering gentle honkings which served to keep the flock

together. Tanner, Jonah and I were alone at the camp and had
no means of shooting them, so we sat very quietly and watched
them go past. Each was like a rather long-legged guinea-hen in
shape and size, black except for a delicate mantle of ash-grey
feathers over the shoulders and a metallic purple breast and
throat—one of the most beautiful of all the forest birds.

A little later there came another sound, from behind the
camp: an agitated "Chrr! chrr! yike! yike! werk! wak!" Looking through the bushes, I saw a great fluttering of many small
birds—particularly beautiful little red-tailed fellows with red
collars and high pointed black and white crests. I had never
seen them before, but I recognized them at once—ant birds.
As I walked gently forward, cautious to avoid disturbing them,
I heard a noise as though the scalp of the earth were crawling:
the rustling of myriad leaves. Insects were fluttering and flying
in all directions, being snapped up by these little birds—even
by a hawk, which flew low near the ground. Then came the
great army of ants.

In several columns, each about six inches wide, they advanced over the ground. Like Panzer divisions they moved in
a series of pincer movements, enclosing large islands of ground,
which they then proceeded to explore thoroughly, running in
masses up and down the lower trees to the leaf tips. By stepping
over the columns I was able to get to the centre of the advancing army, which was about 100 feet wide, composed of many
interweaving strands. I thought at one point that the camp
would be in their path, but they skirted it, keeping about thirty
feet in from the clearing. All morning the armies advanced,
moving quite rapidly, about three to five feet a minute. By
lunchtime they had gone, the cries of the birds had faded away
southwards, and the forest was still.

At lunch I had coffee and "bakes"—dough cakes made of
flour and water fried in deep fat—with which I ate the contents
of a small tin of black codfish roe. George and the men had
returned (they had found the waterfall, but made little progress up the mountain as its side was a mass of loose boulders
carpeted with leaves and mosses), and as I ate, Eoka, Yakotá
and Manaka came and watched me, rubbing their bellies and
groaning whenever I put anything into my mouth. I croaked

once or twice and made a leaping motion with my hand to suggest that my roe was frog spawn:

"*Köoto; kiriwanhi!*"—"Frog; very nice!" said they, at which I gave them each a piece, which they loved.

After lunch I took them up the hill behind the camp a little way, and laid out a plot. They were exceedingly off-hand, and with exaggerated gestures alluded to their empty bellies and general weakness as they chopped down specimen trees—although we had given them a perfectly adequate issue of food from our own rations.

A pack of monkeys passed overhead: the gun was away, but Yakotá had his bow and arrows, and shot several times at them, unsuccessfully; whereupon all lay on the ground and pretended to be too weak to stand.

At that Andrew began to chop down a Manaka palm, to get at the soft, edible "heart" near the apex of the stem. Resting for a moment he told them:

"When you are hungry, eat Manaka heart."

All eyes at once turned on the startled, innocent-looking boy, before they realized that he was alluding to the palm. At once they laughed heartily—a little too heartily—and said no, they would eat Mr. Guppy first!

The palm came down, and gorged, feeling much better, we returned towards the camp. Half-way down the slope was a hole in a freshly dug mound of earth: mosquitoes were hovering inside, so the occupant was at home. Our quarrels forgotten in the excitement, we stood ready round the entrance with cutlasses in our hands while Eoka drove a spike into the earth a few feet back and levered it about. For a moment nothing happened, and we all bent down to look closer. Before I knew what was happening an enormous creature like an armoured car rushed out of the hole, planted its feet on my chest, covered me with earth, flung me violently on my back and was away. Up we sprang and gave chase. It was an armadillo, clumsy looking in its domed carapace, with pointed nose and pointed tail at opposite ends, but running so fast that in a minute it was out of sight.

In the evening all the Wai-Wais except Manaka and Mingelli came to have wounds dressed. They were in a very hostile mood.

After I had finished they loitered around, hoping, I saw, that I would go to bathe so that they could steal from my ration box. I picked up a book and began to read, and a couple of them casually strolled up to the box and began to examine the lock; then they idled away a few feet and sat down. A minute later the padlock, of its own accord, fell to the ground. I picked it up, put it on and snapped it shut. At once they lost interest and went away.

An hour later Eoka returned, saying he wanted to go out early in the morning to hunt and would like to borrow the gun and a few cartridges. I was a little suspicious, but I let him have it.

Not five minutes had passed before Andrew came bustling up:

"Mr. Guppy—you let Eoka have the gun? That was a very dangerous thing. They could desert tonight, or they could murder us all while we sleep and make off with everything. Nobody could catch them. We would have no defence, for they are more than we. Once they fire one shot they could take us by surprise. What are we going to do?"

"Well, if we take the gun back now, we really will arouse their suspicions. We must just hope for the best; and I don't think anything will happen."

Nevertheless, I felt very insecure—I had no means of defence except a penknife; and Andrew went off saying he would sleep with his knife under his hammock in case he had to spring up suddenly.

It was an anxious night: I think we all slept lightly. Towards midnight the most appalling series of screams awoke me. I jumped up from my hammock at once. There came a beating of wings overhead and then again the eerie, bloodcurdling banshee-yell. Andrew came running up.

"Don't worry, sir—that is a hawk-owl; an oil bird.[1] They are very rare since the Indians begin shooting them at nesting-time. They nests only round about Mount Roraima in caves. I have seen them, they lives in thousands."

"What are you doing up?" I inquired.

"I was strolling to see that everything was all right. The Wai-Wais are all asleep so I guess we're O.K."

[1] *Steatornis caripensis.*

But at breakfast as I ate my bake and farine, the Wai-Wais gathered, gazing pointedly at the food—hypnotizing it, as Andrew said. And afterwards, while I sorted some plants, they lay around my tent in a wild abandoned mood, munching palm hearts and singing rather beautiful, but distinctly warlike, chants. Occasionally they would hack down a tree with a show of savagery, or rush up into the branches of another and swing about in a manner calculated to annoy. Under other circumstances I would have been very much amused by these antics; as it was, I think the fact that they knew I was not taking them too seriously helped preserve some semblance of control.

"Come along," I said at last, when I had finished, "let's go and do some work—we'll do a plot on the way to that waterfall, and then go and have a look at it."

Andrew translated, and conveyed their reply—they were much too hungry and tired to work. Yakotá was the most mutinous, so I turned to him and said, "Yakotá, come on," picked up the gun and walked off down the trail. Reluctantly they followed.

"Well, Andrew," I said, "I'm glad they've come. But what bad luck we've had—there's plenty of game around, yet we never seem to shoot any."

"You don't know how lucky it is that they know me, sir," said he. "If I didn't know them from three years back when I come in with the missionary, they would be gone by now."

My own food was beginning to run short, and when we returned I found that three of my remaining six tins had been affected by the jolting of the journey, and were swollen and gas-distended. I threw them into the river, and one, which hit a rock, blew up with a bang and discharged a column of beef stew into the air, to the delight of the watching Wai-Wais. Opening one of the others—a tin of very inferior pork sausage meat—I gave Mawashá a bite. He did not like it, and spat it out, and off they all went. The ants with their attendant thrushes were returning along their former line of advance, rustling over the dry leaves in their millions.

Before dark George and his men returned. They had cut for about three miles beside the river, to a point where it was about 100 feet wide, and open to the sky. They had passed three large cataracts, one very strange, where the river rushed under an overhanging mass of rocks, almost forming a natural arch; but even below the last of these had been unable to catch any fish. I wished that I could go and see these things for myself, but it was too late already, for I had decided we should have to start back at dawn, as there was now no chance of waiting another day without serious trouble.

George had also seen some very large jaguar footprints in a soft patch of earth. They were almost eight inches broad.

About nine-thirty the men were still awake, chatting among themselves, under their tarpaulin 100 feet away. Suddenly, between us, a jaguar snarled and growled—a savage and very unnerving noise. I lay tight in my hammock. I had the cartridges, but the gun was at the men's tent. I could hear the bushes shaking only a few feet away. Andrew spoke up.

"Tanner—go fetch cartridges for the gun and we kill him."

Tanner laughed. "I go wait till he eatin' my toes before I start."

There were a few chuckles, but nobody moved: then we drifted off to sleep. Two hours later a jaguar roared mightily far off down river. Then there was silence.

At 5.30 a.m. the cold, breath-steaming blackness was full of hollow uneasy flappings as guans, the earliest rising birds, flew from branch to branch overhead. It was as if the ghosts of primitive flying-machines were gathering in the tree-tops. With weird creakings and gruntings, produced by special wing feathers, they laboured their wings up and down. A cowbird emitted a yawn, a mot-mot hootooed, as I washed in the warm river.

George, Gabriel, Andrew and Jonah were talking in a grumbling, uneasy way as they came and loaded my baggage. Breakfast, eaten in the glare of the incandescent lamp, was a rather soggy dough-cake, and the remnants of my can of appalling pork sausages washed down with weak coffee, but it was sufficient to arouse their comment.

"Don' let them bother you, chief," said Tanner, as he refilled my cup. "It's mostly deir own fault dat we run out of food, though the Wai-Wais stealing make it worse. I'm all right, because I bring my rations, but dey leave behind most of what you give dem. Dey just didn' want to carry de extra load, and dey feel sure dey will get some game."

When I heard this my feelings stiffened. The grumbling ceased, and packing went on in silence.

A grey light was filtering through the leaves as I turned out the lamp and started along the trail, leading the way back. As I passed Jonah and Andrew I warned them that nothing must be left behind. It was their job to supervise the men's packing, but they hated responsibility because it was bound to make them unpopular. The only thing to do was to place it squarely on their shoulders. They were in a mood for argument, and would no doubt have suggested leaving equipment behind, but I walked ahead, climbing fast up the long steep hill behind the camp, and was out of polite earshot before they could reply.

At our previous camp I waited, and a few of the men passed: the Wapisianas sullen, the Wai-Wais indolent and couldn't-care-less. Yet they were doing their work, which was what mattered.

Half a mile beyond the Urana River, which I crossed an hour later, the ground became rocky, the forest low and irregular, tangled with lianes, and with every twig moss-coated, giving it a deeply mysterious feeling, so that sounds seemed muffled in this little area, though they came clear and bell-like from without.

Suddenly I saw a flaming orange bird settle on a twig—a cock-of-the-rock. Then, ahead, many more—the place was alive with them. I gazed enraptured, for they were impossibly exotic, like spirits of fire, luciferic haunters of these glades. Each was about the size and shape of a pouter pigeon, neatly clad in brilliant tangerine plumage, with curling, fluffy yellow tail and wing edges, black and white bars on the wings, huge helmet-like crests, edged with black, which almost concealed their beaks, and tiny bright eyes, like buttons on their smooth cheeks: overdressed creatures, like fantastic hats.[1]

They sat quietly in the branches, making cracking noises, and dropping fragments of nut or fruit on the ground. They

[1] In captivity they lose all brilliance of colour, become a yellowish dun, and usually soon die.

were very inquisitive and when they saw me came hopping from branch to branch to within fifteen feet, peering intently with heads on one side, yet cautious and highly nervous, flitting away suddenly with rapid jerky flight.

My heart stood still with excitement; my worries about the Indians were forgotten. Here was I in one of the few places where these birds are abundant (in all accessible parts of Guiana they have been wiped out or driven away), by luck, at their breeding season. Great was my anxiety to see them dance.

Very gently I walked on, pushing my way through the undergrowth towards a group of orange bird-flames flickering in the dimness. Then, almost at my feet, I saw the first dancing-ground: a circular area about three feet wide, roughly cleared of leaves, but with a tiny seedling with a few ragged, chewed leaves still standing in the middle.

Twelve feet away was another circle, and as I cautiously moved towards a group of bushes where I would be fairly well concealed, it seemed to draw the birds like a magnet. Keeping very still, I watched them as they flew nearer and nearer, a foot at a time. They would stop eating, look around, and then hop and flutter to a lower and nearer twig. Finally there were about nine birds present, all males, so far as I could see, six of them three or four feet above the ground, three only a few inches above it.

Suddenly one of these hopped into the circle, fluffed its feathers out, and strutted round with a bouncing motion, raising and bowing its head and half-spreading its wings and tail. Then in a flash it rolled over on its back and on to its feet again, then jumped aloft onto a branch, where it stood quite still, looking a little startled and sulky, as if ashamed of what it had done. Another hopped into the circle—but at this juncture Mingelli passed on the trail, about fifteen feet away, and off the birds flew, on broad powerful wings. Only then did I see, flying off above, an inconspicuous bird, speckled greenish-grey —a female.

Two more men passed. The birds were now frightened— probably because they had been shot at so recently, perhaps because my continued presence and clumsy efforts at concealment alarmed them. I stayed on for about an hour, hearing their short questing whistles all around, and sighting several through the screen of leaves and twigs, but could never get a clear view of one; and although they remained near their dancing-places they kept to the tree-crowns, about twenty or thirty feet above the ground.

Dejected, I continued along the trail, and soon caught up with Chekemá and Mawashá. When they saw me they scowled, gesticulated, and spoke to me in menacing voices. Not understanding, I shrugged my shoulders and smiled: probably they suspected me of either spying on them or eating secretly. But as I stepped ahead Chekemá laughed harshly and strummed his bowstring. I half expected an arrow in the back but did not turn my head.

Half an hour later we reached our first camp, and I sat down on a log and considered our position. Before we left this neighbourhood there was one thing in particular which I wanted to do: somehow to open a view southwards from a hill-top, so that I could get an idea of the sort of country through which we would be attempting to pass. It was frustrating to wander submerged in the jungle, unable to see where one was going. It made one feel choked, enraged, helpless; and it made planning ahead very difficult.

But how could we stay the extra day needed with so little food? I resolved to remain at the camp with only Andrew and one Wai-Wai tree-namer, and to send the rest of the men out under Jonah.

At this point Andrew arrived. At once he voiced his opinion:

"Mr. Guppy, you can't say I didn't warn you we would be having trouble. As I was telling you, we should have brought more food—I know, 'cos I been on these sort of trips before."

"Andrew," I said, "it is easy to be wise after the event, but I know all about this shortage of food. It is because nobody carried the full rations I issued them."

He looked sour and chopped at a piece of wood. He was about to reply when from a few yards away across the stream there came a snort and a scuffling. Astonished, we looked up and saw a peccary, then behind it several more. We were across wind from them. They saw us and paused, confused but not alarmed.

Chekemá seized his bow and arrow, Andrew his gun—and bending low and running forward he fired and killed one ("Food!" I thought). At once in wild alarm they scattered, plunging through the bushes—about twenty or thirty so far as I could see.

Simultaneously the rest of the men arrived. Little Manaka, heavily laden, thrust his bow and arrows forward into the hands of Yakotá; and he with a single graceful movement swung round and loosed an arrow at a running pig, fifty feet or so away, only flittingly visible through the undergrowth, and drove it in behind the shoulder. Even with a gun it would have been a wonderful shot.

"Ai!" shouted Jonah in triumph, as it collapsed.

Gabriel tore at Eoka's pack, and came running up to me with the box of cartridges. I gave him five, and away he went, his ancient shotgun in hand, while the others flung off their loads and raced forward, slashing with cutlasses at the pigs, or beating with sticks and trying to head them back to the river. The chase receded into the distance, and then in half an hour the men began filtering back, having lost touch with the herd, but bearing a third pig, shot by Gabriel.

We now had about 150 lb. of meat, and everyone was happy, though weary from the arduous walk. Fires were built, and the cutting up and smoking of the flesh begun. All could now stay with me; but three—Manaka, Yakotá and Eoka—who wanted to return home that night, I sent ahead with lightened loads, in company with Gabriel and Mingelli, who had volunteered to go to the mission and return on the morrow with a few extra supplies.

As they set off I saw that Eoka had a peculiar object sticking out of his bundle—a smoke-dried alligator about four feet long. A gift for his wife, explained Andrew, which he had been lucky enough to find on the New River. Alligator was so great a Wai-Wai delicacy that all had been killed and eaten on the Essequebo, and even on the Kassikaityu they were scarce. Two pigs would not have made so fine a gift.

Chekemá and Mawashá, to my surprise, volunteered to stay. It was puzzling—could I have misinterpreted their earlier behaviour? I decided not. Most likely they thought that by being pleasant now that there was plenty of food they might get more pay.

The next day, near the high bare look-out point from which George had obtained his view northwards, we felled a patch of forest on the southern slope of the rolling hillcrest, and obtained a patchy view to the south-east, over the valley in which the camp lay. Opposite us rose a mountain about 1,800 feet high, with a sheer rock face falling away for hundreds of feet below the summit, crested above with just such a tangle of *Clusias* as we had at our backs. The cliffs were about a mile and a half away and barred all further view. They showed nothing new —simply the same sort of country as we were in.

But from another point, looking more southwards, the pale blue pyramids of higher mountains twenty or thirty miles away could be seen, over the humps of a series of intersecting hills. Standing above and beyond the rest was a cone of rock: from a different angle it might have been the horse's head I had sighted from the plane. Could it be Schomburgk's Pirikitu, I wondered?

Even if not, there, undoubtedly, were the southernmost peaks of the Acarai, revealed at last in a maddeningly inadequate glimpse: a rugged, frightening country.

We walked back to camp tired, but a little triumphant. Gabriel and Mingelli had returned, with the news that Basil and his men had already left on their way upriver. One more worry was over: our supplies were assembled, and Basil had proved reliable. From now on our efforts would be directed to getting as much food and equipment as we could over the mountains. Then our main explorations would begin.

At Yakka-Yakka the next morning we stopped to disembark the Wai-Wais. Fleet as a fawn, with his bundle of arrows, bow, and hammock under his arm, Chekemá ran along the path and into the darkness of the house. Perhaps tactlessly, Jonah and I followed—he was kneeling beside a hammock in which lay his wife.

I felt a strange sensation as I saw him there, on the earthen floor. When we had been sharing the same life in the forest, his personality had been formidable. Now the difference between our ways of life was suddenly revealed—and he, whom I had so mistrusted, was reduced, a naked savage. For a moment I felt a wave of pity and condescension towards him.

I was uneasy, strongly disinclined to return to the mission, to resume the appearances of a cordiality I did not feel. I hated to think of taking advantage of Mr. and Mrs. Leavitt's kindness when I disapproved of their work. I felt like coming into the open, declaring my feelings, and building my base camp somewhere else. But then, I reflected, they had made no demands on me, whatever their views; and now that I had experienced them for myself, I sympathized with their difficulties with the Indians. It would be an act of the greatest surliness to ignore all that they had done for me already.

As the mission hill came into sight, columns of smoke were rising above it, flames licking over the ground: the felled ground on the riverwards slope was being cleared of debris. Attracted by the sound of the motor, the Leavitts and a crowd of Wai-Wais came down to the landing to greet us.

I enquired at once after Manatá, from whom I was determined to exact retribution for his theft. Great was my annoyance to learn that with two other men and their wives he had just left to return to his home on the Mapuera.

Mr. Leavitt was also annoyed with them: they had arrived unexpectedly a year before to stay with the chief; they had eaten his food and lazed around the place—and now, just as planting time had come and they might have helped him, they had gone off to look after their own fields. It was outrageous, grossly selfish. It was against all the rules of hospitality.

Perhaps some other time, I suggested, they might repay the chief, by welcoming *him* on a long visit. Could they really leave their own fields to go to ruin?

After dinner, to which I was invited with the missionaries' usual kindness, they offered me a special treat: would I like to listen to the news? Mr. Leavitt had been tinkering with his wireless all day and now he wanted to try it out.

The electric generator was set going (a rare event, because petrol was so expensive to bring in) and we walked over to his fellow missionary's empty house, in which the receiver was kept.

Through the blackness I could see flames leaping up all round the men's camp while one or two figures were beating them out and brushing off sparks as they settled on the canvas. In a room at the top of the house we seated ourselves, and with a curious sense of strain listened to the vague mutterings of the ether. Reception was appalling, and few words came through —something about a train disaster in London, something about a ship which had—could it be? been torpedoed by the Russians: we could not hear; and though this last would have been a terrible piece of news, it all seemed odd and unimportant in the isolation and remoteness of the jungle.

6

A Handful of Beads

Churumá, one of the handsomest of the braves, came out of one of the little thatched shelters behind the mission and watched me, as, the next morning, I collected the flowers of a small tree that grew beside them. On his head was a double tiara of toucan feathers, one arc vermilion, the other deep yellow. A light dancing-club, shaped like a small paddle, hung from his wrist.

"You see that?" said Andrew. "These Indians don't know about fighting—all they got is these clubs, just for show, when they pretend they is warriors when dancing."

"Why do the clubs have a spiked handle?" I asked.

"So they can stick it in a man's face. Sometimes they quarrel, you see. When they want to kill a man they shoot him with a bow and arrow, like a pig. But when they have a fight at a dance they spike a man's face and they crack his bones with these, and a week later it's all right."

Old Waniu, or "William", Fonyuwé's father, was seated nearby making a hammock on a rectangular upright frame. He passed the shuttle to and fro with his hand, weaving with a strong, hard cord made out of palm fibre, cold to the touch, and rather cheerless to think of as one's sole covering at night. He was a wrinkled little old man with pop-eyes and a salacious grin, very much like the aged Voltaire of Houdon's bust.

In an amused manner, to which his splay-toed, rather deliberate walk added an ironic dignity, he came up to me a little later with a few very ordinary arrows in his hand, which to humour him I bought. With him was his sister Kachamare, the Wai-Wai wife of my Wapisiana boat-builder, Charlie Wai-Wai. She was a gaudily painted, wrinkled creature with a gay smile, and long, skinny brown legs which protruded

97

beneath the two dresses her proud husband had given her: an old shapeless one, dingy with years of dirt, and above it a new one with scarlet and white flowers on a blue ground.

"Mapuer-wau?" said William, grinning his rascally grin and pointing up river.

I nodded. Yes, that was where I was going.

"*Kiriwanhi! Kiriwanhi!*"—good, good! He held out his hand and slowly counted his fingers: 'Mawayána—*Kiriwanhi*; Powisiana—*Kiriwanhi*; Fishkaliena—*Kiriwanhi*"—evidently three nice tribes who lived on the Mapuera.

Then he smiled broadly and laid his head on one side, lolling with eyes closed and tongue stuck out, and said "Fishkaliena", pointing at me and roaring with laughter. Charlie's wife roared too. Evidently the Fishkalienas would kill me.

Suddenly William imitated paddling, counting one, two, three . . . to ten on his fingers, then two more: twelve—twelve men in a boat. Then he drew an imaginary bow and loosed a series of arrows . . . all the men were killed—Fishkaliena . . . ha! ha! ha!

Charlie's wife nodded. Then, struck by a thought, she pointed at her apron and William's little loin-cloth and shook her fingers—they were completely naked. Then she touched his pigtail and pulled her fingers, held together, right down to his ankle—they had very long pigtails.

Andrew, who had wandered away, came up:

"You know why they have long pigtails, Mr. Guppy? It is so they can tie all the heads together from their enemies when they kill them. I seen it on the Mapuera with Dr. Holden."

With Andrew interpreting, I spread out my few poor maps of the region and called out names from them. First a few tribes: Japy, Tucane, Maopityan, Chiriue—none evoked a response. Then a few of Andrew's names: Shilliau, Kalawian, Katawian, Aika, Areka, Powisian. This last only was recognized: William had said they were *kiriwanhi*, but Andrew and Dr. Holden had had their narrowest escape from them. Perhaps they were two different tribes with the same name? Each tribe has its own name for itself, as well as the names given it by each of its neighbours, so several names might refer to a single tribe, and vice versa: all very confusing, giving a vagueness to every piece of information, so that one listened for any, the slightest hint, that connected with something else.

"Kashima?" I asked—the big village mentioned by the missionary as supposedly being somewhere on the Brazilian side.

Far, far away, said William—but perhaps that was only a rumour—a legend of his tribe?

Tunayena—the Water Indians?

He nodded, but he could say nothing about them. But there was another interesting thing, he added, with brightening eyes—a village with nothing in it but women, just a short way down the Mapuera.

The Amazon had been named after a tribe of warrior women whom in 1542 Orellana had seen fighting beside their men at the mouth of the Trombetas. The Mapuera was a tributary of the Trombetas . . . It would be rather wonderful to discover them when all other travellers had failed.

Yet this sounded very much like wishful thinking on the part of the old scoundrel.

Where did the Wai-Wais live on the Mapuera?

Many weeks' journey down, on a tributary called the Yaimo.

This was not on any map, though a tributary called the Barracuxi was marked; but William did not recognize this name. What of the Fishkalienas? They were below the Wai-Wais. And the Mawayána? They lived on the River Oroko'orin.

Ever since I had read it in the Brazilian Boundary Commission's report, this name had stirred my memory. Now, suddenly, the association became clear: in 1728 a Jesuit priest, Father Francisco de San Manços, had written about a journey he had made on the Trombetas. Among the tribes he had heard of was the Mayoyaná Naucú, who were supposed to live in the remote interior of the Trombetas drainage, on the River Urucurin. Could the Mawayáns be the Mayoyaná? No one of whom I knew had ever mentioned them since, and the river was not marked on my maps. Out of the mists of the very earliest exploration there seemed to stretch forth a clue.

I asked William if he would like to come with me, and at once he quivered eagerly. Yes, said he, and his son Fonyuwé wanted to go very much, as he had been born there, for his mother, now dead, had been a Mawayán woman. He could still speak the language.

This was important news. Yet again, we might never see any Mawayáns, and Fonyuwé, if appealing, was a complex creature who might be troublesome.

A few more names drew blanks—Apiniwau, Biloku, Pirikitu —yet when we parted I felt that something solid had been added to what vague information I had about the country ahead.

A few hours later Gabriel, who had been out hunting, returned, bearing a large, coarse-haired peccary, while Eoka came in with the news that he had shot a tapir only a short way away. Great excitement reigned when the huge dismembered beast was brought into the Wai-Wai encampment: the dogs writhed in paroxysms of impatience on their perches, and howled soulfully as it was cut up and the delicious aroma of fresh meat was wafted to them. For a handful of beads Mr. Leavitt purchased a leg weighing 19 lb.; the strange pig-like head, with its curled-over nose, was placed on a log, and everyone, down to the tiniest child, seemed to become enwrapped in yards of intestine, or to be carrying a bowl of liver, half a penis, or a couple of trotters.

Mawashá, digging with his kitchen knife, stripped off several pounds of white fat, and standing aside, began combing out his beautiful waist-long hair, and rubbing in the fat between his palms. Then, when his hair was as glossy as satin, he bound it carefully with string into a pigtail and pushed the end into his enormous pom-pom of bird-skins. Straightening himself, he caught my eye, and beamed with pleasure that I should see him so elegant.

By sunset a deep torpidity had descended upon the encampment: the Wai-Wais had eaten the entire tapir, about 200 lb. of meat. Now I understood why they had all been starving in the forest.

The missionary had kindly offered to help me pay the six Wai-Wais so that there should be no misunderstandings:

"One thing that is most important," he said, "is to be strictly and scrupulously honest with them. Calculate in front of them what you owe them, and pay them the exact amount. Let them see just why they get what they do. One must never break one's word to them—they are such thieves that they need an example of strict honesty. I always give them one dollar a day—in goods, of course: and the young boys like Manaka and Yakotá get seventy-five cents. I make a point of telling them the value in dollars, because I am trying to get them to understand what money is."

Quite late in the morning he had appeared at the door of his kitchen and viewed the throng. Then strolling down the steps had pointed to the sky—at a place where the sun had been an hour before. At first I thought he had mistaken the direction. Then I realized he meant that he would deal with the payments at that time the following day. He was deep in prayer, he explained, and intended to spend the rest of the day in contemplation. There was no reason why the Wai-Wais should not wait.

I was a little taken aback, but I saw the advantage to him, for the longer the Indians stayed at the mission the greater his influence over them might become. They were far too independent at present. All they wanted to do was get paid and go back home. It was most important that they should begin to want to live like civilized people.

When the sun reached its appointed position the next day Mr. Leavitt appeared and a crowd assembled to watch the payments being made.

When the first of my three bags of beads, each about the size of a lady's handbag, was opened, eyes popped and a hiss of astonishment escaped, followed by a screeching excited chatter which as quickly lapsed into silence. Such wealth!—it was incredible! Even those who had nothing to expect left all their tasks and came rushing up to look: babies were left untended, dogs unfed: it was as if a sack of doubloons had been flung down in the middle of Wall Street. And I, measuring out my payments in teaspoons (for these were minute glass beads, almost as fine as sand) felt like Mammon himself. Dozens of eyes followed my hands as I poured each tiny stream of red, white or blue into the little folded palm-leaf its trembling recipient proffered.

"You must remember," Mr. Leavitt said, "that one has to add on the cost of bringing in all these trade goods. That is why the prices have to be stepped up a little."

My original intention had been to issue the goods to the Wai-Wais at cost price—goods which had cost a dollar for each day's work—but by some oversight on the part of the packers very few of the bills for the trade-goods had been sent, and I had no idea what most of the articles had cost. I did not want to make a loss and had no desire to undercut my hosts, so I was charging the prices they suggested to me as fair; but from the few bills that *had* come I was able to guess, as payments proceeded, that I was making quite large profits. This, as it turned out, was a good thing, for I had brought too few trade-goods, and if I had issued them at cost price I should never have been able to get as much done for them as I did; and from the missionary's point of view it was also good, for it preserved the economic *status quo* on the Upper Essequebo.

Even at a wage only one-third of that prevailing elsewhere in the colony every Wai-Wai would soon acquire all the beads, knives, fish-hooks, cooking pots and mouth-organs he needed. Trade goods would lose their value, and no one would be able to get the Indians to do any work. They would disappear into the forest and lead their own happy lives hunting, fishing, cultivating their fields, and trying to procreate children. There were only two ways of keeping them working: by the creation of artificial scarcities (in such simple conditions, by raising prices) and by education. Already education by example had created several promising new demands—notably for aluminium and enamel cooking utensils (so much better than the Wai-Wais' own primitive, if beautiful, pottery that they had ceased to make it) and for cartridges: two Wai-Wais had guns, and before long the whole tribe would have abandoned using bows and arrows, except perhaps for fishing.

The wearing of clothes would merely replace one want—beads—by another, cloth. Far more important economically would be the introduction of imported foods (like rice, corned beef, sugar, salt fish, condensed milk) and new industries, which would lead—if events followed the pattern familiar elsewhere—to the Indians' gradual neglect of their fields and their way of life, and their dependence upon employment for a livelihood.

It was upsetting to realize that any expression of generosity to the Wai-Wais would the sooner bring them to this stage. Meanwhile, as they received their fifty cents' worth of goods for a dollar's wages they were revealed as the simple folk they were: for his fifteen days' work Chekemá got an ounce each of red, white, and blue beads—more I would not allow him, for these, the most portable and desirable of all trade-goods, had to be rationed strictly—a cutlass, a file, a hundred yards of fishing-line, an axe-head, a reel of cotton and a bar of soap; while the rest chose similarly, save Mawashá, who was credited with $15.00 towards the purchase of a gun.

As they walked proudly away, pleased with their pitiful purchases, I felt downcast. I thought of them carrying their huge loads through the forest, and perhaps, after all, going hungry; of the fact that though they had been discontented, they had always been approachable directly, as human beings, and had never lost their sense of humour. They were good men, and worthy of respect.

The payments over, I began to issue rations for the coming part of the expedition, calculating as I went along how much spare food I would have with which to feed the extra Indians I needed.

Mr. Leavitt stayed on, in case he could be of any help, and to chat with the watching crowd. Little flaxen-haired Calvin, his son, clambered about over the packing-cases, or played with small red- and black-striped creatures of his own age. Fonyuwé (quite recovered from his tooth extraction) and "William" were there, several withered old grannies who with long fingers poked the various sacks or pried into boxes, and a mountainous, majestic woman who carried a tiny baby clad only in a necklace, and earrings made of tufts of feathers. It was adorable. Suddenly, held at arm's length by its mother, it released a stream of urine on to the earthen floor. Everyone was a little embarrassed, but obviously it was only to be expected from a baby.

Then there was a stir, and a heavy, fine-looking man entered the storeroom. He had a jowly face with a large mole under the right eye, and was suffering from a severe cold. With him was the most beautiful Indian woman I had ever seen: about sixteen, with a turned-up nose, down which she had painted a

line of red paint, a pretty mouth parted in a smile, tiny white
teeth, shoulder-length hair, and big laughing brown eyes. Her
figure was charming, with plump, erect breasts, a smooth, firm
belly, well-shaped hips, and legs which met all the way down
to her toes when she stood with them together. She wore a
simple working apron of red cloth, earrings, and a necklace
made of seeds and beads, with a large safety-pin hanging in
the middle where a civilized girl might have a crucifix.

She gave us all a dazzling smile, sat down and chatted gaily
to everyone in turn, even to me, though I could not understand
a word. She would look at me sweetly or avert her gaze in
confusion; and then a moment later dissolve into smiles. The
men were stunned, and could not keep their eyes off her. Her
sunny disposition was in complete contrast with the strong-
willed, rather shrewish characters of the usual Indian women.
She exuded feminine softness and appeal: she was a sort of
Wai-Wai Lollobrigida.

Her husband, Yukumá, said the missionary, had just returned
from paddling the three untrustworthy Wapisianas back to the
trail leading to the savannahs. He had gone on to Karardanawa
with them to trade a few cassava graters, and that, undoubtedly,
was where he had picked up his cold, for colds were normally
quite unknown among the Wai-Wais. They always seemed
to get ill when they went to the savannahs, and as a result
feared them very much.

Yukumá looked miserable with his red eyes and streaming
nose. He hawked and cleared his throat continuously and spat
on the floor, rubbing the gobs of sputum in with his heel. It was
far worse than the baby. There was nothing I could do but
try to ignore it. But by the end of the day I felt quite disgusted,
and when at last the room was empty I scattered acroflavine
solution on the floor to disinfect it, and swept it out when it was
dry.

Two days later I took Andrew, Jonah, Chekemá and the
three Wapisianas up the Onoro Creek to study the riverside
forests. Yukumá's wife came with us as far as Yakka-Yakka
village, where she lived. Her presence in the boat tickled the
men, just as would the presence in any boatload of men of a

charming, pretty, and completely unselfconscious nude girl. I did my best to take a photograph of her, but she became so absorbed by the camera, perhaps the first she had seen, that I had no chance of a candid shot. All I ever saw in the view-finder was her intently serious face as she leant forward to examine it.

Where we laid out our plot many of the trees were actually lianes, which in this place, where they were submerged part of the year in swift-flowing water, had proliferated into a criss-cross of slender upright stems and twiggy bushes—so tangled that we had to slice our way about inch by inch. Everything seemed to have loose, flaking bark which fell down the backs of our necks and made us itch, and leaves and branches filled the space so tightly that often we could not see more than a couple of feet ahead, and we were continuously being hit in the face. Underfoot, things were just as bad: our feet went down through thick, wet, dead leaves to slippery wet clay. Everyone became restive and ill-tempered, and things got lost and had to be searched for all the time.

It was a relief, at lunch-time, to re-embark in the boat and sit peacefully munching under an overhanging branch of swamp acacia.[1]

Gabriel threw a line over the side, and at once there was a bite. With a powerful jerk he pulled a big, savage perai aboard. It snapped through the wire leader almost before it touched the canoe bottom, and for a moment there was a scramble as it leaped about in the boat grunting and biting at everything. Then with a cutlass stroke it was killed, and lay, its eyes still gleaming red, its razor teeth showing in the short, blunt snout.

Beside perai, sting rays (which live chiefly on sandbanks), electric eels, and crocodiles make the waters of Guiana more dangerous than the land. It is not only that these creatures are unseen, but they are far more abundant than the snakes or jaguars of the forest: an Indian who would walk all day alone through the jungle would hesitate to swim a river 100 yards broad.

Yakotá passed in a canoe with his mountainous middle-

[1] *Macrolobium acaciaefolium.*

105

aged wife, who was holding a baby in her arms, to which she had given birth a few days before. With them was another man, the child's father.

"He must really love her," remarked Andrew, referring to Yakotá, "for he kill a man to get her—he shoot him in the back with an arrow. Charlie's wife tell me so. Now he is sharing her with that other man. What is unusual is they being such friends. Usually if a woman has two husbands she has to keep quiet which is the father, or the other man would kill the child. You remember that great big ugly woman with the little girl that pee on the floor? Well, she has two husbands, and my, they is jealous of each other."

A little later Andrew was reminiscing about the Terry-Holden expedition.

"You know how many porters we had? Eighty-five. That will tell you what sort of an expedition it was."

"Did they all go down the Mapuera?"

"No, sir. Only six of us, Dr. Holden and myself, and Mr. John Melville who lives out at Wichabai, and three others. You know what, sir? The doctor wasn't afraid of carrying loads. He *always* carry eighty pounds. Just like the rest of us."

"Good for him!" I said.

"Yes, even though we have *eighty-five* porters, he carried his load."

"When he was carrying it did he stop all the time and take photographs in the forest, and make notes of all the different trees he saw, and collect plants?"

"No, sir, he didn't bother with no such stuff. He was after important things. Why, at night he would disappear completely. And do you know what I found? One night I saw a light in the forest, and when I went, there he was, in a deep pit he had dug in the ground, looking at the soil. What do you think of that? What was he up to? That's what I ask myself."

"Well, what was he up to?"

"Guess what I believe, sir. Now I think I know. It was only last year that I read in the papers, and then I know. He was after that radio-active stuff. You know what they say is the reason the Indians no longer live on the Kassikaityu River?

They say its waters are radio-active. And I myself saw the doctor testing the water."

"That's very interesting. Do you think he found anything?"

"I don't know. But he made me swear never to tell anyone that I seen him in that pit. Once he had a great fight with Mr. Melville. Mr. Melville beat him up bad. He was very afraid of him after. It might have been about what he found. But perhaps it was money. Anyway, he was a great man, and he had a lot of instruments, you know, scientific instruments. Yet even so, he always carry eighty pounds."

"That's wonderful. Do you think that I should carry eighty pounds, Andrew?"

"Well . . . I'm not exactly saying that, sir . . . I only mean, a load is a load, isn't it?"

"That's just what I say, too. And if ever there is a time when I *really* see you can't manage the loads, then I'll carry one. Meanwhile I'm paying men to carry loads so that I can do *my* work. I have seen much bigger loads carried than any that anyone has carried so far on this trip."

"I don't doubt. But we still got too few men for the loads. Would you mind telling me, sir, how old you are?"

"I am twenty-six."

"Well, we is a good deal older, Jonah and me."

"Perhaps you should be in charge?" I said, rather acridly.

Andrew saw he had gone too far, and relapsed into silence. Jonah grunted and busied himself with some plants. We untied the boat and drifted downriver.[1]

We paused at a sandbank in the Essequebo just below the Onoro mouth. Clusters of yellow butterflies were all along the water's edge, dipping with their long tongues into the moist sand exposed by the falling river. Among them were larger ones of a rich reddish orange, and a single day-flying moth of the genus *Urania*, a marvellous insect of velvet black with emerald green ripple marks on its wings, and long silver tails.

A few straggly bushes grew on the sand, and in the centre

[1] I should emphasize, for the sake of my friend Dr. Holden, that he has since told me that he never carried a load on his expedition, never fought with Melville, cannot remember digging a pit and was certainly not looking for radio-active minerals!

a clump of an extraordinary-looking *Astrocaryum,* or star-nut palm, of a species that has never been properly described or named, called Awaraballi in Arawak, Yawarda in Wai-Wai, and very characteristic of swampy places in certain rivers of the interior of Guiana. It grows to about thirty feet tall, sometimes erect and quite stately with its pale, straight stem, ringed with darker brown, and its crown of stiff, dark-green leaves rising like ostrich plumes above it, but more usually leans gracefully out over the water in a gentle curve, or even lies flat, parallel with the surface, curling upwards only at the tip—like one of those beautiful marine worms which live in tubes, from which they protrude delicately waving fan-like gills.

Every inch of this palm, of stem, and leaves and leaf-sheaths, petioles, flowers and fruit is covered with horrific spines, sometimes four inches or more in length, black and shining so that they reflect the light and make the greens and browns into greys, and give the whole tree a grizzly, unshaven appearance. Even a small clump of yawardas imparts a melancholy, primeval touch to any landscape, as though they had lingered on from an age-long past. They are like resurrections of dreams, figments of a false nostalgia.

At Yakka-Yakka, Yukumá, Eoka and their wives, and Wayama, all completely naked, were talking quietly as they idled in the shallows under the trees, where the water poured over shelves of smooth rock. When we arrived they slipped discreetly out of the water to put on their laps and aprons before coming to greet us.

Watching them, I realized how much I enjoyed the sight of the Indians' bodies, at rest or when they moved. Old as well as young had their beauty: hollow chests, flabby stomachs, pendant breasts, huge or shrunken, stringy legs and arms, had ceased to seem ugly, repellent. One felt instead the richness and appropriateness of the different aspects of the human body, as of the face, and developed many standards, instead of the absurdly limited ideal of the young adult. And as the Indians went about their daily tasks, and one saw the play of muscles, the movement of backs and loins and buttocks, of breasts and shoulders and arms, of turning necks free and unrestrained, of bodies of every age and degree of preservation, one felt one was witnessing an heroic spectacle—rediscovering a kind of beauty giving the most profound joy, and lost to our civilization, for the sight of civilized bodies is not the same thing at all. From childhood our movements have been circumscribed by the fitted containers in which we live, and by our surroundings, and cultivated to conform with them and emphasize their elegance, and not the grace of the naked body—and the difference is like that between Watteau and Michelangelo.

Eoka's gentle-faced wife looked sick, and we learned that all his family had fever, so we took them—much excited, despite their illness, by our tiny yet powerful outboard motor—back to the mission where the nurse could treat them.

I was surprised to discover that many of the Indians wanted to come to the Mapuera with me, because I had feared that Chekemá or Mawashá would have spread such awful stories about our trip to the New River that no one would want to work; but apparently just the opposite—they had said how much they had enjoyed themselves!

However, a journey to the Mapuera was not a thing to be undertaken lightly, even for trade-goods, and I tried to find out why Wayama, Fonyuwé and "William", the three men I finally selected (apart from the chief, who had returned to his own village upriver, and of the sincerity of whose intention of accompanying me I was unsure), were so anxious to go—especially as I had announced that they would have to feed themselves, which they normally did when travelling on their own, as the small surplus we had was enough only as a reserve.

Fonyuwé, I knew, wanted to revisit the country of his birth, and perhaps see his mother's tribe; but "William" and Wayama were in search of wives. Both complained of the shortage of women on this side of the mountains.[1] "William" was particularly doleful about his loneliness and the fact that he had no one to look after him and make him cassava bread. But this, I

---

[1] There seemed to be about twice as many men as women of childbearing age, attributable partly to mortality from too early childbearing, but also to the fact that girl babies were not much wanted and sometimes killed—a survival, doubtless, from former times, when there were more women than men; but nowadays one of the causes of the decline in numbers of these

discovered, was his own fault; three months before, in a fit of spleen, he had given his wife away to another man, who now refused to return her—a meanness that rankled. Wayama, on the other hand, actually had a young girl, who had been promised him years before, waiting at a village on the Mapuera. No doubt she was with some man, but he intended to try to get her, and even if he failed he could probably pick up a few cassava graters cheaply and make a trading profit on the trip.

As for the other men, Andrew certainly, Jonah probably, did not want to cross to the Mapuera. But I was determined, despite their forebodings—not that I was at all sure what we should find, except rare plants and wonderful forests. We were going to such a remote land, shut off to the north by mountains crossed only by a single trail, to east and west by trackless jungles and to the south by fierce tribes, made yet more savage by their past contacts with people from the outside world, and by terrible rapids on the rivers. Much would depend on luck —and food.

We had about a month's rations—too little to be able to linger on the way. A man can carry, together with his personal effects, only about three weeks' food, so if he is going for longer he must either have a supply column or live off the country. I had already done my best to provide the first of these: Basil's men would be returning to meet me at the beginning of the Mapuera trail in a week's time; and when we reached the Mapuera I intended to send back as many men as I could and continue with the combined total of food.

But we should still be short—we simply had not been able to bring in enough on the plane. We might find villages and be able to purchase food, but I could *plan* only on what I knew. At some point, if we were to continue, we should have to live off the country: good luck in hunting and the spirit of the men would decide our success.

Indians, together with the general low fertility of both sexes. According to Dr. Jones this is probably caused by chronic malaria. He says ". . . the constant interchange of sexual partners may be a desperate attempt to find fertile combinations". Regularization of marriages under such conditions might lead to the extinction of a tribe.

PART TWO

Across the Acarai

7

Bewitched River

"Mr. Guppy! Mr. Guppy!"—despairing, agitated shouts, and just as we were pushing off there was a sudden confusion at the back of the watching Wai-Wais, and up rushed Chekemá. A small fifteen-foot dugout, heavily laden, had already gone ahead an hour before, paddled by four men. We were late in starting—what could he want?

Was I quite certain that I had paid him everything—that I didn't still owe him a few beads, or a fish hook?

Reassured, he gave a sheepish smile—the engine started, and with a loud drone we moved off upriver. Behind, I caught a last glimpse of the mission hill with its buildings brilliantly sunlit in their arena of forest. The main part of the expedition had begun.

The river widened into a broad lagoon bordered by yawarda palms and swamp acacias, then narrowed again as we came to hills and strained up a series of gentle rapids.

We reached Mawiká, the chief's new village, in mid-morning: a conical house like Yakka-Yakka, with several lean-to shelters and outbuildings. In front stood a ten-foot pole, painted with black and white spots to represent a snake, with a distinct head, from the tip of which protruded a long red and blue macaw feather. It was to bring good luck to the village, said the chief. He walked with an unconvincing limp, saying that he could not come with us, as only that morning he had hurt his foot, and led the way into the cavernous darkness of the house, where we sat and ate and drank from bowls placed before us.

His was a most unusual face, rather orang-outang-like with its roll of chin and jowl, its thin, upturned mouth, and crescent smile. He would have been a congenial companion, and one from whom I should have learned much. But who could come in

113

his place? Could I take Kirifakka? He thought for a moment. I knew that soon the village would be planting its fields, and everyone would be needed to help, but he turned at last, and nodded; and Kirifakka jumped with delight and ran to fetch his belongings.

Among the men who came to the landing to see us off was Kilimtu, the Taruma, tall and courteous, carrying his little son, and accompanied by his Wai-Wai wife, an intelligent-faced, cucumber-breasted woman. I asked him where the other two survivors of his tribe were living, but he did not know, for he had not seen them for years; except that they were somewhere on the far side of the mountains.

Soon we came to the mouth of the Kamo-wau, the River of the Sun, where at an old camp-site littered with tufts of peccary hair we stopped for lunch. Then onwards, slumped and sprawled amidst the boxes, trying to sleep or rest. The day grew hotter and hotter, the sun streamed its unmitigated glitter on the water. It burned in round the edges of my dark glasses and heated the top of my head till it was like a corrugated-iron roof in summer. I developed a pulsating headache. We were all feeling a little ill, sniffling and sneezing from a cold which we must have caught from Yukumá. Digging in my luggage I found a black oilcloth sou'wester hat which gave a little shade, though it got so hot that it had to be cooled frequently in the water. Andrew, it seemed, was suffering more than anyone. He began to describe his complaints. His side, back, neck, legs and eyes hurt, and he had a bad cough. What about his toes and ears, I asked, hoping to tease him into better humour. But he remained doleful. I felt sorry: if only I had had another interpreter I would have found some way of sending him home, for he seemed so genuinely miserable at being on the expedition.

Towards evening, when the sun was getting lower, we reached Yawarda, the most southerly Wai-Wai village in British Guiana, named after the spiny palms which grew around the landing. A tangled path led inland to the enormous house, deserted temporarily Fonyuwé informed us, for the Indians had left two months before to help the people of Yakka-Yakka cut their new field up the Onoro. Already the fields and clearing were waist-high in weeds, ravelled with creepers, while inside the

"SHE GAVE US ALL A DAZZLING SMILE" (*p. 104*)

THE CHODIKAR

"As we continued, the river became more and more choked" (*p. 121*)

huge gloomy interior, fifty-five feet across and about forty feet high, eerie etiolated plants of abnormal slenderness and paleness spread and trailed their stems and leaves, and fungal candelabra sprang from the posts and woodwork. It was easily the most substantial house I had seen, with graceful, firmly constructed doorposts, overhung by eaves, strong walls of split *Euterpe* stems to protect the dogs inside from jaguars, and a roof of thick palm thatch, reinforced near the apex by extra layers. There were five fireplaces inside, indicating that fifteen or twenty people normally dwelt here, a hammock frame, a few cassava squeezers, and a shapely new bowl of ringing pottery.

The Wai-Wais slung their hammocks in the house, the rest of us among the trees near the river. As night fell, I felt ill, and shivered and sneezed violently. A golden, hairy spider, four inches across, flipped back a leaf on the ground below me, and stood in the mouth of its hole; a cicada came buzzing up to the lamp and settled at its base, stridulating piercingly. Its mouse-big elegant pale-fawn body was sheathed by beautiful green-veined cellophane wings, and it had scarlet eyes. I picked it up to see how it squeaked, and felt a strong vibration in my hand, but could detect no external movement. I released it and put out the light: the forest was black, the river and sky pale, darkening every second. Deep night-blue clouds were in the sky and hanging reflected in the water, with occasional gleams of yellow light on their flanks; the boat with its muffled outboard motor, the coiling lianes, the leaves, stood in fretwork silhouette.

When I awoke the river was curtained in blue transparent mist, slowly thinning in the warmth of the sun. Overhead a small kind of guan was raucously shouting its Indian name: "Hannaqua! Hannaqua!" and occasionally one heard a little tune like a Mozart minuet, the song of a quadrille wren, with, whenever it came close enough, an undercurrent of soft chrrr-chrrrs, like the clockwork of a musical-box, beneath the gay lilting melody. Surely, I thought, of all song birds this would be the favourite if tamed? By whistling in tune I persuaded the little bird to draw near, and finally saw her, sprightly and brown, with a speckled breast.

My cold had dried up, and I was feeling better, but thinking that perhaps I was suffering from a lack of green vegetables, I collected a few leaves of deer calalloo (*Phytolacca rivinoides*) from beside the house, an acrid plant whose red-stemmed, purple berries are used as fish-bait; but it was too pungent to eat even after Tanner had boiled it.

Distances were still veiled, the banks blue and hazy from midstream, when we set out, an hour after the small boat with its paddlers. The sun hung a brilliant orb in the woolly sky, flashing gold from the smooth olive-green water.

All morning we saw animals in the river or along the banks. First, as we rounded a bend, a group of five or six giant otters clambering out of the water with looping, seal-like gait, showing their massive tapered tails, to which the hind legs are joined.[1] With loud cries of "Ump! Ump!" they slithered into the river, and came popping up all round to inspect us, standing high out of the water like immense champagne bottles. Soon after they disappeared a large and exceedingly surprised face stared up at me from beside the boat and simultaneously a beast about the size of a St. Bernard dog rushed in headlong lolloping flight through the open, grassy-floored riverside woodland, flung itself with an ear-shattering belly-flop into the water, and vanished, swimming away fast beneath the surface: two capybaras, guinea-pig like rodents very good to eat, but useless to attempt to shoot swimming as they would sink and be swept away by the current. A little further Fonyuwé said that he saw an ocelot in the trees, and then we passed for about two miles through yet another blizzard of migrating yellow butterflies, all flying upriver.

"That is a very bad sign," said Andrew; "it means the rainy season is not finished yet. At the beginning of the wet season you always sees the butterflies heading upriver, and then when the dry season is starting they flies downriver. We going to have bad rains soon. Maybe we should have delayed."

"What do the butterflies do at night?" I asked.

"They just goes to sleep. If we was here tonight we would see them flying into the side of the river and settling under leaves. Sometimes they all sleep together in one tree on top of the forest. Then in the morning they wake up and go on again."

[1] Scientifically, Fin-tailed otters, *Pteroneura brasiliensis*.

He sat back for a moment, like a sleepy bear. Then leant forward, aroused.

"You know what surprise me most? That we seen no white-headed maroudis [a kind of guan]. In 1938, on the Terry-Holden expedition, they was flying across the river all the time."

"Dr. Jones told me he shot one on the Kujuwini River three years ago."

"That may be so, but still, all the wild life seems to disappear from this region. When we came that time, we saw bush cows [tapirs], tigers and wild hogs all the time from the boat—just like that, by the water's edge. At that time there was only two families of Wai-Wais living in British Guiana—they all ran away into Brazil after the epidemic kill off the Tarumas. That was a terrible time, dead men in their hammocks, and no one to bury them. Well, now they come back, and there is fifteen or more families living here, something like fifty people. That is what scares the animals away—so many people about. Anyways, food is going to be short again, I wouldn't be surprised."

I could hardly believe that fifty people could reduce the game in an area about the size of Wales. Yet it was always noticeable how away from settlements the number of edible creatures seemed to increase rapidly.

We passed the Puda-wau, or Black River, where Fonyuwé told me Charlie Wai-Wai once lived, and Mingelli was born. The river narrowed rapidly, hills approached on either side and soon we passed an outcrop of a curious rock we had seen the previous day, evidently part of the same eroded formation—a broken mass of strongly metamorphosed shales, unlike any other rocks of the region. At one point where the river wound between steep hills, a clump of colossal trees, called Ichekelés[1] soared fifty or sixty feet above the rest of the forest. Their hundreds of small individual canopies, joined in clusters and bunches, and finally all arising from the great main trunk, looked like a cloud of parachutes lowering some vast cylinder into the tree-tops.

Then rounding a bend, we saw for an instant the low outlines

[1] Probably a species of *Pithecellobium*.

117

of blue mountains twenty or thirty miles further south. The river widened again, and we stopped for lunch at a high bank, with grassy slopes—described by Jonah as an otter's playground, and kept clear of undergrowth by their activities.

"This would be a good place to come at night," he said. "Sometimes the otters will bring their fish one at a time and leave them till they get a lot before they settle down and eat. Then you chase them away and take the fish. But it must mean for sure that there is plenty of fish here. After lunch I go throw a line."

Behind the bank lay a still, brown-watered lagoon fringed with thorny palms, and centred with a dome of granite as big as that of St. Paul's. Settling down with my back against the trunk of a swamp acacia, I ate my lunch and watched the preparations for fishing. A trogon, a beautiful bird with sky-blue back and breast, and yellow undersides, settled on a branch, and was quickly shot and cut up for bait; a small brown squirrel rustled in the bushes.

Wayama paced the shore and then stood on a rock with bow and arrow poised. He whistled reedily, hoping to attract a fish: then shot, transfixing a sunfish. Fonyuwé flung out a line bearing a six-inch steel hook, baited with half the bird, and with a twig lashed the top of the water. A minute later he hooked a twenty-pound haimara (*Macrodon trahira*), a vicious needle-toothed creature which flapped violently as he drew it in, and in a final burst of savagery leaped out of the water at him with open mouth. Mostly quite harmless, lurking in still waters and under banks, they have, none the less, been known to attack men and tear swimming dogs to pieces.

An hour later, as we were travelling along a straight, mile-long stretch of the river, a *Grand Bassin* with high walls of delicate, light-spangled leafage, Fonyuwé began to shiver, his eyes red and unseeing, his brow feverish. I gave him two aspirins, and settled back, worried about him, because of his previous collapse after the tooth extraction, and because if anyone became ill we might have to turn back. Cooling my sou'-wester, it floated off downstream, and as I desperately clutched at it and caught it, he laughed—an encouraging sign.

When long evening shadows lay on the water we came to

the mouth of the Chodikar, the tributary up which we were to ascend into the foothills of the Acarai. Opposite a small island, crowned by spiny palms, which separated it from the equally-sized Essequebo, we camped. I slung my hammock close to the water and bathed in the deliciously cool shallows where it ran over loose yellow sand, not venturing too far out for fear of perai or sting rays.

Refreshed, I went to look at Fonyuwé: his temperature was 103°. I diagnosed an attack of malaria, and treated him with paludrine, and aspirin to relieve his headache. William had the same symptoms and a temperature of 102°, so I gave him the same dosage, and advised both to eat nothing but plenty of thin porridge, and to drink warm water. Any abnormality of behaviour might have made them collapse from nervousness, so I smiled, and they too remained cheerful and animated. I had often treated malaria before, and was not particularly worried. Nearly all the Indians, of whatever tribe, have chronic malaria, with enlarged spleens, and on practically every expedition someone has an attack. I saw them to their hammocks, and left.

The other two Wai-Wais, Kirifakka and Wayama, went fishing below my hammock. They caught several large haimaras, and as I lay looking at the running river, full of black reflections, I could see the eyes of the fish shining in my lantern's light as they drew them struggling through the water. Even after they had gone the river seemed full of living creatures, and fish or cayman splashed loudly up and down it all night.

In the morning both men's temperatures had fallen. I continued the courses of paludrine, warned them off indigestible foods, and placed them where they would not have to do much work during the day.

We travelled for a hundred yards up the Essequebo's continuation, to see what it was like. On both sides the land was low and swampy, covered with a bright green vegetation of small trees, shrubs and bushes netted with lianes, and with an occasional thorny palm, grey and hoary, leaning out low over the water. Coming to a long log lying across the river just below the surface, we put on speed and tried to shoot over at the deepest point, but stuck, and swung slowly sideways:

"Over we go," I thought, rather dreamily, for I was in a curious fatalistic mood; but just as water began to pour in old William pushed a paddle into the sand and Andrew leaped into the shallow stream and held her. Straightening we slid backwards, and floated downstream again towards the Chodikar.

So far as history records the Essequebo valley above the Chodikar has never been inhabited. It was on a mountain at its headwaters that Schomburgk hoisted the British flag in 1837, to mark the boundary of British Guiana, and since then it has been revisited perhaps only once, at the time of the Boundary Survey in the 1930's. Standing on this mountain-side, Schomburgk described the scene:

"The Sierra Acarai, which averages a height of 2,000 feet above the savannah, is more densely wooded than any other I remember to have seen. At times the stream meanders at the very foot of the mountains, at others recedes to some distance: but even here the Sipu (Essequebo) retains its peculiar characteristic of being studded with granitic boulders. . . . We were surprised at the scarcity of animals or birds, although probably no human foot had ever before trod on this spot, yet, with the exception of the smaller birds, and from time to time a single heron, or an eagle soaring on high in the air, all was still as it might be the sandy desert of Africa. . . ."

The Chodikar was about forty-five feet broad, a muddy yellow in contrast with the Essequebo's green. After passing through a few yards of low swamplands, from which grizzled palms leant out over the fast-flowing water at spectacular angles, wreaths of mist, spotlighted by the shafts of brilliant early morning sunlight, rising from their drying dew-drenched leaves, we began climbing a long steep incline of choppy, racing water full of protruding boulders. Trees with pendant fruit spread above, their lower leaves in dark shadow: ahead, the water curved, the sun shining on its waves. Then we came to smoother, wider stretches: a marmoset gave a shrill bird-like whistle as we passed; pale peacock-coloured kingfishers flew ahead with rapid undulating flight and alarmed cries of "Kek-kek-kek"; snakebirds flapped in panic and rose, ungainly, through the tree-tops; and little butterflies of velvet black, sky-blue spotted on their forewings, red-banded along the back—of a kind I had never seen before—sunned themselves on leaves.

Soon we caught up with the small boat, in which George and three paddlers were making as good time as we. They had stopped to transfer Fonyuwé to my boat, for he was ill again. Beneath his coating of red grease-paint he looked ghastly: pale, trembling and weak. I draped him with one of my own thick towels to keep him warm, and cleared a space so that he would be comfortable. My headache was worse than ever, and the smell of old William, who sat in front of me, was almost unendurable. The Wai-Wais washed frequently, but now their usual spicy or fishy paint smell was accentuated powerfully by the fact that neither he nor Fonyuwé, because of their illness, had bathed the previous day.

As we continued, the river became more and more choked with fallen trees, the debris of years, lying criss-crossed in the channel. We had to cut our way through tangled crowns and branches every few moments, or chop through thick tree-trunks with our axes before we could pull the boat forward. At times there were evidences of Basil's passing—axed logs, holes cleared through masses of dead or living vegetation; but mostly these were of no avail to us, for the water level had altered.

In mid-morning we passed an open space in the forest, another otter's playground, opposite the dark tunnel of a small river mouth, the Pwat-wau, or Monkey Creek. Stirred by memories, William, now in good spirits, told us that this place was often used as a camp site by hunting parties; and that moreover, in the olden days, a path from the Wai-Wai villages on the Essequebo had crossed the Chodikar here by an enormous fallen log, and had led on over the mountains for four days' walk to some villages on the River Tutumo, "on the other side"; a river (about as wide at that point as the Chodikar) on which in those days the Wai-Wais had lived, before they moved to the Mapuera. I asked him whether one could still go along that path; but he said no, like the villages, the path had disappeared.

Above here the river was even more nearly impassable: narrow, winding and swift, and so stifled with vegetation that we drew ourselves forward mostly by main force, clinging to lianes, branches and rocks, chopping, hacking and struggling to push the various impediments away, jumping into the water and shouldering the boat over logs where we could save the time of chopping them through. We seemed to be making no more than a few yards an hour; we were smothered in masses of dried mud, dead twigs and scaling bark, insects crawled in our hair, and we were hot and ill-tempered.

Practically every log was inhabited by oval five-inch long insects with mother-of-pearl wings, stalked protruding heads and pincer jaws: Neuroptera presumably, and females, for they rested on broods of eggs. We saw spiders, large as tea-plates, carrying cocoon-like egg-sacs beneath their bodies; iridescent flies ran on leaves, waving their wings; butterflies, bluebottles, brilliant bees coruscating like emeralds, hovered in the air. Strangest of all were the tiny, solemn-looking membracid bugs, shaped like minute space-ships or police cars, bearing on their backs futuristic apparatus of knobs and hooks—T.V. antennae, lightning conductors or death-ray tubes. They rotated on twigs until disturbed, then leaped away, sometimes looping the loop, and flew off on little wings.

Occasionally, as if to tempt us, there would be an easier stretch, and we would start the motor hopefully. Sometimes it would be a place where the entire river surface was covered with proliferating masses of greenery—piled floating tangles of lianes, carpets of *Polygonums* or other plants. Then our bows would part the lush herbage, our propeller would stir the mud —until of a sudden it would be wrapped round by yards of cable-like stems which took fifteen minutes to unwind or cut away. Or we would come to clear sweeps where high, magnificent forest grew right down to the water's edge, arching overhead, forty feet above, to form a dark tunnel, from the ceiling of which, like so many swords of Damocles, hung the large, flat scimitar-shaped fruits of wallaba trees, singly, or in clusters at the ends of ten-foot long, bootlace-like pedicels, or sometimes the beautiful rose-pink flowers that preceded them.[1]

In such places the steeply-sloping clayey banks were often

[1] A new species, *Eperua glabra*, so named by Dr. Richard Cowan of the New York Botanical Garden.

marked by little paths descending to the waterside made by tapirs or other animals. Once we saw a large round head swimming away . . . then it reached the shore and a brightly-spotted ocelot, yellow, white and black, emerged and bounded into the bushes.

We were aware all the time that we were climbing, winding our way between hills, and sometimes glimpsing them, swathed, like all the country, in densest jungle. When the river drew near them we breathed with relief, for we came to realize that it was upon them that the high forest grew, and that though there might still be logs to chop through, submerged branches, rapids and rocky runs to negotiate, the going would be easier than through the lower growth of swampy levels.

Wherever we could we would rush the submerged obstacles and try to slide over, boosting the engine full speed ahead and at the last minute raising the propeller so that the whole boat shook with the sudden roar of power, then as we reached the other side lowering it again and shooting away. Sometimes the propeller would entangle a liane, or strike a snag, forcing us to cut the motor to avoid injury to it; then we would have to start our laborious paddling and clawing again till we came to another clear stretch.

At one point George, very black-skinned and flashing-eyed under his bushranger hat, and his three paddlers overtook us in the smaller canoe, passing with loud shouts of "Overboard! Overboard there, everybody! Out and push!" Soon after which, in a comparatively open patch of swamp woodland, we emerged from beneath a screen of low branches and beheld, towering above, an immense tree: a silk-cotton one hundred and fifty feet tall, mushrooming into a circular crown as broad. Crouched in our little boat it gave us a new perspective to gaze at its outflung branches with their millions of minute-seeming palmate leaves, their tiny fruit-pods—and then to follow down the smooth and silvery column to the tangled stuff which was our concern.

Just beyond we came to a channel which, according to William, led to the Irai-wau, Kamocoko, or River of Blood (the beginning of Wai-Wai territory forty years before, when Farabee had visited the village of Wakakulud on it), shortly above the mouth of which, where the Chodikar became too shallow for canoes, the Mapuera trail began. Hopes were raised, but by 4.15 p.m., when we were all weary from our struggles, there was still far to go; so, coming to a low-lying bank in untidy, scrubby forest full of coiling lianes—a wet, unpleasant place, but the best we could find—we made camp.

Fonyuwé was a little better, and I gave him more paludrines and a dose of Epsom salts. William seemed to have recovered completely, and my own headache had gone, though I was so tired that I left all the riverside plants I had collected in my vasculum, postponing their pressing till another day. Only Andrew was full of complaints—he could not breathe because his lungs were congested; so I gave him a large dose of nasty but effective cough medicine, and an inhalation of Vick's Vaporub.

During the night, as I lay in my hammock, chilled and damp in the misty riverside air, I was woken by a strange sound, like that of a great ship moving relentlessly through the water, cleaving it with its bows and pushing it asunder; but so magnified that it filled the entire darkness as it drew nearer and nearer, a demoniac rushing as with unbelievable force, a whirlwind passed through the forest, tearing the trees up by the roots. There was a loud, continuous rolling of thunder in the distance, but immediately around the air scarcely stirred. Rain fell, but not violently, and then it was all over.

In the early dawn a new kind of guan manifested itself with a noise like a rusty door-hinge creaking; then, overhead, like the chattering of a machine-gun: it was a white-headed maroudi. Andrew fired and missed, and for an instant as it flew off I beheld its broad rounded wings silhouetted against the sky.

George went ahead in his small boat equipped with an axe to clear the way. The river had risen a little as a result of the storm, and the going was easier than before: it was becoming broader, shallower, rockier, but there were still many fallen trees where everyone had to get into the water and heave the heavy boat over.

For a long time Fonyuwé and William, who were both well again, and Kirifakka refused to wet themselves. As they wore only a few beads and a tiny lap, it was hard to understand this, but they explained that it was because if their red paint were washed off they would be naked, and evil spirits would be able to see them and do them harm. Indeed, Fonyuwé went on, it was obvious that there were large numbers of evil spirits around, else why were there so many fallen trees? The only explanation that he could think of was that a powerful witch doctor had died, and that in anger at the loss of their ally they had got together and thrown down all these trees as a revenge on human beings. However he and William became at last so incensed at the delays that, amidst laughter and cheers, they plunged into the water and threw themselves against the side of the boat with the rest of us.

Jonah for the first time in many days was in good humour. He had been very silent, exuding disapproval of the way things were run and making occasional comparisons with previous expeditions, but now, his little yellow body elf-like in pink bathing trunks, he was enjoying himself splashing about and giving advice. At one place he was knocked backwards and stunned for a second by a falling branch, but got up again looking no worse.

"He must have offend a piai-man,"[1] said Andrew. "Watch out, Jonah! They is after you!"

With his great strength, and his skill as an axeman, Andrew performed prodigies of heaving and chopping: he was magnificent, and now that he was able to show what he could do he had forgotten his discontents.

We stopped for lunch in a sparsely undergrowthed swamp of tall slender trees, drawing the boat up to a beach which was nothing but a soggy mass of dead leaves. There was a mouldy smell, the soil was sticky, squashy clay, everything was soaking; yet before long fires were alight and meals cooking.

"Jonah," I asked, "how do you start fires when everything is so wet?"

"That's not difficult, sir. Any wood will do, if you get a big stick and cut away all the wet wood outside. Then you make shavings of the centre. But it is good to know that there are some sorts of wood which burn even when they are green. The best is trysil,[2] but I haven't seen any about this part."

---

[1] Witch doctor. [2] *Pentaclethra macroloba.*

As I sat munching my bread and peanut-butter sandwiches, tiny stealthy black flies—bloodsuckers as I discovered when I crushed one that had settled on me—hung in the air all around, looking very much like mosquitoes, except that they rubbed their legs together. There were plenty of real mosquitoes as well: culices; anophelines; a giant inches across, of a kind which breeds in the water collected in the leaves of epiphytes, which came whining through the jungle with a noise like a police car in pursuit, and settled upon a leaf, where it vibrated its body until it was a mist of legs and wings almost invisible until struck by the sunlight; and small sapphire blue *Haemogogi*, dangerous creatures, conveyers of jungle yellow fever (endemic in the blood of monkeys and certain other animals of the tree-tops where these mosquitoes usually live, and from which, inquisitive, they occasionally descend to the ground to investigate noises).

As we continued I saw that in many places everything in the water—rocks, roots, even living twigs and leaves which had hung in it only during the flood seasons—had a coating of some black substance giving it a dull, dead-matt surface. This was an interesting discovery, for it might indicate the abundant presence nearby of manganese ore.[1]

The country was changing: we had ascended to a level plain and now the river wound and twisted continuously, so that looking through the forest we often saw light shining through the trees where a part of it several bends away had swung round near us. There were open places where we sailed under the unobscured sky, where tangles of a *Bauhinia* vine smothered the riverside plants in drifts of flowers (from a little away like pyramids of pink horse-chestnut); silt banks where grew low mauve starry-flowered herbs: then, unexpectedly we found ourselves gliding beside an arching wall of delicate Chinese-green bamboos, a sight I had never seen before in Guiana, where wild bamboos are generally supposed not to exist, though mentioned by one or two early travellers.

For years I had been curious to see the strange poison bamboo reputed as growing at the mouth of the Rappu River, a

[1] Tests of a coated stone which I brought back led to the dispatch of a geological expedition to the area. Its results have not been published.

tributary of the Essequebo in an extremely remote part of its middle course: "The islands in these rapids," wrote Barrington Brown, "and a river near by are so called from the existence of a peculiar species of tall and graceful bamboo which flourishes there, not being found further north. Pieces of the stem of this bamboo are dried and used by the Indians as arrow heads, which are said to possess similar properties to the far-famed Wourali (curare) poison. They split up the stem and dry the pieces over a fire, and then shape them into lance heads, which they fasten on the ends of arrows. Wild animals wounded by these arrows are at once completely paralysed, and in that condition easily dispatched. This bamboo is tall, growing singly, and not in clumps from a mass of matted roots like the common bamboo."

Though this grew in low clumps, and, said Fonyuwé, was only used for making flutes and pigtail tubes, I collected a specimen for analysis,[1] for since I had seen Yakotá shoot the pig on our way back from the New River, I had been certain that the Wai-Wais did know the true poison bamboo, and were perhaps keeping it a secret from me: the pig had given an agonized cry when the arrow had driven into its shoulder, had run on for about a hundred feet, and then collapsed, dying seven or eight minutes later. The arrow point had been of bamboo, but not coated with curare; and the wound had seemed too superficial to have caused death.

A mile or so further we passed the mouth of the Irai-wau, and soon after heard the sound of axes: the river divided, and a few yards up the smaller left-bank tributary, still called the Chodikar or "Chororikar", we came to a cluster of canoes—Basil's, Charlie Wai-Wai's, old "Manatá's" and a battered half-sunk dugout.

George and his three men were already clearing a space and constructing frames for the tarpaulins, and camp was rapidly made.

Then I noticed that Kirifakka had turned a pale yellowish colour: his temperature was 103.5° F. I was horrified. It seemed extraordinary that in an area where malaria was endemic all these Wai-Wais should suffer such high fevers from it. I felt

[1] And in so doing ran a sliver into my thumb, which ached for a week.

deep uncertainty about the wisdom of going forward, yet so far my treatments had been successful: William, Wayama, and Fonyuwé were now as fit as ever.

I gave Kirifakka a slightly more vigorous dosage than usual —four paludrine tablets, and two aspirins—and fed him twice that evening on warm diluted condensed milk. In the morning his temperature had fallen to 99.8° F., but this did not mean that he was cured, for I had noticed that, as is typical of malaria, the Indians' temperatures were always highest in the evenings. I dosed him with Epsom salts and continued his treatment with paludrine, then began the pressing of the specimens I had collected on our way upriver.

No sooner had I settled down than, ghostlike, a crowd of pale, sullen Indians began to drift into the camp. Silently they came up to me and shook hands, then moved off and sat down —Basil's Wapisianas, come to help carry our loads over the mountains to the Mapuera.

8

Discontent

The Wapisianas were a discontented-looking crew, yet it was a relief to see them, for I had worried, wondering how Basil was getting on. I had had to trust him, and now my confidence seemed justified: without question or argument, he had accomplished a most arduous task—the opening up of the trail across the Serra Acarai to the Mapuera, and the transport there of a great deal of equipment, including drums of petrol and oil. He had remained behind at the Mapuera, said his men, with Charlie Wai-Wai, Albert, and James, working on the boat I had ordered them to construct. They had only just begun it—because Charlie had forgotten his adze at the Chodikar, and had had to return for it, wasting many days—but they had spent them as profitably as they could, preparing the camp-site.

All this through Andrew, for evidently none spoke English.

There was a pause. Then they launched their complaint: I was giving them short rations, and they could not live on them.

Surprised, I answered that I was giving them the full Government rations; and produced an official list to prove it. This mollified them somewhat, so I then told them that we had brought two large sacks containing about one hundred and fifty pounds of farine with us, in case anyone wanted more food, and that I would issue them an extra half-pint a day from that.

One man then asked for a pair of shoes and a shirt, as an advance on his pay, for he had worn out those he had brought with him; and, when he had received these, asked for tea and coffee. How many days' rations had he and the others left? I questioned—they were supposed to have ten. About five days' said he complacently, as they had all eaten ahead—they had not bothered to ration it out.

When I heard this I flew into a rage: How could food ever

be expected to last if everyone gorged himself? Turning to Andrew, who was translating, I said:

"Tell them that regular Government rations are all I have to offer, and that they must make up their minds now that they are going to work on them, or they can all go home and we'll call the whole trip off. The only thing extra I can give them is a little farine. I'm not going to have any more complaints—there have been enough on this expedition."

Andrew looked startled: "Mr. Guppy, if you tell them that they will all go. You don't know these Wapisianas."

He was an over-cautious fellow, but I wanted no more nonsense. "Well, what would you do on your own ranch with people like this?"

He deliberated. "Well, sometimes I give them all I have and do without myself. Other times I think to hell with them, they're a bunch of rogues."

This made me smile. "So tell them nothing?"

"No, sir. We better not."

"O.K., then—we'll see what Basil can do with them. He brought them, and he's responsible for them."

For this gentle word of caution I forgave Andrew much of his past vexatiousness. Indeed, looking at the big, clumsy fellow, I realized what a good sort he undoubtedly was—kindly, well-meaning, simply tired of wandering. Yet between him and Jonah I was exhausted—every order was carried out so ungraciously, every move had to overcome such unwillingness.

Saying nothing more about food, I asked what the country ahead was like. It was very rough, said the Wapisianas, and it would take five or six days to reach Basil, carrying the loads across in stages. We would just reach him as his food ran out.

It was still morning, so after they had eaten and rested I sent them off again with the first batch of goods, and instructions to deposit them near the highest point of the crossing at a place where we could camp—where, while the rest of the carrying was done, I could study the forests of the divide. The other men I put to enlarging and tidying the clearing, and making tables and benches of sticks, axe-handles, and extra paddles for our eventual return down the Chodikar.

Then with Jonah I paddled a short way downstream, collecting along the riverside. By far the most interesting plant was a Bromelaid, *Pitcairnia kegeliana*, growing on the deep clay soil. Unlike most of its family its leaves were not stiff and water-catching, but grassy, so that with its vermilion flowers it looked much like a garden *Montbretia*. Hanging from the trees were *Peperomia macrostachya*, with fleshy, pale green leaves and whip-like inflorescences, and occasional sprays of a lovely liane of the family Gesneriaceae, an *Episcia*, its little yellow flowers hidden in heart-shaped, translucent scarlet bracts, set aflame by the slanting sun rays.

Silvery whirligig beetles raced about on the water, and chrysomelid beetles, marvellously shaped and coloured, like the jewels encrusting an ikon, roamed on the leaves. Breaking off a twig (suspended from which, on long threads, were several little white fluffy balls, about three-quarters of an inch in diameter and pierced with holes: moth cocoons), I nearly touched an extraordinary furry caterpillar. About four inches long, it was covered in a forest of beautiful branching pink and green poisonous spines, contact with which would have caused painful, even dangerous, irritation and swelling. Insect life seemed particularly abundant here, doubtless because the surface of the vegetation-sea was close to the ground along the river and in the clearing.

Back at the camp Andrew gave me a fresh Brazil nut, the first I had ever eaten, brought from the watershed region by the Wapisianas; a sure sign that we were penetrating into a new forest-world. It was so soft that I cracked its shell between my teeth, and its white, crisp flesh was of a delicacy and sweetness unknown in London, Paris or New York, where the nuts only arrive months after they have been gathered by Indians beneath their remote, gigantic trees.

That evening Kirifakka had no temperature, and everyone seemed in high spirits. Andrew and Gabriel had built a special powis-tail for themselves, from which, lying in their hammocks, their faces illuminated by the firelight, they hung out and chatted with the other men. Pots were stirred, flutes were tootled, and there was much joking and singing and telling of stories.

The four Wai-Wais with us were very different from the

irresponsible, alarming ones who had come to the New River. My respect for them grew when I saw how carefully they conserved their few rounds of cassava bread, the strips of deer meat and fish they had smoke-dried—instead of glutting themselves and then causing trouble when they ran short. How easily I might have generalized from the others' behaviour! Perhaps Mingelli and Eoka had been of the same calibre, but they had been overshadowed by the barbarousness of Chekemá, Mawashá, Yakotá and Manaka.

All day my feet had itched acutely, and, examining them after dinner, I saw beneath the skin the round black marks which indicate an infestation of jigger or chigoe fleas, probably picked up at Yawarda, for they are often common in deserted Indian villages—and indeed may have caused their desertion. The females of these fleas burrow gently into the flesh, gorge themselves with blood, and swell rapidly to the size of a pea as their abdomens distend with developing eggs and young. Left alone, the larvae escape and repeat the process in multiplication, and I have seen a photograph of a man's foot after more than a hundred had been extracted, even from under his toenails, several of which had had to be removed. Now Tanner with a needle gently and skilfully opened up my flesh and squeezed out a mere dozen. One or two had burst, and carefully he scraped to get the last fleshy shreds of flea-body out of the little cavities; then I covered the holes with plaster. It was a little painful to walk. Apart from this I was beginning to feel the excellent health of jungle life. Providing one keeps free of malaria and dysentery (there is no need, in Guiana, to boil drinking water except near settlements), no more healthy, even invigorating climate exists than that of the South American rain forest.

In the morning I sent off ahead more men with loads, and with Andrew, Jonah, William and Kirifakka laid out a plot in the forest of the river flood plain—a forest of one hundred foot high trees, buttressed and with spreading surface roots, ragingly inundated during the wet season to judge from some of the smaller trees, which had been bent sideways, even horizontally, and from the thickly silt-coated leaves of the undergrowth plants.

Common here was the Karia palm, apparently a species of *Bactris*, whose immense spiny leaves arose close to the ground, from a stem only a few inches high, and curved out for twelve feet or more, dark green and motionless in the still air. Very rarely the stem had elongated, raising the huge armoured crown six or ten feet aloft. As we worked *Morpho* butterflies, big as birds, flashed their electric-blue wings along the riverside, pugnacious insects, whirling in combat whenever male met male; and a quadrille wren lilted its own Mozartean tune, different from the one I had heard before.

Andrew was full of excitement at a jaguar he had heard in the night—it had roared far off, then later gnashed and cracked its teeth on the opposite side of the river, only a few yards from the camp.

"It could have come across if it wanted, I'm telling you, sir. Water ain't no barrier to a tiger. You know what I once saw? I was in a boat with my brother, near Karanambo, where you pick us up in the plane, and we see a tiger feeding on an alligator. When it see us it leave the prey and swim off into very deep water, so we decide we going to run it down and crush it against the bank, which was rock and form a cliff all along the riverside. So I turn the boat straight on it, and race the engine to get up speed, and my brother shoot an arrow right into its side. Just as we think we going hit it, it jump up right out of the water onto the top of the bank, which was about twelve feet high. What you think of that? It shows just what a jaguar can do in water."

"Are you sure it didn't jump from a submerged rock? I can't believe it could fling itself twelve feet out of deep water."

"That is just what it do. We search all about and find the bottom was so deep we couldn't reach it with a pole. You remember what the chief was telling you the other day about hunting dogs, Mr. Guppy, how it is most important that they must have long tails? That is because of hunting jaguars. A short-tail dog is no use, because it will always get killed. When the jaguar springs it jumps backwards and hits a tree, or gets itself tangle up in bush ropes. But a long-tail dog use his tail for a feeler, or a antenna, and all the time he is feeling behind, to know which way is clear for him to escape."

133

The plot finished, we began to collect specimens, and this necessitated felling a certain number of trees.

"You know, Mr. Guppy," Andrew went on, leaning on his axe at one stage, "this timber work can be very dangerous. Once I was with a man cutting down a greenheart tree. At the last minute I left him to finish off the job and stood aside to watch. Now when that tree begin to fall it knock down a dead branch of a Baromalli tree which was suspended up there on a fork, and the wood come down with such force that it sever that man's head clean from he shoulders and bury it in the ground. And that headless body it wave its arms and it make sound 'Mm! Mm! Mm!'

"It's terrible, everything happens to me! Yet I don't know why. I is a innocent person. I don't do nothing! You know, twice my own half-brother Manny Bishop tried to knife me. He was a real wild man. Purely due to his wildness he loose all his money. He start out as a rich rancher, with plenty of cows. Now he is just a poor cultivator, just cutting a field once in a while. He killed several people, you know. One time he find a woman stealing from his field, and he knock her down and jump up and down on she belly, even though she was pregnant. But they could never catch him, though he was wanted for murder in both Brazil and B.G., and after eleven years they drop the charges."

"He sounds a very bad man."

"The first time he tried to knife me was at Figueredo's Store.[1] There was a big dance there, and he was drunk, and he try to drag a woman out of the house agains' she will. So I say to him, 'Come Manny, we are the only British here, let's set an example for all these Brazilians.' At that Manny draw a knife and rush on me in a corner of the room. So all I could do was spring aside. Then I kick him on the elbow, and den in the belly and I drag him away. That is a real terrible man, I'm telling you. And you ever hear of Victor Gomes? That is another man who try to kill me."

"William," obscene old rascal, could not take much part in our conversations, but he kept the men amused by his numerous

[1] This store, the only one in thousands of square miles of savannah country, stands on the Brazilian bank of the Ireng River.

phallic gestures. We sent him up a tree to collect its flowers, which were comparatively low, and on sliding down he pretended to hurt his genitals badly on a projecting knob on the trunk. With chuckles and groans he rolled around clutching himself. Then with a slash he cut off the knob, shaking with laughter, carved it into a perfect resemblance to a penis, and replaced it on the tree at an appropriate height. Everyone was so tickled by this that work stopped for several minutes, while the popular old creature was clapped on the shoulder and made much of.

Several times while collecting we mistook for sprays of flowers the brilliant young leaves of various plants—for in these jungles it is the immature, not the old leaves, which are brightly coloured. There is no autumn, and trees shed their leaves at all times of year, the old leaves withering and falling inconspicuously, often one at a time, so that there is a continuous replacement; but sometimes all at once, in which case the flush of tender young leaves—lemon or honey yellow, pink, mauve or crimson, slowly changing over a week or two to the sombre greens of maturity—may be as spectacularly showy as any flowering.

In this almost seasonless climate the wood of trees shows no growth-rings, so it is impossible to tell their ages or their rate of development. Over vast areas the patterns of soils and climates change little, yet the forests that cover them vary from place to place, both in species and in consequent structure. The greenheart, one of the commonest trees in northern British Guiana, was not to be seen here. It seems to have spread slowly, dropping its heavy seeds in an ever-widening circle, from somewhere in the centre of the colony, where, perhaps, it was evolved. Nor had we seen trysil or mora, which give the riverside forests further north their characteristic appearance—seemingly only because their distributive mechanisms had not yet brought them, and not because they would not have thriven here; while the Brazil nut was apparently only just venturing northwards into British Guiana.

Perhaps the mysterious trees, utterly isolated, which from time to time one finds in the forest are remote advance-guards of such a vegetable invasion. Near Bartica, in northern British Guiana, for instance, there stands a giant, 180 feet tall, which, over many years of observation by the Forest Department, has never been known to flower, has never been identified, and of which only one other specimen has been found—by myself, one hundred miles further south. Where did it come from, one wonders? Is it the furthest flung of a tribe abundant elsewhere in the endless sea of leaves; or a survivor of a once-common, now disappearing species?

Another unidentified, mystifying tree was quite small, growing only about twenty feet high, but most distinctive because its dark reddish-brown bark was crowded with stout, stud-like thorns, and when cut with a knife gushed forth thick white milk. Since I had first found it near Bartica, and later near the goldmine of Omai, I had always looked for it. By the New River I had seen two specimens, and now, today, a third: we seemed to be approaching its native land. But still there were no signs of flowers, no means of telling what it was.

How do such trees spread, and how produce their fruit and seeds? They must be self-fertile (for surely crossing is out of the question), or apomictic, dispensing with all need for pollination. But one only guesses, for the great field of genetic studies, of hybridization and the intermingling and evolution of species in the tropical jungles has scarcely even been glanced at.

In these enormous, uniform lowlands, time—not, as in most lands, climatic zones, mountain or water barriers—seems to have set the geographical limits of the various species of the dry-land forests. Even over quite short periods one learns of species spreading from one region into the next, and slowly we are beginning to see that the flora has come from certain focal points: mountains that stood as islands above the waves when, in Pleistocene or late Tertiary times, seas covered half the continent, and which bear today some of the world's most ancient vegetations. In most parts of the globe man has destroyed the forests, or altered them so much that those that remain appear largely of secondary origin. But on these uninhabited South American mountains there still exist, if anywhere on earth, true primeval forests unchanged, except by their own internal evolutionary processes, perhaps since before man himself had evolved.

Everything I had seen of the forests on the Acarai Mountains seemed to confirm the geologists' belief that they too had remained above those seas, and that they constituted one of the source regions from which plants had recolonized the lowlands exposed when the water receded. First and most important was their extraordinary richness in species of big trees, unparalleled over such a large area anywhere else that I had ever been. Many times I had counted and named all the trees beside the path for miles on end, as I had done on the way to the New River, and found the same bewildering diversity. In one place I had walked nearly half a mile before any tree had repeated itself! And it seemed certain that at no time in the past had more than a few hundred people lived in these thousands of square miles—and then only near the bigger rivers.

To me, even without the geological evidence, this diversity of species alone suggested that this might be a residual area of ancient forest. Physically there was no barrier to prevent all the species of these low mountains migrating into the regions around. But to invade successfully a species has to find the right niches—and some species, perhaps because they have light wind-borne seeds, or seeds that float or are carried by birds, move faster than others, and once established make it difficult for late-comers to find a foothold—for which reason one would expect a reduction in number of species per given area away from the point of origin. North of the mountains this was very much what occurred; southwards I had yet to see.

Jonah could understand why I wanted to travel on both sides of the mountains, to see if their plants and forests were distinctive from those of the surrounding regions. But to try to find reasons for this was beyond him. To him the fact that there were no moras, or greenhearts or trysils here showed that they could not grow, despite the resemblances of soils and climate. I tried to explain that perhaps they had not had time to spread here, whereas other trees that are found everywhere, like the *Cecropias*, spread fast because of their light seeds; but he shook his head—to him there were so many strange new plants here that God must have created this part differently, and that was that; and all my various efforts and studies were just a waste of time.

George and his men returned wearily just before dark, ten

hours after they had set forth. They had gone, he said, about ten miles: a remarkable feat, for it meant that they had averaged two miles an hour—very fast walking for the jungle. Wayama had wept under his load.

It was a hateful thought: just then, however, he passed, smiling at us.

"How much was he carrying?" I asked.

"About eighty pound. But it's not so much the weight, sir, as these Wai-Wai don't understan' how to carry things. As soon as I show him how to pack he warishi, so the weight between he shoulders, instead of fallin' behin', he was O.K. and he gone ahead of us all."

"Thank Heaven for that. You had me worried. We must move camp tomorrow, because we must get to the Mapuera as fast as we can. I'm sorry, because it's Sunday, but then you all had several days' rest while we were at the mission. Do you think you can manage it?"

"Don't bother about that, sir, that's O.K. with us. It will be good if we reach soon."

However, it was not O.K. with Jonah:

"Mr. Guppy, we can't shift things tomorrow. The men is weary."

"Well Jonah, George says he can manage it, and he thinks the others can. We have no more work to do here. When we get across we can rest."

"That is no good, sir. We expects our Sunday's rest, even when we have rest on other days of the week. Besides, if we work tomorrow you will have to pay all these men time-and-a-half."

"I am prepared to do that. You see, Jonah, if we delay we'll run out of food before we get anywhere. Once we reach the Mapuera and have our party and all our supplies assembled we'll be able to plan better, and we'll know more about what lies ahead. I'm sorry about it being Sunday, but will it matter if you rest on a Thursday, or a Tuesday instead?"

"Sunday rest is different, sir."

"What about Basil, Jonah? We must try to reach him before he runs out of food."

"All right, sir, if that is what you say."

He turned, shrugged his shoulders, and walked slowly, grudgingly, away.

Early next morning the Wapisianas reappeared. They estimated now that it would take only three, instead of five or six days' effort to reach the Mapuera, picking up the various loads deposited ahead as we reached them.

On hearing this I decided to move only as far as their previous night's camp, three miles away at the base of the main climb, for it would give the men a short and easy working day and allow me to lay out a plot on the way. I instructed Jonah and Andrew to take minimum loads so that they could walk with me and help me, for now that the Wapisianas had come no one would have much to carry, and I warned them that they must supervise the breaking up of the camp and the loading of the men, about which they had been so negligent on our journey to the New River.

Despite this I soon saw that things were being left behind, and I ran after the men who had gone ahead and sent them back to the camp. Summoning Jonah and Andrew, in whom I could sense stubbornness, indifference, and uneasiness about their authority, I spoke sharply to them:

"You are not doing the work I have assigned to you. I do not expect to have all this grumbling and shirking—it is setting a very bad example."

"The loads are very heavy," murmured Jonah.

"They are lighter than those we took to the New River and back. Today the way is level and we are only going about three miles. Do not let this sort of thing happen again."

Andrew then spoke up, abashed but feeling he must make a show.

"I'm a hasty man . . . . All I say is when Mr. Angoy send me on this trip he never tell me nothing about what work I is to do. I'm like a blind bat. . . ."

"That's perfectly all right, Andrew," I interrupted. "You are doing well for a blind bat. But now you are here you must do as I say. When you return to the savannahs you can complain about what a bad time you had."

They were both silent. Then they moved over to the men and began to allocate the burdens among them. To their surprise (and a little to my own) the men accepted their additional loads cheerfully, satisfied that they would not have to return for them, and in a few moments the atmosphere of sullenness had dissipated.

One of the best examples was set by Kirifakka, who took the heaviest load of all, a box of tinned food, carefully moving aside his pigtail, cased in a bright new bamboo tube, as he shouldered it. As he walked off, George, in admiration, gave a comic leap, pretending to jump on his back, and even Jonah smiled:

"He is a good boy," he remarked, seeking to gratify me. "I have been thinking how good it would be if there was more hard-working boys like that. He is keen on learning about the different trees and animals too. It is very rare to get anyone like that among we Arawaks today. I wish I could take him back with us and train him to work for the Forest Department."

It was extraordinary how popular with everyone this slender youth, so full of smiles, with his husky breaking voice, had become: so far superior was he to all the other men in manners, that it was only when one saw him eating with his fingers, and deftly tossing the bones of monkey or alligator over his shoulder, that one realized that he was a "savage".

At first we walked through flood-plain forest in which almost every big tree was a Wallaba. Their columnar stems rose pale and blotched into the ceiling of foliage, from which, like mobiles, the dangling Damoclean fruit hung motionless, or swung and turned in the slight breezes, glowing ruby when a spot of sunlight caught them.

Then came a slope of deep, spongy black loam, about a foot deep, on which the Wallabas grew even taller and more densely: it was a remarkable soil, very much like that of the old Taruma village site near the mission. Digging in it and looking around, I realized that this was indeed the site of an old settlement, though there were no signs of pottery. Doubtless, if I had searched more widely I should have found them, but the proof lay not only in the presence of this soil, which seems to occur only where there has been human occupation, but in the forest, for it still had a scattering of secondary growth species, such as always spring up after clearing.

From my reconstruction of his journey it must have been near this very place, if not actually here, that Schomburgk found a Wai-Wai village in 1837, before the tribe had moved northwards into the Essequebo valley. Because my chief concern was with forest indubitably undisturbed, it was most important to know where there was even a suspicion of former human interference, and I began to consider how an archaeologist might try to discover the past history of the region. With aerial photographs it would be possible to locate patches of second growth, or re-grown primary forest, even hundreds of years old, and from them the village sites; without them the task would be almost impossible, for all these forest tribes are shifting cultivators, moving every three or four years. It would be sheer chance if one came upon traces of any of the older villages, the ones abandoned beyond living memory. The Indians have certain favourite sites, particularly hills above flood-level close to a river, to which they return again and again, and possibly one could find all of these more obvious places. But even if there were stratified remains at them this constant shifting would make it difficult to date the periods of settlement. Worse, all evidence of the existence of these older villages, except what is intrinsic in the structure and species of the forest, might easily have been washed away, for the whole land surface above flood-level is continuously being eroded by water.

A little further we glimpsed an opening in the trees, and turning aside came to the shore of an eerie morass, a great grey expanse of water in which water-lilies and other aquatics grew, and above which mist floated in wisps amidst the crowns of decaying swamp trees and the dark green fans of *Mauritia* palms. It stretched away as far as we could see. An evil place, said old William.

Then, after passing through a gloomy forest full of gigantic trees (Ichekelés with coarse reddish-black trunks twenty or more feet in circumference, and, to my delight, several Brazil nuts, their globular fruit decayed on the ground below them—for the fruiting season was long past and only the rare late fruit contained good nuts), we descended a brief slope to the undulating sandy meander-plain of the Upper Chodikar; scrubbily forested, the taller patches full of straight slim stems of bamboo, thorned at the joints, bursting above the tree-tops into nodding ostrich plumes.

We crossed and recrossed large jumbled swathes of trees uprooted a year or two before by a wandering cyclone, and came at length to where the camp stood, beside a deep swift-running stream with a bed of coarse quartz sand.

After lunch, while tarpaulins were being put up, and powis and maroudi tails constructed, I took the gun and went with Kirifakka across the river and up the long steep rise beyond, walking on red clay like that we had seen near the New River. This was again the mixed forest of many species, with trees slender, straight and very tall, and the cries of greenheart birds ringing joyfully all around. On the right a mountain-side showed slaty, and far away falling water tinkled. Everywhere curious toads hopped: first a fingertip-sized one of velvet black marbled with brightest buttercup yellow, motionless beneath a fern, then one heard, but did not see, like a dripping tap—plink! plonk! plonk . . . plonk! plink! then several of the abundant leaf-toads, three inches long, flat-backed with upturned pointed snouts, pale fawn, and marked with a mid-rib and various blotches to simulate a fallen leaf; and walking slowly and confidently through the leaves every few yards, two-and-a-half inch long creatures of vividly conspicuous royal blue, with darker blue-black legs and sides. One which I picked up made no attempt to evade capture, or even to escape, and when returned to the ground, slowly, doubtfully, began to climb a tree. *"Kirifakka!"* said Kirifakka, smiling, pointing to it and then himself.[1]

A tinamou flurried away on whistling wings, then we scattered a dozen small partridges, picking their way through the underbrush. I fired at a toucan, forty yards up in a Silverballi tree, and missed; and returning, stalked a shaking bush to which Kirifakka pointed with urgent whisperings of *"Maipuri! Maipuri!"* (Tapir): a bush which parted to reveal a Wapisiana just as I was taking aim, to my companion's endless amusement.

[1] Later Andrew told me he believed that this was the toad of which he had heard, with the deadly poisonous juice of which certain tribes coated their arrows: smoking the animals alive above a fire in a little cage, and dipping the points in their flesh.

At the camp I had once more to speak to Jonah. It was his duty each time we moved to build a small framework of sticks, which, with a piece of canvas wrapped round it and a paraffin lamp inside, formed a stove over which I dried the specimens, which mouldered and fell to pieces if this was not done regularly each night until they were quite dry.

"Jonah," I said, "you've forgotten to build a stove."

He looked doleful and upset, but stubborn.

"What are all these long faces for? I want to see some cheerfulness. Don't you *want* to go to the Mapuera? This has been a short day, the loads are not so heavy, we haven't run out of food—life ought to be good!"

He pursed his lips: he was determined not to give an inch.

"The work is not good, Mr. Guppy. We will have certain trouble with these men. They intend to desert, that is what I feel: they is full of complaints."

"So far all the complaints I have heard are from you and Andrew. Both of you should be finding ways and means of doing the work, not lamenting that it can't be done."

"Planning is one thing, Mr. Guppy . . ."

"Come on, Jonah! You know as well as I do that this work is not so bad. We've been together on many trips before. I'm sorry if we are moving too fast, but we've got to get ahead. Now I'm going to bathe. Please have that stove ready when I return."

He was frowning thunderously when I turned round after a few yards.

9

The Lonely Walk

I was extremely worried: with all their grumbling and criticism Jonah and Andrew were making it very difficult for me to get anything done. It seemed as if they would stop at nothing to prevent the expedition going forward. It was not that they disliked me, or resented my powers, or that they were being disloyal—far from that! It was just that they were convinced that they knew best. They thought that I was driving the men too hard, that the Wapisianas would desert, that the Wai-Wais would attack us, that we were heading into certain trouble and danger. They were so worried wondering which way the cat would jump that they were prepared to force it to jump, on what they thought the side of safety: of staying where we were, or going forward inch by inch.

Even so, their conduct was inexcusable: it was their duty to support me, and to set an example for the older men of what could be done. From my own experience, I knew that we were not doing anything so very arduous; but in the face of all the uncertainties of the country, and our remoteness from familiar places, their courage and judgment had apparently deserted them. I would have sent them both back if there had been anyone to replace them, but Andrew was the only man who could speak Wapisiana and Wai-Wai as well as English, and without Jonah my botanical work would have been twice as heavy. As it was, I was so tired by the end of each day that I had no strength left for internal politics.

Basil, a few days' walk ahead, seemed a more dependable type of man. Once I reached him I could decide what to do about them.

In the green stillness of early morning, amidst the wood smoke and the damp pendent leaves of the bushes, we packed our heavy loads. Jonah and Andrew were glum, avoiding my glance. I waited until every item was safely stowed, sensing the possibility of trouble, then followed last with the four Wai-Wais.

Fonyuwé walked just ahead as, balancing on a prostrate log, we crossed the Chodikar and commenced the long slow ascent. He carried a warishi on his shoulders, the weight taken largely by a band round his forehead; but, immensely strong, he seemed oblivious of it.

"*Atchi?*" I asked, pointing at a large tree, for he was an expert tree-namer.

He turned and smiled, revealing his pointed, filed teeth. "*Wana*"—a kind of monkey-pipe.

This might almost as well have been spelt "*Wada*", for Wai-Wai, being an unwritten language, has no respect for the fixed values of consonants; and even those which do seem constant may be intermediate, like the Chinaman's L and R, or even quite different from our own: the F in Fonyuwé, for example, being not an F at all, but a "fricative" P, made by pronouncing P, but not quite touching the lips together. One of the pleasures of getting plant names from Fonyuwé was that his pronunciation, unlike that of the other Indians, was so delicate and precise that even this subtlety could be detected.

For half an hour we walked slowly together, I with my notebook open, he with his keen eyes arove, pointing out each new tree. Like the other Wai-Wais, separated from the rest of the men by their language, he was obviously enjoying the trip and judging his work purely on its merits.

Then I walked rapidly ahead, observing the changes in the forest until at about 2,000 feet the path levelled off as it reached the broad ridge-top. Two miles further, at a small, deep-lying rivulet, I found George, Jonah and Tanner resting: Jonah and Tanner friendly, but George a little surly. But then it might have been his manner, for he and I were often at unintentional cross-purposes. I framed my thoughts in the wrong way, and he, over-eager to please, got confused and thought he had offended me.

After a drink and a moment's chat I continued. There was little undergrowth and the path was often almost invisible—a faint line of disturbed leaves among a million others, dry and brown, that had fallen to the ground. I kept a sharp watch for its signs—tiny scuffle-marks on the ground, or cutlass-cut twigs. Three years before I would not have been able to tell that there was a trail even if it had been pointed out to me.

For two hours I was alone, except when I passed a pair of Wapisianas, with no sound in the world save the gentle stirrings of the wind far overhead, and once a bird calling somewhere on my left; then, descending sharply to a tumbling silvery stream with the remains of one of Basil's camps beside it, I found Andrew and the rest of the men preparing lunch, though it was only 10.30; and looking very much as if they felt that their day's work was over. They were huddled, talking in low tones, and looked displeased to see me.

"Well, Mr. Guppy, this is the place where George bring his things, near the highest part of the main ridge. For that was the highest place you just cross. Did you see the tree?"

"No, Andrew, what tree?"

"There is a tree just off the trail, about a mile back, which has initials carved on it by the men of the Boundary Commission seventeen years ago. That is the boundary—so now we are in Brazil."

"That's very exciting. It means we can't be so far from Basil. But where did the Wapisianas leave their loads?"

"Sir, they say they leave their loads a good way further."

"Was it on high ground?"

"Yes, it was on higher ground even than this. This is the watershed, and we is in Brazil, but the highest place hereabouts is further on, and it is near there that they drop them."

"Ask them if we can make it today."

He turned to the Wapisianas, who were sitting quietly, eating their farine and dried meat, and spoke rapidly. Slowly they replied, looking suspiciously at me with their peaky yellow faces.

"Yes, sir, they say they could make it."

I could see that this was not what any of them wanted.

"Fine. I shall go ahead and have my own lunch in about an hour's time. It is only ten-thirty now."

"O.K., Mr. Guppy. I only stop because you say to come up to George's load."

He was wary of me but continued:

146

MAKING A POWIS-TAIL

FORDING THE TARUINI

(p. 154)

KIRIFAKKA AND FONYUWÉ

"How about William and Jonah?"

"They're coming up like steam-engines," I said, at which the Wapisianas laughed—they could evidently understand some English; tension relaxed a little, yet I was still not popular.

Judging this to be a good note to leave on, and before anyone could say that he could or would go no further, I passed through them and set off alone ahead, following the scarcely detectable trail. I was deeply uneasy because I was almost certain that some sort of a sit-down or go-slow strike was in the air: yet I had made up my mind. The best way of getting an order obeyed is to act as if the possibility of its being disobeyed does not exist, and by going ahead I was forcing the men to follow. I was also placing myself in a very difficult position, for if they decided to draw my bluff and stay where they were, or come on only a short way, I should have either to return to them, defeated, or to remain alone in the forests. My chief hope was that the Wapisianas, who had only just met me, would be unwilling for an open break so soon. I decided that if they had not caught up with me by evening I should try the following day to reach Basil, though the Mapuera might still be two days' walk away. There I should wait for them, and if and when they appeared threaten them with a Court of Enquiry. Very likely they would feel ashamed; but my position would still have been weakened, for I could never try the same manœuvre again. On the whole I relied upon their fundamental decency to make them follow. My chief danger, I thought, was of getting lost. Once over the brow of a hill from them I could shout for ever, and never be heard.

As I walked I kept my head down, glancing up and around constantly at the trees, the insects, the birds, but always returning my gaze to the path and fixing it firmly in my vision. Years in the jungle had developed an automatic attentiveness without which I should soon have been lost. Sometimes, at difficult places, I would pause, and with conscious effort scrutinize the ground: certain trees littered the earth with giant brown rustling leaves which looked disarranged in any case, or sprang back quickly after being trodden upon, and under them the path melted away as if into a quicksand; sometimes it was lost beneath the immense crown of a fallen tree or vanished crossing a patch of bare rock, or became entangled with false trails made by wild animals, running water, or even ants. If necessary, I would turn round to make sure I could see the path behind me, and break a twig which I kept always in view as I searched behind, around and ahead. Sometimes I had to return many times to my twig and start all over again, patiently, before I was certain of the way.

Near rivers my difficulties were always worst, for there the false trails multiplied. Minute as the evidence of a path is, once made it is preserved, in these gloomy depths where growth is slow, as if in a vault. One saw the traces of men or beasts who might have passed twenty years before. Indeed, it entered my head that perhaps already I had taken a wrong path that was leading me, not towards Basil, but to a long-abandoned village or far-away hunting-ground. It would have been easy to do so, for when they went in the right direction, our path often followed these old or alien trails; and when it diverged from them again I always walked on bearing a little residue of doubt that I had chosen rightly.

What if I did get lost? I had a compass, and from it knew that I was travelling mostly just east of south. I could continue in the same direction, hoping to find the trail again, but I might recross it a dozen times without seeing it. Unless by chance I stumbled upon Basil's camp there would be very little hope of my ever being seen again: Indians who had lived all their lives in the jungles had disappeared far nearer civilization. It would seem to matter little which way I turned—north, south, east or west—I had not even a cutlass, and once I got down into the denser-forested lowlands I could probably not make more than three or four miles a day. On all sides the forests rolled, full of cliffs and swamps and rivers, foodless, uninhabited.

And so I walked on in the gloom assailed by rather bitter doubts, unable to see much more than twenty feet in any direction through the enveloping mist of leaves. The enormous columns of the canopy rose out of sight through the lesser forests of twenty-, fifty-, eighty-foot tall trees, and higher even soared the black crocodile-barked Ichekelés, infrequent colossi.

There were many interesting and strange species—one in particular, which I tried to memorize in case I saw it again, had scattered the path with yellow corollas from the mouths of which protruded long crimson stamen tassels—but I could do nothing to collect specimens of the complete living flowers out of sight above.

Sometimes I skirted a gully, or a saddle between hills; sometimes a waterfall rushed and boomed, and then half an hour later had faded out of hearing. I was in noble scenery, and could see nothing. This blindness infuriated and obsessed me. I was filled with a claustrophobia, overwhelming at times, so that I longed to tear the forest asunder, roll it back like the curtains of a stage and gaze upon the scene. I was like a mole crawling underground—but I could not come up for a breather when I wished.

What, I wondered, had ever induced the first Indians to leave their cosy open riversides and wander from the Mapuera to the Essequebo? How had they ever found their way across these dark forests, never able to see far, or guess what lay ahead or on either side? No wonder their minds were full of rumours; no wonder they knew nothing of the existence near them of a great river like the New River. Only after years of scouting would they begin to know a landscape like this and feel it friendly.

After crossing one plunging rocky stream that flowed eastwards, and a long hour of rolling waterless upland, I descended a couple of hundred feet to a level terrace through which flowed a beautifully transparent river. A mossy, rotting trunk led down some twenty feet to water-level, and from this I clambered onto an iron-hard ancient log half-sunk in the glistening silvery sand-bed. Sitting there, I ate my lunch—two peanut-butter sandwiches and a piece of tinned sultana pudding. I had a bar of chocolate and a boiled sweet left. I was singularly ill-prepared for any venture.

I waited for a while, then clambered up the orange-red clay bank collecting: there were cushions of mosses, liverworts, and selaginellas, and two attractive herbs quite new to me—one with sprays of purple tubular flowers,[1] the other, milky-juiced, with sinister little orange-centred purple flowers, the petals of which were bordered with green.[2] After an hour there was no

[1] *Ruellia graecizans.*   [2] *Matelia?*

sign of the men. I had walked quite slowly, taking notes, and if they were following at a normal pace they could hardly be so far behind.

Scouting on the bank, I found an abandoned powis-tail. It was years old, decayed and full of scorpions. Perhaps I was on the wrong path? I began to despair: should I return until I met them, with some face-saving gesture? A green fallen leaf gave me hope, for it appeared to have been picked recently.

The onwards trail, distinct beside the river in the heavily underbrushed swamp forest, led steeply up the valley wall. At the top, where I could see the river crossing, I sat and waited for a further half-hour, intending to go on unseen when the men appeared: but still there was no sign of them. The sun had passed its zenith—it was about one o'clock. I watched the shadows slowly move.

Suddenly I started—a faint distant sound came to my ears, like a shout: far, far away. Standing up I hallooed, and then again, and my voice rolled among the hills and echoes, but there was no reply.

Impulsively I turned and hastened on. The forest seemed peculiarly dark and lonely, the sun spots few and far between. Little brown ghostly butterflies flitted over the leaves, and settled, invisible, on the ground. Whenever I stopped to listen for the men I could hear faint noises all around, low down. They might be the wind, or a little bird walking along, or a jaguar. What should I do if I came upon a jaguar? I could not imagine. I had a small penknife, but that would not be much use. Obviously I should be afraid: I should have to face it with resolution, if not courage. I should probably do nothing and hope that it would go away.

I was looking back, moving slowly, straining my ears for sounds. Rounding a corner, *there* was a spotted beast, lying flattened in the path about thirty feet ahead. But no sooner had I seen it than it jumped up and aside with a crash, and ran off softly. For the first second I thought it was a jaguar—but it was only an ocelot. Still, my heart beat so fast that when a minute later a tinamou started up at my feet I nearly dropped. Then I laughed to myself, and feeling oddly reassured, walked on fast, determined that when I reached the next likely place I should build myself a small shelter and try to light a fire.

In a small bog of feathery palms a baby crocodile splashed its tail at me; two deer sprang off, their brown bottoms, white-streaked in the middle, bouncing up and down over the dark carpet of glossy green leaves.

Further still another tinamou, a homely domesticated chicken-like bird, was stepping softly along, unaware of my approach. When I was only a few feet away it turned, aghast, and leaped into the air and away.

From ahead, after I had crossed several more hills and bog-filled valleys, came a multitude of small sounds: moving cautiously I saw through the leaves a flock of about fifty trumpeter birds, ash-grey footballs wandering slowly along on stilts. As soon as I revealed myself they scattered with violent honkings, running away or flying into the lower branches of the trees, where they teetered, watching me.

A few yards further the long gentle downwards incline flattened into another alluvial terrace, and I came to an enormous dark river of shallow water, silently rushing over a bed of black rocks, with the high tree branches meeting far above it—wrapping it in mystery and gloom.

It was seventy feet broad, bigger than any river I had seen since leaving the Essequebo. Beyond it the path faintly zig-zagged up an almost vertical hill-side. On one side stood a recently-made tarpaulin frame—one of Basil's. Relieved to discover that I was still on the right trail, but utterly weary, I flung myself down in a patch of sunlight.

The ground was cold and wet, and before long I had to move again to keep in the sun. I scraped together a few dead leaves—water oozed out when I pressed them. Clad only in my cotton vest, shorts and tennis shoes I had little protection against the cold and damp. The night would be an ordeal.

Restive, I got up and searched for the dump of rations. There was no sign of them—could this be the right place? The men had said that they had left them in a rocky place—but the last rocky place was far behind: surely I would have seen the cases of goods beside the path? Without food my position was very unpleasant.

With my penknife I set to work gathering a pile of branches: wet though they were, they would keep me a few inches off the ground. Then, realizing that the sun would soon be gone, and that I had no matches, I tried to light a fire with my camera lens. But it did not bring the rays to a sharp point, and not even paper from my notebook would smoulder. The rocks in the river were soft and decomposed; I could see none of the trees used for lighting fires by friction.

I waited.

Slowly the sun patches moved across the ground. If the men had been following they should have been here an hour and a half before.

Four o'clock came. I was in a fever of impatience. I knew that if I started back at once I should have just enough daylight to reach the river where I had lunched, where perhaps they had stopped. There I should confront them. I blazed with fury.

At 4.15 I jumped up and started back, but I had not gone twenty yards before I realized how weary I was, that I should scarcely be able to make it; two hundred yards, before I met the first porter coming in.

It was Mark, the only Wapisiana who spoke much English, a pale, foxy fellow with a forage cap, carrying the gun.

I was excited, ebullient, relieved, cheerful.

"Any luck?" I shouted to him.

He shook his head morosely.

"I should have had the gun," I said, "for I saw two maams [tinamous], two deer, a flock of trumpet birds, and a small tiger."

He put down his load: he was dead beat. Then he went to the river and drank, and came back shaking the water off his hands and sat down near me. He was plainly glad to see me, and began to talk about the wages I was paying. I was paying well for the region, he agreed, but the food was not enough for the work, which was the heaviest he had ever done. The load he had just carried was not so bad, but the three ten-gallon petrol drums had been terrible. Everyone in Basil's party had taken turns in carrying one, and slowly, in stages, they had been moved across. As for the rations that I had not found, they were on the hill just over the river.

He was shy at first, somewhat reserved, for probably he had

not seen many white men in his life, or been with them much in circumstances where he could talk to them. But soon, finding that I had no wish to be standoffish, and was as worried as anyone by the problems of food and getting the loads over the mountains, he became more open and friendly, and we began to discuss the best ways of managing things.

As we chatted the rest of the men came in. From being angry and nervous I was now disarmed, anxious not to appear cruel, for I realized that I had won my victory. I could tell, from their uneasy glances, that they had waited, thinking I would return, and now did not know what sort of reception they would receive: they had heard my halloo from far ahead, and eventually had picked up their loads and followed. I realized that I was extremely lucky.

After they had rested, Jonah and Andrew came up, guilty-looking but very nonchalant, and were most attentive and interested in everything—examining maps, discussing what lay ahead, talking about what they had seen. They had never been like it before. I pretended not to notice, but joined in in a direct, man-to-man manner.

"This is the Taruini River," said Andrew, "which means the Caterpillar River in Wapisiana. The Wai-Wai name is Horo-ko-wo. The other creeks we pass is the Yurua, or Blowpipe, where you meet up with us, and the Yai-imo or Kukui or Harpy Eagle River, which we cross over twice."

We searched on the vague, delicately-coloured maps: one, the vaguest of all, showed an area marked "Morros do Tarou-ene" with a river, hopelessly misplaced, flowing through it. There was no sign of the other names.

"When we reach up to the Mapuera it is going to be smaller than this," continued Andrew. "It is going to be half this width. We will have to follow down it for days before we can float a canoe."

"Mapuer-wau: *Kiriwanhi!*" said William with rolling eye, puzzled by what we were doing but hearing a familiar word. He hummed a song, doubtless obscene.

"The ol' man feelin' good," said George. "He say that two days down the river there is a village entirely of women. He is nothing but a John Thomas."

Everyone was being exceedingly friendly: it was a most pleasant change.

The next day, while most of the men carried the baggage a stage further, I studied the forest of a hill-top with Jonah and Andrew. Energy, quickness, anticipation of my wishes were now their watchwords, and far more was accomplished than usual. As night was falling I bathed in the cold dark river, and watched the men coming back, carrying loads of firewood. William had caught four haimaras and a string of smaller fish—plenty of food for us all. To celebrate, I opened one of my tins of black-berries, chosen as a deliberate contrast to jungle fare; and for an instant was transported away by their tart flavour.

The Wai-Wais also were celebrating: a monotonous, nasally intoned chant, broken by periods of rapid muttering, came from their fireside. Then William sang a sinuous, varied song that might have been Hindu:

"Spirit of the haimara fish we are eating please do not hurt us, and please don't give us bellyache. Leave us alone, for we mean no harm by eating you."

After each verse Kirifakka would repeat it, for it was a music lesson as well as an entreaty.

The following day we moved. The loads were quickly stowed, in everyone's eagerness to show what he could do, and almost before the sun was up the men were away—strange robots beneath their cumbersome piles of packages—stagger-ing across the uneven bed of the Taruini and up the slope beyond.

William, Andrew and I followed and soon came to a shallow rocky river, the Shururucanyi (waterfalls, in Taruma), which swept from the south and away eastwards through beds of purple-flowered *Ruellia graecizans* and Gesneriaceae. For a mile or two we walked beside it, up and down over a series of spurs, until, crossing, we caught up with Jonah, George and the Wapisianas, seated beside a tributary streamlet. Laughter, pointing, and sounds of mimic copulation greeted the arrival of William, who seated himself among his admirers, while I strode on ahead alone through an increasingly wild landscape.

Rocks projected between the trees, and gullies and crags showed on either hand: I walked fast, feeling a return of confidence in my path-finding, until I came to a curious knob of many-faceted rock beside the path. Try as I might I could not detach a fragment, so I sat on it, waiting for the arrival of an axe.

Near me there was a rustling and scuffling, as of animals playing, but I could see nothing. Then with loud scratchings a black jaguar slithered face-downwards down the trunk of a tree some thirty yards away, and leaped off onto the ground. It ran in a half-circle around me, then stopped. Projecting from behind the bushes I could see its hindquarters and long thin lashing tail, then, as it crouched low, its head: it was watching me intently, with yellow eyes and flattened ears. A moment, and it ran on again for a few yards, and again stopped half-hidden, but now much nearer. I turned, keeping my face to it and wondering what to do. I could see it more clearly: it stood about three feet high, and its back was about four and a half feet long—a very big jaguar indeed.

There was more rustling on my left, where it had come from, and I realized that another might be approaching. At that moment it rushed off with a violence that was quite startling— which would have overwhelmed me before I could think— and I heard the voices of the men.

"Sir!" said Jonah, horrified, "that is a lucky escape. If we had not come you would be dead now. That is a Maipuri tiger, which is the worst kind."

"They is very common round here, though elsewhere you scarcely sees them," said Andrew. "If you had not seen it first it would have attack you right away. That is how they always acts. They jump on you and they kill you at once."

We descended a long continuous slope, the southern edge of the Serra Acarai; and soon after midday reached what was evidently the Mapuera flood plain, a sticky clay level intersected by muddy creeks and covered by dense, low forest. Rain began to fall heavily as we passed the advanced loads, under a palm-leaf shelter beside a swampy stream (overshadowed, where the path crossed it, by an unusual Apocynaceous tree), and it was vilely uncomfortable in the soaking forest. Tanner floundered, splashed and slithered just ahead of me, singing "Buttons and Bows", the wet branches and liane tangles he pushed aside continually flipping me in the face or showering me with mud; behind came Kirifakka, under a box of trade goods.

Briefly, on our right, we saw a broad river, open to the sky: the Mapuera! Then we were in the dense forest again.

"*Kanawa*," said Fonyuwé, pausing ahead and pointing; and a minute later we skirted an enormous half-completed canoe— the canoe that would carry us down the great river!

To our surprise we now came to cultivation, and then saw a conical Wai-Wai house ahead. Old "Manatá", the thief of our rations, "Sam", Manawanaro, a quiet, pleasant man whom I had employed as a tree-namer at the mission, and two women came smiling out to greet us. Tanner and Kirifakka were as much amazed as I—it was totally unexpected. Why had the Wapisianas not told us that there was a village ahead? It was typical of the lack of communication among us all, and of the difficulties that arise when either side does not know what the other wants. Probably they had thought we already knew so simple a fact.

A hundred yards further, down a broad gently sloping path, stood a green tarpaulin; and Basil advanced smiling, hand outstretched:

"Welcome, Mr. Guppy, to your camp. I have tried to make it a nice place for you."

No more gratifying words could have been spoken.

Beyond the tarpaulin lay the Mapuera: not at all Andrew's narrow stream, but broad, fringed on its far shore with plumy lettuce-green bamboos, curving away in a long prospect of forested banks full of flowering trees—yellow cassias, violet jacarandas[1]—to an abrupt 1,500 foot high conical mountain.

One by one as the men came up and saw it they dropped their loads, and stood, exclaiming with delight. It was one of the most beautiful stretches of river I had ever seen.

"What lies ahead, Basil?" I asked. "What have you found out from Manatá and the other Indians living here?"

"Sir, the river is full of rapids. One day and a half down we will pass the Taruini mouth, and then it will broaden out. A day further and we will come to the Tutumo, and six days down

---

[1] *Cassia lucens* and *Jacaranda copaia*.

from there is the first Wai-Wai village. Below that is the Fish-kalienas."

"What about the Tutumo? I would like to go up that a little way because it will lead back to another part of the mountains."

"Ah, sir—that is the country of the Mawayáns, which very few people has ever visited. Charlie has been to one village, and I know two men there, Foimo and Kwakwé, who are the last Taruma Indians. They say there is a huge village there of hundreds of people, Mawayáns and Wai-Wais and other tribes all living together. There is supposed to be an abundance of women: some men have even three or four wives."

I turned to Jonah, Tanner and George. "Well, that's where we want to go—shall we go?"

"Sure, let's go!"

"We haven't much food, you know."

"Don't worry about that, sir," said George. "We will live on cassava bread. We will buy some yams and plantains from Manatá which will last till we reach."

"Sir," said Jonah enthusiastically, "we can set everyone hunting and fishing, and babricot [smoke-dry] all we get."

"Right! Then I'm going to divide up everything we have. There'll be no more issuing of rations. Everyone will have to look after his own food. Anyone who doesn't want to come can go back home, and that will mean extra food for us. Is that agreed?"

"Sure!"

"And for every day that anyone works after the rations are finished there'll be extra pay."

Why were the men so keen of a sudden? Why prepared now to endure hard work, discomfort and shortage? Jonah, George, Tanner, Andrew, had, it was true, been reassured: the Wapisianas had not deserted, the dreaded Mapuera had turned out not so bad a place after all—there were even people here that they knew—Manatá, thief though he was, and Basil and Charlie, safe and sound.

But there was more to it than that—what about the Wapisianas? Their enthusiasm showed that their imaginations had been seized: they wanted to sail down the river and see what was away below, to reach the land of the Mawayáns. And the river itself had probably a lot to do with it; instead of being melancholy and sombre, like most forest rivers, it was quite amazingly beautiful. Perhaps if the path had emerged at an uglier place a mile away their reactions would have been different.

10

Last of the Wai-Wais

Basil, by reason of his tact and more polished manners, formed a marked contrast with Jonah and Andrew. He was a type of man almost unknown in the jungle, very much "at your service"—yet no fool, and a strong, independent personality. He looked like a jockey—small, slender, bowlegged, with tiny feet and hands, and a greyish, wizened, broadly-smiling face. His gaze was disconcertingly steady, his physique tough as a nail. It was no surprise to learn that during the first World War he had served as a volunteer in France—to see a little of the world, he said.

While Andrew and most of the men went to fetch the last of the baggage (and, as a result of Andrew's absence a pleasant peacefulness fell over the camp), he and I walked through the forest to inspect the canoe.

"You have done very well," I said.

"Thank you, sir. It was hard, and I had to persuade the men, but I am very interested coming here. I always wanted to see this part."

"How is it that you, an Arawak, are living on the savannah among the Wapisianas, instead of near the coast?"

"I am a prospector, and I came up here originally to work near Maroudi Mountain. And that is why I have my own reasons for wanting to come with you: I am looking for gold and diamonds."

"Have you seen anything good?"

"Just a few indications, but it is hard to be sure. I wash a little in every creek we come to. But I would like to come back and spend a year, and move around slowly. If I can get a grub-stake to last me one year I am sure I can find something. Presently I just pick a living bleeding balata. I think I will sell all I have in store at Lumid Pau, and cut a field somewhere here. Then I can live on that while I search."

We came to a thirty-foot log, partly hollowed, but cracked at both ends.

"We work five days on that, then just as we was adzing the interior, it split open. That, and Charlie forgetting his adze, delay us so much that we make one big boat instead of two small. I hope that is all right, sir?"

"Yes, it was a sensible decision. Though we may have more trouble in the rapids with a big boat."

A quarter of a mile further, in a tiny, palm-fronded clearing created by the fall of the immense tree from which it had been made, lay the nearly finished boat on a mound of butter-yellow chips. The wood was of such a blazing transcendent goldenness that our faces and the whole clearing were bathed in light reflected from it; while in its hollow interior there played a pink radiance like that at the heart of a yellow rose.

Charlie, James and Albert were chipping with axes and adzes, shaping and smoothing the hull.

"It is now at one of the most difficult stages," said Basil, "trying to get the wood of an even thinness. Often, even at this stage, a boat will burst right open, because of the strains in the wood. But I have some bad news. Charlie have to return to his camp on the Kassikaityu River, because Gabriel bring a letter from his sons which say all his balata there is spoiling, and they need help to get it out to the savannah."

I was much taken aback at the thought of losing a man of such solid worth, who had constructed this marvellous-looking boat. But in face of the pathetic tale of sickness and misfortune in his letter I could not hold him, so I told him how sorry I was he had to go.

"He is sorry too," translated Basil, "but he will see you have a good boat in the water before he leaves."

Returning, we stopped to exchange greetings at the village. George and Jonah were there, already very much at home. They had cut sugar-cane and were crushing out the juice in a press shaped like an old-fashioned water-pump, consisting of an upright post with a hole in the top, in which a stick was inserted and levered up and down upon the stalks.

"These are a very primitive bunch of people," observed Jonah, smiling contemptuously. "Look how badly they make this press. We Arawaks have a much better design. And do you know what I discover?—they don't know anything about how to treat sores! They must really be stupid, because the bush is full of medicines, healing barks, and such-like things."

"Are you sure? Because I want to find out about any they use."

"Yes, sir. All they have is a lot of nonsense. This old man Manatá is a sort of witch doctor. He dresses up and makes noise and blows tobacco smoke on a sick person, and he believes he can cure people that way. Think of people believing that rubbish."

He was plainly delighted that, he, an Arawak, should be so superior.

Old Manatá sat a little way off, weaving a cassava squeezer. As I approached he rose and shook hands, smiling a rather hypocritical smile. About his face, with its shaggy mane of whitening hair and its pale shifting eyes, there was something that made me distrust him profoundly: it was lucky that I had had no chance of punishing him for his theft, for he might have been a dangerous enemy, instead of an ally selling us provisions.

After him "Sam", who had been standing on one leg and scrutinizing me in his puzzled way, came forward, and with him the third man of the village, Manawanaro, and his wife, a lovely girl with raven-black hair down to her shoulders.

She was pregnant, but breast-feeding a small boy of about three, a very shy creature who ran away and hid every time I attempted to make friends with him. He regarded his mother as a sort of drinking fountain; quite suddenly, with pursed lips he would bend his knees and spring upwards, catching her teat in his mouth, and with any luck clasping her round the waist. But sometimes he missed with his hands, and fell, and the swollen breast would suddenly come away from his mouth, and bounce back into place. He would even leap at her for a quick swig when she was walking along, and I realized why the Indian women's breasts so soon lost their shapeliness.

"You know, Mr. Guppy," said Basil, "I learn that Manatá

stole some food from you. But you must not worry while you are here because everything will be safe. It is only at the mission that they steal all they can get. Even if we go away and leave things they will be all right."

Because of his past hospitality to Basil and present friendliness I was prepared to forget Manatá's theft—indeed, how could I judge him? Perhaps he had been short of food; and we *had* appeared to have a lot. The elaborate plans of an expedition, and their dependence on the possession of reserves were something he could not be expected to understand.

But why did the Indians steal at the mission only? I was beginning to understand. It was because they could not see why the missionary, one man, should keep such hoards of goods under lock and key. In their society a man can make everything he needs: if he gives away something, he can always make another, and as a result their tradition is one of free hospitality. I had been surprised how frequently in their villages things I admired were given to me, and instinctively I had tried to reciprocate. But they could not understand why it was impossible for the missionary to throw open the doors of his storehouse and say, "Here, take all you need, I have more than enough for myself; and give me in return all you have that I want." And in resentment at this non-conformity with the rules of good behaviour, they stole to force his observance. They could not understand his ideas of right and wrong, based upon a world where people use things they cannot make and have to buy, and where in consequence surpluses are accumulated, personal property is sacred, and fixed values have developed for buying and selling. It was hard not to envy them their simple outlook, and feel that their practice was more perfect than our own—but from the materialistic point of view the missionary was undoubtedly right, from the evolutionary, on the winning side.

Charlie now arrived, and through Basil and him I asked Manatá about the Parukutu or Barokoto Indians, who from Schomburgk's and Farabee's accounts had lived just south of the Wai-Wais.

"Mr. Guppy," said Basil, "Manatá says that he and 'Sam' are the *only* real Wai-Wais still living, and all the rest are

Parukutus, but they *calling* themselves Wai-Wais because they marry into the Wai-Wais, and adopt their language, and live in their country. At one time all these tribes keep separate, and thought it was a bad thing to marry with one another. But since they began to die out they start to move together, and forget their own ways. Although the Parukutu language was very much like Wai-Wai, nowadays nobody speaks it."

"What about the Wai-Wais down the Mapuera?" I asked.

"They are mostly pure Parukutus," replied Basil. "In this village Manatá and 'Sam's' wives is both Parukutu. But he says that Manawanaro, who is married to Manatá's daughter, is a Mawayán, and that now the Mawayáns also are dying out and coming to join the Wai-Wais, though they are also a different race."

"Whereabout do the Mawayáns live? How could we reach their country?"

Charlie began to trace a map of rivers in the dust, and to tell me of the names of the tribes of which he knew. First, east of the River Tutumo, or Buna-wau, a tributary of the Mapuera, were the Mawayáns.

It looked as if they were exactly where I wanted to go— east of us, and a little south of the Acarai. But if Tutumo was another name for the Buna-wau, the river that Farabee had ascended in 1913, then the Mawayáns were probably the same as his Mapidians, and Schomburgk's Maopityans—the Frog Indians, supposedly extinct! It would be an interesting discovery.

"Can Manawanaro tell us how to get there?"

"Charlie say he has never been—he is like Fonyuwé, his mother dead and he bring up among the Wai-Wais. But Charlie *himself* has been, and he says it will be almost impossible for us to reach without a guide, because the trail is far up the Tutumo River, and very hard to find. And after, you have to walk for two days over mountains to the Oroko'orin River, where their first village is, which is the one he has been to."

"Well, we can try, anyway. What other tribes does Charlie know about?"

"He says there are four Wai-Wai villages down river, and he has been to the nearest one, called Cacheré. He has only heard of who lives below: first the Karafayans, then Paoran, Fishkarayan, Shawayan and lastly the Kamarayan, who are famous fighters."

This list only added to my confusion. I now had lists of tribes derived from Schomburgk, Farabee, Andrew, the Missionary, William, and now Charlie and Manatá, and the points of coincidence among them were few. About the Tarumas, the Wai-Wais, the Parukutus, the Mawayáns and the Fishkalienas there seemed to be general agreement. Of the rest, the Powisians, the Shilliau, Kalawians, Katawians, Aikas, Arekas, Karafayans, Kamarayans, Shawayans, Paorans, Wai-wĕs, Chikenas, Sikianas, Diaus, and yet others, all seemed to be just names, perhaps derived from misunderstandings, perhaps merely different words in different languages for the same tribes —or even different villages of the same tribe.

"What about the Tunayenas, the Water Indians?"

"They live beyond the Mawayáns, but nobody knows about them any more."

Charlie's sand-tracing coincided quite well in parts with several of my maps—enough to suggest a possible derivation for some of them from similar tracings. All, from what I had seen myself, contained scatterings of information and misinformation: they bore the same sort of relationship with reality as the cartography of the sixteenth century, had the same sort of interest, and were about as useful as guides.

"Ask Manatá if he knows the Big Village, Kashima."

Charlie brightened, and in halting English explained that he wanted very much to see this, and was very sorry to go back, because he thought we might discover it.

"Where about is it?"

"Manatá says it is by the Mawayán country. But Charlie says he does not believe it is there, because when he went all he saw was about seven or eight old men and ten women. But that was a long time ago. He says he was always hearing about this one Big Village—but he only once met with any man who had ever been there."

The Big Village was probably a legend, anyway. What was far more important was finding a way of striking eastwards into the Mawayán country. So far as I knew, Farabee and his companion Ogilvie were the only Europeans who had been there. When Schomburgk had seen the Frog Indians they had been living much further north, near the Rio Alto-Trombetas. None of the Indians, except an occasional adventurous spirit like Charlie, seemed to do much travelling. They knew next to nothing of what existed beyond the narrow bounds of their own territory. Or perhaps this was a false impression caused by the confusion of trying to find out through a series of interpreters, none of whom understood the other's languages well? In either case, it was frustrating. If we did *not* find the Mawayán trail, I knew from my New River experiences that it would be hard to get far.

As I got up to go I asked if I might look inside the house, and on being courteously waved in, entered. Manawanaro's wife rose from a dish in which she was scraping yams and suppressed the crescendo of frantic barkings which at once arose. The dogs, sixteen in all, seemed even more savage than usual. One was so fierce that she bound its muzzle with string to prevent it biting through the wooden stick which served as a halter between its collar and the wall; another, evidently a favourite, sat upright, ears laid back, canines exposed, in its own small specially-woven hammock. Two were pure brown, the rest largely black and white like those on the Essequebo. All, as usual, were well cared for, plump and sleek—unlike the dogs of other tribes, which are kept skeletal in the belief that a hungry dog is a keen hunter.

Even more than the English the Wai-Wais deserve to be famous as dog-lovers. Their dogs are, collectively, the world's most pampered—nothing is too good for them. When puppies are born they are washed at once in a special infusion of roots to make them strong. If their mother dies or runs dry they may be suckled by a woman. They spend most of their adult days reclining, in the ease of Oriental potentates, on their shelves, or even in their own hammocks, above the ground out of reach of jigger-fleas (one wonders indeed if these dogs' eagerness in the field may not be due in part to forced inactivity). They are fed on the pick of the kill; and they are washed two or three times a day, partly for cleanliness, but mostly to prevent them suffering from the heat: at all the Wai-Wai villages in the mornings and afternoons I would see the Indians taking their dogs down to the river, the women carrying armfuls of puppies and children, and sometimes a favourite grown-up dog (often wearing an absurd but charming necklace of beads and feathers) slung on one hip and supported by an arm under the forelegs, in a manner awkward-looking but apparently comfortable for both, the rest of the pack gambolling through the bushes near by. The Indians would immerse and splash themselves, then carefully dip the dogs, before taking them, miserable and in fits of shivering and sneezing, back to their perches.

These dogs are so savage and fight so much among themselves that a short stick, hard to chew through, is always placed between collar and lead. They are a menace to strangers—against the approach of whom, and of wild beasts and evil spirits, they are kept partly to give warning—yet very affectionate to their owners, who seldom strike, though often threaten, them with shouts and raised sticks; and they are astonishingly well house-trained, howling when, unable to wait till the next ramble to the riverside, they want to be led away into the bushes.

Emerging by the far door I found "William", wasted and ill-looking, lying in his hammock, screened from the sun by a line of palm leaves. His temperature was 102° F. I had given him the complete curative course of paludrine tablets prescribed for malaria, so it was worrying to find him with the same symptoms again. Puzzled, I began a course of atebrin, hoping that it might be more successful.

By tea-time Andrew and the men had returned, and with them the feeling of tension. As if sensing my thoughts, Jonah, who was working with me, spoke.

"You know, sir, it would be good if Andrew went back. He does not seem to like this sort of work."

"True—he is always saying so. Yet he is a valuable and experienced man, and the Wai-Wais know him."

"Maybe that is so, Mr. Guppy. Yet it is bad that he is always complaining. It unsteadies us all. He could go with the five men who are going back to the savannah."

Just as the sun was up next morning, Fonyuwé and Kirifakka

burst upon me painted from head to foot in brightest orange and vermilion, with stripes of black. The green gloom of the forest was shattered. They seized me by the hand and led me to the riverside, to a little slope of grass, and there posed—Fonyuwé very clownishly, with an enormous piece of sugar-cane clamped between his jaws, pretending to be a baboon.

They wanted their photographs taken. As neither had ever seen a photograph it simply meant that they wanted that particularly gratifying amount of attention and fussing over that I gave to anyone who was specially well dressed, whenever I had my little leather-covered box with me.

Pointing to the sky, I indicated that it was too early, at which they stroked and parted my beard for several minutes, pretending to be looking for insects. Stealthily taking a grasshopper from a leaf, Fonyuwé gave a shrill scream and with popping eyes signified that it had come from just under my chin.

Then they took me to see an abandoned "woodskin", or bark canoe, which they had salvaged by stuffing its numerous holes with bast. It seemed the very thing in which to make a trip down the beautiful canal-like eastward swing of the river, to Faiafun, the little conical mountain at its end, now like a smoke-grey cardboard cut-out against the burning red sky.

Ever since I had seen Faiafun I had thought of it as a possible look-out: it rose so steeply from the level plain, it was so isolated, that from it I was sure that I could obtain uninterrupted views over immense distances—I might even, on a very clear day, see the Amazon! A wild, romantic fancy, for it was at least 250 miles away.

While some of the men began clearing a path and laying down a series of sticks and logs as rollers over which to drag the boat to the riverside, and others shaped paddles and seats, or went hunting or fishing, George, Jonah and Sam, my two dazzling comrades and I set forth in the perilous, leaky little craft. We glided under the delicate shivering bamboos, past little bays of sand and silt where aroids grew,[1] towards the mountain, which, as we approached, stood over us like a wall, sixteen or seventeen hundred feet high.

[1] *Dieffenbachia.*

167

Where a four-foot thick log lay across the river—a bridge, said Sam, used for many years by the Wai-Wais when hunting on the mountain—we landed, and I set George to chop it through, to allow the big boat to pass. Sam cleared a way towards the foot of the mountain, and Jonah and I followed slowly, scouting in the tangled riverside, and finding an unusual passion-flower vine with a single flower and many hexagonal elliptical fruit, all of the palest rose pink;[1] and, in a rocky place, a delicate *Begonia*.

After a short patch of swamp forest we began to climb by a winding path, the hunting path used by the Wai-Wais, at an angle well above 45° in places. The ground was hard clay, from which projected numerous rocks, evidently volcanic, but some of the honeycomb texture typical of lateritic ironstone. As we ascended we caught thrilling glimpses of the plain spread below, and at last, at a point where fallen trees made an opening, a clear view northwards. There, to my astonishment, I saw what was unmistakably the peak I had viewed a month before from the New River: almost certainly, from its position, Schomburgk's Pirikitu—a cone of rock, largely forest covered, but with bare patches. It was at least 3,000 feet high, and right and left, as far as I could see, there was no other mountain like it.

Nearer, rolling hills (the Morros do Tarouene, I presumed) extended on either hand. The section of the Acarai which we had crossed was further west, hidden by the trees; but I determined at a future date to open up views so that I could see it and all round.

Returning, Fonyuwé and Kirifakka cut poles, and standing up, punted us at a good six knots up through the small rapids we had descended. Their style might have raised eyebrows along the Cam, for they "climbed" the pole, but I know that I, once proud of my punting, would not have had a chance against them. Then in the open water above they worked off a little more of their excess energy in a spasm of vigorous paddling, sending the water surging and swirling along the sides of the canoe, making it buck and bounce on the waves. Our motion was rather like that of an eight in rough water. With six of their

[1] *Passiflora fuchsiiflora.*

fellows I would have backed them against the Leander Club; and at the end of the journey they were fresh and beaming.

After dinner, while we worked on our collections, Jonah launched forth:

"You know, sir, this man Manatá; well every one of these Indians seems like they are very afraid of him. I believe he may even be a Kanaima. Anyway, he is a very powerful piai-man."

A piai-man was a sorcerer or medicine man, but a Kanaima was something much stranger and rarer.

"What is a Kanaima, Jonah?"

"Well, sir, what they always say is that they are people who can change into animals at will. Sometimes they do it for revenge upon someone who harmed them, but mostly for pure wickedness. Once I met a man who told me about how his brother died. He came in one day and complained that he had terrible boils on his seat, but he would allow nobody to dress them, or even see them, and he refuse to go into Georgetown to hospital. He died a few days later, and they found he was full of buckshot. Now what is so strange is that the day he first complain a jaguar was shot from behind, but it got away. And another time I hear of a man who saw two jaguars swimming a creek. Then when he look again, two girls are standing on the bank. They beckon to him, but he paddle on fast."

"But do you believe in this?"

"I really can't tell, sir. But once, when I was a boy, I had a strange experience. I was paddling along a small river, and I heard a peculiar whistling low on the water ahead, just as they say a Kanaima does. So I paddle round the next bend, and it was still in front, like two creatures calling and replying, one on each side.

"Then I hear a noise like a labba[1] swimming under water, and the whistling was only a few feet away, but no matter how hard I look I could see nothing. It was night by the time I reach the landing, so I tie up the canoe and run along the path till I reach home, and when I tell my father he was afraid, and he close up all the windows and doors.

"I went to sleep but he stay up all night, and about mid-

[1] *Agouti paca:* a large rodent.

night he heard the whistlings coming up the path, and they circle all round. We all wake up and lie quiet. We was trembling and frightened, but they say the Kanaima can never reach you unless you go out to him of your own free will, as if you go out to see what the noise is.

"After a time they go away down the creek, and then for two more nights the same thing happened. Then they never came back. But I always remember that, and that is why if ever I could meet a man who was a Kanaima, I would like to study with him, to see if it is a genuine thing."

Darkness had long fallen when he bade me good night. Soon peals of thunder awoke me. Heavy rain rolled over the camp and through the forests, lightning flashed, and a whirling spray rose from the open ground. I got up and shone my torch around, half-expecting the usual streams of water underfoot, but Basil had dug drains around the outside of the tarpaulin, and my belongings—my deed-box, shoes, haversacks, cases—stood covered with towels on logs near the centre of the tent. I retired again, and slept on with a faint spray dampening my mosquito net, and the wild drumming of the rain on tarpaulin, ground and forest.

Rain was providential, for the river, whose dropping level we had been anxiously watching, would rise again, and ease the passage of the boat.

Mawayáns Come

Wandering downriver along the bank, Charlie had found a small dugout sunken in the sand, abandoned by Chekemá when he had left the Mapuera to live on the Essequebo. In the morning, with Andrew, Gabriel, and Wayama (elaborately coiffed, striped and spotted), I followed him to inspect it.

Insects had become so pestilential that it was a pleasure to leave the camp. Commonest of all were minute "eye-flies", which Jonah said bred wherever there was damp, rotting vegetation. They hovered perpetually in front of one's eyes, like spots during a bilious attack, settling gently on the moist corners, or on nose or lips, whenever they saw their chance, and so elusively that I seldom managed to kill one.

Dimethylphthalate smeared on face and arms repelled them for short periods, but was useless against the larger menaces, such as cowflies, gay, waspish creatures with green cat's-eyes. Looking up through the translucence of the tarpaulin the shadows of a dozen or so were always to be seen, sunning themselves on the warm canvas. Sometimes, in the mood for blood, silently, delicately, one would alight on my clothes, and probe until it found a place where it could push through; then with tail up and the whole force of its little body plunge its pointed mouth-parts deep, puncturing the flesh as if with a blunt needle. An unknowing spectator would have been surprised to see me every few minutes, as I sat in my tent, give a sudden jump and squirm, a reflex wriggle which I and all the other men developed to dislodge them before they bit.

Deer-flies also were annoying, honey-coloured insects with brown-banded wings which slowly circled over one's head as one walked through the forest, and specialized in biting the back of the neck; but sluggish, and easily killed by a clap of the hands.

"Andrew," I said, when we were alone together, "you know that five men are returning to the savannah. If you like, you may go back with them. I shall be sorry to lose you, for without you as interpreter and guide we would never have been able to get so far. But now I can spare you, for I have Basil. But you have done wonderful work"—an exaggeration to gratify his vanity.

"I don't think I have, sir. I think I have been wasting my time and yours. I'm a blind bat. I don't know the work, the forest doesn't suit me, I have felt sick since I came. I was forced to go on this expedition. The District Commissioner say he will make things easier for me if I go. I never wanted to come over to Mapuera again. Once is enough. Three years ago the missionary beg me to come over here with him, but I refuse. I say to him I am come to see he don't change the Indian's habits in B.G., not in Brazil. Anyways, sir, I'm glad you give me the chance to go."

He looked downcast. He had been generally discredited in the eyes of the men by the fact that nothing we had seen had corresponded to his descriptions. Obviously the Terry-Holden expedition had reached the Mapuera at a different point. Now, on top of all, he would be returning, a little as if in disgrace.

We had by this time walked about a mile, skirting the Indian field, crossing a streamlet or two, and were in thick gloomy forest. Suddenly Charlie, in the lead, stopped: approaching was a file of Indians, carrying laden warishis, and bundles of arrows and arrow shafts tied up like Roman fasces.

They too halted: there was silence and surprise. Leading was a scared-looking young man with a sensitive face and big gentle eyes—the image of Jean-Louis Barrault; then an old woman, a tall giggly man with a big nose and a scholar's stoop, a timid boy, and an old, bent man, thickset, with foxy features, shrewd eyes, and wobbling mouth.

Solemnly we shook hands. Then Andrew, who had fallen behind, burst forward and seized the old man's hand warmly.

"Foimo!" he cried; then turning to me: "This is Foimo, one of those two old Tarumas you hear about. I know him because he live for a time on the savannah. The rest are Mawayáns! They are trading and visiting Manatá. It is a great piece of luck. Foimo will tell them we are good people and they will help you. *Now* maybe you will reach the Mawayán country!"

Foimo had been scrutinizing me penetratingly. He shook his long hair, swept out his arm in a dramatic gesture, and pointed to each of the Indian men in turn:

"Icaro" (the scholar); "Wacoro" (the boy); "Makata" (Barrault).

To my surprise Makata was deathly pale, and trembling; and the others, too, except Foimo, were evidently terrified—perhaps of me, what with my whiteness and my beard. So, after a little more conversation, and a series of friendly smiles which palpitated them all the more, we walked on, leaving them to recover.

We passed two cataracts which our boat would have to descend, and came to a bay overhung by a monkey-pipe tree of curious kind, whose creamy flowers turned an evil blackish-green instantly upon being bruised, at the foot of which was Chekemá's canoe. Leaving Charlie and Gabriel at work patching it, Andrew and I turned back, embarrassing the Mawayáns, whom we found seated in a circle, their loads off, painting and primping each other in preparation for meeting the people of the village.

In the afternoon, everyone, including the new arrivals, was mustered to drag the boat along the prepared path to the riverside, for it was best to move it while the wood was still fairly thick, to avoid damage. Ropes were attached to bow and stern, and a milling mob of Indians stationed themselves around it wherever they could exert leverage.

At a signal from Andrew the pushing and pulling began. His hair tousled, his pointed teeth glittering, he was inspired —heaving gigantically, bolstering everyone with mighty shouts as we urged the boat along. "Oh, Liza!" and "Wapès!" he bellowed whenever it got wedged among the trees, and the Indians would laugh and pull harder. In little more than an hour it was at the camp, and rolled up a foot above the ground on trestles, where the last adzing, shaving, and smoothing could conveniently be done.

Besides Andrew and Charlie, four Wapisianas were returning: Albert, shy, charming, Jouvet-like in features, James, swarthy, wavy-haired, glittering-eyed, moustached—both middle-aged, hard-working men whom I should be sorry to lose—and two of Basil's men, whom I hardly knew. First I issued rations to them for their journey, then I divided all that was left among the rest of us, so that we should each start down the Mapuera with the same amount of food, reserving less of the staples, such as rice and sugar, for myself, as I had a few individual luxuries such as tins of meat and vegetables, which could not be divided.

By hard experience I had discovered that simple mathematics do not apply to the sharing out of rations. Twenty pounds of sugar or dried meat taken from forty seldom leaves twenty—— usually twelve or fifteen, and when these fifteen have to be divided among ten men, quarrels often arise because they all say they are entitled to two pounds as before. Part of the loss comes from waste, but most from the evaporation of water as the lower or inner layers of the food are exposed; indeed, in this humid climate, volume and weight may vary even between morning and midday. It was therefore with relief that I saw the last of the ration cases empty. We might have grave food shortages in the future, but at least I should be spared the disagreeableness and niggling that accompanied each issue. Each man now had to ration himself, out of the two and a half weeks' supplies everyone had been given, supplemented by as much as we could shoot, fish, or buy from the Indians.

Next, I paid the returning five with combs, mirrors, pen-knives, trousers, shirts, shoes, etc., and cheques which I had arranged to be honoured at the Government post on the savannah. While this was going on, Mark, who was remaining, hung around slyly, watching, listening, and taking note of the prices I charged for different things. Finally he came forward and said, "I want soap. It very cheap. Far less than savannah. Take out of wages"—which precipitated a rush upon the trade goods that kept me up late into the night.

Even Fonyuwé and Kirifakka were infected. Basil had gone to bed, so they were forced to use sign language. Vigorously they pretended to comb their hair, then Kirifakka showed me a comb with many missing teeth. From a box of trade goods he selected a blue one, solidly made, with a long handle. Then I offered him the mouth-organ that I had promised to keep for him when he joined the expedition. Reverently he handled it, but did not blow through it, awed that so beautiful a thing should be his. Then Fonyuwé cautiously blew a couple of notes, and paused, as if scared.

I pointed at Kirifakka, asking, "Do you want it now?"

But he slowly shook his head, handed it back to me, and said, "Kanasenay"—the name of the mission.

Surprised at this unusual and admirable restraint, I wrapped it in tissue-paper, put it back into its cardboard box, and before their watchful eyes placed it carefully at the bottom of all the trade goods.

In the morning Andrew and the returning men came to take their leave, heavily laden with plant, wood and rock specimens, and equipment we no longer needed.

"Sir, I hope you don't have any hard times like we had with Dr. Holden. Only don't go too far from your boats, or you may suffer from the Indians. But I wish you the best."

"Thank you very much," I said. "When I come back I'm going to come and visit you at your ranch. I want to see how you catch those big Arapaima fish which I have heard about!"

He seemed to take this as a dismissal, very hastily shook hands and said, "Goodbye, sir." Then, a little later, his burly figure with its piled warishi disappeared down the path and into the darkness of the jungle.

12

Burning our Boat

"You know, Mr. Guppy, it is good that Andrew has gone. We men didn't think so much of him. Do you know, over by New River he always sleep with a knife by his hammock? I notice it myself. Just as though he was frightened of someone attacking him."

No sooner had Andrew left than Jonah was full of such remarks.

Tanner was kinder: "I don't think he like this trip at all, sir. I believe he thinks a lot of himself. After all, he is a rancher, and we are just ordinary folks. He has a jeep, and here he was working just like anyone of us, except that he was a foreman. He even offer us work on his ranch—any of us boys, he say, we could have a job any time we like, working for him. That shows he must have feel his position bad."

I felt rather ashamed when I heard this. Poor Andrew, all his bellowings, his violent opinions, had been efforts at self-assertion. Without him life felt quieter, soberer.[1]

Often the Indians from the village would stop to chat with me on their endless perambulations to and from the water, and we would carry on long conversations, neither side knowing what the other said unless Basil and Fonyuwé (who spoke Wapisiana and Wai-Wai) were there to translate. Manatá I still felt was hostile, Sam friendly and inquisitive, while Mana-wanaro's wife was openly flirtatious. She would smile at me and flutter her eyelashes prettily, while pretending to examine my

[1] I know now that Andrew was a very sick man when he came, so I am glad of my decision to send him back, and sorry for any sufferings I may have caused him. I raise my hat to him, a very gallant man in my estimation of whom I was deeply mistaken.

belongings, until her mother, losing patience, spoke to her; then off they would walk, she sometimes with a backward glance, her little boy running beside her, and a circle of dogs leaping and barking all around.

The newly-arrived Mawayáns also soon became friends, though Makata was suspicious at first. Complete with bow and arrows, prepared for anything, he came and stood away off up the path, and watched me for half an hour. Then Icaro and Foimo came walking along, and he raised resolution enough to join them as they approached me. Rather stupidly I raised my camera and photographed him: he did not know what I was doing, and I did not know what he would do. His face twitched; the hostility and fear on it alarmed me. But a little later he laid aside his weapons and gradually tension eased. Then, in two or three days, he was coming and going as happily as the others.

What interested me most was the shape of his head. It was extremely tall, flat-sided and flat-backed, exactly the type of head described by Schomburgk and Barrington Brown as typical of the Maopityans, or Frog Indians. This, and the fact that "*Mawa*", as I had discovered from Mawashá's name, might mean a certain type of frog, seemed strongly to confirm my growing belief that in the Mawayáns I had rediscovered the Maopityans. Yet strangely, neither Makata nor the other Mawayán boy, Wacoro, recognized the word "Maopityan". It was, I knew, a Wapisiana word—perhaps it was unfamiliar to them. If ever I reached the Mawayán villages I might be able to come to some more definite conclusion.

Icaro also presented a problem: he was not a Mawayán, but a Mayena, or Emayena—he pronounced it both ways; a tribe of which none of us had ever heard before, perhaps totally unknown—though, like "Mawayán", the name bore a resemblance to San Manços' "Mayoyaná". There was a further possibility: "Uma-yena," I discovered, might mean any tribe living a long way away, "over there" (pointing down river): even so the question remained, which?

With Basil and Fonyuwé to translate, I began to piece together the newcomers' story, and try to find out how we could reach their country:

"These five is travelling with four others, who stay behind to fish, and are following in a few days. They are all running away from the Fishkalienas, who attack and killed many of them and are trying to wipe out the whole tribe."

An alarming thought—what if we should encounter them, unarmed as we were?

"But, sir," continued Basil, "I don't believe this is the truth. I was talking to Foimo and he say that is just an excuse they always give when they comes to stay at a village for a good while. It appears this attack was many years ago, and there are still plenty of Mawayáns left behind in their villages."

"Ask them what happened when they were attacked."

"A party of Emayenas was camped near some big rapids near the Mawayán country, but far from the Mawayán villages. All of them got ill and died, so the rest of the tribe thought that the Mawayáns had bewitched them and were trying to kill them out. At that the Emayenas decide to kill out the Mawayáns first, so that is why the Mawayáns are leaving their territory and joining up with the Wai-Wais."

It appeared from this that these particular Emayenas were the Fishkalienas of the first story and that Icaro was one of that dreaded tribe—one, moreover, who had married a Mawayán girl, and adopted his enemies as his own people.

Gabriel, standing near by, now spoke: "I believe that all that happen is that Icaro steal Mawayán girl for wife. Foimo and his brother Kwakwé, the two Tarumas, save him, and now they is all three living together in a village, with a few Mawayáns who is friendly to them. Foimo is now fed up with Icaro, and he try to leave him behind on this trip, but Icaro want to come, so he come."

Where the truth lay among all these stories, and who the Emayenas really were, it was hard to discover. In this land of rumours, where last year and yesterday are confused, and long ago is very much the same as today, it seemed almost as if tribal history, its myths and legends, were absorbed as personal memories: people move, villages move, all is uncertain; the very names of the people seen by past explorers may have changed, and they may today regard themselves as belonging to a different tribe. It is like a Yugoslav who was born an

Austro-Hungarian. But he has a written history to fall back on, while the Indian has only memory and legend.

Passing on his way to the boat, now receiving its finishing touches, Charlie stopped to talk to us. He began unwrapping a small palm-leaf package:

"Charlie bring you a present, sir. It is a poison arrow point which he get from the Mawayáns."

It was a six-inch long slip of bamboo, shaped like a stiletto, with the base of the blade flat, designed to be inserted in the slot at the tip of a special arrow. The upper two-thirds of the blade had been lightly coated with a brown gummy substance —curare: if it penetrated the skin this light sliver would cause death within a few minutes.

"A large well-fed ox," wrote Charles Waterton in 1812, in his *Wanderings in South America*, "from nine hundred to a thousand pounds in weight, was tied to a stake by a rope sufficiently long to allow him to move to and fro. Having no large Coucourite spikes at hand, it was judged necessary, on account of his superior size, to put three wild-hog arrows into him; one was sent into each thigh just above the hock, in order to avoid wounding a vital part, and the third was shot traversely into the extremity of the nostril. The poison seemed to take effect in four minutes. Conscious as though he would fall, the ox set himself firmly on his legs, and remained quite still in the same place, till about the fourteenth minute, when he smelled the ground, and appeared as if inclined to walk. He advanced a pace or two, staggered, and fell, and remained extended on his side with his head on the ground. His eye, a few minutes ago so bright and lively, now became fixed and dim, and though you put your hand close to it as if to give him a blow there, he never closed his eyelid. His legs were convulsed, and his head from time to time started involuntarily; but he never showed the least desire to raise it from the ground; he breathed hard, and emitted foam from his mouth. The startings, or subsultus tendinum, now became gradually weaker and weaker; his hinder parts were fixed in death; and in a minute or two more his head and forelegs ceased to stir. Nothing now remained to show that life was still within him, except that his heart faintly beat and fluttered at intervals. In five-and-twenty minutes from the time of his being wounded he was quite dead. His flesh was very sweet and savoury at dinner."

So stable is the poison that even after it had been preserved for forty years at Waterton's home in England, it was still found effective. Many have been the attempts to discover how it is prepared since he wrote his account, many the expeditions sent to find its ingredients or to purchase it for testing. Even today it is largely mysterious, though various components have been isolated, and some have proved important in inducing relaxation of muscles, such as is required in treating tetanus or in abdominal surgery. The most active ingredients are derived from vines of the genus *Strychnos*, but are not at all like strychnine (which comes from a tree of the same genus), either chemically or in effect. They are called curarines, and produce a paralysis of the nerve-centres if introduced into the blood (but no effect in the stomach, for which reason animals killed with curare may be eaten), resulting in relaxation of the muscles, and death primarily from slow suffocation, because the lungs cease to work. There is no known antidote, except artificial respiration and oxygen. The Indians themselves, if accidentally poisoned, are said simply to lie down and die.

"Have the Mawayáns any more to sell?"

"No, they only bring four quivers, which they sell to Manatá and Sam, and they wouldn't sell again because the Wai-Wais don't make poison, and it is very scarce."

"What else did they bring to trade?"

"They bring also graters, and bows, and arrow grass, and arrows, and red paint made from roocoo,[1] which they sell to Manatá, and it is he sells them to the other Wai-Wais in B.G."

Except for the poison these were all things which the Wai-Wais made themselves. Yet they were willing to accept them and give in return articles from the outside world which grew increasingly precious as they were traded on and on away from civilization—and yet which *were* traded on, so that even the remotest, most-hidden tribes possessed a few of them.

"Why do they give trade goods for things they can make themselves?"

[1] *Bixa orellana.*

Charlie grinned, and spoke in his stumbling English direct to me:

"Wild Indians no know about trade. It for make friends. Give even when want for keep. He give something else or maybe he no pay back now. No matter. Next year—any time. Every Indian make arrow. If I make, save you make. You make something else."

No economist could have expressed it better.

Old Foimo, who was standing near, had been eyeing me shrewdly. Now, with a shake of his long greasy locks, he turned to Basil and spoke rapidly.

"Sir!" said Basil, after a moment, "a wonderful thing happen! Foimo say he would like you to come to the Mawayán country. He will turn back now and guide you there. We will go to the Oroko'orin River and beyond. And when we reach he will send Icaro ahead to fetch all the Mawayáns to come and see you, because none have seen a white man before, though they always hear about them."

Fonyuwé, listening to Foimo, suddenly raced round in a circle making a noise like an outboard motor, stopped, flexed his monstrous biceps, smiled broadly, and burst into a loud gabble directed at Basil:

"Fonyuwé is very pleased, sir, because he says now he will see his relations. Sir, you do not know how lucky we are—we should never reach there without guides. It would have been no use even to try it. And even if we reached and nobody gone ahead they might think we was enemies. But now it will be easy!"

Even the dry Basil was smiling.

"That's marvellous—but how long will our journey take?"

"He says it will be many days by boat and walking, but when we meet there will be great rejoicing and feasts. He says he will show us something very strange, which is two savannahs in the forest—a small one, then a big one, by the big village of the Mawayáns."

I had never dreamed that such a thing existed—the rare aviators who had flown over the region had reported no savannahs or even large open spaces in the forests, except Gunn's Strip, far to the north; even Colonel Williams, that veteran forest flyer, had never seen one. To be able to examine such an isolated patch of grassland would be, botanically, one of the most exciting achievements of the expedition.

The time came for the penultimate stage in the construction of the boat—the "burning", or opening up of the hull.

"We have to light fires under her," explained Basil, as we joined the crowd of Indians gathered to watch, "and keep turning her on the trestles till she is heated evenly right through and the wood becomes soft. Then we will pull the sides apart, so she becomes flat and wide, and force in ribs so she sets correct."

"You mean you will *heat* her to soften the wood? But I would have thought that would dry and harden it?"

"Well, sir, it is green wood——"

"Of course . . . now I see. It must soften because the heat turns the moisture in the cells to steam. But then that will set up a lot of tensions—she might easily split if it isn't done very carefully?" It was worrying, because we could not afford time or food to build another. The expedition's continuation depended upon success.

"Exactly, sir. It is very skilful work at every stage. And what is bad we cannot find any Ité palms round here, and their dead leaves is the only good fuel to give a slow steady heat. We has to use ordinary wood. It is lucky we have Charlie, because nobody else is such a good canoe-builder. None of these Wai-Wais knows how—all they makes is woodskins and small dugouts."

First the boat was rolled over, bottom up; then torches carried the flames from one end to the other of the bed of faggots. As the flames licked up, burning brands were pulled away here and there, or more fuel added to keep the distribution of heat even.

Meanwhile implements like gigantic clothes-pegs, three or four feet long, had been prepared; and when, after an hour, the outside of the canoe was as hot as the hand could stand, and it had been turned right way up again—releasing a puff of smoke from the interior—they were slipped over the sides, and used as levers to pull them apart. Feet planted against the hull, the men heaved and sweated—but the wood moved not an inch.

Jonah watched all this in a fever of impatience and interest. Soon he was so worked up that he lost all control:

"My God, what is this man Charlie?" he kept saying in a loud voice. "Everything he do is wrong—the wood is going to split!"

The labouring continued. Slowly, with terrible agonized strainings, the sides began to yield. Charlie, like one demented, leaped into the hot charred interior and ran to and fro, blackened with soot, streaming with sweat, forcing in ribs to hold each millimetre gained. He was in torments, seeing and hearing nothing but the stubborn wood, lest at any minute it might crack and destroy all his work.

"This will never do!" shouted Jonah, capering like a fiend. "He should have heat the outside as well as the inside—and he should have built fire *right* inside, and keep water in case the flames get too high—then the sides will fall open. This way she go split for sure. He shape the boat fine and now he go spoil it."

Hours passed: I could not keep away, yet I hated to see the terrible wrestling.

Perhaps Jonah was right, for the wood was very hard and was plainly being forced. But I had to have faith in Charlie. He had brought her so far, and he had made many boats, even with his clumsy methods. I turned on Jonah:

"Have you ever made a boat yourself?"

"No, sir, but I seen plenty made—I know well how to do it. Besides, we Arawaks . . . "

As an Arawak he felt he belonged to the cleverest tribe in Guiana. I walked up and down, gazing in uncertainty at all that was being done. Small holes and cracks began to appear in the sides: it was evident that all was not well. At times it was almost more than I could bear to see.

I went to my tarpaulin and tried to write, watching the heroic struggle from a distance: the enormous hull of the canoe, the blackened men, the licking flames, the puffs of smoke, all in the darkness of the overarching trees. Sometimes a sun ray pierced down, in its wanderings over the forest floor, and shone through the blue smoke and picked out a yellow twisted face or shoulder. Then far above the leaves would shift, and it would flicker away to the quiet earth a few yards off.

By lunch time she was half open. Afterwards heat was applied again, to the outside. Then the work of prising, of hammering in ribs began again.

After four more hours she had been opened as far as Charlie judged safe. Wiping his brow, tottering with fatigue, he came to tell me.

As he spoke there was an almighty crack, and with a shudder one side broke loose at the stern: before our eyes the split began running down the length of the boat. Like a madman he leaped forward and hugged it while lengths of liane were brought and bound round and round.

It had run only about three feet; if it did not extend in the night it could be patched. There was nothing more we could do—we had to leave her to cool.

Ill, trembling, and exhausted, Charlie begged for aspirins. I tried to cheer him up.

"No worry, Chief. She all right. I mend," said he, doing his best, in turn, to reassure me.

The following morning as the splintering coat of charcoal, the soft mantle of soot, were washed and scraped away, the superb lines of the boat began to appear in wood now a deep honey colour—long and slender, with a high poop where Tanner would sit with the tiny outboard engine, and a beaked prow. The split in the stern—which had, if anything, closed a little—was drawn together by twisting stout cords between upright planks set on both sides, then bound tightly round with wire and secured with nailed steel tape torn from a pack-ing-case; a large hole burnt in one side was mended with a metal sheet made from a flattened kerosene tin, lined with a piece of sacking. Finally, all cracks, crevices and joints were sealed with "Impervion" roofing cement, and the seats fitted.

Then she was launched: down a grassy bank near the camp, plunging and settling softly in the water, sitting nicely and evenly. A few cracks oozed, which could be caulked if they did not swell and seal themselves. She looked wonderful.

"She looks very dangerous, Mr. Guppy." It was Jonah's voice. "She is round bottomed, she will roll over very easy."

"Are you coming at least to try her?"

"Hm. No, sir. I don't want no wetting."

Despite his crusty gloomings I and eight others stepped aboard, and with paddles merrily clicking against the sides, Indian fashion, made fine speed upstream until, after a few hundred yards, we came to small rapids at an old black basalt flow, criss-crossed with channels and fragmenting into *cubes;* then back to the camp, passing a curious platform of sticks built high in a *Cecropia* tree—a platform where men disguised with leaves would lie with their bows and arrows waiting to shoot birds eating the fruit of a neighbouring tree.

A white-headed maroudi peered down from a branch overhead as we tied her up. Stepping ashore from the gunwale I nearly overturned her: she rolled rather too much, it was true, but was large and safe-feeling. The general verdict was favourable, though Jonah still voiced his views:

"I don't like how she looks at all. She is so deep she will strike rocks in the falls, and she is too slow and heavy to turn when the water run fast—she is going to be very bad to handle. That boat is not safe, Mr. Guppy."

"Then we'll all drown together," I snapped.

While the rest of the men began making ropes with which to lower the boat through the rapids, twisting together hanks of stout fishing-cord, Wayama and William (now well again) started downriver in Chekemá's small canoe, armed with an axe and cutlasses, to clear the river of obstructions.

PART THREE

Frog Indian Country

13

The Stone Staircase *(first part)*

Charlie, a man known and respected by all, acted as Master of Ceremonies and began the circulation of the drinks—three huge bowls, which had been set before us by our hosts—passing them to each in turn.

"You will have to go back across the mountains all alone, Charlie?" I asked.

"No. Three Mawayán go mission. Wacoro, Makata, an' he mother. But first rest two three day."

Staggering, with distended stomachs, we rose after half an hour, leaving much undrunk, shook hands with Manatá, Sam, and the Mawayáns, and made our way along the broad path through the forest to the boat.

Packed with all our goods and provisions, sacks of yams and drums of fuel, it still had six inches of freeboard.

"I go walk first, just to see how she goes," said Jonah.

"We won't come back for you!"

Protesting strongly, he squeezed himself in last and sat beside Foimo and Icaro, our two guides, on top of the tarpaulin which enveloped and protected everything from sun and rain, settling himself comfortably with feet extended.

We were off!

We slid over a long shallow sandbank, twisted through a network of fallen branches and trunks below the camp, and then, with engine singing, turned down the long straight avenue, with its selvage of fluttering bamboo points, towards Faiafun.

At speed she rolled with a slow, majestic roll, bringing each gunwale in turn to within three inches above the surface. Then, unexpectedly, she struck a rock, and ground to a standstill until two men leaped overboard and dragged her clear.

More rocks—the beginnings of the rapids. We floated down a sinuous tide, and then a long gradual, tumbling slope into a basin of slowly revolving water, glassily clear and full of fallen leaves swimming in the depths. From ahead came the turbine sound of the first serious falls.

The men, tying ropes to bow and stern, swam to various points and gently eased her over a few more rocks and rills. From comparatively calm water we looked towards white surf (overhung by sweeping sprays of a gnarled, torrent-tortured tree with tufts of paddle-shaped leaves and pink shaving-brush flowers), foaming down an incline between smooth grey boulders and bleached twisted driftwood branches. We tied up, and began the portage—unloading, and carrying everything for half a mile to the lower end of the falls, through mossy, ferny forest in cool air trembling with their sound.

Then came the task of "streaking" or lowering the boat by means of ropes, for these rapids were too powerful and irregular to shoot, even unladen. The men were in fine form—laughing, plunging and splashing: Mark full of eager smiles, even Jonah inexpressibly boyish in purple trunks and white vest, stealing from rock to rock, leaning back and testing each foothold for firmness with his toes, as he carried a rope forward.

Meanwhile, scrambling along the sides of the river, I collected a number of unusual plants: the pink-flowered tree, which proved to be of the mimosa family[1], two 18-inch high shrublets, one with pink[2], the other yellow[3] blossoms, and several flowering Podostemaceae, or paku-weeds—curious plants that live in the highly oxygenated water of the rapids, passing most of their existence in a state of suspense, as dark, gelatinous-looking blobs firmly attached to rocks many feet below the surface, and only proliferating into foliage when the river-levels begin to drop in the dry season. Then they rapidly produce masses of frilly, seaweedy fronds, green or reddish in colour, part leaf, part stem in nature, the favourite food of the fish from which they get their common name, the paku: a delicious and beautiful fish, flat, rather discoid, powerfully built, and much in appearance like the perai (to which, though a pure vegetarian, it is closely related), varying in colour from

---

[1] *Calliandra tergemina.*   [2] *Turnera* sp.   [3] *Oxalis sepium.*

black, bluish-grey or silver to tomato red, and growing up to ten pounds in weight.

As the weed bourgeons into leaf, in certain rivers vast shoals of paku come crowding into the rapids from deeper water to browse on it, and the Indians make special trips to shoot them with bow and arrow. Then as the rivers drop further, the weed is exposed to the air and begins to decompose along the water-line in slimy, succulent masses, and simultaneously bursts into clusters of ethereal pink, lilac or silvery-white flowers, which in their thousands rim the rocks with a changing band of colour as each successively lower contour of plants is exposed, brought into blossom, and dies away above—a process which, if the level is falling fast, may be completed in a few hours. Finally, after fertilization, as the remains of the plants desiccate in the sun's warmth, the flowers wither into brown, poppy-like stalked seed capsules which stand like dead grass, twitching in the breezes and showering the hot rocks with seeds, that germinate when the waters rise and repeat the cycle.

Below a broad weir of rock, over which the waves rolled, we embarked again, and were swept, bumping and scraping, down several small descents. Rounding a bend, we saw that the river was divided ahead by a shelving rocky island with the green and red finned paku-weed thick along the water-line—and, despite the efforts of the men, were whirled sideways towards the deeper channel, from which there wafted a wonderful, terrifying booming.

By strenuous paddling we managed to reach a sugar-loaf rock at the brink, crowned by a *Clusia* with table-tennis-racket leaves and swollen pink buds, to the crooked roots of which we clung. Leaping ashore to lighten the boat, we pulled it into the shallows. Ahead, in a long sweeping curve, the water toppled another twenty-five feet over the reddish rocks, dazzling white, creaming and fulminating until, at the bottom, it rose in a positive fountain of dancing spray.

Cautiously, along the edge, we worked the boat stern first downwards. Just as we reached this final frenzy one of the Wapisianas, mistaking a shouted command, slackened the bow line: slowly, she swung broadside. I sprang into the stream towards her: George seized the rope: we pulled, faces strained, heels slipping on the smooth rocks, knees buckling under the force of water: she struck a rock, heeled side-ways—then a wave entered, and she was full, jammed against the rocks with the water thundering along her hull and pouring out at the stern. Specimens, papers, a scatter of oddments fled away on the current.

Now she weighed tons, and all efforts to move her seemed unavailing. But she was intact: Charlie's hull was proving itself. After hours already spent in the water the men were exhausted, but somehow the strength was found.

The sun was declining red in the west when at last, by levering with herculean lengths of tree, we managed to shift her. Bailed out, loaded with a few heavy items like petrol-drums, we shot the last insignificant rapids, rolled her broadside over a submerged log, and reached the end of the portage and the piles of baggage.

There, in semi-darkness, the tarpaulins were put up, and after a bath, I sat with Foimo and Icaro. They had lighted a fire and slung their hammocks, red-stained from their bodies, between the trees on either side of it. Fireflies with twin headlights circled around, insects hummed, sandflies stung, the water thundered far off, the smoke of the fire drifted up against the dripping leaves, the dark sky. We had only come about a mile, yet I felt content. We were under way, the worst rapids for a long while ahead had been passed in safety and with small loss, and it was delightful to be sitting with the scholarly-looking Emayena with his thin, beaky face and protuberant twinkling eyes, and the genial, pot-bellied old Taruma.

Very early, a blue haze under the trees, the sun a flaming onion on the oily olive water, we started, leading the boat like a horse through the rough places where black bars of rock broke the river. Superb tonka-bean[1] trees overspread the rapids, their boughs a surf of purple flowers.

Then there were broad meandering stretches where the river was bordered by beaches of sand and silt and trembling bamboos, where scrambling pea-vines with yellow flowers, the pink pom-poms of a prickly sensitive plant,[2] grew on the mud.

[1] *Dipteryx oppositifolia.*   [2] *Mimosa polydactyla.*

Manatá had gone ahead, by a boat he kept below the big rapids, to an abandoned village field to fetch fruit for us; and rounding a corner, the morning sun painting the scenery in blues, golds, and greens, the air iridescent and cool, the water shimmering-skinned like a butterfly's wing, we saw his small canoe approaching, laden with bananas and sugar-cane.

By midday my mood had changed: the river was very low, the water-level dropping fast—I foresaw trouble in returning unless it rose again; we had come only a very short way, and had not once been able to use the motor because of the succession of fallen logs and small rapids, each, though with a drop of only two or three feet, full of rocks which the propeller struck. We were meatless: although birds had flown overhead and animals called from the bank, we had shot nothing.

Tea, yams, rice, bread, made a stodgy filling lunch, eaten in the boat while a barrier log was axed. The heat simmered, spirals of air rose from land and water. The vertical sun covered each object with a hoar of hideous whiteness. I was restless, uneasy, impatient.

Irritably I signalled Tanner to use the motor, to try to get some speed up between obstacles. At once, as he lowered the propeller, free-spinning with the clutch in, into the water, there came a series of sharp raps—perai. Looking over the side I could see the light flash on their bodies as they turned in shoals and launched themselves against it. How fortunate that they stayed in quiet pools! Their presence in the rapids, where the men had had to work for hours in the water, would have made travel almost impossible.

A minute later we hit a rock again. It was useless trying to work the motor: patience was the thing, for a single mishap could irreparably damage it. Bumping, drifting, paddling, we continued.

By late afternoon the men showed signs of wanting to stop and make camp, but I knew that we must move as far as we could, or we should again run short of food. Lips were pursed when we reached a large fallen log which I insisted must be cut through so that we could go on. Then, wonderfully, the country-side changed, and there were miles of level land through which the river meandered, bordered by overgrown mudbanks, bamboos, and irregular tangled woodland above which the globular leafless crowns of jacarandas were bursting into mauve flower.

Occasionally low hills approached the river, and tall, dark forest closed in again; then, though there might be no rapids, often there stood in the still water groups of boulders smoothly sculpted into eggs, totem poles, skulls, teeth, globes, the backs of elephants, whales, brontosauri—all on a monstrous scale, and bleached and stained, striped by running water, fractured into discs and plates. Perhaps of everything in the interior of Guiana it is the spectral quality of such rocks that one remembers most: megalithic natural statuary, relics of ancient subterranean lava injections, now risen to the surface through the washing away of the softer covering earth—the bones of the planet, showing like a skeleton after the flesh has rotted.

After nine hours of travel we landed at a sandy cove crinkled with sharp black rocks, a very cold place where the saturated air was kept in motion by the swift water. Five and a half hours had been spent in negotiating rapids, two and a half in drifting and paddling, half an hour in having lunch, half an hour in travelling with the motor: we had come, I reckoned, about fourteen miles by water, perhaps nine in a straight line.

Unbroken sleep is almost impossible in a hammock—every time one moves, one wakes—and as I twisted and shivered, frigid, I realized that for much of my time in Guiana I had not had a night's undisturbed sleep (indeed, that away from the coast few of the country's inhabitants had ever experienced those eight hours of continuous slumber that civilized people consider necessary); despite which, now I was accustomed to one, I found sleep in an Indian hammock much more refreshing than in a bed—perhaps because, unlike the long narrow garden or naval hammocks, they are woven as broad as long, and lain in diagonally, with the body level, supported evenly and firmly at all points, the head low, and the legs high—an attitude of perfect restfulness.

Stirring the fires occasionally, warming ourselves with cocoa, we passed the hours of darkness. Here on the open, rocky riverside the diurnal variations of temperature were much greater than in the forest, even at higher altitudes—sometimes as much as 30° F. At 5.30 a.m. the temperature was 63° F.

Our onwards way was easier, with the motor steadily in use except where we had to disembark at cataracts: an undulating descent through beautiful and varied scenery which late the next morning took us past the mouth of the Taruini—the first fixed point on the journey—a small opening with a cluster of rocks opposite.

Our course had been largely east, or even north of east, and only after passing the Taruini did it begin to veer southwards as expected. As we went I examined my maps: inaccurate though they were, they still held a certain fascination. One showed two Mapueras, side by side, one with the Wapisiana names for the tributaries, the other the Wai-Wai, and neither, from what I had seen, more than hinting at the true position and flow of the river. Even the Boundary Commission map, showing only the frontier—presumably with great accuracy— and the chief rivers, was inaccurate where these were concerned only a few miles from the border.

We approached an incline where for about an eighth of a mile the river ran down a narrow, shallow, straight gorge, falling about twenty feet. The water was rough and full of boulders, especially at the upper end, but George, the bowman, saw what seemed a clear channel winding down the middle. Swinging towards it, we felt ourselves launched forward.

At that moment the engine cut out, and try as he might Tanner could not restart it. We paddled furiously, but we could not cope with the speed of the current. Floundering, with water pouring over the gunwales, we struck rock after rock. I stood up and shouted to George, who was levering with the enormous bow-paddle, a special instrument for steering and fending off. I could see rocks rising like peaks out of the clear depths. Sometimes their sharp edges protruded above the surface, sometimes they showed dark and massive a foot or two down; and over and between them the water rushed, carrying us with it.

Then came a long bubbling slope. The branch of a tree swept us, and a saucer-sized tarantula leapt from it on to me, scrambled about on my head and chest, and then onto the tarpaulin, where it was squashed by Cyril. It was strange, as we hurtled along, to see insects come fluttering out to us over the lathering wastes as if we were an island haven.

Then we were through, with a lot of water shipped, but safe, and the forests closed in again, with white rocks gleaming at every turn, like towers and castles afloat on the still, black, river.

"Tutumo: *gashin?*"—are there rapids on the Tutumo? I asked Foimo, sitting beside me.

He raised one finger, gave me a sharp, foxy glance, laughed, and said something; then returned to his complacent smiling, a comfortable-looking old fellow, with a huge belly and thin legs.

14

The Brothers

Once again the boat gathered speed, and standing up I saw the drop ahead—the most formidable yet, for we were running towards a deep valley with half the height of the trees growing in it hidden from view.

Almost simultaneously I saw a cluster of red bodies on a ledge of rock to the right: William, grinning his scatological grin, and a group of strange Indians who waved and smiled as we turned towards them. The noise of the rapids filled our ears as we drew up and tied the boat secure.

With great courtesy we were helped ashore, shaken by the hand, and then introduced by these strangers to their wives and children. Wai-Wai women were usually ignored and never introduced, but these were Mawayáns, the four whom Foimo had said were following him.

As he landed, Fonyuwé had rushed forward and embraced one of the men, and now, smiling, he led him up to me, a young man with a silly, broadly grinning face, missing front teeth, and an upturned nose.

"Yapumo," said Fonyuwé, holding him by the hand and raising two fingers close together—from which I learned that they were brothers; and then, through Basil, that this was the first time they had met since childhood.

"Where is Wayama?" I asked—who had accompanied William in the small canoe.

"He is sick," translated Basil. "For days he has been talking wildly all the time. Now he is better. He and William do not want to come any further, because evil spirits must be plotting against them."

Wayama got up from his hammock when I approached. His

temperature was normal, but he was very weak. He had evidently suffered severely.

"William say if you give him the medicines he and Wayama will take them as you say. He is sorry to turn back, because he wanted to find a wife. But he will be rich when you pay him so he is going to ask the friend he give his old wife to to give her back."

Sadly I agreed, and gave them a supply of atebrin tablets, and a few articles to carry back to the mission. It was really best that they return, taking things slowly and easily while Wayama convalesced, though it would make me two men short for the journey back over the Acarai.

Fonyuwé now drew my attention to a pigtail-tube that Yapumo wanted to exchange for a cutlass. It was decorated with the skins of the rarest birds—the cock-of-the-rock, the pompadour and cayenne chatterers, troupials, humming-birds, honey-birds, kingfishers: it was the most beautiful pigtail-tube I had ever seen. The beads with which the tubular part was encrusted alone would make a field of research, I speculated, for some must have come hundreds of miles, perhaps hundreds of years ago, from the places where originally they had been traded, they were so old and worn, of such delicate, faded colours.

I looked at Yapumo—I could tell that he did not really want to part with it. Yet having shown it, he felt that he could not withdraw: smiling, he pressed it into my hand. Then he brought forth an elegant cylindrical bamboo quiver, tufted with sapphire and carmine feathers, capped by a single piece of leather miraculously worked and stretched into a perfect fit, and containing thirty or forty curare-coated arrow-points: a great treasure, which likewise I bought; then several bows and arrows, longer and even more beautiful than those of the Wai-Wais.

"Yapumo wants to come with us," said Basil. "He is so glad to see Fonyuwé that he does not want to leave him. And the other man, Yeimiti [a tall, rather silent, young man] will come too and help us carry our loads. The women and children will go on to Manatá's and wait for us to return there. Now we will be all right. We will have plenty men."

Lunching by the waterside, in the full sound of the cataract, I had a dish of boiled yams, a "bake", and Nescafé. Four feet away, sitting on a mass of feather-pluckings (two large guans had been shot by Jonah), sat the younger, brightly-painted Indians, devouring a pot of stewed alligator. Kirifakka held out a claw to me.

"*Kiriwanhi*, Meeshterguffin," he urged.

In return I flung him a poisonous hairy caterpillar on a leaf, pointing down my throat.

"Sank you," he said—and burst into laughter, at my amazement at his cleverness in picking up English.

The meal over, with farewells all around we embarked. We paddled towards a group of rocks at the brink from which we could plan the descent. I had lost my love of the beauty of falling water in my hatred of it as an obstacle—yet the sight of this particular flight of rapids revived it in me. The river, very shallow, flowed like waving green hair over a broad fan of reddish rocks, and then, in a multitude of small silvery-foaming cataracts descended, as over a grand staircase, into the valley. Never had I seen so many kinds of paku-weed as here: frizzly, curly-fronded, they burst into showers of pink stars wherever the rocks were exposed; while elsewhere were swards of a dense emerald-green growth of sedges, all of a tiny species with three snowy bracts round the flower-heads, flowering profusely in white drifts and tussocks both above and below water. It was as colourful a scene as an Alpine meadow, and made doubly vivid by the glassy greens and blues and pinks of the breaking water.

There was little danger. The problem was chiefly one of finding deep water to lift the big boat while jockeying it downhill. Jonah and Icaro in Chekemá's small canoe, Yapumo and Yeimiti in their own, went to either side of the river, searching out possible routes for themselves. Foimo, patriarchal, pointed first one way, then another, not realizing that our boat could not follow theirs, while Yapumo, whose intelligence had by now greatly impressed me, lifted a hand to bid us wait, and walked and waded forward from his canoe till, discovering a way, he came back and led us on.

Turning to me, with vigorous gestures he described an even

more colossal series of falls, then arched his finger across the sky three times to indicate days, and pointed downstream.

After three hours the boat was at the foot of the main rapids and we embarked; too soon, for we were nearly holed in a further downwards rush of six or seven feet.

Below the falls was a large island, circled on its left by the main branch of the river. When we were half-way down its shore, and almost before I realized what was happening, we swung abruptly left past a pile of bare boulders, and up a tributary river, a dismal flood of dark water which poured towards us in an undulating rush.

This was the Buna-wau, Tutumo, or Calabash River. We had entered the territory of the Mawayáns.

For an hour we made our way upstream, the motor useless because there were so many rocks, progressing by poling or paddling—the standing men in the smaller boats ahead making graceful figures of eight, like the opening and closing of butterflies' wings, as they swung their long poles first on one side and then the other.

While camp was made on a rocky point Tanner produced a pot of tea for Jonah and me and we began to sort out my riverside collections—all in good condition, except the paku-weeds, which had disintegrated into masses of sugary cellulose.

I was weary, yet triumphant that we should have got so far.

"It seems like things are not going so well, Mr. Guppy," observed Jonah.

"What on earth do you mean?"

"Well, how long do you suppose we are going to stay, sir?"

"Another four weeks, or so."

"Sir, I don't see how that is possible. I must go back to Georgetown, because I have things there I must do. I cannot stay out here in the bush without food."

"But Jonah, only a few days ago you wanted to come. You said you did not mind if we went a bit short."

"Ah, but sir, we haven't got enough food to last."

Tea, and this unexpected treachery rallied me: "But *you* were the most enthusiastic of all. You said you did not mind how long we lived on yams and cassava bread and any fish and animals we got. It was *you* who told me how wonderful you thought it would be to see strange tribes, and that if we had Indians with us from this part we should have no trouble, because they would know the best places to fish and hunt, and tell all their friends, when we got to villages, to sell food to us."

"All the same . . ."

"Jonah, you mustn't look at the gloomy side of things—look at Basil and the Wapisianas—they are all very keen."

As soon as I said this he brightened:

"Yes, that is true. I've been thinking the same thing—they are very eager boys. And we are going to have many strange experiences, and see all sorts of dances and costumes."

It was an extraordinary and rapid change of outlook. Was it because he realized that he was the only complainer? Was he, indeed, the only complainer, or were the other men also, unknown to me, discontented?

Yapumo had come down to the riverside where we were working and was watching curiously all we did ; and when Tanner lit the paraffin lamp he stood beside it and examined it with great intentness. The moon had risen, nearly full, but veiled slightly with clouds.

"*Nunyi*," he said, pointing to it.

"Wai-Wai?" I asked.

He nodded: "Mawayán: *kushu*."

There was a strange whistling, "pip.peeeeeeeeeeep", very shrill, repeated from the oddest places all along the river-banks, where, when I flashed a torch, nothing was to be seen. Through Basil and Fonyuwé I learned from Yapumo that it was made by a large kind of spider which dwelt at the water's edge and caught small fish and sucked them dry.

Flickering sheet-lightning had of late begun to appear in the night sky—a sign that the good weather might be breaking up and the Amazonian rainy season drawing on. Now it flashed brilliantly, and then, far off, thunder rolled:

"*Dedabaru.*"

The Mawayán language was decidedly harsher, fuller of con-sonants, then the Wai-Wai.

"Sir," said Basil, "can you come and see Foimo? It looks like he is very sick. And I am not feeling too good either. I catch a cold from him."

It was most worrying—as fast as I got one Indian well, another succumbed. At least Basil had only a cold, and was only slightly feverish (100° F.); but Foimo was in a very bad way. His temperature was 103.9°, and he lay crumpled and pallid, with one leg dangling over the side of his hammock.

I gave him four paludrines, and retired, wondering who would get ill next, and what I could do to prevent it. I dreamed, for the first time on the expedition, of other places, of England, France, even Georgetown on the coast.

In the morning Foimo's temperature had not fallen, as in the past had those of all the other sick Indians I had treated. Instead, horrifyingly, it had risen to 104.1°. I became seriously worried. What would happen if he or one of the Mawayáns died? If the blame were laid on me or any other of the men we might have difficulty in getting out of the country in safety, for the Indians believe that death can only be caused by witchcraft, and that it is incumbent on the relatives or friends of the deceased to revenge themselves on the sorcerers.

My heart went out to the old fellow, looking so composed despite his fever, and I kept as cheerful a countenance as I could to buoy him up. Remembering Dr. Jones's advice concerning malaria—paludrine for prevention, atebrin for treatment— I switched from paludrine to atebrin hoping that it would be more successful, but began each of the other new Indians— Yapumo, Yeimiti, and Icaro—on courses of paludrine. When we embarked I placed all of them, and Basil, whose cold was still troubling him, in the smaller boats where they would be dryer, for there was a great deal of splashing and jumping in and out of the big boat in shallow places.

Our general direction was mostly east, and during the morning there were long clear stretches where we were able to use the engine, towing the other two canoes. This was far, far more wonderful than anything the Mawayáns had ever dreamed of! Amid shouts of delight the heavy-laden boats, strung like sausages, careered round the bends of the river.

Racially, we were now a most heterogeneous crew : three Mawayáns, a Taruma, an Emayena, a Wai-Wai, two Arawaks, three Wapisianas (one with a large admixture of the blood of the vanished Atorad tribe), a half-breed—part Hindu, part

Arawak, with dashes of Portuguese and negro, a negro and an Englishman of French, Huguenot, descent.

At one series of low bars we had to unload the boat. Here, when the Mawayáns refused to wade more than knee-deep, their excuse was not that if their red paint were washed off evil spirits might see them, but "*Camisha*", which they uttered loudly, pointing to their little red cloth laps. Admittedly, it was uncomfortable to get one's *camisha* wet . . . then Basil explained to me that it was a fish they were afraid of—probably a tiny elongated catfish with spiny fans, of which I had heard, which has the habit of forcing its way up the human orifices, from which it cannot be dislodged without causing severe mutilation or even death. These fish are unknown in Guiana, but we were now on a tributary of the Amazon and they were possibly common.

Above this rapid there were more long curving meanders in which we kept up a good speed. Several times we passed areas, similar to that I had seen near the Chodikar, where swathes of trees a hundred yards wide lay dead and splintered, uprooted by another, more recent, whirlwind.

We stopped, unsuccessfully, to try to shoot a curassow which flew low ahead of us into the trees. Game birds were abundant, but shoot as we might we could not kill one. Particularly common were bush curry-curries—black ibises—unpleasant, hasty-flying birds as large as hens, with harsh voices, a uniform, motheaten, undertaker's garb of greenish-black feathers, naked black leathery cheeks, and long curved bills like surgeons' probes—designed, one felt, for picking out eyes. It was not difficult to understand why their ancient Egyptian counterparts had been depicted on the walls of tombs.

"Kurri! Kurri! Kurri!" they shrieked, flying low ahead of the boat: excellent eating, and easy shots, but always just out of range.

Clinging to rocks, or running and jumping rapidly over the water were occasional long and thin-legged spiders, about four inches in diameter—the whistling, fish-eating spiders, said Yapumo. They were a speckled grey-brown, and almost invisible when at rest flattened against the rocks, or the side of the boat, where sometimes one would pause briefly before flitting away again over the surface in its quest for prey. Once we saw swimming across our bows a long reddish-brown snake, a "fire-snake": the fifth snake seen on the whole expedition (and like two others, harmless), making an average of less than one a week, or one poisonous kind every two weeks—for we were now at the beginning of the seventh week of our journey.

Heavy clouds gathered in the sky ahead as the afternoon drew on, and we could see rain falling from them. Often, far off, we heard wind or rain rushing through the tree-tops. Then a steady downpour descended, chilling us, and the sky grew totally grey.

We might reach the path to the Oroko'orin that afternoon, said Yapumo ; and this spurred us to keep going despite the lateness of the hour. But as the dim twilight prematurely deepened, and the driving rain enclosed us, lancing into the water all around, we became more and more dismal. I had removed my clothes to keep them dry, and was naked except for a towel on my shoulders. Thinking of the two sick men I signalled that we should land—but the ground was swampy, slushy mud coated with dead leaves.

"Real *chichibé*", said George Gouveia.

We kept on, though we could hardly see the banks, whistling to keep our spirits up, until, riding through one small rapid, a steep firm slope at last appeared.

Here while the tarpaulins were put up, I shivered uselessly beneath a dripping palm-leaf, while old Foimo, rattling with fever, cowered in a hole among the roots of a leaning tree. All around the heavy liquid poured from above, through the leaves, on to ground and water, while in the distance thunder prowled through the darkening sky.

Foimo's continued high temperature depressed me bitterly: Why should I spend my life struggling through mud and rain and forest, I thought, continuously wet and miserable? Scientific curiosity seemed a very poor reason.

A little later, while wind and rain raged outside, Tanner brought me a delicious soup made from yams and a freshly-caught haimara fish, a tender slice or two of white-headed maroudi, and a cup of cocoa; revived, brimming with optimism, I then retired into my blanket-filled hammock.

It was still early morning the next day when we reached a shallow left-bank tributary of the Tutumo, the Kurudu-wau or, in Mawayán, Wenye-yoku—the farine porridge river—and ten minutes' journey up it, the beginning of the path. Without guides, we should have passed the small hole in the riverside forest which was the mouth of the Kurudu, and even if we had entered it, might have sailed past the landing, for it was merely a bare shelf of rock at the water's edge, with little sign of disturbance in the vegetation behind.

Inland a short way was a small clearing with a derelict palm-leaf shelter in the middle, and here we made camp for the day, for it was important that messengers go ahead to announce our coming, a task for which the two brothers, Fonyuwé and Yapumo, eagerly volunteered.

"How far are the villages?" I inquired of Yapumo.

"Four days' walk," said he. "Two over fairly level ground, called Imai-bau, or the Mud Hills; and two over high hills, called Shiuru-dicta by the Wai-Wais, and Serernap-naw by the Mawayáns. When we arrive we will make everyone gather vegetables and make cassava bread, and send out huntsmen to kill game so that there will be plenty to eat when you come."

"That sounds very good."

But a moment later Fonyuwé announced, after talking with Yapumo, that they would reach the first village on the morrow, because they would walk all night without stopping.

It was most confusing trying to gauge distances for someone accustomed to keeping his concepts of time and distance separate. But the Indians' use of days or parts of days as units of distance was quite logical, for what use is it talking in miles when everything depends on the kind of country you go over, and how you travel? If light, you get there sooner, if heavy, or with a white man or a sick old man, it takes longer.

"Well, Jonah, we will rest in camp today and follow early tomorrow—that ought to please you."

"One day in camp is nothing, sir, when you always missing Sundays, and tomorrow is a Sunday. Besides, how do we know the Indians will sell us food when we reach? I think we are running risks of starving. We should stay for a week and catch fish. Then when Fonyuwé returns we will know for certain before we start."

"By that time we really *might* be starving."

"And what if Foimo die? The Indians might murder us. It is better we turn back."

"I agree—that would be serious. But it is another reason why we must get to their villages as fast as possible. If we get him home they will at least think that *we* we can't be the people who put the spell on him. It would be much worse if he died here."

At midday Foimo was no better. His temperature was still 104·1°. He had a slight cough, vomited occasionally, and complained of a pain in the stomach. I gave him three more atebrins, cough mixture, and Epsom salts after a cup of tea.

"Sir," said Jonah casually, "it looks like your bottle is running out."

"I have another, but we *are* getting low on drugs."

"Hm. Then why did you leave medicines at the mission? Why didn't you bring them all?"

"Jonah, I have used more drugs in the last three weeks than on all my expeditions put together during the past three years. That's why we are short."

He gave me a withering glance. He was much too wise to argue with.

"Don' worry about him, chief," said Tanner, as soon as Jonah had gone. "And he carrying plenty food—more dan anybody else. He make sure he is all right."

Late in the afternoon I went to see Foimo again. Basil, whose kindliness and attentiveness to the old fellow had very much won my respect, was seated near him, watching a big metallic blue hunting-wasp dragging a tarantula it had paralysed across the ground under his hammock.

Foimo was so pale that I was frightened. He looked as if he was dying. He was coughing continually, and breathing with a terrible effort. His temperature was 105°.

How I wished that I had more medical knowledge! If only there were some small and adequate guide to modern methods of treatment for people such as me, forced to be their own doctors—something between the professional medical books and the first-aid manuals.

I had to make some sort of decision, for plainly my treatment had failed. His symptoms no longer seemed in the least like malaria—more like bronchitis. Suddenly a great light dawned . . . I realized how stupid I had been : Basil had caught a cold from Foimo. I remembered the snivelling, hawking Yukuma at the mission. None of the sick Indians had had malaria!— they had all been suffering from the common cold to which in their isolation they had no natural immunity. I was in the midst of a mild but potentially serious epidemic in which the virus seemed slowly to be changing the nature of its attack, manifesting itself in weirder and weirder forms. By luck, palu-drine and atebrin had formerly been successful in reducing the fever, but the virus or germ had survived and been transmitted —and already Fonyuwé and Yapumo, almost certainly carry-ing it, had gone ahead to the Mawayán villages. There was no way of stopping them. At least I had some drugs left.

The first question, obviously, was how to cure Foimo. I was so certain now of the origin of the disease that I abandoned all thought of anti-malarials. I had a sulpha drug—sulphathia-zole—and I decided to stake everything upon it. If it did not work Foimo would be dead in a few hours.

To start with I gave him four tablets, then two more after two hours, and four last thing at night, because I did not want to disturb him later in case that might weaken or frighten him more than if I kept up the pretence that there was little wrong.

There were no signs of change before I retired: if anything, he seemed weaker. I began to feel hopeless.

All night long he coughed, long, slow, agonizing coughs that seemed to take all the strength out of him, and grew feebler and feebler as his life drained away. There was nothing I could do. I had reached the limit of my knowledge.

Then I suddenly awoke. The coughing had stopped. It was dawn. I sprang up and hastened to him: he was asleep and breathing peacefully. An hour later, when I took his tempera-ture, it was down to normal. The sulphathiazole had worked. I thanked Heaven with deepest relief.

Obviously Foimo could not move, but so outright had been

the cure that I no longer feared the disease. I had plenty of sulpha tablets, and I decided to walk on with the men towards Mawayán land as planned, leaving Basil to feed him, tend him and give him his medicines, and to help him follow slowly when he could.

Several fish had been caught during the night, and when I came to say goodbye he was sitting up and drinking a large bowl of fish broth, chatting in a lively way to Basil, and obviously fast recovering his strength and spirits.

15

The Deserted Village

The undergrowth was thick, irregular, untidy, wet; the path so vague, tortuous and branching that that across the mountains seemed in recollection a tourist trail by comparison. The general direction was a little south of east, roughly parallel with the Wenyaufu-yoku (a tributary of the Wenye-yoku), a large stream glimpsed occasionally deep in its mud-sided channel, with murky, boulder-studded branches which we frequently crossed.

To lighten the loads we had left a cache of supplies behind under the powis-tail, and as we walked I was surprised to find how much my mind returned to it. Two tins of bully-beef, a tin of sardines, a tin of condensed milk, a packet of tea, a little rice and farine, and a small towel—how pleasant it would be to uncover my personal hoard on our way back! It would represent an instant rise in the standard of living. Then there were our stores at the mission. But the mind rejected them— they were too near and too much. Only on things fantastic or far out of reach, like London, Georgetown, or the world of "Moby Dick", which I was reading, could it dwell with pleasure.

The ground was a maze of peat bogs and low riverain levees flooded during the wet season, and everywhere waist-high in small palms with pretty spikes of white flowers.[1] We passed a new powis-tail shelter, evidently made by Fonyuwé and Yapumo the previous night, with fresh fish-scales on a rock near by; and the mouldering remains of one which Icaro said that he and Foimo had slept under on their outward journey. From this and other signs I gathered that it was extremely rarely, perhaps only once in several years, that the Mawayáns

[1] *Geonoma* sp.

left their fastnesses. We had been very fortunate in meeting them.

By late afternoon, when we camped beside a wide shallow stretch of the river, we had come about seven miles. Rain was beginning to fall, and it was only with difficulty that I persuaded Yeimiti to move his hammock so that Icaro, who had developed a high fever, could also lie under shelter and near the fire—for the Indians have no conception of the care needed by a sick person, and often cause death through neglect.

I gave Icaro four sulphathiazoles to begin with, but unlike Foimo he was a difficult patient: he held the tablets in his mouth to deceive me, but was forced to spit them out because of the taste. He retched and vomited, wasted several and became hostile at my insistence. It was only through tact that I at last got him to swallow some, persuading him that they were what had cured Foimo.

"They will have to give you part of Dr. Jones's salary for all the work you are doing," remarked Jonah genially. All day he had been in good humour, but in the evening, as we worked together, there were disapproving silences and flatly contradictory remarks.

His support would have meant much to me. Instead, he was becoming so increasingly disagreeable that I began to consider detaching a few men to take him back to the mission. My patience was giving way, not only with him but with the rest of the men. They were beginning to grumble again—a senseless activity, aimed at lowering my morale so that I would make the work easier; and against their own interests, for the quicker we moved, the quicker we should reach new supplies of food. It sprang from an attitude of being automatically against the boss, based perhaps on past ill-treatment. It could not be reasoned with. Telling them we might run out of food was useless—they didn't seem to care, being unimaginative—and I had no means of forcing them. They resented strong measures before the brink of actual disaster, but reserved for themselves the right to lay blame. It was a dilemma resolvable only by arousing their enthusiasm. Whenever they realized how far away this ordinary-looking bit of forest was, and thought of all that they would tell their friends and relatives when they got

"IN A TINY, PALM-FRONDED CLEARING . . . LAY THE NEARLY
FINISHED BOAT" (*p. 160*)

"IMPLEMENTS LIKE GIGANTIC CLOTHES-PEGS . . . WERE
SLIPPED OVER THE SIDES (*p. 182*)

MISTY MORNING ON THE MAPUERA

back home, they worked like furies. But the onus of keeping them in this state rested on me, and it was beginning to exhaust me. I hoped sincerely that my strength would continue equal to it.

From my hammock I contemplated their vague, heavy shapes outlined against the flaring fires, the sparkling, sweeping sprays of rain and mist: swinging, insensible hulks, like lumps of plasticine which I was trying to force into shape. Only occasionally was there any response from them. It was like wooing a dozen frigid women. Perhaps it was the forest itself of which we were all victims? Endlessly crawling in the green dungeons, walking the dark corridors and catacombs of leaves—no wonder we all felt gloomy and rebellious. Man is a creature of open spaces: even the Wai-Wais lived in enormous clearings. There were two or three more days of forest ahead before we reached the villages. Testing days I felt sure they would be.

"Sir, we must stay here," said Jonah with granite countenance in the morning. "Icaro cannot move, and it is impossible to take his load because everybody got more than he can carry."

Icaro's temperature had fallen to nearly 100°, but the shock of the illness and the cure had left him very staggery. I offered to leave one of the men with him so that he could rest and be looked after. No, said he: he would feel worse if he stayed. He would come with us, if someone would carry his load.

"See?" said Jonah triumphantly. "What are you going to do about his load?"

"Oh, don't worry about that," I said very casually. "He hasn't much, anyway. You forget Basil and Foimo will be coming along carrying practically nothing. I'll leave a note for them."

"I will take his hammock and a few things," volunteered Tanner.

Jonah's face fell, and he set his mouth.

The country became rocky, though still low lying; and the forest, from being a tangle of lianes and swamp trees, more open, with sometimes a sight of the sky, and full of small-stemmed trees with naked reddish trunks.[1] We walked on soft springy moss, and passed patches of wild pineapples and silk

[1] Chiefly *Myrtaceae*.

grass,[1] ascending gradually while as gradually the forest grew mightier, until the stems of the trees were towering clean and smooth a hundred feet out of sight into the upper canopies.

These were the Imai-bau, the Mud Hills.

Now the streams began to flow south, at right angles to our general direction: we had crossed some sort of a water-shed; then, by lunchtime, another, for the brook we stopped beside ran northwards, and was possibly a tributary of the Alto-Trombetas.

Just beyond it Yeimiti trod with his bare foot on a snake. With a loud expectorant hiss "s-s-s-s-s-s-s", it darted straight at me, struck my bare left leg, lashed round, touched the other and was away—evidently confused, for it had not opened its mouth and bitten, as so easily it could have. The Indians had heard but not seen it, but I followed it with my eye to where it came to rest in a small bush near the path. It was a fer-de-lance, one of the deadliest of snakes.

Cutting a long stick Mark broke its neck, for it might have been a danger to those following. (We could hear much joviality behind as with relish they discussed the different Indian words for the genitals of man and woman.)

On the long easy slopes we now trod there were fresh signs of pigs, and soon we smelt them strongly. Cyril, with the gun, dropped his load and ran, loping lightly, until he was out of sight in the undergrowth, occasionally snicking a twig to guide him back. There were shots, crashings and snortings, then another shot far away; but an hour later he returned with nothing. He had, however, already shot two tinamous. With any luck, if it were my turn, I might get some of their meat in the evening: meanwhile I was feeling rather ill and growing increasingly hungry, for there had been very little to eat.

Food was very low. From the very next day, I reckoned we would be in serious trouble unless we could get some from the Indians or were successful hunting or fishing. We had reached the point where we had not enough, unaided, to return to the mission.

I had three boiled sweets in my pocket, which I had refrained from eating in the morning. Rather gloatingly I occupied my

[1] *Bromelia* sp.

mind in thinking of how many minutes there were to go before I would have the first, then the second and the third—spacing them out through the afternoon at hourly intervals. Suddenly an awful thought struck me: what if I only had two?—in that case I would have to wait an hour and a half before I ate one. I decided not to look: if there was one over at the end of the day it would mean an extra one for the morrow.

Then Cyril and I came to a Brazil-nut tree, and surprisingly found three unbroken fruit under it, each containing a few fresh nuts, golden brown outside, white, light, and crisp-kernelled among many that were full of stinking juice. Six, and I felt a new, happy man. There were more trees further, but no more nuts.

The sun was low, and the long slopes continued, with never a sign of a camping-place. Every river was dried up, its bed a crust of mud, until we found a trickle eighteen inches wide in a soft swampy place, beyond which peat covered the ground so thickly that it formed high walls almost enclosing a minute tributary rill.

Mosquitoes filled the air with an incessant whine, driving us all to our hammocks as soon as we had eaten. I was depressed, more so perhaps than at any time on the expedition; yet determined. One of the few reassuring, familiar things was the sight of my own face, even if now horrifyingly bearded, in the mirror twice a day when I brushed my hair.

In the morning Icaro's temperature was slightly subnormal. He sat in his hammock with an idle smile on his learned countenance, with a fledgling in his hand whose mother was fluttering in distress in the bushes nearby. When I produced my medicines he looked at me sneeringly, gave me a slight push, and turned away.

Slowly he began to pull the fledgling apart by the two legs. I took it from him, and instead of continuing the process, as he thought I would, put it on the ground. His face flushed with anger, and raising a stick he smashed it down just short of the little bird, then flung it hard after it as it hopped away, but missed. He got up, but not feeling well enough to pursue it, sat down again, shrugging his shoulders. Very firmly I made him swallow the tablets I had brought.

A mile beyond the camp we came upon a rectangular patch of second-growth forest—an old Indian field, abandoned a hundred or more years before, the first sign of human settlement in the region that we had seen, and indicating some degree of permanency of habitation. To me it was as exciting as the discovery of a ruined temple, and as sure an indicator of the past. At sight of it I began to feel much less despondent.

Two and a half hours later, after passing through another patch of second growth, the very low undulating hills flattened, the swampy dells broadened, and we came to a sandy, brown-watered river about sixty feet wide, flowing southwards—the Oroko'orin!

We waded across, waist deep, with a consciousness that we were nearing our destination.

Beyond was a flood plain three or four miles wide, which we crossed mostly along the broad, sparsely-grassed, cracked-mud floor of a dried-up drainage channel, to another slightly narrower river, the Mara-yoku, or Haimara River, a tributary of the Oroko'orin.

Along its banks grew bristly yawarda palms, which I had last seen on the Chodikar, and a solitary-stemmed bamboo, whose single green shoots, up to eight inches thick, rose from bulky rhizomes, the tops of which protruded from the earth, and soared straight up for 50, 60, or even 70 feet to a plume of fine lanceolate leaves. It was extraordinary to walk through a grove of these stems, like green-painted Victorian structural ironwork. At each node there was a pair of two-inch thorns and a large brown scale-leaf, like a piece of wrapping-paper, enclosing the stem above. Nothing I had ever heard of was at all like it, except, perhaps, the poison bamboo described by Barrington Brown.

The path on the far bank of the Mara-yoku was wide and well worn, at first through dense shrubbery with the sky open above. Knee-high sedges, their leaves still dew-spangled, grew beside it out of the deep black loamy clay, and on them, in hundreds, butterflies were emerging from their chrysalises: heliconiids[1] with long narrow black wings, splashed on the hinder pair with a sunburst of red and yellow rays. Slowly,

[1] Butterflies of a family typical of the deep jungle shade.

214

sleepily, they waved their drying wings, and offered no resistance to capture even when able to fly a few yards. It looked as if the whole area had been under water only a short while before, so perhaps they had survived submergence as pupae.

Another hour's walk over undulating ascending ground took us past one more old field to a narrow, leaf-choked stream, the Napmanana, a-hover with mosquitoes and full of small, actively-swimming guppies. On the far side were low bushes, not high forest like that from which we gazed; and a broad path, made firm in its lower, muddy portion with a flooring of logs, led from the landing-place up a long steep slope.

At the top, in a circle of bare red earth backed by a hundred acres or more of cultivations, stood the village, a conical house, taller and more graceful than any we had seen, but in other respects similar.

It was deserted.

This was the village of Titko-tirir, or Minyew-bau, the Place, or Hill, of the Brazil-nut tree. Inside was Fonyuwé's warishi, the presence of which, Holmes-like, the men interpreted as meaning that we were to wait until he came to fetch us.

With Icaro leading the way we walked through ranks of sugar-cane, bitter cassava, yams, plantains, bananas, pineapples, silk grass, tobacco, cotton, past clumps of arrow-grass and patches of gourds. As we went he pointed to different patches and said this was his, that Foimo's, or Kwakwé's (Foimo's brother, the other Taruma), that Kofiri's (a Mawayán), that Wacoro's (another Mawayán), this from this year, that from three years before. The crops were in excellent condition, with few signs of insect, virus, or fungus attack. The whole field, so well tended, bespoke immense labours: with his family, each of the five men of the village had felled, planted, and tended between five and ten acres a year.

Each crop, said Icaro, had been planted on the soil best suited for it, which was why the field was so patchy.

Who was the chief?

Kwakwé, Foimo's brother. He and Foimo had built the village according to their own ways. It was not like the way the Mawayáns built.

This, then, was a Taruma village, the only one in existence. To have stumbled upon it was alone worth the journey.

"This is a great disappointment," said Jonah. "I was expecting a great village and many people. This is just an ordinary sort of place. There is no Big Village here at all."

"Perhaps it is further on, Jonah? Or perhaps it does not exist at all? I can't say I really expected it. On this sort of expedition you just have to wait and see what you find."

We walked for about a quarter of a mile, grilling and prickling with sweat in the unaccustomed glare of the sun, clambering over the hulks and skeletons of felled trees, scrunching their charcoal branches, ducking between tangles of crisscrossed timbers, to Icaro's own sugar patch.

Here, with a wave of the hand, he bade us welcome, and we cut ourselves lengths of cane and sat chewing and chatting in the shade of the big waving grasses for half an hour. Then sticky and happy turned to the work of camp-making.

Food now was assured: even Jonah had no complaints.

The following day, waiting for Fonyuwé, we returned to the Mara-yoku and cut down one of the giant bamboos, leaving a section of its trunk beside the path, to be picked up on our return journey, and walked back slowly to the village collecting. There were several trees new to the expedition: an *Eschweilera*, or monkey-pipe; a lovely Sapotaceous tree[1] with clusters of yellow buds near the ends of the twigs; and an unusual tree of the family Moraceae with tiny flask-shaped flowers.[2]

While we were felling the last of these Basil and Foimo appeared, Foimo walking slowly with a stick. With great pluck he had set forth, after only one day's rest, on a walk of about thirty miles through the rough forested country.

All afternoon I worked with Jonah, telling him a little more about the way in which our method of sampling was designed to give a general but useful picture of the forests of this enormous region. In the Acarai the myriad species almost certainly represented a survival of very ancient primeval forest types, perhaps even, though changed, with their constituent plants,

[1] *Pouteria.*   [2] *Trymatococcus.*

of those archetypal forests in which the higher plants had evolved. Few such remote, undisturbed forests had ever been examined ecologically, but in the brief time at my disposal what could I do to justify myself? However hard I worked, what were my few hundred specimens, my few plots, when one could walk miles without seeing the same tree twice? Perhaps I should have stayed at the mission? Yet each time I moved I was lured onwards again, and each time found something strange and rich to reward me. Already Jonah and I sensed that we were in forests a little different from those of the Acarai. They showed signs, at least near the trail, of disturbance in many places—and, despite the difference in species, indefinably reminded us of the British Guiana lowlands.

When we had finished, in the late sunlight I strolled up the path to the village, Icaro following me at a distance. Outside and inside, except for a greater perfection of finish, there was little to distinguish it from the houses of the Wai-Wais. There was the same remarkable utilization of space—the storage lofts, the hanging shelves, the various objects stuck in the thatch, the dog platforms. Culturally the tribes of the region were on much the same level: such close similarities showed that they must have imitated and learned from each other.

After taking a photograph I went outside. At once there was a loud cough, much rattling of sticks and palm leaves, and up came Icaro, very casually as if to show that he had not been watching, but carrying his cutlass in his hand. For a moment I was a little apprehensive. What did he suspect? Perhaps it was simply bad manners to have entered the house without his permission? Such a slight misunderstanding of motive could be as serious as a genuine offence.

I smiled, and pointed to various trees round the clearing, saying, "*Atchi? atchi?*"—asking their names in Wai-Wai; then re-entered the house with him, saying "*Kiriwanhi*"—good—about various things, and with gestures questioned him about their uses.

He relaxed a little.

Then I noticed a faint prickling sensation, and felt a series of light taps on the calves of my legs: they were covered with jiggers, and more and more were landing every minute. Like minute springs, each about the size of half a lentil, they came hopping across the floor—plop! plop! plop!—towards us.

Stamping hard we both ran outside, brushing them off with our hands. We looked at each other and laughed, and while I took off my shoes and searched about in my clothes he fetched a soft, deliciously juicy pineapple, which we shared.

I began to like him again. He was a generous host, his suspicions of my medicines were, after all, only natural considering their strangeness and taste, and his cruelty towards animals was the common callousness of all these Indians towards pain, even when suffering it themselves.

Seeing his good humour I pulled the folder of maps out of my haversack and began questioning him about the names on them. I had very little idea of where we were. So far as I could guess, however, we were heading towards a large, low, upland region between the Mapuera and the Trombetas rivers called the Serra Irikoumé—certainly one of the most isolated places left on the face of the globe.

"Irikoumé?" I asked.

He thought, then slowly shook his head. He did not recognize the word.

"Itapi, Itapi-wau, Itapi-yoku?"—the name of a river.

"Itapi: Kura-kura." He laid two fingers side by side and pointed down the hill.

The Itapi, marked on one of my maps far to the south, flowing into the Trombetas, and on another as the name for the lower course of one of the two parallel "Mapueras", was evidently the same as the Kura-kura, a mile or two away, of which the Napmanana was probably a tributary. "Kura-kura-nawa" was marked on this map also, somewhat to the south of what I estimated our present position to be. Farabee had visited a village of that name, doubtless situated beside the river. It was exciting to discover this faint link with a past explorer, to feel in consequence not quite so lost in an amorphous wilderness.

"Casuro-wau?"

He pointed vaguely to the east; then shook his head.

"Fishkaliena?"

Slightly west of south.

"Emayena?"—the name of his tribe.

He pointed south again, but this time a little eastwards, and waved his hand away from him to show that it was a long, long way to them. From his manner it seemed that they were a separate tribe.

I pointed east:

"Mawayán," said he.

"*Anoro?*"

But he did not know of any other tribes in that direction. North, north-west, south, south-west? But each time he shook his head and shrugged his shoulders.

Later, wrapped in a towel, I was returning from a dip in the mosquito-ridden Napmanana when, like a couple of bombs, in the wildest high spirits, Fonyuwé and Yapumo burst into the camp, rushed up to me and dug me in the ribs with shouts of "Mawayán! Mawayán!" to indicate that I had been adopted into the tribe; then away to shake up everyone else.

Basil and Foimo, who had been resting after their journey, came to me after dark, as I was eating a dinner of yams and fish.

"Fonyuwé is very excited," said Basil. "He says everyone is waiting for us at the Mawayán villages. They have prepared a big welcome, with plenty of food and drink."

"Good!" I exclaimed. "Let us start early. When will we get there?"

"We should reach by noon."

There were many questions that I had not had time or opportunity to ask Foimo about his own tribe:

"What happen to Foimo after all the other Tarumas were killed off?"

"He and his brother leave everything and go to the savannah, because they knew some Wapisianas from trading with them, and live there until just about five years ago. Then they leave because it was growing too civilized. So they came to the Mawayáns because their language is close to Wapisiana, so that they could understand it well."

"What about Kilimtu?"

"He was only a small boy at the time of the influenza epidemic. Some Wai-Wais take him across to the Mapuera and he live there until they move into B.G. He don't even know how to speak Taruma."

Heavy rain began to fall—quite exceptionally heavy, and Fonyuwé, Yapumo, and Mark, who had been sitting outside, crowded under the tarpaulin. Then a humming and throbbing arose—a most extraordinary wild, dynamo-like sound—from the direction of the valley of the Kura-kura: a whirlwind, the second one we had heard, but this time very near, and drawing closer.

For ten minutes we sat while the noise steadily increased, till an atrocious groaning and crackling and crashing filled the whole world. The lantern shone brightly on the glossy red-striped faces of the Indians, catching cheekbones and temples. Outside was darkness, tangled impenetrable forest, torrential rain. The monstrous flailing mill was dragging trees out of the ground, shattering them to fragments. A human being would be scrunched in an instant in a vortex of flying timber.

Then, when it was seemingly only a few hundred yards off, the noise began slowly to recede, until it was out of hearing.

We resumed our discussion.

"What was the chief difference between the way the Tarumas and the other tribes lived?"

"Foimo says that one time the Tarumas used to have separate houses, but a long time ago they decide it is better for all the people in a village to live in one big house. Another thing is they lived much longer in one place than the other tribes."

"What about the Wai-Wais and Mawayáns?"

"The Mawayáns are much nearer the Tarumas. They stay far longer in one place, but the Wai-Wais are always moving about. They make a new village every two or three years.[1] They are a very restless and quarrelsome bunch of people. But people of each tribe usually live in just one neighbourhood, a good way from other people—they don't like to live close to another village because they are frightened they may quarrel

[1] The Paripi palm, *Astrocaryum munbaca*, found only in cultivation and taking several years to fruit, is typical of abandoned Taruma settlements. The Mawayáns, as I learned later, grow nothing slower-fruiting than Anatto, *Bixa orellana* (three years), a small tree or shrub; the Wai-Wais than bananas and papaws (one year).

and fight one another. So they choose a place they like, and they cuts their fields all around. Then they get tired of it and move somewhere else, but not too far away."

All these tribes, even the savannah-dwelling Wapisianas, use the same methods of agriculture: they find an area of forest land above the level of floods, fell the forest, burn the debris, and plant their crops on the rich soils exposed. Then about three years later they abandon this field and clear another patch of forest.

Why, one wonders at first, do they not continue cultivating the old field, when it is so much trouble to fell the forest— whose timber they do not even use? The answer lies in the nature of the forest soils. Above flood-level in this part of the tropics they are what are called "lateritic earths", and their fertility, though extremely high at first, disappears within three or four years of clearing. No method of keeping them under continuous cultivation has ever been found—if it were, we could happily increase the world's population by half again. They become as sterile as a heap of bricks, and fertilizer will not restore them: even fifty tons an acre would be wasted, washed away in the first few rains, because their structure is such that they do not hold the nutrients. Only under the shelter of forest, protected from drying sun and eroding rain, do these soils develop and retain any worthwhile degree of fertility. Then a layer of rich organic matter accumulates slowly, over many years, in the top few inches—hence the spreading roots of the forest trees, in effect feeding on their own litter—and it is this that gives these soils their initial productivity. Clearing and burning liberate the nutrients in this layer, but also expose them to erosion, and in a few short seasons they are washed away.

Where the population is low and a field is abandoned as soon as its yield begins to drop, forest springs up quickly again on lateritic earths—second growth forest to begin with, then, over hundreds of years, the primary jungle; the rich top layer builds up again, and fertility is restored. Under these con- ditions the Indian practice of clearing, cultivating and abandoning is the wisest and best method of agriculture that has been evolved for dealing with them, except that it wastes the trees and involves an enormous amount of labour for a relatively low return. But where the population is high the soil often is overcultivated and so damaged that forest comes back only slowly and perhaps in a debased form, or may not be able to return at all, but is replaced by grasslands which will no longer support crops of trees.

Yet, by planting certain trees even savannah grassland soils have been restored, and by alternating trees with crops on strict long-term rotations soil degeneration need never take place, and a high population can be supported. Such a rotation system may, some day, make Amazonia a great region of agricultural as well as timber production. Meanwhile, it is an expensive system, and there are other and better soils at hand, fertile and high-yielding, which can be planted year after year, but which the Indians never use because they lack the necessary knowledge: the alluvial soils of the river valleys, periodically inundated, the cultivation of which requires a system of flood control and irrigation.

Without strict, scientific rotation, it is inconceivable that the cultivation of lateritic soils could support a large population in the forest without converting huge areas into second-growth or even savannah. Otherwise big, permanent, self-supporting settlements can only be expected in lateritic areas where there is a knowledge of irrigation. A lost city in the Amazonian jungle almost certainly presupposes somewhere the existence of irrigation works; and, except perhaps among mountains, where simple damming and terracing might be sufficient to produce regular high yields in a small area, such irrigation works would have to be on an enormous scale because of the heavy rainfall and vast inundations—for all of which reasons—without conspicuous damage to the forest or a fundamental change in the character and economy of the Indians—no "Big Village" of thousands or even hundreds of people seemed to me at all likely or possible in the unbroken forests of this region of northeastern Amazonia.

Yet, the legend still had its fascination, and the name "Kashima" still seemed to mean something.

At its mention Foimo now pointed south, towards the lower Mapuera: was it the name of a real village, perhaps quite small, but magnified by distance? Was it perhaps a place that someone

had visited years before, and the story of which had changed
as it was passed from mouth to mouth—a small Brazilian town,
or a place like Karardanawa, the Wapisiana capital, a village
of about two hundred people, whose existence yearly caused
the destruction of much forest and the spread of savannah?

There were so many stories afloat in this closed world where
a man seldom sees more than a few yards—what about the
Indians who lived under water? Fonyuwé was quite carried
away when I asked about them—he waved his arms wildly and
told about a tribe who lived far away on the River Casuro,
who had colossal arms and legs, as big as the trunks of trees.
The Water Indians were *nothing* to these, he said.

At first I thought he was trying to tease me. Then I saw that
he was serious. Perhaps at the back of his mind he believed in
such things, beyond the borders of his known world? After all,
outboard motors and aeroplanes were stranger still, and *they*
existed. His father, mother, uncles, aunts, had told him tales—
how could he tell if they were true? I had asked: he simply
repeated what he had heard.

16

The Mawayán Capital

The Welcome

We had not walked for half an hour when we saw two Indians approaching, one a tall man with a kindly face painted all over a smooth dark red, carrying a hand of bananas and several rounds of cassava cake, the other a small, slim, and fiery individual who pranced along like a Nijinsky, bearing a bowl of drink. With breath-taking magnificence he flung out his arm in welcome when he saw us.

They had come with offerings to entice us forward: greetings were exchanged, and we sat down for a few minutes and ate and drank.

There was about the smaller man's face, as about his figure and movements, something quite extraordinary. His tousled curly hair,[1] his delicate aquiline countenance, his huge burning sparkling black eyes—he was the revolutionary, the poet. Thirty years younger, in a butterfly collar, he could have been Shelley at Oxford.

Sometimes, as we talked, he looked at me, his head on one side, nodding, considering me. With Foimo I had felt in the presence of a strong mind, but with Kwakwé—for it was Foimo's brother, the third surviving Taruma—it was the rarest, firmest intelligence that glanced out of those eyes.

When we rose he led the way, walking again with that wonderful freedom and grace that I had first noticed—like an angel in a drawing of William Blake's.

Nowhere were there signs of destruction from the previous night's storm: even from the crest of the hill, as we passed through the village field, there was not a missing tree in the

[1] Like Foimo, he wore his hair nape length, not in a pigtail.

whole circumference of forest. But then its track could so easily be hidden by the thinnest line of trees.

Suddenly, as I saw Foimo, Kwakwé, Fonyuwé, Yapumo, Icaro, all leaping along the path ahead, I felt an inward burst of exultation. What a short-sighted creature I was, I thought— so wrapped up in the cares of the expedition that I had forgotten all the joys of life!

The Mawayáns, it had begun to dawn upon me, were *thrilled* by our visit! For them, in their isolation, it was one of the most exciting of all possible events. They had rounded us up like a travelling circus and were bringing us to show to all their friends and relatives: a white man, such as only the two Tarumas and their chief had seen before, and a black man, Charles Tanner, an even stranger creature, of whose kind the merest rumours had reached them. Now, phenomena rare as comets, we were approaching their villages, and soon all that anyone had ever heard would be consummated in our persons! No wonder they were so lighthearted! No wonder such promises had been used to lure us forward—of food, and drink, and dancing, and wonderful things to buy, such as I had seemed to want (only better), and savannahs, and a big, BIG, village.

The forest lightened: low hills, swampy places, an abandoned and a newly planted field, a hunting hide—a sentry-box of palm leaves in which men with bows and arrows could watch for game walking along the path—then a stream, and in the distance the sound of barking. Here Kwakwé told us to leave our burdens and make our camp; and while we washed and tidied ourselves, and the wilder Indians put on paint, he went forward to herald our coming.

Beyond a field of about forty acres, newly burnt, with silvery logs twisting upon crisp blackened earth, the land rose to a ridge from which we saw the distant turquoise dome of a mountain. A few yards further, at the entrance to a path between low bushes entwined by a passion vine bursting with big bluish-purple flowers, like gas flames,[1] Kwakwé met us, playing on his flute a greeting to which our own flautists replied.

Amidst a panic-stricken dog-barking we entered the village:

[1] *Passiflora pedata.*

at a glance I could see that it was quite unlike any other we had come across, standing in a small area of smooth-swept bare earth, surrounded by its gardens.

All the people were in a cluster, silent or talking in low tones. Yapumo led me forward at once and introduced me and then each of the men to the chief, his grandfather. Then one by one the people of the village came up as I stood next to the chief, each man with his wife and children, and I shook hands with them all, even the babies-in-arms dressed in their scarlet feather earrings; and passing me, they went on to greet the rest of our party.

As I watched the introductions proceed I realized, with humility, how charmingly and warmly they were playing their part of hosts, welcoming as friends and equals a group of strangers to their village. There was none of the slight awkwardness of a first meeting with the Wai-Wais, or of the glum inferiority of the "civilized" Indians. They had their own code of manners—natural, informal, without gravity, yet with both grace and dignity. Courtesy could not have been more perfect. Beside their scanty, painted neatness, I felt a shambles in my khaki shirt and shorts, tennis-shoed and bearded.

Four basins of earthenware, glazed a shining dark brown or red and delicately striped and zigzagged in black, were set on the ground in our midst. From man to man they were handed in a circle, so heavy that I nearly dropped the first—containing about three gallons—when it reached me.

I drank: in it was a rich thick purple liquid made from crushed yams. I was frantically hungry. For days I had had little to eat and no meat at all. A syrupy banana drink, pineapple juice, a cool, sweet mixture of cane juice and fermented cassava meal, followed; then a bowl of meat stew, very peppery, in which I dipped cassava bread.

I began to feel wonderfully replete.

Once the drinking had begun, men and women resumed their tasks and we were free to perambulate, returning when we wished to the bowls, which were kept replenished by an old woman.

There were two chief houses, the main one, in which about six families lived, circular, its roof forming a low shallow cone exactly like an immense Chinese coolie's hat on stilts. It was completely open all round, unlike the Wai-Wai or Taruma houses, and was consequently much lighter, airier, and pleasanter to be in. The fireplaces were near the sides, from which the smoke escaped (there was no central smoke-hole), and the dog-shelves were low so that their occupants could peer outside. In a special lean-to, attached to the side of the house, a monkey, a marmoset, and two dogs lived, leashed, on a couple of broad shelves of sticks.

This openness of construction bespoke a greater sense of security from man, beast, or spirit than among the Wai-Wais, and as if to support this, the house appeared to be prodigiously old for a wooden thatched building in these parts. All its interior timbers were covered in a hard, shiny layer of smoke blackening, so thick that a penknife had to do much scratching to reach the wood beneath. It might have been built, I guessed, twenty, even fifty years before; and the whole region, to judge from the abandoned fields we had passed on our approach, had certainly been settled for generations—perhaps hundreds of years.

The second house, evidently the guest-house, was smaller, and similar in shape except that a triangular section (like a big slice cut from a cake) was missing from the roof, and had been built on at an angle, as if hinged out from the main circle, giving an open space in the centre where work was done in fine weather. In it stood a small square wooden frame on which a man's lap, or loin-cloth, was being woven from cotton thread; and all around the apparatus of cassava preparation, placed conveniently for use.

Besides these two houses there were a number of small shelters containing baskets and pots (some up to four feet in diameter) and several rectangular frameworks of poles on which, produced for our consumption, vast numbers of white discs of cassava bread, like enormous oatcakes, were drying in the sun.

Mountains of cassava roots had been dug, and everywhere the women were furiously at work preparing it for eating. It is hard to guess how the use of this vegetable, the staple food of tropical South America, was ever discovered, for it is virulently poisonous unless its juice, which contains prussic acid, is extracted. First the roots are grated into a coarse moist meal, which is sieved to remove large fragments and then packed into long basket-work tubes hung from the rafters of the houses. These have a loop at the bottom through which a stick is placed, and on this the utmost leverage is exerted to elongate the tubes and squeeze the contents until the last drop has dripped out. Then the meal, almost dry, is sieved again, and spread on earthenware griddle discs where it is baked into the white rounds of bread; while the deadly juice, after repeated boilings, forms an excellent dark brown condiment and pre-servative, used in all the Indian stews, called cassareep.

Tanner and I strolled together, and wherever we went we were greeted with friendly smiles. Frequently the Indians would produce articles for us to admire, and then press them into our hands. Yapumo, beckoning, led me to his hammock, and from the thatch above pulled out a six-foot bow of pink-tinted wood, a sheaf of arrows as long, a pair of wristlets, a pigtail-tube, a quiver of poisoned arrow-tips.

"These people must really like us! It seems like we can have anything we want—only trouble is when they ask for something we can't spare," said Tanner thoughtfully. "You mus' hide your camera, sir, in case dey might ask for it."

"What are you getting that pigtail-tube for?" I questioned.

A shy smile flitted over his features. "Sometimes we give fancy-dress party where I lives. I go wear it—den you will see fun!"

The sky was azure, cloudless, the sun vertical: later, when it was lower, the day would be perfect for colour photography. I resolved therefore to return as soon as I had unpacked at our camp by the stream, because the weather had been so uncertain that I might never have another chance.

At 3.30, just when the angle was right, I set forth back to the village, but as I left a dozen Mawayáns arrived and Basil came running after me: they had come to visit me, he explained and, as we were their guests, and depended upon their good will, it would be a good thing if we paid them at once for the various articles we had taken and all the food they had prepared for us.

I was annoyed, but I could do nothing except try to pay them as quickly as possible. So I unlocked the trade goods and began

measuring out the beads. A hiss of amazement: I was a millionaire again, a bead-Croesus, an inconceivably wealthy and
powerful man, as I counted out the fish-hooks, knives, files,
safety-pins, before their delighted gaze, while they clustered
round or wandered, examining my possessions as I had theirs.

Then, when the settlement was over, there was still no escape:
the charming creatures produced a bowl of drink. In unutter-
able contentment at all they had acquired they settled themselves down and slowly the bowl was handed around from man
to man—the wives remaining in the background, one with a
tiny fish clasped in her hand, another a small boy who clambered all over her, or stood at her side, all the time holding
one of her nipples between finger and thumb.

I was beside myself: I looked up—the long shadow of the
forest had crept right across the newly cleared field and was
almost at the hillcrest, beyond which lay the village. The light
was almost gone!

To everyone's astonishment, and with abominable manners,
I sprang to my feet and strode off rapidly towards the village
with my haversack of cameras. Suddenly I realized how badly
I had behaved. I looked back: they were following, a long way
behind. There was nothing for it—I walked on; but at the
village all work had ceased and the sun had sunk so low that
it was useless even to attempt to take a picture.

I was disappointed, ashamed of myself, and unsuccessful.
There was only one thing to do, and that was to try to make
amends. When the little straggling group arrived I smiled
brightly, pointed at everything and said "*kiriwanhi*" cheerfully
over and over again. With gestures I tried to explain to Yapumo how much I liked the village and preferred its open-sided
houses to the ones I had seen before. I teased Kirifakka on his
long plain bamboo pigtail-tube, pointed to it, twiddled my
fingers and pretended to blow down it as if it were also a
flute, and feigned surprise when no sound came.

At that they laughed, and we sat down together in front of
the big house. Kwakwé, who had looked especially worried,
began to feel more comfortable, and soon he too smiled. He
realized that I was sorry and had not meant to hurt anyone's
feelings.

Such an act as mine, among the Indians of convention, might have meant war. Hide-bound savages exist, but the Mawayáns at least were not among them. If at a pow-wow I had refused to smoke the Pipe of Peace (presuming they possessed such a thing) I am sure they would have thought simply, "Well—perhaps he doesn't want to smoke." Rigidity would have been much more likely near a mission, where an alien morality has been forced on the people. Often I had noticed, at semi-civilized villages, how at my appearance—a strange white man —the Indians would become self-conscious: their face muscles taughten, their thoughts become hidden, a mask cover all their feelings. They would withdraw out of reach, and only slowly later emerge as they saw that I had come as a friend, and not to judge them, or bully them, or cheat them, or stop them enjoying themselves in their own way.

Among so many strange new faces I had almost forgotten Kwakwé, yet glancing up, I saw him watching all I did: his eyes lighted, with an instant and flickering change a smile spread across his face, he waved, elegantly, and was transformed—an Ariel, whose every move was an arabesque. He was extraordinary—it was hard to believe that such cultivation could exist in the jungle. It was something only found, surely, in old civilizations?

Other travellers have surmised, from the perfection of their manners, that the Indians of the remotest South American forests are refugees of higher cultures driven into their fastnesses by barbaric, more warlike and materially successful tribes—and perhaps they are. Yet there are so many different groups, apparently unrelated, with graceful manners, that to postulate the former existence of a higher culture for each is absurd: it is more profitable to look to the environment. What could there be in common between life in those civilized circles where manners are held at a premium, and in these inaccessible forests? Most likely, it seemed, a relative stability—for everywhere, whatever their degree of polish, good manners must be based upon consideration for others, and therefore upon at least some lessening of the struggle for personal pre-eminence; and if there was one profound difference between the world of the forest Indians and that of our civilization which will soon overwhelm it, it was that while in the latter ambition is so important that it is hard to conceive of existence without it, in the former it is almost absent. And it was precisely this lack of struggle between men, I believe, that produced the happy, beautifully mannered societies of the forest depths.

Wide horizons—grasslands, mountain ranges, the sea—are what stir men's minds. Here, where one can seldom see a hundred yards, where the forest, limitless as far as the imagination can reach, overwhelms and encloses, the mental horizon is also restricted, and it is impossible to conceive of a great civilization arising or flourishing. People live in small groups, presumably compatible; there is little or no tribal cohesion or organization—it would seem absurd. One man is as good as another, there are no heights to scale, needs are simple, any man can make all the things he requires, and his wants as a living creature are fully and easily satisfied. The smoothness and pleasantness of life is the most important thing of all, and good manners is the oil that makes it run easily.

Civilization, viewed from the forest, is a neurosis, its progress measurable by such things as the incidence of sudden death from hypertension.[1] The pity is that in its advance its more beneficial aspects are usually seen only after these old, rich but weak societies have succumbed to the assault of the crude destructive elements which it throws ahead.

Away from other men these people obtained directly in life much that is obscured by our own mode of existence, and for which in our moments of weakness we still yearn: they had life itself, instead of the earning of money; happiness instead of ambition, manners instead of drive, simplicity instead of increasing complexity. By living among such people, isolated, harmonious, a civilized man could never escape from his own mental world; yet from the comparisons to be made there he might learn much about the value of his own ways.

A few yards away Yapumo had moved to his hammock, where he lay, fondly stroking the cheek of his tiny shy young wife. They were obviously deeply in love. Though I had never doubted that such sweet and open feelings must exist among

[1] A condition unknown among the forest Indians, according to Dr. Holden, who took the blood pressures of all the tribes he encountered.

the Indians, I had never before been allowed to see them; but here I was accepted as a friend.

Even more wonderful was the sight of the old chief, Waruma's, joy at being again with his grandson Fonyuwé. They reclined facing each other in a hammock, Fonyuwé listening, warbling softly on his flute, the old man chatting gently; then in turn Fonyuwé telling of his adventures while Waruma took the flute and breathed out a few notes: a comfortably built old fellow, not fat, but a strong man beginning to relax, his complexion as pale as many a white man's, his face kindly, with that look of contentment that a simple life sometimes gives to the late middle-aged; and absolutely at peace. His eyes were half-closed and little laughs of bliss from time to time escaped him as he talked or fluted. I thought that I had never seen a man more overflowing with happiness.

I too was happy. It was dark, and flickerings from the fires competed with the fading glow from the sky. A bowl of stew, a few rounds of cassava bread, were brought out by an old woman.

I returned to camp quite late, musing upon what I saw or guessed, wondering how long I could stay, how long keep the men content, and feeling a little uncertain, despite these good beginnings, of the food supply and the future.

Village Life

As I was walking round the village the next day, a furry, long-tailed kibihi, or coatimundi, leaped onto my shoulder and put its arms around my neck. By the time I left, a week later, it had become my devoted companion, and would sit inside my shirt with only its nose poking out, or walk round and round inside above my belt, in an unbearably ticklish way. It was an insect-eater, in temperament half-kitten, half-puppy, restlessly inquisitive in its quest for bugs. Its long, soft, pointed nose would investigate my ear; then a minute later it would jump on to the table of palm slats, scattering my papers—even, on one occasion, blowing into the ink-bottle and drenching me.

Numerous pets roamed the village, as they roam the villages

of most of the Guiana tribes, unconfined (and in the case of birds, with unclipped wings), free to go away and lead independent lives whenever they wish, yet preferring to stay among human beings.

Most conspicuous, perhaps because most active and aggressive, were three trumpeter birds. They would come up softly, stand on one leg and incline their heads to be scratched, yet a moment later one might see one leaping ferociously, with lunging beak and claws, on to the back of some animal. Whenever we returned through the village from a plant-collecting foray they would dash up to inspect the flowers we carried, for they have a great passion for bright colours—and sometimes follow us, gambolling and somersaulting, darting at the blossoms and displaying their wings, for several hundred yards.

Three monkeys—two very intelligent ring-tailed capuchins and a large black female spider-monkey (affectionate and cuddlesome, but so mischievous that it was mostly kept tied up)—roamed the rafters and roof-tops, while a fourth, a baby howler whose mother had been shot for food and which the Indians were trying to rear, was kept in a wooden cage. It was a gentle little creature which clung as if for life to one's hand, pathetic to see because howlers never survive long in captivity. Occasionally it would open its mouth into an O, throb its throat, and give a tiny growl, the merest embryo of the wonderful soaring song of the adults.

Sitting bolt upright, bright-eyed and alert, or nuzzling bits of debris on the ground, were four creatures, each about a foot long, like miniature barrage balloons in shape but with the soft, puzzled faces of Thurber dogs: baby capybaras. They grow to be the world's largest rodents, about as big as a large dog, but even when adult remain tame. They become so possessive towards their masters that they will attempt to drive away anyone who speaks to him for too long. These were long past the suckling stage, yet whenever I sat near one it would approach, take a finger in its mouth as soon as I patted it, and remain attached, gently chewing and sucking. Sometimes I would stay with fingers spread for half an hour, giving bliss to all four; but one day I proffered a pencil, and with a snick its end was removed—there was no doubt that they had well-developed incisors, and henceforth I was more cautious.

Several powis or curassows, stupid, turkey-sized black birds with snowy breasts, bright yellow legs and beaks, and crisp curly black crests, wandered pensively, inquisitive but with troubled eye, as if realizing what excellent eating they were. Almost as good were the various maroudis or guans: smaller and slenderer, black with red or white wattles (or, in the case of the smallest kind, the hannaqua, of an overall olive-green), they sat quietly most of the day in the rafters of the houses, but in the early morning flew from branch to branch around the clearing with harsh cries and weirdly rattling wings—looking, with their short stubby wings and long rounded tails, like reconstructions of early fossil birds. But the commonest village birds were, of course, the parrots, of which there were about eight, and the macaws, of which there were four: glorious green, yellow, scarlet, or blue fellows who walked solemnly about in the dust or clambered over the houses. One parrot—a small, very friendly green and yellow bird with a black head, which uttered a short, sharp cry to call attention to itself whenever I passed —was of a type unknown to me, but perhaps common in Amazonia.

A pair of toucans completed the list of tame creatures at the Mawayán capital. Other villages to which I had been had had more pets, including deer, pacas, peccaries, ocelots, jaguars, agoutis, parakeets, hawks, owls, ducks, cotingas, even half-grown tapirs, the largest mammals of the South American continent. Indeed, at one time or another I had seen tame practically all the large, edible, or unusual creatures of the region—sometimes only the young as in the case of the various cats or the tapir,[1] but more often adults as well. Some, un-

---

[1] Jonah knew of the case of a fully-grown tapir, several years old, living in the forest near a village on the Pomeroon, which still occasionally returned to visit its former owners there; and I once saw at an Arawak village an ocelot which I was told had been kept for nearly a year—a beautiful beast with its soft thick fur and rich coloration of browns and yellows, which during the day was seldom far from its owner's house, usually lying lengthwise along a rafter or branch—so difficult to see because of its perfect immobility that recognition often produced a shock—but was still willing to be handled, if undemonstrative.

doubtedly, were kept purely as pets; baby animals perhaps helped satisfy the strong maternal yearnings of the frequently childless Indian women; trumpeters acted as watch animals—guardians against spirits, jaguars, and human enemies; macaws and parrots provided feathers, used in headdresses and other ornaments—they were, as a result, frequently rather moth-eaten-looking—while there were possibly beliefs, such as those known to occur elsewhere, connecting the prosperity of the family with the health of its animals, or the possession of animals with the propitiation of the spirits of their species. Yet most, and certainly all the more edible of the tame creatures (curassows, guans, trumpeters, deer, tapirs, peccaries, capybaras) were without doubt largely kept as a reserve of food—the Indian equivalent of refrigeration.

It is a curious fact that captivity nearly always made these birds and animals sterile: there might be plenty of adults of both sexes in a village, but only rarely did they breed, and none, therefore, could be considered domesticated. Perhaps, one wondered, our own domesticates—dogs, cattle, geese, horses, ducks, chickens,[1] etc.—were also kept originally, together with other species, primarily for food, and were selected simply because they continued to breed in captivity? There are many species apparently just as suitable as some we use—the powis, for example, as tractable and far more delicious than the turkey—which are not widely kept largely because they have not crossed this psychological barrier.

But how could one account for the Indians' success in taming, perhaps unparalleled elsewhere? Either the South American jungle animals by nature must be particularly easily tameable, or the Indians must have some secret—only those animals and birds apparently least intelligent (such as sloths, opossums, tinamous) seemed unamenable.

With baby creatures attention, tenderness and care were undoubtedly the important factors. Creatures scarcely emerged from the womb or egg—parakeetlets the size of a finger-tip,

---

[1] Chickens certainly, and domesticated dogs probably, are not native to South America. I did not see chickens among the Mawayáns, but the Wai-Wais kept a few for their feathers, crowing, and pugnacity. Neither the birds nor their eggs were eaten.

baby humming-birds no bigger than peas—were taken back to the villages and reared to adulthood: newly-born mammals were suckled by the women, birds fed with pre-chewed cassava bread forced into their beaks, or even directly from the women's own mouths, in imitation of the mother birds; and if a creature were naturally shy or savage it was given to many people to handle, so that it became accustomed to human beings. Yet despite this there seemed to be little *kindness* as we understand it: animals were shot in the hopes of merely wounding them (sometimes with arrows coated with a non-lethal amount of curare), mother animals killed to get their young, nests robbed and all the fledglings destroyed except the one or two wanted. And while the pets were often affectionate towards their masters, the Indians, at least the men, lost interest in them once they had grown up, and might even be savagely brutal. Once I tried to stop some Wapisianas using a tame deer which had broken a leg for target practice with bow and arrow, but nothing I said was of avail. Just as the Indians are stoical or indifferent to their own sufferings, so they could not understand why anyone should object to the maltreatment of an animal. So for an hour, because care was taken not to hit the deer in a vital place, the sport continued, until at last it died of its wounds.

Probably the idea of cruelty does not even arise to the Indians—the means are simply directed towards the ends. This attitude is shown in the taming of adult birds or animals—a treatment designed to produce submission: they are put in darkness in a box or under a large bowl for a day or two without food or water, and at the end of that time, if still alive, are usually prepared to eat and make friends. Then their faces are rubbed into the owners' armpit or smeared with his red body paint so that they get to know his smell, and they are released.

Nothing else seems necessary: thereafter, though perhaps wary of strangers, they are usually attached to their master and his family, come when called, allow themselves to be picked up, and return home even after long foraging trips into the forest. They are never treated in any special way, but along with dogs and children form part of the family, move when it moves, and share its food. And undoubtedly this casualness, together with the Indians' feeling of the nearness of man and animal (as exemplified by the women's suckling of young mammals), and the open-air existence so intimately connected with their former natural environment, contribute to the ready acceptance by these animals of their new existence.

The day after our arrival one of the Mawayáns, called Yuhmé, a fussy, oldish man, set forth to bring the rest of the tribe—two people, from what I could gather—from the distant mountain where they lived, intending to return on the morrow; Kwakwé, the best fisherman, went fishing, and Ka'i, a tall, handsome, rather grave man of about twenty-five, came to lead us to the two savannahs of which we had heard.

He was a splendid figure as he strode ahead of us, red-painted from head to toe. We were crossing the newly burnt field towards the village, when in the very centre I saw a spot of green—a single young cassava plant, newly inserted in the ground.

"What is it doing there?" I asked through Basil.

"It is planted to deceive animals. All the time that men have been working here, clearing, and cutting trees and burning trash, the animals in the forest have been watching—deer, and porcupines, and pigs and armadillos and bush cows [tapirs] and every sort of animal, come to see what is happening. And they have all been saying to themselves 'this looks like it is going to be a field full of good things. We must come back and eat them.'

"So just as soon as the ground cool the Indians takes one plant only, and puts it right in the middle. Then, when the animals come out to see what there is, all they find is this one small plant. So they don't bother with it—you see, nothing has touched it. They just say to themselves 'this place is no good'— and they never come back. But if you were to put nothing in they would return again when you plant up and eat everything."

Beyond the village, to my surprise, the ground underfoot began to change. Soon we might have been in the lowlands of British Guiana, for we were walking upon the peculiar soil of that region: a beautiful, loose, snowy-white or pale brown sand with rounded grains. I had last seen such sands 350 miles to the north of the Serra Acarai, many months before; and now here they were again some thirty miles to the south. If they were in origin the same as those in British Guiana, it might be a very exciting piece of evidence in support of my belief in the isolation of the Serra Acarai above the sea in Ice Age times, and the antiquity of their forests. But how could I be sure?

Long before the Ice Age a vast plateau of sandstone covered the greater part of northern South America, overlying the harder and more ancient crystalline and volcanic rocks of which the Acarai Mountains are an elevated part. Over millions of years this plateau has worn away, exposing those older land surfaces again, until today all that is left of it is the Pakaraima Range, between Venezuela, Brazil and British Guiana, and a number of isolated mesas in the forest. From its erosion came the British Guiana sands. Particle by particle they were washed down from the uplands by rivers, and sorted as they rolled along—the larger grains moving more slowly—until, when they reached the great shallow sea (called by geologists the White Sand Sea) that once covered what are now the lowlands, they were deposited in thick, loose-lying layers of very even grain-size. Then, when the lowlands emerged from the sea, these layers of sand were themselves subjected to erosion, so that now they form a gently rolling plain at most a few hundred feet above sea-level, with steep gullies where the rivers have cut back into them. Their original colour of pale brown has been washed out in most places, leaving them a glistening white; and high forests cover them—forests very distinctive in character, for not all trees flourish on loose, free-draining sands.

In some places they have been washed away completely again, while in others merely the thinnest layer of them remains over the underlying rocks. But to a geologist this is enough to enable him to reconstruct the history of the region, if he can be sure that they are true sands of the White Sand Sea—for confusingly, the underlying rocks, if granites or gneisses, themselves sometimes break down into sands which may also be white and, if they have been sorted by a modern river, of even grain-size. Fortunately there is one fairly consistent criterion— the White Sand Sea sands are rounded, the others angular.

Bending down, I ran a handful through my fingers, then

looked closely at a few grains: they were rounded! But a few yards further the soil changed to a typically granitic sand—and the previous patch was too small to draw any conclusions from.

Then we stepped out into the savannah: before us an expanse of meadow curved away for about a hundred yards, bordered on all sides with yellow and purple blossomed bushes,[1] and backed, in the distance, by a line of palms.

"This is the big savannah," translated Basil.

"But it is quite small," I said; "besides, I thought it was supposed to be on top of a mountain?"

"We *are* on top of a mountain—this is Shiuru-dicta, or Shiuru palm mountain, and the village is Shiuru-tirir—the place of the Shiuru palm, which grows around here. But there is a higher mountain far away. Yuhmé has gone to fetch the people who live there."

The ground was covered with thick sedges among which slim herbs held their heads—grasses, xyrids like minute primrose-yellow flags, green- or purple-flowered *Polygala Timoutou*, wiry stemmed *Utricularias* with flowers like almost microscopic pinkish-mauve orchids, melastomes with hairy leaves and mauve petals. It was a delight, a relief, to walk free of the all-enclosing forest, to stand under the stately *Mauritia* palms and listen to the rustling of their leaves.

In the middle of the open space, on a long low sandy mound four or five inches above the general level, stood clumps and islands of small trees,[2] their branches laden with orchids and spear-leaved bromeliads aflame with vermilion flower spikes. Around them the sand—indubitably white and round-grained— was completely bare, except for a puff or two or a thin crust of lichen,[3] sparse tufts of a curious dry grass-like fern,[4] and a strewing of crisp dead leaves. Such dry bare sandy places occurred in British Guiana only on true White Sand Sea sands, and this small patch was exactly like those there both in structure and species. It was hard to believe that it was the only such patch in the region—there *must* be more, perhaps eastwards on higher ground in the Irikoumé; yet the Indians knew of no others. Could it be that these few square yards in the

[1] *Byrsonima* and *Rhynchanthera*.
[2] *Humiria balsamifera*.
[3] *Cladonia*.
[4] *Schizaea pennula*.

middle of a tiny extent of grassland were the sole relict in this part of Amazonia of a once much wider-spread vegetation?

Through an opening in the bordering bushes we made our way to the small savannah. This, instead of dry and rank, was cool, moist, succulent, full of palms. *Heliconias* and *Costuses* waved banana-like leaves, and underfoot stretched the thickest, moistest, brightest-green carpet of filmy ferns imaginable: *Trichomanes heterophyllum* and *Lindsaya Schomburgkii* in soft tussocks and cushions.

We collected a few specimens, then returned to the village to eat with the Mawayáns—a stew of little red river crabs and fish, and a bowl of pineapple cordial.

Life was so ordered, I noticed, that there was an appearance of leisure. For the men, who on the whole did the work requiring the greatest physical strength (though it might be more sporadic than that of the women), the day's tasks were done—they had been out fishing and hunting before dawn. In a few days or a week, at the first rains, they would begin planting the new field, and then they would be busy enough. Meanwhile, at midday they made bows and arrows, mended various things, wove, or simply lay in their hammocks.

For the women, though the heaviest work—the gathering of vegetables from the fields—had also been done in the cooler, earlier part of the day, there were still children and animals to be looked after, food to be prepared, pottery made, floors swept; yet they too had time for chatting or rest. Their position was obviously a dignified and satisfying one, and the differences between their work and the men's considered appropriate, even enjoyable. There was little disparity in its intellectual level, and there seemed few hard and fast rules, for sometimes either sex could be seen helping the other in its rightful tasks.

I had sometimes sensed a certain harshness in the Wai-Wai men's attitude to their wives, but the Mawayáns were gentle and loving. Only that morning I had noticed how tenderly Ka'i and Kabapböyö, his elder wife (for he had two), seemed to regard each other. When he had arrived to take me to the savannah she had come too, bringing a load of cassava bread for us to eat. A woman was entitled to separate payment for the work she did, but in this case they considered their labours equally divided: she had dug up the tubers and made the bread, he had cleared and planted the field, so I agreed to split the payment between them. But instead of choosing separately, they had consulted each other, and it had been touching to see how she had shared his excitement when I gave him the most coveted thing I possessed—a steel axehead, of which there was only one other in the village, and that very old and blunt.

Now, to my surprise, as we sat drinking, Ka'i drew me aside and handed me a small but very pretty brown terra-cotta bowl, thickly embellished with black stripes.

"It is for you," said Basil, "because this morning you paid him too much for what he did."

As we talked, I watched the village children (about a dozen, the offspring of ten men and ten women) playing games, cuddling their puppies, or helping their parents. They were the prettiest creatures—the little girls in their tiny bead aprons, the little boys in nothing but necklaces and earrings—and full of high spirits—yet it was amazing to see how responsibly they behaved: little girls of three or four, who in civilization would have been scarcely more than delightful but helpless pets, carried still younger children on their hips and washed and fed them, while boys of the same age ran about with large sharp knives in their hands, or stuck naked in their belts, and came to no harm.

The world of the forest Indians—without electrical devices, automobiles, staircases, upper floors—is so much safer, despite its occasional snakes or jaguars, than our own, that almost from the first children can be left untended to explore it, and so much simpler that a child can readily understand it and share nearly the whole of his parents' life. No mysterious or complicated things like money or employment intervene between him and the sources of life's necessities. Food comes from animals, birds, reptiles, fish, which have to be sought and killed, or from vegetables which have to be cultivated; houses are made of trees and leaves—and before long a little boy can help in making a real house. Even the tame animals with which he plays will be important to him in his later life, for upon his knowledge of their ways will depend his success as a hunter.

All this must make the world seem a wonderfully warm and

understandable place, and help the rapid growth of a child's self-confidence; and because the knowledge and skills developed are the same as an adult's, childhood is a direct preparation for adulthood, and not a thing apart. The effect of this is particularly noticeable where sex is concerned. Under the intimate conditions of communal life, copulation, pregnancy and birth are familiar spectacles, and soon form part of a general realistic picture of human and animal behaviour; and because adult practice is plain to see, there can be no development of labyrinths of opposing or inhibiting beliefs, attitudes and practices. As a result, growing up is straightforward, without any of the bewilderment or even misery familiar in civilization. Soon after puberty boys and girls are initiated into adulthood by means of tests of two sorts—of ability to endure pain or discomfort, for both boys and girls, and to shoot straight with bow and arrow, and thus provide meat for wife and family, for boys alone—after passing which girls remain with their parents, but boys become attached to the chief and under his authority, where they have comparatively greater freedom—not that there is much restriction, beyond the general loose rules of conduct of the tribe, upon the freedom of either sex.

For both there follows a period of promiscuity. In civilization, despite the fact that puberty generally occurs earlier in girls than in boys, their sexual life usually begins later, and sometimes does not reach its peak until middle age—a strange distortion, which can probably be accounted for by the fact that the sexual life of adolescent girls is usually suppressed even more strongly than that of boys. But among these Indians, where the right of the adolescent to satisfy his sexual needs is openly acknowledged, the activity of both sexes appears to be parallel. Unmarried girls seldom become pregnant, because there is a knowledge of birth control, and marriage follows as soon as a partner is chosen. The girl makes the choice, showing her acceptance of a particular man by working as his wife. There is no ceremony that I could discover, though there may be an exchange of gifts: the man simply moves his possessions into the girl's father's house, or part of the communal house, and slings his hammock above hers. As soon as possible, dependent on the time of year, he begins cutting and planting a field so that he

THE RAPIDS ABOVE BUNA-WAU MOUTH (*p. 199*)

OMANA-GASHIN (*p. 300*)

THE MAWAYÁNS DANCE

can support her, if he has not one already; and until it bears
he is fed by his father-in-law, for whom in return he works for
a period which varies largely according to his age.

It might seem that as with animals, so with societies, the
higher the type, the longer the period of dependence of the
young—but in civilization this has reached the dangerous stage
of being prolonged beyond sexual maturity. And the attempt
made in civilization to suppress sexual activity and the seeking
of independence—two natural consequences of puberty—in
the interests, ostensibly, of giving greater time for learning and
adaptation, constitutes an even greater attack on the spontaneous maturing of the individual than that which produces
the pet-like helplessness of younger children. The result is the
deranged condition we call adolescence. From studies made in
other societies it seems that the difficulties we associate with it
are not natural at all. Certainly the sexual troubles, the struggle
between the generations, the powerful and occasionally anti-
social combativeness, the awkwardness and ill humour, the
listlessness and evasiveness that result from capitulation to, or
avoidance of, parental authority at a time when naturally it
should be shaken off (the very fact that adolescents are forced
to live at home may sometimes in itself produce delinquency),
all appear to be absent among the young Wai-Wai and Mawayán men and women. Their desire is to learn about the world,
to discover their own position in it and in their society, and to
fit into it as adults and make the best of it—not necessarily to
change it—and in this they are helped clearly and practically
by their elders.

In medieval Europe, when men and women commonly
married as young as do the Mawayáns, adolescence was
probably as simple a period of bodily growth as with them.
Perhaps its struggles are appropriate, even important, to our
age? Just as likely they are damaging.

It is the common theory that sexual energy can be sublim-
ated, or turned into other forms of energy, and that suppression
of the sexual life of adolescents increases the energy available
to the brain, though it may retard the maturing of character.
If this were true one would expect in civilization a greater
mental vigour in women—in whom suppression is much more

extreme—than in men; yet the opposite is the case: it is only where women have comparable freedom that they attain equality, as here among the Mawayáns at a simple level. This alone suggests that there is a fallacy in the theory of sublimation, and that a vigorous sexual and mental life usually go together— that neglect or suppression of a bodily need lowers vitality.

Fortunately suppression is seldom completely successful, for the sexual needs of adolescents are so powerful that boys nearly always, girls frequently, find means of satisfying them.[1] But if only because they have to be furtive in civilization, these means are undesirable, while at worst they may be permanently damaging—though other factors, such as heredity, may be as important as upbringing in originating perversions, deviations and neuroses. Homosexuality and bestiality are both known to occur among the semi-civilized Wapisianas—by most of whom, however, to judge by their joking references to them, they are despised—but during the long periods when the various tribes-men of my party were separated from women there were no signs of them. From what I observed, and from all the stories and discussions I heard, desire seemed centred entirely on the opposite sex, at least among the Wai-Wais and Mawayáns— which is hardly surprising considering the firm directional push towards heterosexuality given after puberty, and the freedom of both sexes to indulge it. And this view is supported by the loose nature of these tribes' polygamy, in which when there are more men than women, women have several husbands, and vice versa. Even in their mythology, where stories of sexual intercourse between humans and animals are common, I heard none involving homosexuality.

Kofiri joined us, a boy of about twelve with that extremely well-brought-up look which had first impressed me, among these Indians, in Manaka. Like many of the Indian boys, he was married to a woman much older than himself—Mawa ("Frog", a salutary name for such an enormous ugly woman) being twenty, if not thirty years older.

In civilization most people would have regarded such a

[1] Precocity is often associated with early sexual activity. Though the advantage sometimes disappears in later life, large numbers of infant prodigies grow into long-lived, prolific adult geniuses.

union, legal or otherwise, as repellent. They would have thought of the shock caused to the young mind by such an early seduction and not of the possible benefits. Here, among the Mawayáns and Wai-Wais, the first marriage of a boy or girl was frequently with someone much older. There were always older people in the tribe whose partners had died or left them, and who wanted a new one, and instead of marrying among themselves they nearly always chose someone who had only just attained adulthood. In this way they obtained a young, strong companion, while the girl or boy got a partner who was almost a father or mother to them, and upon whom they could lean and trust while growing up and learning the duties of a husband or wife.

Such marriages, oddly assorted in our eyes, were frequently both happy and long-lasting—Kofiri and Mawa were clearly devoted to each other, as had been Yakotá and *his* older wife—and one got the impression that the Mawayáns were very affectionate, and that this open relationship between young and old was a source of great pleasure and benefit to them.

I asked Ka'i, who as well as Kabapböyö had an extremely young wife, if the two never quarrelled.

Very seldom, said he; otherwise, one or the other would leave. There was nothing to make people stay together if they did not want to. Some people lived together happily all their lives, but others moved about from person to person all the time.

It was a restful, undemanding attitude, contrasting strongly with European ideas of possessiveness and (often despite a succession of marriages) life-long partnership; but like the rest of these Indians' philosophy, it implied a degree of individual liberty and a simple, limited outlook hardly possible in our own complex, tightly-knit, competitive society.

We make no attempt to solve the problem of how to give adolescents a normal sexual life—indeed, make it as difficult as possible for them to have one; we give no clear, practical heterosexual guidance, and may inadvertently encourage homosexuality; we instil inhibiting ideas about sexual behaviour often so contrary to what is later held allowable that readjustment is as upsetting as failure to readjust is retarding. We may even, through suppression, diminish the potentiality of a bulk of the population.

It might be argued that we can learn little about upbringing from a society like that of the Mawayáns, because our own requirements are so different, and that in our society early sexual freedom would carry no responsibility, and so might undermine the respect of each sex for the other. Yet it is hard to see how the *difficulties* of adolescence encourage learning and successful adaptation, or are necessary in giving more time for them—or even, though they may subdue the weak and increase the determination of the relatively fewer strong—produce any desirable diversity of character. What seems axiomatic is that the closer we return, compatible with civilization, to the natural requirements of human beings, the stronger we shall be: the question being one of discovering the minimum deviation from nature necessary to secure the gains we have made.

So I reflected, sitting next to Jonah. The bowl was handed to me, and as I passed it, I asked him about his own upbringing as a child in an Arawak mission village. But he was not at all enthusiastic:

"Mr. Guppy, I had a miserable time. Arawak parents is cruel to their children, not like these, who never punish them. They make them obey strictly, and sometimes they beat them so hard you wonder that the child live. They try to teach them how to obey the commandments. White people is much nicer."

Despite my affection for him, Jonah was the worst thorn in my side. His continuous disapproval, his mulishness whenever we deviated much from the fixed routine of ordinary departmental surveys, moved me to desperation. Perhaps he meant no harm, and did not realize the effects of his grumbling? Perhaps I was over-irritable, or suspicious—or simply by nature averse to grumblers? For my own sake as well as in the interests of the expedition, I knew that his grumbling must be stopped, yet whenever I was on the point of being stern with him, my old fondness and respect would come flooding back. I had known him so long, and he had been my first guide in the forests.

The real cause of his behaviour was probably that he had no authority: he was very proud of the privileged position he had won in the Forest Department through hard and outstanding work, but over the years, as my experience had grown, so also had my independence of his advice; and here, away from the territory he knew, his usefulness was purely botanical. He was not even officially my second-in-command, as he had been on previous expeditions, and doubtless his self-importance had suffered.

Now, as I looked at him, so tiny, so bright eyed, so wise, with his wrinkled face very serious, I decided that I would make a last effort to win him:

"Do you think we will be able to hold out a little longer without discontent?" I asked him as we returned to camp and the pressing of our specimens.

"It is just a matter of food and work," he said. "We must take things easy. Then we can fish and hunt. I don't mind for myself when we get back."

"How about going a short way down the Mapuera? Do you still think we could do that? Food is very low."

He was his most conciliatory:

"Sure, Mr. Guppy—it would be a pity now we come so far not to go down there a way. I wonder how far the Amazoons is? It can't be more than two or three weeks down—it would be wonderful to see it. Yet I doubt we would ever get back up that river or plenty people would be up here already."

"I think it is a very long way, Jonah. Anyhow, this is the really unknown country where we will make our discoveries, and we've still got a lot of work to do, on the way back. We came across the Acarai so fast that we had no time to collect properly. And then there is the country on the way out to the savannahs. So all I want is to go a short way down to see where the changes begin."

"Well, sir, what I would say is this: let us leave in about three or four days, for then we will still have plenty of food from these people, and later they may not have so much to give us. If we go steady and easy we should reach the boats on the third day of walking, in the afternoon, and we can go out and camp on that last camp we have on the Buna-wau. We should reach the Mapuera the next day, and then we will go as far as the food will let us or we want to go. And if we reach villages we can stop and buy food. That way things will not be so bad."

"That sounds very nice, Jonah—our problem will be getting the men back to British Guiana if it is as good as that! I will see if we cannot get two or three extra men from the village to help with the carrying, and that will make it easier still."

For the moment he was on my side; but I knew that at the first straits his opposition would begin. Tolstoy, whose *War and Peace* I was reading, pictured leadership as a formal hierarchy, a cone supporting the leader at the top. My own experience, I reflected rather ruefully, was nearer that of the revolutionary who heard the mob raging past his window and shouted to an aide, "Find out where they are going, for I am their leader!" My best supports were Basil—reliable, unpresumptuous, encouraging—and Fonyuwé and Kirifakka, who, oblivious of all the dramas in human relationship that raged around them, lived in bubbling spirits and did all their work as if it were fun.

The Party

Thundery, cloudy, the next day dawned, ominous for the party the Mawayáns had decided to hold for us that evening. Fonyuwé, enraptured by his rediscovered relatives, had been excused from work, but the other men were hunting, fishing, drying meat, gathering vegetables or boiling down cane-juice to make sugar, which we had run out of.

Kwakwé came along the path, a bow and a sheaf of arrows in his hand. I indicated the sky and made motions of descending rain: he waved aloft with a smile, as if to reassure me that all would be well. I undulated my hand forward—a swimming fish: at once he rose on tiptoe, and, half-turning on his foot, loosed an imaginary arrow into the stream; then smiled, pointed and went his way.

Slight showers, then wan sunlight, as Jonah, Basil, Mark, Yapumo and I made our way to the centre of the newly-cleared field, to scan the encompassing forest for flowering tree-crowns. Already planting had begun. Ka'i and Kofiri, with ten-foot long pointed sticks, were driving holes into the hard earth, in irregular patterns but fairly even spacing. After every two or three dozen they would stop and plant, inserting a long slim sucker of silk-grass[1] into each, from a laden warishi near by, before beginning digging again.

Axe, cutlass, fire and pointed sticks were the Mawayán implements of agriculture, and with them and their bare hands they had produced the fine crops in the fields around—crops, nearly all of them, which bore for several years and could be harvested continuously. Their yams were the best I had eaten, their sugar tall and juicy, their cassava high in quality and yield: only their bananas were of inferior varieties.

In such an isolated place it was interesting to see so many introductions—bananas and sugar-cane, for example, among the staples, being natives of the old world—but so rapid has been their spread that almost no tribe is without some. Only a few years after Columbus,[2] perhaps, they had arrived here, carried from tribe to tribe, and been incorporated into the economy; and now no one can say when or whence they came.

But even before the arrival of introduced species the Indians must have been well fed, with, among cultivated plants, cassava, yams, pumpkins, pineapples, peppers, sweet potatoes, papaws, deer-callaloo (*Phytolacca rivinoides* and *P. icosandra*) and doubtless also maize, which I did not see. Besides which, as wild vegetable foods, they had Brazil, palm, and other nuts, palm hearts, and the fruit of forest trees of such genera as *Eugenia* (which includes the rose-apple), *Psidium* (the guava), *Rheedia*, *Moronobea*, *Chrysophyllum* (the star-apple), *Spondias* (the hog-plum), and *Anacardium* (the cashew)—many of them delicious, though mostly unknown in the outside world; while besides foods, they possessed tobacco, silk grass, cotton, gourds, arrow-grass, anatto, among cultivated plants, and a variety of wild useful plants.

Two large crowns of vivid blue drew us. Next to yellow, pinkish-blue is the commonest flower colour of the forest canopy, though supposedly most attractive to bees, which are rare; but in both these cases the colours proved to have been deceptively brightened by distance and the hazy air.

---

[1] *Bromelia* sp., used for making string.

[2] Bananas, for example, were first introduced into the New World by Spanish monks in the West Indies, in 1519.

One tree was the lovely *Erisma uncinatum*, with massive inflorescences of a feathery ash mauve—stalks, flowers, bracts, buds and all; the other, a *Lueheopsis* (of the Linden family, Tiliaceae), with flowers of a deep rose-pink, among large golden-brown velvety buds. As I clambered along its fallen trunk reddish-brown quarter-inch long ants swarmed up my legs, dropped onto my shoulders, and bit and stung me savagely, screwing themselves into contortions; a dead branch weighing half a ton, suspended above and disturbed by the felling, crashed to earth ten feet away, a green tree-viper slipped from a twig I was about to chop through with my knife, and, as if to complete the picture of the dangers of plant-collecting, Jonah warned me not to touch the sap oozing from a liane I had slashed lest it blister me.

Exploring further, following the trail Kwakwé had taken beyond the camp, we soon came upon more loose pale-brown smooth-grained sands; but now for miles they led away, undulating up and down hill, and unmistakably like those of British Guiana. Even more astonishing were the forests upon them. With exclamations of delight Jonah and I recognized tree after tree that we had last seen hundreds of miles to the north—here the commonest species were the same as there! *Swartzia leiocalycina*, an ashy-barked tree with blood-red sap, *Eschweilera sagotiana*, one of the finest of the monkey-pipes, *Alexa imperatricis*, *Tachigalia rusbyi*, and several *Licanias* and *Pouterias*: there was no mistaking it—we had passed right through the mysteries of the Acarai region and come out again on the other side among familiar things.

In the flat valley bottoms were patches of a little palm—the Shiuru palm, quite new to us, and apparently to science.[1] It was one of the prettiest palms any of us had ever seen, scarcely fifteen feet tall, with great feathery leaves of the palest green curving down on all sides almost to the ground, like the tresses of a weeping-willow. Its stems were a smooth grey, and at the top, half-hidden, were bunches of corn-yellow flowers and yellowy-green spindle-shaped fruit filled with a juice like coconut milk, which we drank.

We measured a plot on a hill-side, to compare with those of

[1] Provisionally it has been placed in the genus *Syagrus*.

the other forests of the region and of the forests on the sands of British Guiana, then Jonah and I returned to camp, ebullient. At last everything I knew about these forests had begun to fit together, to form a pattern in which I could perceive the logic: speculative perhaps, but supported by the evidence and in accord with what was known from other areas. Clearly now came the picture of the great sandstone tableland of ancient times crumbling away to reveal yet older landscapes beneath it, including the Serra Acarai; of first those sandstone mountains, and then the Acarai, standing above the sea as a peninsula or chain of islands bearing their ancient forests, from which, when the sea ebbed away or the land rose, species began to spread, colonizing the newly emerged lowlands; of the sculpturing and washing away of these sandy lowlands, the slow evolution of new species, and finally, of the landscapes of today, still evolving, with their clues to the past.

And within this larger picture I now felt surer of my smaller one—of my hypothesis of the nature and distribution of the forests themselves, upon which I had based my survey methods. Instead of these forests being classified largely by their structure —which is, after all, only the result of the species present, their proportions, and their individual development—I was convinced now that I had been right in classifying them first by the landscape-forming process, such as erosion or deposition, which they accompanied and influenced, secondarily by the soil and its stage of development, thirdly by the influence of such outside agencies as man, animals, fire, high winds, and only fourthly by species and structure.

All these forests, uniform-seeming yet infinitely varied, were, like works of art, the solutions, to date, of the working out of problems. Their patterns were patterns produced by variables— species, climate, soils, landscapes—interacting upon each other, their beauty that of the close approach of all these interacting quantities to a point of rest, or equilibrium. Only in the early stages of the interaction—after a landslide or a windfall, for example—when the problems were stated and little progress had been made towards their solution, did one encounter ugliness in them.

I surmised that these sands we had discovered stretched

away to the east and were what comprised the Serra Irikoumé. If only I had had time and food enough to explore them thoroughly! But it was hard to travel further east, said the Mawayáns—no paths led in that direction, and there were no villages there—at least none of which they knew; and already the rainy season was drawing near, and soon we should have to leave.

Perhaps, I consoled myself, we should find further clues down the Mapuera.

The women of the tribe appeared while we were working at the camp and bathed a few yards upstream, removing their ornaments and aprons before submerging shoulder-deep, talking, splashing, washing their children and dogs. Then we and the men followed.

Dressed in our best we walked up to the village as soon as the day's heat was past, at about four o'clock. The sky had cleared, the thatched roofs and gardens sparkled in the slanting sunshine, the shadows slowly lengthened.

The people were still making up, transforming themselves into polychrome zebras or Edwardian bathers: rubbing red paint on to their hands from waxy-looking rolls of clay tinted with anatto and scented with *Protium* gum) and then all over their bodies; the men slashing crude black or darker red stripes across their chests and the women all over their bodies, in horizontal rings from neck to knee.

Even the pets were painted: occasionally one would see a man wipe his hands on a nearby dog or monkey, smearing it irregularly, but most thickly on head and shoulders, then adding a few careless stripes.

Bodies painted, there then began the absorbing task of facial making-up. With tiny greasepaint-paddles, lines, crosses, zigzags were added to cheeks, foreheads and noses; each man and woman concentrating with the utmost intentness on his own features, now that everyone had one of my small circular trade mirrors, instead of being forced to vent his artistry on a neighbour. Finally ornaments of feathers and beads were put on, and with delight wife examined husband and husband wife.

Although at first they had seemed alike, already I had begun to see differences in dress between the Wai-Wais and Mawayáns

—most noticeable, perhaps, being the relative "poverty" of the Mawayáns. Instead of an abundance of beads, they had to make do with palm seeds, nuts, dried fruit, Job's tears,[1] for their necklaces, and bands of bast, palm-leaf, or cloth (sometimes bordered with a few beads) for armlets and anklets. Their ornaments were scantier—there were no signs of the feather crowns, head-dresses, plumes and pendants, the dancing paddles, nose-feathers, or bead under-chin slings, from ear to ear, which the Wai-Wais donned at the slightest excuse—yet often they were better made and more artistic. The men's laps were longer, feather-fringed, and, instead of being rolled tight at the top under the navel, were fixed in a loose decorative fold in front; the women's aprons larger, differently and more attractively patterned, and their hair much longer and worn in a bun, instead of loose-hanging about the shoulders, as with the Wai-Wai women.

As we wandered among the houses we came upon a magnificent, powerful man standing like a block of hewn stone in the path, surrounded by dogs and relatives:

"Machira," said Yapumo, introducing us—the man who lived on the mountain, who had come with his family to see me.

My hand was grasped and firmly shaken, and Machira looked at me intently from clear eyes under a low forehead. He had a flat head, high cheekbones, a protruding mouth—the head of a Frog Indian—and his arms, shoulders, chest, calves, thighs were massive and solid. He was a Titan, beside whom even Fonyuwé shrank to a chicken, and evidently a straightforward, honest, no-nonsense type of individual.

After gazing full in my face for a minute he drew back, his expression serious, and swept his arm out in a broad gesture, towards his mother, wife, children, dogs.

"*Anoro*," he said—all are mine: meet them.

And I shook hands with each in turn, admiringly, for like him, down to the smallest of his ten dogs and the youngest of his three children, they were physically splendid, healthy, well cared for.

Together we sat down to drink, and he spoke to me long and

[1] The hard pea-like fruit of a grass, *Coix Lachryma-Jobi.*

earnestly. He was utterly perplexed by my inability to understand him.

As the bowls were passed to us, thunder rolled.

"*Dedabaru*," said I, pointing—it was one of my few Mawayán words.

"*Aha! Dé-dabaru!*" and he raised his arm and shook it, and pointing his finger, snaked it down to earth like lightning.

"Thunder," he pronounced, but with poor success.

Pointing in various directions, asking through Basil and Fonyuwé, from him also I tried to discover the names of other tribes and where they lived, but he knew little. Many years before, he said, the Mawayáns had known people to the east—Diaus, and Tunayenas, and Katawians—but then there had been a fight, and now nobody ever went that way, and the trail was lost; perhaps those people no longer even existed.

What about white men—had any come here before?

No, said he. None had ever been to this village, and I was the first he had ever seen. But in his father's time two had visited the tribe, and more recently some had come up the Buna-wau and the Oroko'orin and some of the people had seen them; and far down the Mapuera, below the mouth of the Oroko'orin, he had heard that one had come, with some Indians, and had begun to cut a field.

Most certainly the travellers on the Buna-wau and Oroko'orin had been Boundary surveyors, while the first two could only have been Farabee and Ogilvie, in 1913. Their map showed that they had followed a trail close to mine. Shiuru-tirir was unlikely to have been built in their time, old though it appeared, but they must have passed close to its site. They had seen Parukutus in the country between the Buna-wau and the Oroko'orin, now deserted, where we had seen only a scattering of youngish second-growth Mapidians and Waiwĕs (a tribe different from, but apparently related to, the Wai-Wais) in the region in which we were, and further east the tribes mentioned by Machira as once having been friends.

Even here the epidemics were reaching, the tribes vanishing.

Who were the Emayenas, Icaro's tribe? Were they indeed a tribe unknown before, as I now began to suspect, or was this merely another name for the Fishkalienas or the Katawians (with whom also the Mawayáns had fought)? Most important of all—who were the Mawayáns?

Though the Brazilian Boundary Commission's report had concluded: "Nothing is known about the Maopityans (Frog Indians) found by Schomburgk about 100 years ago . . . It can be presumed that this tribe is extinct," it seemed very probable to me that the Mawayáns were that tribe, but a detailed discussion of their history was difficult through a series of interpreters. Without it, the most important evidence in tracing relationships was language, and on my return I compared, with the aid of the missionaries, a few Mawayán words for simple things such as the sun, hand, eye, with those given by Farabee for the Mapidians—from which it appeared that the two languages were identical, and therefore almost certainly the tribes also; though, to the hypercritical eye there might still be a shadow of a doubt, for just as the Parukutus now spoke Wai-Wai and called themselves Wai-Wais, so might something similar have happened: the Mawayáns *might* be the Mapidians, or they might have absorbed them or been absorbed by them.

So many tribes had disappeared in the region, died out or moved, that it was next to impossible to discover where each that survived began and ended: almost certainly, whoever they were, the Mawayáns were mixed with the remnants of other tribes that had dwindled until they could no longer maintain a separate existence, and now they too were dying out. There were few women, few babies were being born—the whole tribe numbered only thirty or forty.

Perhaps instead of or as well as being Mapidians, they were the same as the Mayoyaná Naucú reported by Father San Manços in 1728 as living near the Urucurin River?

If so, they became even more interesting, for they thereby acquired a known history unique for such a remote, undisturbed tribe, as a stable group that had lived in one locality for at least 224 years; and if they are also the Mapidians, their history, though dateless, went back even further, for legend says that the Mapidians originated from a branch of the Atorad tribe (now extinct or mingled with the Wapisianas—their territory was in the South Rupununi Savannah region of British Guiana) which, a long, long time ago, "disappeared over the mountains".

Whatever mixture of races they were, the Mawayáns had abandoned the practice of deforming new-born babies' heads, for none of the children showed it, and among the adults only Machira and Makata. Perhaps these two were the only true surviving Frog Indians? If they were, then we had traced to one of its sources the most mysterious of all the legends of Amazonia, that of the underwater Indians, for most probably it arose from the misinterpretation of the name of the "Frog Indians", and of that of the still unvisited Tunayenas, or "Water Indians".

Piles of banana leaves were brought out and set before us. They had between them layers of a delicious yellow glue a quarter of an inch thick—a paste made from bananas—which we scooped up with our fingers. Then more leaves, this time containing three-inch slabs of a substance like wet doughy bread, of a mottled greyish oatmeal colour: undiluted piracarri, the basis of many of the Indian drinks, made by moistening freshly made cassava bread in water, sprinkling it with a powder (doubtless containing yeast) made from certain leaves,[1] and putting it to ferment between banana leaves for four or five days—at the end of which time it has swollen to several times its original thickness, and is sweet-tasting and very good to eat.

Next, a bowl of a dark-grey whipped cream—made, though it had quite a different flavour, by diluting this same piracarri dough with a little water, straining and beating it; after which came basins containing piracarri in its final forms: as a series of drinks of different consistencies and tastes, to produce which the dough is crumbled and put into covered pots for two or three days' further fermentation, mixed with varying quantities of water, and in some cases fermented yet more and strained to a clear liquid of indubitable potency.

I had hardly put down the last of these when another large earthenware bowl was handed me, this time filled with a frothing dark-brown liquid, thick but refreshing.

"This is made in a different way," said Basil. "First the women make extra-thick cassava bread, then they burn it black on both sides on the griddle, and mix most of it with

[1] Of *Trema micrantha*, among tribes living northwards.

water in a pot. Then they wash out their mouths and sweeten them inside with honey or sugar cane, and chew what they have put aside until it is soft, and spit it into the pot. Then when it is all mixed, they boil it, and stir it up and strain it, then mix more water with it and put it aside for five days to ferment. Then you must drink it soon, or it will spoil."

Perhaps nowhere else is such variety of form and flavour produced from so simple a raw material—not even the hen's egg is as protean as cassava. I had scarcely begun to sample the range of Indian cookery, to appreciate the delicacies lost with each advance of imported foods—for in more accessible places many of these recipes have been forgotten, or are considered too laborious to be bothered with.

As I drank, or dipped my cassava bread into the bowls of stew that had now appeared, an occasional cooked cockroach or other creature floated past. But hunger had made me callous: I simply drank or dipped at the other side.

Looking up, I noticed that the whole inside of the great circular house was crawling with the tiny beasts—not the obscene cockroaches of civilization, but delicate little forest insects, protectively coloured to resemble fallen leaves; repellent, none the less, in their sheer numbers, for not a square inch was without them. They had not been there a few days before, when I had scratched the timbers: there must have been a sudden hatching.

I pointed them out to Basil:

"Tomorrow they'll be gone. All the tame birds will eat them," was his calm response.

While fermented drinks are very important in the Indian diet as sources of vitamins which they get nowhere else, their stews, flavoured and preserved with cassareep and often highly seasoned with peppers, are their means of eking out their very limited supplies of meat and fish. Whenever (and it is not very often) there is a successful hunt, the Indians gorge themselves and then lie torpid, because fresh meat has to be eaten at once or it goes bad, and even if smoke-dried will last only a few days. At other times they live chiefly on vegetables, taken in the form of cassava bread, fruit, or thick, gruelly drinks.

A basin containing a liquid very much like cocoa in appearance and flavour was passed round the circle: I drank as deeply as my bloated condition would allow.

Jonah put forward a restraining hand:

"Be careful, Mr. Guppy, it will tie up your insides. It is made by soaking ripe palm fruit in water. It is good, but you must not drink too much."

Sitting, drinking, wandering, talking, the afternoon passed.

Flocks of macaws flew overhead, and the tame ones on the housetops flapped their wings in the last sunrays and screamed, but made no attempt to join them. The chief sat near us, carving a flute; then, as dusk fell, he went to the door of the big house and played a short tune.

Immediately Machira came out, a shack-shack in his right hand, an arrow in his left, followed by the men of the tribe. They stood in line, and a woman carried a bowl of drink and held it to the lips of each in turn. Then, with the bowl still in her hand, she stood in the middle of the cleared space before the houses, beside the rest of the food.

We withdrew to one side and seated ourselves on logs: the dancing had begun.

Machira, with a low muttering, led off to the right in a circle facing the woman, the rest of the men following. They moved sideways, with a curious stamping of the leading foot that gave a rhythmic undulation to the line.

"Yowp! Yowp!" suddenly shouted Machira, when they had danced once round.

"Yip! Yowp! Woohoo!" came a high-spirited chorus of replies, and the men swung round and danced back in the opposite direction.

This was the Howler Monkey dance. For half an hour it continued without noticeable change, then, as abruptly as it had begun, it stopped, and the bowl of drink was again passed by the serving-woman.

Then it began again, but now we had accepted the invitation to join. It was not a difficult dance, but I was so full of food that I could hardly move. Others felt like me, for with a rending noise one of the Mawayáns upped and emptied the contents of his stomach on the ground a little way clear of the dancing space.

By the time, hot and breathless, that we stopped for further drinking, it had grown dark, and the only illumination was the occasional flaring of a fire within one of the houses, from the cavernous interiors of which hammock-borne faces of old women and young children peered forth.

The women, who had been watching, joined the men in the next dance, and a man stood in the centre as server. They formed an inner circle, the leaders holding a stick parallel with the ground on the inside like a barrier, and danced in counter-rotation, their voices rising high and strong, in a wailing, rather liturgical chant, blending with the men's, or sometimes replying to them. Then they formed a column in threes, with the men behind, and in this formation moved first a few paces to the right, swayed, then a few paces to the left, then to the right again, and slowly forward.

I had three flashbulbs, and wanted to photograph the dancing—but knew that, friendly as the Mawayáns were, if unwarned they would undoubtedly panic at the first blinding flash of light. So, with eminent caution, I had proceeded through Basil, Fonyuwé and Yapumo, to tell the entire tribe not to be alarmed.

The night sky was full of shooting stars, the darkness almost complete, so that it was impossible to see anything except a row of faintly silhouetted moving figures.

A little tense, I pressed the shutter.

There was not the slightest tremor, or flicker of notice, but what a scene was revealed: the cavern of blackness, the palm-leaf roofs, the bright red bodies soaked with sweat—but it was far from the uncontrolled orgy the missionary had led me to expect. Perhaps the Mawayáns were quieter people than the Wai-Wais?—though obviously everyone was enjoying himself.

Darkness again. Sometimes above the singing there was a scuffling in the bushes, sometimes the sound of vomiting as room was made for more drink.

Unobserved, towards midnight, I got up and crept away to sleep.

Tumblers of the Mind

Beside my tarpaulin, leaning over the swift-running stream, grew one of those mysterious thorn-studded, milky-latexed trees—the sixth I had seen—for whose flowers I had so long and unsuccessfully searched. Several times I had examined it, hoping to find even one, but without luck.

Weary from the party, the men lay late in their hammocks. It was a Sunday, and partly to appease Jonah, but mostly because on the morrow we would begin our return journey, I had declared it a day of rest.

Though the general Amazonian rainy season is from late November until May, and this was only November the 9th, we were in a mountainous region where it apparently started earlier, and steadily the threat of its onset had been increasing. The air was a-tremble with distant thunder; heavy storm clouds rolled low overhead; rain could be heard far off. Soon, perhaps very suddenly, we would be overwhelmed: already the Mawayáns were planting their new field with all haste.

Heavy rains would not only make it almost impossible to work—more serious, they might maroon us. Deposits on leaves showed that floods sometimes covered the low-lying country west of the Mud Hills to a depth of ten feet, but a rise of even four or five feet in the level of the Buna-wau or the Oroko'orin would be enough: a couple of days' continuous rain and Mawayán land would be isolated—as it undoubtedly was for many months in each year—so that even if we could get through with our burdens to where we had left our boats, we might find them swept away, or sunk unsalvageably deep in turbulent waters.

It was best, therefore, to start back at once, especially as I wanted to go a little further down the Mapuera, and lay out a few more plots in the Acarai forests on our return crossing. Besides I had, in the back of my mind, a certain date for our return to civilization: just before he had taken off from Gunn's Strip, Colonel Williams had told me that on December 9th, in exactly one month's time, he would be landing a Dakota at Lumid Pau, where every three months a plane called to pick up a load of balata gum. By leaving at once and working fast we might be able to do all we wanted to and still catch it—and that would save us not only the cost of a special charter, but much delay, for otherwise we should have to cross the savannahs to an airstrip nearer civilization.

I was sorting through a bundle of specimens when by chance I glanced into the crown of the mystery-tree—and there, above a branch where I could never have seen them from directly below, were two flowers, side by side. At last we should be able to identify it!

Climbing a stump, I drew the thorny branches down. Puffs of a gardenia-sweet scent filled the air; the flowers, slender, tubular, orange-centred, with spirals of palest cream petals at the edge of the corolla tube, grew in a small cyme in the axil of one of a pair of glossy, dark-green, opposite leaves: the tree could only belong to the periwinkle family—the Apocynaceae; and indeed later examination showed it to be most likely a species of *Lacmellia*.

My work over, I went to the village, now sleepy in the mid-morning sun. Yuhmé was making arrows, and I sat and watched, for I had heard that he was considered the most skilful arrow-maker among the Mawayáns.

For the shafts Yuhmé had cut down a few inflorescent scapes of arrow grass, straight, slim, pith-centred cylinders, fifteen or twenty feet tall, from among the thick, high clumps that grew around the village. He discarded the flowering apices, with their clouds of yellowy-silver spikelets, then dried and chopped them into five- or six-foot lengths, the slenderer from nearer the tip for bird, fish, or poison-arrow shafts, the stouter portions for the heavier missiles used against big game.

With a loop in a piece of string he carefully rolled, squeezed and tapered the last few inches at each end of these lengths, bound them neatly into shape with waxed fibre, then into their tips inserted like plugs (to fit snugly, held firmly by the pith) the slender conical stems of previously-carved wooden heads and tailpieces—the latter, notched to receive the bowstring, at the narrower ends—and made these secure by yet more binding. Then holding each arrow straight, he rotated it, made final adjustments, and tightened and knotted all these threads.

When several arrows had been brought to this stage Yuhmé opened a box woven of palm-leaf strips containing feathers, and a few inches in from the head and tail of each bound a pair of small fluffy red or yellow toucan breast-feathers to the shaft by way of decoration. Next, to the rearward of these he attached the flights, made from the wing primaries of a harpy eagle or macaw, and bound them tight with carefully-patterned stringwork. Finally, when these were fixed to his satisfaction, he wetted his finger and thumb in his mouth and gave the rear end of each flight-feather a little twist, so that the arrow would spin in flight like a rifle bullet, and go true to its mark.

Each arrow must have taken twenty minutes to assemble, perhaps half a day in all to make if one included the carving of the parts and the collection of the material. Each was different, exhibiting some little ingenuity or variation in design—some even being made largely for fun, to buzz in flight, or with a loose pebble inside the shaft which rattled when the arrow was shaken. Far more trouble had been taken over them than was strictly necessary, especially when one considered their frailty and shortness of life, for most would not survive a single shooting. Yet Yuhmé would not have made them in any other way. To him they were a means of expression, for like everything else made by the Mawayáns and Wai-Wais they were works of art as well as useful.

Practically everything these Indians made was decorated. Little tufts of feathers, bunches of beads and seeds were hung wherever they could be attached: on bows and arrows, baskets, combs, hammocks, cassava-sifters, and other strictly utilitarian articles, as well as on their own noses, ears, wrists, ankles, and on pet monkeys and dogs—a light-hearted frippery, like the covering of a cigarette-lighter with rhinestones, absurd perhaps, but no more so than the crests and combs of birds, from which they might have been derived by imitation.

More serious in intent were the painted patterns, in red or black, which covered every flat wooden surface. Frequently these were semi-naturalistic, showing jaguars, sloths, monkeys, squirrels, lizards, frogs, scorpions, in lively silhouette from the most easily recognized viewpoint; but sometimes they were almost geometrical, so abstract that it was impossible to tell on one's own what they meant. Yet nearly all, even the most hieroglyphic and fragmentary, had their meaning: numerous small crosses meant savannah grass; a pair of spirals stood for a fly—its eyes; a triangle was a fish's tail, while a zigzag might mean running water, or a snake if it had a thicker head, a lizard if hooked at both ends, or even the folded young leaves of a palm, if imbricated with other zigzags. And sometimes one could find whole series all representing the same thing, lizards or sloths, for instance, ranging from semi-naturalism to extreme abstraction. Farabee explained the origin of many of these more abstract designs in Wai-Wai art (with most of which, at least today, the Mawayán designs are identical) by showing from their shape and cross-hatching that they were derived from woven basket-work designs, and these in turn from a naturalistic painted art—probably more naturalistic than anything at present found among the Mawayáns and Wai-Wais and more like that of some of the related Arawak and Carib tribes[1]—from which they had been initially modified towards abstraction by the fact that in basketwork curves are obtainable only by weaving the strips in a step pattern, which at once imposes some degree of formalization.

No action was expressed in these designs, there was no attempt at the representation of space or of three-dimensional solidity, at the maintenance of correct proportions between the sizes of the different objects grouped together, or at objective structural analysis of limbs, joints, etc. One might therefore have been tempted to compare this art, especially in its clumsier manifestations, with that of 9–11-year-old European children. But such considerations were quite irrelevant if naturalism was not its aim; and in its clarity of conception and design, its highly complex, stylized, decorative patterns, the aptness with which the various media were used—even in the absence of representations of human beings, the first things usually depicted by

[1] The Mawayáns are an offshoot of the Arawaks, who centuries ago spread northwards from somewhere in central Brazil; while the Wai-Wais are part of their rival nation and frequent conquerors, the Caribs.

European children—it was quite unlike any children's art, and all too obviously the product of technically skilled, even sophisticated, adults.

There was also no doubt about its indigenousness, for there was nothing in its designs or technique which could be traced back to any environment other than the forest. From the forests, apart from a few imported articles like beads, knives, coins, safety-pins, came all the rather limited range of materials used: feathers, seeds, fibres, strips of bast and leaf, split stems of reeds, soft woods,[1] vegetable dyes, gums, bones, leather. And the limitations imposed upon the Indians' society by the forest— the small, isolated, impermanent villages, the lack of open spaces, of objects of ambition, of wars, catastrophes, of organizations like church or state, to stimulate the mind—have led to it being as nearly a personal art as one could imagine, giving pleasure perhaps to a few people around its creator, but far and away most of all to himself. Yet it was hard to believe when one considered the intricacy of some of these designs, especially in basketwork, that there was much room for spontaneous invention. Surely they and their meanings must be completely traditional? Yet the increasing abstraction, and the presence simultaneously of different stages, showed that this art, like our own, which is also going abstract, perhaps for similar reasons, was still evolving. Besides which, some of the most complicated designs were confined to beadwork, and beads had certainly only been introduced within the last hundred years.

As I watched Yuhmé, who had now turned to the weaving of a small basket with a scorpion pattern, it seemed to me that this was to him a form of intellectual activity. His absorption was total, like that of a chess-player, as slowly beneath his fingers the clear geometrical pattern of three right-angles took shape. He had complete control of the numerous tiny strips which sprang up from the base. One felt that he could invent any design he wished—not merely reproduce those he had learned by heart.

I felt suddenly, as I had never felt before, that I was close to

[1] Most of the woods are too hard and heavy for carving without excellent tools; as are the rocks which, at least in modern times, are used solely in making chips for cassava-graters.

264

the origins of artistic creation. Why should a man, living in isolation in a vast forest with practically no one to observe him, with nothing to gain from it, transform and beautify the things around him? Why do men do this everywhere? There must be some convincing explanation for this mysterious activity, apparently so separate from the rest of life, than self-expression or the imposition of order on the universe. Where does the *need* to create arise? Where does the energy come from? What directs it into its particular form—why should the Mawayáns and Wai-Wais produce these distinctive angular shapes and patterns, these rich ornamentations, and not something else? If one could answer these questions one would be able to penetrate far more deeply into the human mind than is at present possible, and understand far more about the differences between individuals and races. Not to attempt to answer them—and no comprehensive psychological theory does—is to disregard all that has raised man above the animals, and that is most relevant to our own state and the state of our civilization.

Living creatures have few essential requirements: food, oxygen, moisture, a certain range of temperature, excretion, perhaps reproduction. The abundant energy they derive from the oxidation of food is used in attempting to satisfy these and escape from enemies, in doing which the brain's function, even in the most primitive nervous reactions, is one of adaptation, of differentiating between favourable and unfavourable phenomena, and at a higher level of building up as comprehensive a picture of the outside world as possible, fitting in new observations beside old and establishing the organism's relationship with them so that it is best able to survive. Creation, therefore, as it is directed by the brain, must arise primarily as a means of achieving this.

Every creature, even an amoeba, must have a picture of the outside world. But an amoeba's picture must be built up of elements which to our minds would be abstract, for its perceptions can only be of such distinctions as light and dark, perhaps colours, warmth and cold, freedom and contact, a few chemical sensations, perhaps size, and its responses are limited to physical action avoiding the unpleasant, retaining or increasing the pleasant sensations—the sum of such responses constituting what we mean by a "picture". In exactly the same way, as the sum of our responses, we too build up our picture; and infinitely more complex though it is, we must build it up from foundations just as abstract. Just as in our bodies we, in common with all other higher animals, have different levels of organization, the most fundamental, that of the cells, retaining the structure and mode of functioning of the primitive one-celled organisms from which we have evolved, so we have different "levels" of organization in the nervous system corresponding in their increasing precision of perception, analysis, response and powers of association with the various stages of our evolution: protozoan, invertebrate, vertebrate, mammalian, human, racial, family—varying more and more between individuals at each higher level in their inherited, as distinct from their acquired attributes and content, until at the highest or shallowest levels they are entirely personal.

The frequent close similarity of response even to quite specific stimuli between men and animals can well be accounted for by the presence of such "levels", and they enable one to understand how, for example, despite the great difference between my own and the Mawayán's world, and the fact that I could not recognize very many of their designs let alone understand their significance, I could still get pleasure from their art, much as might a Mawayán with no knowledge of Christianity from Leonardo's "Last Supper". For in both cases, beneath the comparatively precise symbolism of things realistically represented, producing an immediate response in those to whom they are familiar, there lie more fundamental and abstract symbolisms of pattern, form and colour, widely understood, associating with deeper levels of the mind, and forming a common language of mankind, perhaps largely inherited.

In human beings the process of building up a picture starts in early childhood, when we begin sorting the phenomena of the outside world into categories, almost identical with those of the amoeba, of how they affect us: pleasing, displeasing, or neutral, which later (sometimes wrongly) come to be associated with our needs. In this way, on a basis partly of heredity, partly of environment and upbringing, a comparatively limited selection of phenomena come to act on our senses as effective stimuli, powerful in proportion to the strength of their associations, while the greater number of the stimuli we receive, including many which at first aroused equal interest (and many perhaps equally important for us), cease to be noticed even when we are alert. The number-plates of cars in the street, the feel of clothing on the skin, the sounds of traffic are such stimuli, consciously perceived by children, who have not yet developed fully their classifications of relative importance, and unconsciously, to a far greater degree than they usually realize, by adults.[1]

At first in building up this picture we respond directly to external stimuli, but once the brain has responded to a stimulus it tends afterwards to respond similarly to others like it, and place the new image in association with the earlier, because of which, though our picture changes throughout life, it does so with increasing difficulty, because what is already there colours later reponses and affects the incorporation of new material.

Such a "picture" of the world, in the case of a complex creature like a mammal or a human being, with a mind on many levels and a vast store of memory, is really much more a three-dimensional "model", for it is built up at all the different levels of the mind: where our perceptions have remained imprecise, as in the case of taste or smell, our reactions are still very much on the level of "pleasant", "unpleasant", "neutral", and our images are vague, abstract; but with touch, sound, and especially sight they become increasingly analytical, specific, precise. Each person's model therefore is a composite of all his responses in their various and fluctuating strengths in the imagery of every sense at every level, and is completely individual; and however false it may seem to others—and it can never be more than fragmentary—it is to him Reality, the foundation of his feelings of security or insecurity, and therefore of all his behaviour.

But what has this to do with artistic creation?

---

[1] That this is so, and that these images may be remembered for a long time, has been shown by hypnotism, drugs, shocks, and tests of subliminal perception. The drug mescalin seems to put out of action that part of the brain's mechanism upon which the varying strengths of our responses depends, and to restore temporarily a microscopic childlike vision: of the world perhaps more nearly as it *is*.

Until a phenomenon's position in the mind's model is satisfactorily established the mind is in a condition of disequilibrium. Interest is aroused, the attention is fixed on it, and it is compared, consciously or unconsciously, with what is already known: it is thought about, in the effort to understand it. Thinking is experimenting with images, mental reproductions of the perceptions of any of our senses; but the difficulty is that images cannot be held: they are fleeting, constantly changing and being blended with other images. When conscious control is removed, these shufflings and transformations—all part of the mind's effort to restore its balance—manifest themselves as dreams. But dreams are influenced by wishes, fears, physical stimuli such as coldness, stomach-ache, noises; and their solutions, though they may point the way, are often unsatisfactory in waking life. Then, with external reality before it, the mind in endeavouring to adjust its inner model consciously needs urgently to be able to control its images—to be able to fix them in a form in which they can be pondered, criticized and altered if necessary—and the only way in which it can do this is by trying to reproduce them, usually with the hands. And this I believe is the origin of creativeness, and indeed of all human achievement, for unless a creator can record his thoughts with his hands or body at each stage he is helpless, and can make no progress to the next.

Creation, therefore, one might define as a form of thinking in which the hands or some other means are used as extensions of the brain, with which to fix images and solve problems—an elaboration in man of the brain's prime role in maintaining the organism in security. And a finished creation is a projection of some part of its creator's inner model of reality, showing the way in which a disturbing feature of the outer world has been incorporated. The creator knows when his solution has been reached, because his balance is no longer disturbed: in fitting this feature into the projection his own inner reality has been adjusted and he loses interest, perhaps long before his work from a technical point of view is complete.

For some people, savage or civilized, words or signs provide the imageries most important to them; for others sounds, shapes, patterns, colours, tastes, smells, the sense of touch, physical movements, even the movement of the bowels or other organic functions. As all these imageries can be experimented with, one must accept that each, even muscular movement, may be a form of thought. And from thinking in them, or combinations of them, come the various forms of creative activity and expression: dancing, cooking, chemistry, acting, athletics, music, mathematics, literature, painting, etc.; while their relative importance and degree of development accounts for most of the differences between the characters of individuals—their ambitions, motives, relaxations, ways of life and thought—between the cultures that races evolve, and even between the ways of thought and communication of different animals. Dogs probably think largely in terms of smell, while the sense of smell of ants must give an imagery no less precise than that of sight with us; similarly one might almost say that bats *see* with their ears. Bees use dancing imagery to convey specific directions to other members of the hive—and in India temple dances can convey entire systems of philosophy.

Individuals may not be able to think at all adequately in any but their special imagery—a painter or mathematician may be incoherent, a writer insensitive to music—yet everyone has to solve problems in his own imagery if he is to maintain his health. A Nijinsky denied dancing will inevitably lapse into catatonia, because for him dancing is a very precise form of thinking, and however well he may be able to think in other imageries, unless he can think also by dancing and before an audience, he is unable to fit his experiences together into a coherent whole, and feels incarcerated in a hostile world. Games, gymnastics, the various forms of exhibitionism, shouting, fighting, dancing, sexuality, contain elements of non-verbal thinking so important that mental health may be impaired if they are denied[1]—yet in Western civilization certain kinds of thinking are so habitually suppressed that they are being systematically evolved out of existence. A great many of our introverts, neurotics, depressives, lunatics—often valuable sensitive people—are probably in their condition because in our society they are denied opportunities for thinking in imageries that are necessary to them—

---

[1] Intuition is the sizing up of a situation by non-verbal thought, hence the intuitive's difficulty in explaining in words the reasons for his conclusions.

and it is because of this that drink and various drugs often become important: they dull the perceptions and allow the conscious mind to wander at will in its own internal reality, and sometimes—as can dreaming, creativity, emergency—break down association barriers and inhibitions on behaviour and allow the minds' model to adjust itself closer to reality. The occasional orgiastic dances of "savages" serve the same function, and perhaps more successfully, because more naturally.

While walking with the Indians one quickly discovers the extraordinary keenness of their perceptions, and how each sense helps the other. After living in the forests for a while one acquires, or re-acquires, some of this as a necessity—or one would get lost, or tread on a snake. Great was my delight and pride when one day Jonah remarked, "You know, Mr. Guppy, you sees just like an Indian." A half-eaten fruit on the ground, and they look up—parrots are eating overhead, they say—but it is only after searching that the parrots are seen: they guess parrots because it is usually parrots that eat that kind of fruit in that way. To the forest Indians nearly all they see is of interest. Their environment may be far more limited than that available to a dweller in civilization, but they are directly dependent upon it for survival. We can, indeed have to, choose one of thousands of possible ways of life, and as a result our field of perception shrinks enormously in proportion to the whole, but they have no choice, and their perceptiveness expands to encompass their entire, smaller world. They think about it in every imagery and means of self-expression. They paint, carve, weave designs of animals and plants, sing about them, dance in imitation of their movements, expressing everything in its own imagery: movement imagery, for example, by dancing, where with us a painter would have developed his visual imagery until it overshadowed the rest of his mind, and would express movement by composition. For this reason alone one cannot expect in these Indians' arts the concentration which in ours comes from the expression of an entire universe-model through one imagery; while the differences between their arts and ours reflect the differences between their universe models and our own, and the ways in which they are built up.

With some people the building up of this model proceeds

smoothly. Their minds shuttle images to and fro rapidly and efficiently, fitting them together in different ways, forming and rejecting associations, and their model, however incomplete, is not at odds with the reality around them. Their problems therefore are chiefly outside them, in seeking security by exploring and assimilating as much as they can of the outer world, and their creativeness is chiefly concerned with this—with reproducing with greater and greater accuracy their perceptions, and with classification and analysis. Other people, however, build up a model which is unrealistic or disordered, perhaps because through upbringing they have specialized their imageries too much or are prevented or inhibited from forming associations freely or thinking in imageries necessary to them, or because the different parts of their minds have not developed proportionately. In any case they have difficulty in fitting images together and achieving a realistic and coherent model, and their will, the energy of the mind used in seeking security, is therefore turned inwards trying to do this. It is only as they succeed that they attain the feeling of confidence needed to release their energy in outwards exploration again.

What such people create or express in solving their often painful inner problems, whether in the form of a work of art, an hypothesis, a religious revelation, a poetical inspiration, a mathematical formula, will be quite unlike anything produced in the first instance, and may be unlike anything already existing in the outer world, for it will be a complex of many images and even imageries—yet it will be an attempt to compound them in as simple and realistic a form as possible. Such complex symbols, or systems of symbolism, reflect the structure of the human mind in their three variable dimensions—their degree of specificity, of complexity, and of fusion. The first of these, specificity or generality (or abstractness) of the images concerned, is dependent in the first instance on the precision of perception of the sense organs, but even more upon the level of the mind at which the image is analysed; the second, simplicity or complexity, is a matter of the number of images brought together in the construction of the symbol by the brain's network of nerve channels and association centres; and the third, the degree of separation or fusion of these images, corresponds not merely with the mind's ability to shuffle them and fit them together, but with the urgency of the need for unification, and this probably with the degree of insecurity in the environment. Finally, as attributes of the completed symbol, there is its degree of realism, or correspondence with something existing in the outside world, and its strength—the response or responses it produces, which depends upon the combined effectiveness of its various images as stimuli.

The greater the number of images that a unified symbol contains the less likely it is that it will be able to convey them all realistically. Yet while realism is the aim of symbol creation, obscurity as well as complexity may be a strength, because by disturbing the mind obscurity attracts its energy. The more precise and realistic the imagery of a symbol, the more separate its components, the more easily it is fitted into the mind—and the sooner it ceases to be noticed. Thus closely unified symbols are more effective foci for the attention than diffuse ones, and are capable of liberating more energy; and being of necessity unrealistic, may continue to do so even when the reality they formerly summarized has disappeared: thus the Cross survives even though Christianity is always changing; and national flags are more effective bonds than similarities of outlook.

It is a little dismaying to think that the only reality we can ever know is a model in our minds constructed on the model of our minds; that its closeness to Actuality is something we can only guess by how well it works and that the direction of human progress merely multiplies the number of pieces of the puzzle we have to fit together, which only at the deepest levels of our minds, where all sensations are reduced to one or two, can fuse. Nevertheless, human progress is the story of the construction of more and more comprehensive and realistic universe-models, for the sake of a feeling of security, by means of this natural outwards and inwards flowing of the energy of the mind (which Jung calls the progression and regression of the libido, but does not explain). Again and again among different races and at different periods of history the same stages can be found in their evolution, reflecting not merely the universality of human experience, but the identity of brain structure. In all communities various stages of this progression and regression, or extrospection and introspection, are to be found among individuals, but history is the story of how people as a whole are affected. There are times of outwards exploration with an efflorescence of specific language and naturalism in all forms of creativeness. There are times of crisis when the old universe-model can no longer accommodate the prolixity of new knowledge, marked in creativity by harsh conjunctions of disparities, with on the one hand the old tradition, posing problems and working out solutions that have become meaningless, on the other the new solutions achieved by discarding the old proliferation and turning inwards to deeper levels of the mind—and characterized, for those living through them, by a feeling of purposelessness and frustration, and by the separation of morality, art, politics, science, religion, everyday life, from each other.[1] And there are times when a new model has been built up and the mind's energy flows outwards again—marked at first by simplicity and harmony in what is created (because the problems being solved are at deep, abstract mind levels), but in turn leading to elaboration.

Sometimes, however, the old universe-model is too strong: all the facts are referred to it and rejected if they do not fit it, instead of it being altered to accommodate them; and the mind remains turned inwards, for its chief problem becomes the acceptance of incongruities. Then for hundreds, even thousands of years, as in China, India, ancient Egypt, the eastern Roman empire, the Roman Catholic countries since the Reformation—even, one guesses, the Neolithic, following the wonderful

[1] The Renaissance from this point of view is directly comparable with the present day. Both show similar adjustments towards new realities taking place at slightly different times in different fields of thought. In architecture, for example, where reality is constructional method (applied to the solution of problems of requirement), the flowering of late Gothic was followed by such incongruous mixed styles as Jacobean or that of the French Renaissance chateaux—just as today clumsy monstrosities mix features of the elegant simplicity of the new style with those of the old; but the old style is already dead, as Gothic was dead 300 years ago after Inigo Jones introduced classicism into England. It is the same with religion: the Reformation swept away, besides much else, the hierarchy of saints, as Darwin did the Creation myth; but today no new Luther has yet pieced together the durable remnants of Christianity.

Palaeolithic period of realistic art—initiative is destroyed and exploration of the outer world virtually ceases. Peace, stability, high refinement may mark such periods—but history is left in the hands of heretics.

The universe, as the Mawayáns and Wai-Wais conceive it, is neutral: merely a place in which one lives, pleasant or unpleasant as the creatures in it, of whom man is no more important than any other, make it so. As with other primitive peoples (and as in the myths and legends of civilized races), their first ancestors, the heroes and discoverers of ancient times, are described as men who were either made from animals, descended from animals, or could talk to or understand the language of animals. Fire, in Mawayán legend, was discovered by a woman who married a tinamou; and the ancestress of the race, equivalent to our Eve, was the daughter of an anaconda. She was fished out of the deep pool in which she lived with her father, to the Creator's jealousy and surprise (though he had long suspected that there might be such things as women), by his younger brother, the male ancestor of humanity. Even in the act of creating, the Mawayán Creator is a vague figure. He made the earth much as a man might build a house, as a place to live in, and dwelt there with his brother, fishing, hunting with bow and arrows and trained foxes (before there were dogs), among apparently previously existing men (much as Adam and Eve must have lived among previously existing people, for how else could Cain, their son and sole surviving child after the death of Abel, have married?). He is pictured as a man rather like the chiefs of these Indians' own very loosely organized tribes—much as the Old Testament Creator was, like the great leaders of the Jewish nation, a supreme commander whose orders could not be disobeyed with impunity—and this conception of him is another argument against the likelihood of these Indians being descended from a higher culture, for that would surely have had to have a centralized authority. And today, a wise old man, he lives in the sky, paying no attention to what happens on earth—for which reason no prayers are offered to him.

The Indians believe that everything—birds, beetles, scorpions, animals, plants, rocks, running water—has some sort of

SIESTA, SHIURU-TIRIR

2(b)

2(a)

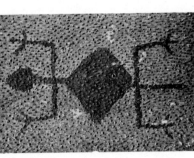

1(a) 1(b)

3(b)

 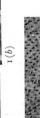

3(a)

5

4

1. (a) Scorpion and (b) Frog (Mawayán woven designs). 2. (a) Flies' eyes and (b) Fish tails (Wai-Wai painted designs). 3. Lizard (a) abstract painted design on centre of Wai-Wai dancing club, showing cross hatching, which appears to indicate derivation of the design from basketwork; (b) semi-naturalistic painted design on a Wai-Wai cassava grater. 4. Mawayán man's vanity basket: two spotted jaguars facing each other with a beetle between. Uprights on either side represent trees; crosses, grass or leaves. 5. Anaconda effigy (Wai-Wai).

life or spirit in it, and that the spirits of dead things go to the sky and live with the Creator. But sometimes they return to earth and wander about, as proof of which people and creatures known to be dead are sometimes seen in dreams—for what can dreams be but wanderings of the spirit, and how else could one see someone known to be dead?

Although most of these spirits are harmless, others, such as those seen in delirium, or which are believed to lurk in the forest and attack solitary men, are evil, especially if directed by sorcerers, and but for them no one would fall ill or die. Perhaps by depicting everything, and especially things feared, the Indians hoped to propitiate their spirits? And the fact that such depictions would have to refer to *all* the spirits of a particular kind of creature might help account for their abstraction— there was little doubt that none of their drawings, at least at the present time, were intended to represent individual things, while many, such as those of beetles or frogs or lizards, stood for whole groups of creatures of which they were well aware that there were numerous different kinds. Their taming of animals probably also had in it an element of propitiation, and it might well be that their arts complemented this, for it was noticeable that their designs, except for those of dogs, were mostly of untameable creatures—jaguars, scorpions, sloths, howler monkeys, lizards.

Why, I asked Yuhmé, were so many things decorated with lizard designs. It was a design of which I had found a whole series, from semi-naturalism to the merest squiggle, like a letter 's'; and there was even a lizard dance.

The reason, he said, was because long ago some Mawayáns had seen the lizard-people—little men dressed as lizards.

Yet propitiation alone could hardly account for the extremity of abstraction of some of the designs, or for the fact that in some cases their meanings had been forgotten. There must be some reason why their external environment had so ceased to interest these Indians that they were turning away from it, and had become more interested in pattern than representation, some reason why only by working out patterns they could restore the balance of their inner model of reality—so different, apparently, from our own or that of their ancestors.

K   275

Similar series, showing a change away from naturalism, can be found in the arts of other peoples, primitive as well as civilized. They are usually dismissed as representing periods of cultural decline or degeneration, yet from what we have seen they far more likely indicate attempts to find a way forward out of an impasse. At one extreme they exhibit an art concerned chiefly with emotion: the deep subjective involvement of the artists is shown by the fact that human beings are the commonest subjects, and even where this is not so, colour, form, proportion all express emotion or relative importance. The essential parts of creatures—their eyes, nose, lips, fingers, toes—are nearly always carefully enumerated, but frequently they look as if they were stuck together to form a composite, and often their proportions are distorted so that the effect is grotesque. Such an art seems to represent an inwards search in which the position of man in a hostile environment is the most important problem—for fear, incomprehension, insecurity are what it usually expresses—and it is only as a solution is worked out that the parts begin to fuse and naturalism returns.

At the other extreme one finds an aesthetic and intellectual art in which colour, pattern, harmony, perfection of finish and decorative effect are the aims: human beings are scarcely depicted, known essentials are unhesitatingly omitted and proportions varied in the interests of design; meaning is relatively unimportant and may even be forgotten, and intellectually interesting techniques such as stringwork, weaving and basketry are elaborated, while painting and carving are neglected. Such an art, of which that of the Mawayáns and Wai-Wais is clearly an example, seems by contrast concerned with a turning inwards away from a comparatively secure world, in which mysteries have been encountered which have to be explained, but with no great emotional urgency.

Both extremes can be found in our civilization, where there is no consistency of belief or direction; but among the Mawayáns and Wai-Wais the arts reflect the simplicity and uniformity of their ideas, the fact that they are merely at the beginning of the long process of universe-model creation, or religious discovery. There is little fusion of design, or imagery—and indeed their conception of the universe is a jumble of vague, incongruous, separate ideas. Yet at their minds' level these ideas probably fit together as satisfactorily into patterns as do the imprecise, disproportionate abstract beetles, jaguars, lizards, and rivers on the sides of their baskets—and as doubtless did the equally fragmentary and contradictory beliefs of the Old Testament in the minds of our ancestors.

If one searched one might possibly find depictions of human beings, such as are occasionally seen among other Guiana tribes, in which people are drawn without special care or emphasis, exactly as animals are drawn. But they have not begun to discover that, by using human representations as symbols, more ideas can be fused and yet expressed naturalistically than in any other way. They have therefore no concept of a man-like God (for their creator is scarcely a god, as he is not worshipped), or of gods personifying fate, death, war, justice, wisdom and other abstract qualities, far less of such later sophistications as a god who *is* the universe or in whose mind the universe exists as a thought, or of a life force. They have not even attained the level of imagining dragons, griffons, sphinxes or other compounds of animals or animals and humans—though the lizard-people may be a beginning in this direction. The only unified symbol they have evolved, and that still naturalistic (the merest beginning of a fertility symbol), is the anaconda effigy, representing good luck and the ancestral spirit, of which I had seen an example at the Wai-Wai chief's village, Mawiká. The rapid decay in this climate of nearly everything made by the Mawayáns and Wai-Wais, particularly of basketwork and painted wood, in which their arts are most highly developed, makes it unlikely that we will ever discover a series of remains from which we could date the beginning of their concern with inward problems. But the simultaneous presence in their arts today of different stages in abstraction shows that the process is still going on, and this is confirmed by the fact that they are still creating myths: thunder, they now say, is a black man in the sky shaking stones in a tin can. Designs, identical with some of theirs, particularly at the realistic ends of the series, can be found among related tribes, sometimes neighbours, sometimes quite distant, from whom they have been separated certainly for two or three hundred years, though with whom they may have maintained contacts; and if we could date the movements of these peoples we might be able to find out when the change began. It is tempting to think that it might have been with the coming of the white man, or the first epidemics, but their arts' serenity suggests otherwise.

It will be interesting, if saddening, to see what changes take place in the next few generations. Very likely almost their entire artistic productivity will come to a stop, for civilization and the missionaries are on their doorstep, and the shock produced by them often so shatters a primitive people's reality and inhibits their thinking that, for a while at least, despair, secretiveness, suspicion replace their former charm and extroversion, and their minds are frozen in a profound, slow, inwards searching, before, after a generation or two, they begin to recover—though by that time their culture is lost.

Fonyuwé had wept (Andrew had said), overwhelmed by his first glimpse of semi-civilization—Karardanawa, with its numerous small mud-and-wattle huts, its chapel, and its people in their shapeless clothing—and had cried out, "I am good for nothing but carrying loads. I am just an animal beside these people."

Yet how much sadder than the tale of his disillusionment was the condition of the Karardanawans! It is hard to say, of all those who form the vanguard of civilization—prospectors, balata bleeders, traders, officials, ranchers, missionaries—which are the most destructive. Probably the missionaries, for even when they view their flocks with love, as human beings and not as sinners and outragers of decency, their aim is to overthrow everything that is fundamental in the heathens' beliefs and ways of life. Old-style missionaries would search for things the natives revered, and destroy them, and stop their ceremonies, but public and governmental opinion have been raised against such behaviour and modern missionaries have to be subtler. Their approach is often economic. They introduce new wants, turn their missions into labour exchanges, and make their flocks subservient before beginning to exert pressure to produce that perfect society which they cannot achieve in civilization. The natives' standard of living (measured by such means as the average cash income, or the consumption of imported goods) rises, they learn to read and write (though they have access only to the missionaries' books), are clothed hideously but "decently", give up polygamy and frequently birth control, receive medical attention, and are baptized—but the joy goes out of their existence. Their horizons roll back and they find themselves of no importance in a world which they do not understand, over whose changes they have no control, and into which they cannot picture themselves fitting—and with no future except that of forming a depressed class of daily labourers.

Usually, hidden to avoid trouble, the debased relics of the old customs continue, but many turn to the missionaries and accept their faith. Indeed, it is only after the destruction that the missionaries begin to build. Yet the effects of conversion may be quite different from what they expect, for in Guiana (as also, one hears, in Africa, Asia, the South Seas) it often liberates the natives from moral restraint. The Indians believe that if a man breaks the laws of his tribe, or harms others, he will suffer because others in turn will do him harm, or will not like him, and that he will go on suffering after death, because in the next world he will find all the people, enemies included, whom he knew on earth, and have to continue living with them. Every man thus has to accept responsibility for his own actions and their consequences for all time—but these consequences are comparatively minor. Christianity inflates them into heavy burdens of Sin and Guilt when it introduces its advanced, unified concepts of a single great force of Evil (far more appalling than a few malevolent spirits or men, who can be dealt with as individuals) and a God infinitely good and wise, who are fighting for control of the world. It exalts man's importance, so that he becomes not merely distinct from animals, but the end and purpose of creation, and puts him in a position to bargain for the surrender of his soul. To the Indians the choice appears to be between continuing to lead a life according to their old ways and suffering Hell, torments, burning fires in the next world, and adopting alien customs in exchange for the promise of everlasting bliss. But at the same time they are offered an escape: belief in the mysterious God's Son and repentance of their sins, even on their death-beds, will apparently get them the bliss anyway.

At last they understand the ruthlessness, lying, cheating, stealing, violence, bullying, adultery, drunkenness of so many of those who belong to this faith; and having accepted the Christian's beliefs, they accept his standards of behaviour. From then onwards it is only their natural goodness, their lethargy, and the threat of the police which restrain them.

That the Indians are capable of accepting responsibility for their own actions at a simple level is shown by their beliefs; and that they are ready for more unified concepts is shown by their search. But that there should be such results from the introduction of Christianity shows the lack of intelligence of many who attempt to teach it—as well as the weakness of what they teach. For until the load of incongruities, acceptance of which the Churches require together with their spiritual and moral teachings, is swept away, Christianity cannot be a credible guide in the modern world, and its teachings, whatever material benefits they may accompany, can only be destructive to the minds of those outside it. Its apparent alternative, the philosophy of science—that nothing must be believed which cannot be verified, and that everything is relevant and interdependent and must therefore be known—drives us on to a phenomenal proliferation of discovery on the one hand, but requires a suspension of belief on the other, and provides only poor, shallow, incomplete unifications to sustain us meanwhile— until all is known, and the grand, final model is revealed. To live by it requires even more strength and resolution than in the past have come from the inner security of a coherent, comprehensive, realistic universe model, such as the Churches provided—yet it is hard to see how, in its rigid adherence to proven truth, it conflicts with the aims of religion, which must also be the discovery of truth. And its acceptance of personal responsibility in the highest degree, and therefore of the necessity of striving to increase self-awareness, extends also to the choice between Good and Evil (concepts which we may have created ourselves, or which may be attributes of that unknown Actuality nearer to which we increasingly attempt to adjust our inner models—and is surely at the heart of Christ's teachings.

Missionaries are frequently educated men, dedicated to their work, altruistic in intent, backed by wealthy societies. If they could begin to view their work objectively and see the horrible un-Christianity of so many of its results, and the loss to the world that it causes of things that can never return; if they could forget their lust to evangelize, their virulent and petty bigotries, despotisms, and intersectarian jealousies, and adopt an attitude of humility towards their flocks, they could more than any others make the transition to civilization smooth and beneficial wherever it is necessary. They could protect the natives during the period when they are trying to assimilate the mass of new ideas being thrust upon them, teach them new techniques in agriculture, medicine, carpentry, metal work, and so increase their self-confidence and their ability to adapt themselves without suffering or loss of independence. But to do so they would have to support the tribal society, and therefore—until the natives voluntarily desired conversion—the beliefs upon which it is founded, and such a course would require a patience and restraint of which few missionaries seem capable.

There is unfortunately, in the absence of such an ideal, nothing like a world-wide organization or agreement to protect primitive peoples. The Mawayáns might be saved for a while by their remoteness, but they were bound eventually to be affected by the fate of the neighbouring Wai-Wais. And the Wai-Wais are so few that it is only a matter of time, speeded up, perhaps, by something like a mineral discovery, before they are dis-possessed of their ancient tribal territories—without redress, as they have no legal claim to them—and lost in the spreading heterogeneous population of British Guiana: Hindus, Chinese, Portuguese, negroes, Indians of various tribes, and mixtures of every kind.[1] And even if they avoid absorption, they will sink into the drabness of the mission proletariat of such places as Karardanawa—whereupon will disappear one of the last remaining evidences that in South America, that continent of sullen, oppressed Indians, there were once gay, even extroverted tribes, as beautiful in their regalia as any mountain peoples of New Guinea, artistic, self-sufficient, happy, living peacefully,

[1] With the approach of independence for British Guiana it has been announced that the Wai-Wais and other primitive tribes will be integrated into the general life of the country: already, legally, they are voters!

morally, creatively, in equilibrium with their environment—and from whom much could be learned about mankind.

It was thus gloomily that I considered old Yuhmé, sitting there in the sunshine, and wondered what his fate and that of his children and grandchildren would be, and when they would cease to make their lovely arrows, and cassava-graters, and feather-hung vanity-boxes. I was glad that I had seen them when I had.

From Ka'i, who was standing near by tickling a red-painted monkey, I bought two arrows, one large as an assegai, with a sheer piece of cutlass-blade for a head, the other more of a harpoon than an arrow, yet feathered for flight—a hideous weapon designed for the largest game, with a wooden shaft four feet long, and a big barbed piece of steel fitting like a cap to its end, held tight by a long spiral band of cording designed to untwist when the arrow struck home.

Machira (who had agreed to help carry our loads as far as the Buna-wau, as he wanted to earn as many trade goods as he could) was a few yards off, weaving a circular fishing-net, and when he saw me make these purchases strode away and returned with a bow and a sheaf of arrows, some tobacco wrapped in a palm-leaf, and a fistful of feather ornaments. We could carry so little, and I had already bought so much from the other Indians that I did not really want anything more; however, so as not to offend him, I selected three superb arrows, flighted with blue and scarlet macaw feathers, and the tobacco, and declined the rest.

He was chagrined: he stood for a moment, his brow wrinkled. I fingered an ornament, whereupon, picking up the fish-hooks and knives I had given him, he dumped all his possessions in my hand, not rudely, but firmly, as if to say, "I want trade goods for three arrows or the lot—take them all!"—and walked away, back to his net.

Ka'i now produced a quiver of poisoned arrow-tips. This was too rare an article to miss, besides being small and light. Through Basil and Fonyuwé I questioned him whether I could also get some of the curare poison itself, or the ingredients.

Certainly, he replied, he would give me some at once: I could come with him to where he kept it.

Agog, I followed as he led the way along a narrow path through the sugar cane to where, ducking beneath a wasps' nest on the underside of a leaf, we found a tiny shelter with walls of palm thatch. This, the holy of holies in which the poison was made, was forbidden to all uninitiated men, to all women, and usually to all strangers. Inside was a stool, the remains of a burnt-out fire, and all about on the floor, and on small shelves of sticks at the sides, bits of bark and root, and lengths of the bamboo from which the arrow-points were shaped.

Amazed that I should have been allowed to come here, I remained silent while he gathered together the three principal ingredients—dusty pieces of bark—wrapped them in a palm-leaf, and handed them to me.

Then to my great surprise he began to tell me how the poison was made. Dozens of people have tried unsuccessfully to drag this information from the Indians, and now, when voluntarily it was being imparted to me, it was most frustrating being unable to speak directly to Ka'i.

What made things particularly difficult was Fonyuwé's mood: he was a necessary link in the translation, and he was at his most annoying. He too had apparently made curare, and instead of repeating what Ka'i, precise and rather learned-looking as he expounded, was relating, he wanted to tell me about himself. He flexed his muscles, puffed out his cheeks, and his eyes shone. He waved his arms and raved about how terrible it was making it, and how thin and emaciated one got, how one could eat only porridge and cassava bread, and how one sat all day long over a fire, stirring and stirring and stirring.

A few of the Wapisianas had followed, and interested, gathered around. Fonyuwé became self-conscious and glanced about him at them, mincing like a showgirl. A devilish smile flitted across his features, and he gave a tremendous groan, thumping himself on the chest:

"Ooh! Ooh! Ooh!" he howled, agonized, wiping his hands down his cheeks to signify tears.

"It is impossible to get any sense out of him," said Basil; "he is just making a lot of noises."[1]

[1] The missionary told me later that the Wai-Wais have a special onomato-poeic "epic" language, or mode of speech, used for the description of very

Eventually, however, by noting down everything that was said I was able to reconstruct the mode of preparation and the sequence of events:

For one month before starting to make the poison a man had to keep away from all women, even his wife, and to refrain from bathing; then he would go to the little hut, where he had gathered the following ingredients:

1. The most poisonous of all, a root called *Ositi* by the Mawayáns, *Barawetu* by the Wai-Wais, and probably the root of a *Strychnos* vine. This he would pound up and boil in a pot with water, adding after an hour or two, chopped and pounded up, the rest of the ingredients in the order given:

2. The next most poisonous, a bark called *Kwitaru-dediyen* by the Mawayáns, *Kwarar* by the Wapisianas, and possibly the bark of a *Lonchocarpus* vine.

3. A leaf found in the mountains, called Snake-tongue leaf (*Wianyuba* in Mawayán; *Okoin-yuro* in Wai-Wai; *Kwarar-nenub* in Wapisiana); and probably the leaf of an arum, used for its glutinousness, as a binder.

4. The stem of a four-foot-high plant called, in both Mawayán and Wapisiana, *Tautau*.

5. The leaves of a vine called *Achuri-tuna* in Mawayán, and *Watwa-matko* or *Tuatua-matko* in Wai-Wai (*Tuatua* meaning alligator).

6. The teeth and venom of a snake called *Shawiti* in Mawayán and *Ko'i* in Wai-Wai, and doubtless the bushmaster or fer-de-lance.[1]

These were all boiled together slowly for nine days—more water being added when necessary, and any scum formed being skimmed off—during which time the brew had to be stirred constantly, day and night, and the maker was allowed to eat only farine porridge and cassava bread: in consequence of which, his sleeplessness and his exertions, he felt ghastly and got very thin.

exciting things, beside their ordinary one; and that this raving of Fonyuwé's was not due to clowning, lying, or exaggeration, but to his love of the use of this special, more poetical, tongue.

[1] The Indians are extremely specific in the naming of plants and animals and there should be no difficulty in a future traveller identifying those of the above list which I have been unable to collect and identify.

By the end of nine days the brew was reduced to a thick, dark, reddish-brown gum. Then bamboo arrow-tips, previously carved, were dipped in it, stuck points-outward into holes in the broken shaft of an arrow that had killed an animal, and turned slowly over the fire to dry. Any poison left over was flung away.

In examining these arrow-tips I had been struck by a curious thin striation beneath the poison, winding in a spiral from point to base of the blade. Now I saw that this was actually a groove which helped to fix more poison, and perhaps aided in its dissolution and entry into the blood. And the blades were notched deeply all round at the base so that they would break off and remain in the wound, instead of being dislodged, if the animal tried to get away among the vegetation.

After a drink of cassava beer at the village, I returned to the camp to do my packing. The sky was clear overhead and in the east, but westwards it was dark: purple clouds and black skeins of mist hung low over the forests we should be crossing on the morrow, as for days past they had done. Rain was falling far away in the Serra Acarai. It would mean higher water for the boats—if it had not washed them away—but uncomfortable travelling.

The sun shone encouragingly bright in the morning. At breakfast, between bowls of farine and dips of cassava bread into black Nescafé, I packed an enormous bowl I had bought from Yapumo's wife, reddish-brown, zebra-striped with black, and highly glazed with *Protium* gum. I filled it with shirts, wrapped it with towels, and swathed the whole mass in my hammock. Even as I worked a fragment broke from the edge. It was one of my greatest treasures: I wondered if it would ever reach civilization.

Then I went to the village, strolling over the tangled earth, under the cloudless blue sky, and feeling sad at leaving. Blue wood-smoke was rising above it, passion flowers and convolvuli were spreading their flowers, the pale morning sunlight was gilding each blade of sugar cane, each leaf of pepper, cassava, calalloo. The earth underfoot was so clean, the air so cool that to be alive was physical delight.

Even on this last morning, when they were accompanying

me, Ka'i, Machira, Yapumo and Yuhmé had brought forth their bowls of drink. On Yapumo's fingers flashed two bright new rings, made from brass cartridge ends.

"*Kiriwanhi*"—nice, aren't they?—he asked, holding them up—and I strongly agreed. What business of mine if elsewhere his tastes would be laughable?

The traveller journeys far, lured on by legends, but I felt that if I saw nothing more I should be content. There is no Golden City of Manoa to be found in Guiana. No great new things, such as Fonyuwé's men with tree-trunk legs, or a buried city, can really remain hidden, even in these vast forests: the news must be noised from tribe to tribe—and one would hear of it, and be able to judge of its possibility. The returns for discomfort and long periods of monotonous travel are few, and the un-expected things are those that are not talked about, because people think nothing of them—gentle manners, kindliness, hospitality, beautiful feather jewellery, superb long bows and arrows. I had found a single village with few people living in it, and they were kindly and simple—and yet those slight things and what I had learned from them constituted a great reward.

We were packed and ready to go—indeed, some of the men had already set off an hour before into the forest. Where, I wondered, was the chief, or Kwakwé?

Then I received an unexpected shock: they were ill, and so again were Foimo and Icaro. That morning our appalling epidemic, the spectre that had sat on my shoulder all through the expedition, had broken out again.

I had few drugs left, but I gave them each stiff doses of sulphathiazole, and left more tablets with them than I could spare, with instructions that I hoped they would follow. We could not remain with them, because there was no food. The only thing that I could console myself with was that no one, not even those, like William and Wayama, who had been untreated, had died so far.

I did not know whether one shook hands on parting, and those who remained behind gave no indication—perhaps they expected me to make the move? So I waved, turned, and strode away from the village, with Basil at my side—and as I walked I prayed that soon there would be an end to all the illness.

17

Jonah Overboard

Striding through the forest, over the low hills, through the swamps and bogs, the problem of Jonah was uppermost in my mind. Despite our conversation of a few days before, his grumbling had become much worse. I should not have minded if our position had been easy: but it was not. The men had spent the past week hunting and fishing, but with little success; more serious, the Mawayáns had been able to let us have only four days' food instead of the ten we had hoped for. They were beginning to run short themselves and needed all they had to tide them over the wet season. It looked sadly as if we should have to abandon going down the Mapuera and push as fast as we could back to Manatá's village—from there, if we could get supplies enough, collecting for a few days on the Acarai watershed.

Basil, even the Wapisianas, faced the issues fairly calmly, and were prepared to help me do the maximum possible. But Jonah's attitude was a triumphant, disagreeable "I told you so" at any least hint of difficulty.

The depression of the forest was heavy on me—the sheer untidiness and volume of twigs, leaves and bark that surrounded and pressed upon me, the flickering half darkness, the wetness, the spider-webs that enwrapped my face, the nameless countless insects that crawled and bit, the sweat, the branches plucking at clothes and hair . . .

The hills were slippery from recent rain, and the continuous dampness had rotted all my shoes. One by one they had fallen apart, been mended, mended again, and finally discarded. Now my only sound pair, the ones I had formerly kept always dry as camp shoes, burst within a few minutes of each other. For a mile, until I found a monkey-pipe tree and was able to bind

287

them with a strip of bark, I flipped along as if in a pair of slippers. I did a little reckoning: excluding water travel there were probably no more than eleven days of continuous walking ahead. If I walked carefully, and if we found a balata tree and could mend them with its gum, I might just possibly be able to make them hold. Meanwhile I swathed them with bandages of bast.

Titko-tirir, the deserted village; the Mara-yoku, with its amazing solitary bamboos, and an alligator swimming away under the grey thorny palms; the Oroko'orin. The heat was vertical, intense; then the sun was ahead, flinging long golden streamers into our faces. At darkness we reached the miserable muddy place of a former camp.

A vast tree came thundering down near by, and I awoke. The stars were still out, but the sky was paling. There was the sound of voices, loud barking: the Mawayáns had caught up with us. They had remained behind at the Oroko'orin, with half of our belongings and all the cassava bread and bananas which I had bought to form our staple diet, to catch fish, promising to rejoin us early this day.

Inevitably I had been worried about when we should see them next, yet I had trusted them. Among all the sullenness of the Wapisianas, the scowlings of Jonah, there was something reassuring about them—perhaps it was the presence of the two women, Ka'i's and Yuhmé's wives, heavily laden though they were (for Indian women carry their husband's belongings, leaving them free to hunt). Somehow it was good for morale to think of this family party staying behind, fishing and cooking in a leisurely way, and planning to walk ahead early in the morning and catch us up. It made us, too, feel correspondingly tranquil.

About noon Yuhmé and his wife were walking just ahead of me when their three dogs dashed away through the forest, yelping and barking. Then a peccary, which they had headed off from a small herd, raced by a few feet in front, closely chased by an old and usually tired-looking bitch, and took refuge under a hollow tree beside the path. There Yuhmé shot an arrow into it, and as it bolted out, finished it off with a swipe of his cutlass.

Two guans, a residue of smoke-dried fish, the peccary—
and our dinners were assured. That morning, fiercely hungry,
I had opened my last tin of meat, anticipating the small cache
at the riverside. It had done me good, yet now I regretted it:
one could never tell when the hunters would have luck.

"First meat for four days," I could hear Jonah saying, by
the camp-fire that night. He had been too tired to help me, so
I was working alone on the day's collections. "How we expected
to go on like this? A man can't work without proper food . . ."

Grunts of agreement.

Yet there were worse diets than bananas, farine, cassava
bread and an occasional taste of meat in the Mawayáns' stews.

A little later he was describing a past expedition on which
the leader had fallen so ill that he had lost his reason. He had
run about naked with a knife in his hand, and had given senseless orders.

". . . So we tie him up, three of us, and we put him in the
boat, and all the time he was shouting and saying he would get
us punished. And we take him back to headquarters. It was the
only thing we could do when things reach bad like that."

More grunts of assent and interest.

At the Mawayáns' camp an enormous fire had been lighted,
to ward away the dampness, and while the two women petted
their dogs or moved about doing little oddments, the men took
turns in singing. It was not so much the tunes—though from
Kirifakka's early morning fluting I had got to know and like
several—as the pure beauty of sounds and notes that stirred
them. Fonyuwé would warble forth a short run of several
words, then, anthem-like, repeat one or two, or the concluding
phrase, in different keys and pitches, ascending or descending,
ending at last in a long cadence with a drawn-out final note,
like a monk singing an elaborate chant. Then came the resonant
bull-like voice of Machira, even more of a taster of sounds than
Fonyuwé, lingering on and lovingly repeating his cadences,
intoning them through his nose and turning his head on one
side so that he could better hear the results.

Following Machira and Yapumo the next day, I had to
walk so fast lest I lose them, for the path was too faint for me to
follow on my own, that I was scarcely able to think. For the

seven or eight miles to the riverside I half ran, half limped, because of a painful thorn in my right foot which I dared not delay to extract. Panting, I flung myself down when at last we arrived, and pulled it out. We must have made at least four miles an hour, a speed exceptional even on a well-cut trail, and we were far ahead of the rest of the party.

With joy I laid bare the little store I had left behind here: whatever the cost, I determined to open the sardines and savour their rankness at dinner and at breakfast the following day. I should still have two tins of corned beef and one of condensed milk left, which I would delay broaching; then I remembered my regrets of the day before at unnecessarily opening a tin. No, the sardines could wait.

With Yapumo I bailed out the canoes. Leaves and inky black water, stained from the tannins in their wood, filled them, and green mildew covered their sides, interspersed with the yellow dust-pushings of boring beetles. They were almost afloat. The level of the river had risen by at least a foot, as I could clearly see from a tree-stump, now submerged, on which I had formerly stepped up from the rocks on which they were drawn.

"How long we been walking, sir?" asked George, when he and the other men arrived an hour later.

I looked at my watch. "Two and three-quarter hours."

"It was longer," said Jonah flatly. Then a moment later, aside, but so that I could hear—"But chief have the watch."

I could see that he had been working himself up, and that he intended to challenge me at some point. I regretted my softness to him in the past. He was marshalling his support. With George Gouveia, whom I liked and trusted, but who was his best friend, and Gabriel, Charlie's son, whom I did not like, because he struck me as being rather a wise guy, he sat a little distance off, holding forth in hectoring tones; and they, more soothingly, were agreeing with him.

My first job was to pay off the Mawayáns, and see if I could not persuade them by generosity to come further with us. Food was scarce but men were needed, and they had proved themselves not only refreshingly willing workers but better fishermen than anyone else. Thinking of their kindness to us, I gave them all the trade goods I could, keeping only a small reserve for purchasing food at Manatá's and hiring one or two men for the journey back across the Acarai. Then I distributed all the salt I had left, about 8 lb., as it was something they valued very much, and of which they had no natural supply.

When this was concluded all, to my delight, agreed to come further, except Machira, who said that his wife and family were expecting him to return. Nothing would make him change his mind. He shook hands, and strode powerfully back along the trail.

Jonah, meanwhile, had been talking to Basil:

"We go stop at the first camp downstream, the chief promise," I heard him say.

I had made no such promise, though I had agreed with him that if we reached the riverside in the afternoon (instead of the morning), it would be a convenient place at which to stop. It seemed that he was planning to make an issue of it. I began to sense what lay ahead.

As we embarked I called him quietly from a few feet off, meaning to make my position perfectly clear, but he moved away without answering and entered one of the smaller boats.

Twenty minutes later we approached our uppermost camp on the Buna-wau, and at a rapid where the big boat had to be led the two smaller shot through and paddled ahead. I saw Jonah's canoe draw in to the bank at the old camp site; the Mawayáns in the other, doubtless feeling it was rather early to halt, hesitated in mid-stream.

"Shall we stop here?" shouted Basil from behind me.

I waved my hand, and past we went, through a short rocky run and on downstream.

There was a shout of rage from Jonah, and in a few moments his long thin canoe, paddled fast, drew abreast. In a hoarse, violent voice, choking with anger, he bellowed at me:

"You gave me your word that we would stop here. I don't like people breaking their word. What do you mean by going on?"

"The conversation has now ceased. We are going on," I replied calmly, and his shouting subsided.

The men were rattled: everyone, I saw now, had been

anticipating trouble. For a moment a wave of uncertainty passed over them, as if their vision were blurred by the sudden release of feeling. The boat yawed towards some rocks.

"Look out there, George," I called, pointing. He was transfixed, his job of bowman forgotten.

Pulling her straight, in unsteady tones he asked the time.

"Twenty past two," I said.

"Start looking for a camping-ground," I called out after an hour and a half, during which time we had continued in silence.

We were delayed at a rapid, and the long canoe swept past close, with Jonah in it avoiding my glance.

"Find camp spot," shouted George to him.

Rain began to fall, lightly, then in grey torrents, but for once it was warm and not at all uncomfortable. A curassow passed low overhead, and I shot it on the wing. Thanks to the killing of the peccary, and the Mawayáns' skill in fishing, we had still almost as much food as when we had left Shiuru-tirir. It might be worth while taking a final chance and continuing a bit further—but Jonah would have to go. It was imperative to teach him a lesson, to stop once and for all his infectious grumbling. I was elated, determined.

His boat was ahead now, and he had the task of choosing a camp site. We passed several good places, and then the long meanderings of the river through level muddy swamplands. It seemed as if he intended going on till nightfall. The rain became freezingly cold. Perhaps this affected him too, because soon after we came upon his boat tied up by a sandy, sedge-swarded beach, backed by peculiarly black and gloomy forest.

While camp was made the Mawayáns huddled under a tree, arms wrapped around themselves, looking very blue but making cheerful, incomprehensible remarks to each other and to me. Then, when the rain stopped, they began to build themselves a shelter.

Jonah was holding forth with animation, directing operations, but when I approached he went off and cut sticks in the forest, occasionally reappearing to deposit a bundle. I began to calculate what stores we could spare for him.

A little later, when we were settled, I called Basil:

"Could we spare enough food," I asked him, "to send an

advance party back to Manatá's village and across to the Chodikar with some of the baggage? If we could do that we could go a few days down the Mapuera."

He saw what was on my mind and brightened.

"Yes, we still have three days' cassava bread and vegetables, and a half sack of farine. It would be a good idea, because they could return and meet us, and help carry. Otherwise we will have to make two trips."

"Fine," I said. "Tell Jonah I want to speak to him."

Jonah had been joking and laughing loudly ever since the camp was made. But now he was very serious.

"What's all this bad temper, Jonah?"

"I'm a bad-tempered man, and even to the most senior officers I'm used to having my say. And you *promised* to stop at that camp. I told the men we were going to do that and have an early day."

"You had no right to tell them that. You only cause trouble by trying to make my decisions for me. Besides, I made no such promise. We never know in advance where we will be when it's time to stop."

"What if I refuse to work? We were coming for four weeks and here we are, long overdue. In the past when I work for Mr. Fanshawe or Mr. Davis they never have any complaints." He looked miserable, like a sulky schoolboy.

"Well, now you are working for me. I would never have brought you if I had thought you would be such a worry. So remember—I will have no more ill manners." I paused. "Anyway, I have some useful work for you. I want you and Gabriel to go ahead tomorrow in the small canoe, with some baggage, and do some collecting half-way back to the Chodikar on the high ground. That will give time for the rest of us to go a little way down the Mapuera."

He was silent, his face jowly, deeply lined with unhappiness. I had not realized that he would be so easily overthrown: it was amazing how even at his most trying he could arouse my sympathy.

"Come, Jonah, don't take it too hardly. It is important work as you must see. I know that this trip has been a strain, so take your time. We will be the ones now who will have to rush.

When you reach Manatá's, get some of the Indians to help with the carrying. I will give you half the plant press so that you can dry your specimens, and all the tinned meat I have, because we shall keep the gun, and you can stop early and fish. You will have about ten days before we catch up."

After a little while I saw that the idea appealed to him. With considerable eagerness he discussed all the things that I wanted him to look out for and do. He had accepted his reprimand and now was on his mettle. What might have been a bitter disagreement, or might even have led to a mutiny, had ended peacefully and in a manner that would further the interests of the expedition. I felt sure that he would do good work.

The rapids on the Buna-wau were worse than I had remembered. In the morning we ran several at speed, and in one struck so hard that Ka'i was flung overboard, water swirled in at the side, and for a moment the boat seemed likely to overturn.

It was an ugly, gloomy river, with dark forest overarching on either hand from shores of black rocks. Then, towards noon, we swung into the Mapuera, and at once our moods changed—between tall walls of sunlit green a long, superb reach of blue sparkling water lay ahead, lined with crescent beaches of yellow sand.

Landing, we were saying good-bye to Jonah and Gabriel and handing over the last few items to them, when I noticed a strange agitation among the Mawayáns.

"What is the matter?" I asked Basil: they were talking heatedly in a small group.

"They say they will not come further. They are afraid the Indians below will kill us all. They are enemies."

"Tell them that some of them know Fonyuwé, who went down the river three years ago, and that we are only going for three days, because we haven't enough food."

"It's no use—they say they have seen fresh fish scales on a rock, which means there are Indians about."

"It is probably where an otter has been."

"They still won't come. They will go with Jonah to Manatá's village, and wait there for you."

"Well—ask them to wait ten days, then they can help us carry."

Pulling Chekemá's boat high up the beach—we with the engine would tow it on our return upriver—we tied it to a tree and pushed off. Jonah and Gabriel embarked in the Mawayáns' long canoe, and a minute later a bend in the river hid them from sight.

"I'm glad to see them go," said Basil. "Now we just have to rely on ourselves."

18

The Stone Staircase (continued)

A light spray blew from the sparkling wavetops into our faces; the excitement of the journey seized me again—we might go on for weeks, months! The world seemed joyous.

There were now nine of us: Basil, George Gouveia, the three Wapisianas—Mark, Cyril and Wapisiana William—Fonyuwé, Kirifakka, Tanner and myself.

Huge capybaras flopped like thunderclaps into the water, but never within range. I shot a "tiger bird"[1] in flight, a huge bittern whose spread wings had a radiating pattern of bars of black and brown, white, yellow and red, inedibly tough but good for bait; then, a little later a fawn which showed its head above the herbs of the riverside—a beautiful pale-bellied red creature, spotted with dark brown, which would provide us with meat for at least two more days.

Perai were common, to judge from the many signs of them. Once a cluster of periscopes appeared in the water ahead— inquisitive otters with mouths agape, and sloping shoulders like ninepins, one with a big perai in its jaws; then a mile further we saw terrible flappings in the water, and came upon a large fish like a bream lying on its side on the surface, half eaten by them. As we watched they dashed at it and flipped it out of the water, and struggled away with its belly. Then at a flight of rapids came a great shout from Wapisiana William, standing in the bow and scanning the slopes:

"Perai!"

The water was seething with sharp fins, and disc-like fishes struggled in masses in the shallows.

But they were not perai, but paku—the first I had seen— lying on their sides as they grazed on the frilly weeds to which

---

[1] *Eurypyga helias.*

they had given their name; pausing, perhaps, on their way upriver to spawn.

As we manœuvred the boat towards them, Mark, poised on the gunwale, fitted a harpoon arrow to his bow. Seeing us, they leaped and fought, skittering to get away. Then he shot, and transfixed one, a lovely creature a foot long, silver and blue-grey. At once it swam towards deep water, but jumping overboard he seized the floating arrow shaft, linked to the detachable head deep in the fish's side by a fifteen-foot line, and played it into the shallows.

We camped at a bend in the river, below a run of steep, choppy waves. Boulders as big as automobiles stood in the clear olive-green water and, while the men cast lines from their summits, I bathed in a pool in between. I felt tired but well, exhausted by the struggle with Jonah, peaceful in his absence.

A little later a haimara two feet long, a spotted "dogfish", pike-like in appearance, and six enormous perai, all caught within a few feet of where I had swum, were being smoked or fried over the fires.

We dined on the rocks in the open air, I on a slice of paku, delicious as Scotch salmon—indeed, to me, its only rival. Behind us, the camp was a cavern in the forest, while overhead two flowering monkey-pipe trees of different species[1] showered us with drifts of small damask-pink, or larger white and yellow scented flowers. Before us, growing on submerged rocks, groves of water guavas,[2] small bushy trees like sallow willows bearing white dog-rose-like flowers, stretched away to where, a hundred yards upstream, the tumultuous rapids foamed.

"Tanner," I asked, "what would you do if you thought wild Indians were coming to attack us?"

"Sir, I would move fast! But if I had to stay I would try to find an island to camp. And I have heard a way you can make sure they don't creep up—you can cut plenty of pimpler palm [palms with thorns] and lay down all round, thick, thick, so they bound to step on them. They would not cry out, but they would go away."

"When they think they are going to be attacked, these Indians usually leaves their villages altogether," said Basil.

[1] *Eschweilera confertiflora* and *E. subglandulosa.*   [2] *Psidium parviflorum.*

"They scatter about and sleep in the forest, and leave a few dogs in the village to make noise. But I believe they very seldom has any fights these days. They is too few."

I got up early, and bathed again just as the first sun rays touched the water, cool and pale as a fish's belly. Fonyuwé and Kirifakka, goat-like, were scrambling from rock to rock, so I sent them up the monkey-pipes to fling down flowering sprays. They discovered, interlaced among the crowns, branches of a third tree in flower,[1] and collected from that as well.

After only ten minutes afloat we paused and collected again. On the edge of a high vertical bank, a colossal tree stood by the waterside—one of those enormous Leguminosae with which the forests were sprinkled—in full flower. Its trunk was straight and columnar, branchless for eighty feet, and flanked at the foot by buttresses ten feet high. Their wood was soft, and in half an hour we had chopped them through. A minute later there came a groan, and the tree began to sway in the direction chosen, towards the river. Then with a rending crash it was down, but to our disgust the crown, eighty feet or more across, sank completely out of sight into the deep water!

Just where the slanting trunk touched the surface was the beginning of the first branch, and this we severed, hoping to hoist it up. But like most of the woods of Amazonia it was heavier than water, and before we could secure it, it slipped from our grasp and disappeared.

I disliked felling trees, even where they were thick as grass, and to have wasted such a particularly fine one was painful. But as we were about to sail on a scatter of tiny objects began to float to the surface—flowers no larger than pinheads, microscopic buds, the leaflets (each the size of a housefly's wing) of the feathery bicompound leaves, and finally a whole leaf, six inches long—enough, it transpired, for the tree to be identified.[2] Content with these, and a wood block from the trunk, we continued.

Vertical 120-foot forest rose from the water's edge, the trees, swathed in lianes, like the buttresses of a Gothic hall—King's College Chapel in green. Where it was lower a pea-vine with flowers like large dark purple pansies[3] rampaged luxuriantly.

---

[1] *Trichilia compacta.*   [2] *Piptadenia psilostachya.*   [3] *Machaerium* sp.

The sunlight was hazy, the rapids presented few difficulties, life was good.

But as the day wore on the rapids became steadily worse. The river was so wide and deep, the current so strong, that a mishap in any of them might have meant loss of life and certainly of equipment and food, without which our plight would have been desperate.

Every ten minutes we shot one, and my heart stood still. As we approached each a mirage would overwhelm the vision, caused by the different, out-of-rhythm swingings of land and boat and water: first the puckering water surface, furrowed by submerged snags, then, as we took the plunge, the fluxing slope, the bearded rocks tossing the waves from their eyes, the foam masses, advancing and receding, rising and falling, in front of each; then, while the bowman rose, his giant paddle in his hand, the boat swaying and shuddering, the water roaring, the whirlpools swirling, the banks fleeing past faster and faster, out of focus across the seething surface . . . till the whole earth seemed to be quaking, swinging unsteadily.

Then the trees on the banks would cease to gyrate, the line of white would be behind, and from ahead would come the first signs of the next descent.

A blue mountain appeared straight in front, down a long reach of the river. Fonyuwé pointed and held up four fingers: there were big falls four points ahead, each point being a bend of the river of ninety degrees or more.

These four points were very long ones. The sun declined to low above the forest. It was past four o'clock and the men were getting restive, for camp-making took at least an hour, and it was dark by six.

There were no more rapids, but the river wound downhill between low hills at increasing speed. The surface of the water got steeper and steeper, the bends sharper, the forest darker, denser, lower, growing evidently out of shallow rocky soil. Then black rocks began to appear, sticking out of the black water. We rounded a bend, and the river divided into two ahead, the far half plunging downhill out of sight, while a vast booming, detonating, filled our ears.

Hastily we turned the boat, paddling to assist the engine,

and headed for the bank—swept, despite all our efforts, relentlessly sideways. Just before the falls came into sight we reached a level ledge of rock behind which a low hill rose steeply.

"We arrive this time very early," said Fonyuwé, to the annoyance of the men, who had begun to complain at the lateness of the hour. "When I come three years ago we arrive after sunset, in the dark, and we nearly get carried over the falls. Fifteen men were drowned here one day. They took the left bank and couldn't stop the boat."

"What are the falls called?" I asked.

"Omana-gashin; or Caban-teroan in Wapisiana, which means House Falls, because there was once a village here."

While the boat was unloaded, he, Kirifakka and I, in a sudden access of schoolboyish excitement, went racing and leaping off along the rocks to view the falls. There was a whole series: above the brink of one we waded perilously through shallow water of such force and swiftness that we were nearly dislodged, to an island in midstream on the far side of which, half-way down, a cloud of spray hung in the air above the main thundering. From a series of stepping-stones we looked down into a cleft some thirty feet deep and a hundred yards long. At its head the river, a great bulk of water, arched downwards in a wall twenty feet high, then in a phenomenal rush of pure white foam descended another thirty along the length of the trough.

Everywhere along the edge was the richest growth of paku weeds, with their curling red and green fronds, half seaweed, half lettuce, their ice-cream pink flowers and pinky-brown fruit capsules forming a strangely prismatic array of colours, outlining the white- and blue-reflecting water as if with a rainbow, and filling the air with the sweet smell of their sugary decomposition.

All around the forest ranged, richer in tint and texture and shape of leaf and crown than I ever remembered seeing it before in the tropics, its solid battlements overbending the white, gnarled dead tree-trunks and driftwood, the yellowish globular boulders of the beaches.

The sun was setting in a pearly overcast sky, and even as

we watched grey clouds descended on the tree-tops, and a sudden rainstorm veiled the scene. Clouds and smoke from the fires were resting on the forest in compact masses: we turned and hurried back, knowing that we were in for exceptionally heavy rains.

Beneath the tarpaulins, in the middle of flying spray, I spoke to Basil:

"What do you think of these falls? How long will it take us to get down them?"

"Sir, we cannot lower the boat, not even along the sides. We will have to cut a trail and haul it through the forest for half a mile, and the ground is very rough. It will take about three days. What is worse, Fonyuwé say this is just the beginning. There are more falls like this for many miles below. If we had small boats like the Indians it would be all right."

"How far is the first Wai-Wai village?"

"Three to five days, if it is the same place as when he came before with Chekemá."

I thought. It would have been exciting to go on, but we had seen other Wai-Wais, and the Mapuera had been ascended and descended several times before. Our triumph had been in reaching the Mawayáns and finding the brown sand forests of the Serra Irikoumé. Our most important work now lay on the far side of the mission, on our way out to the savannahs, for there we should be passing from the zone of heavy rainfall and luxuriant Evergreen Rain Forests through Seasonal Forests, where many of the trees shed their leaves in the dry seasons, into the great grasslands where for half the year there is drought. In any circumstances such a journey, from one world into another completely different, would be an experience; but here it would help round off my knowledge of the frontiers of the Acarai, and might even throw light, at least in my own mind, on the origin of the savannahs—a much-disputed matter.

There was also the question of catching the plane. If we were to attempt that, there was not much time to spare. If we could stay a day more and do a little botanical work I should feel fairly content—perhaps a great series of cataracts would make an appropriate and symbolic turning-point?

"I don't think it is worth going further," I said to Basil.

"Especially as I can't see how we'd drag the boat up again. I'll do some collecting tomorrow, and then the following day we will start back, as fast as we can."

From under my tarpaulin, when night had fallen, I could hear the wild sound of the river and the beating of the rain on my canvas roof. Streams of water, illuminated by the lantern, poured to the earth all round its edges, and a broad rivulet ran across the floor. Before long the men had to move the boat, for it was being carried away by the rising river. Then, the lamp out, snug in my hammock, protected from spray by the mosquito-net, the continuous rushing sound lulled me to sleep, and as I slept it was like the grumbling of all the Jonahs I had ever known; until, in moments of extreme fury, the storm awakened me again.

Half-way through the night the rain was so heavy that I felt the ground with my foot to see if it was flooded, and shone my torch all around, fearful lest the river had risen more and we were in danger of being carried away. I could hear trees breaking, branches crashing, under the sheer weight of water. There were voices—the men were shifting the boat again, lashing it at both ends to the trees.

In the morning the rain continued. The river was like the surface of a grater: the drops, seemingly as big as marbles, splintered into spray and mist as they struck it. The sky was an indeterminate woolly mass; cloud, rain and river just varying densities of water.

"Sir," said Basil, "the boys are like wild horses! They want to get home fast. It would be best if we let them know what you want to do on the way back so they have time to make up their minds to it."

There was only one important thing—to clear a few views on top of the little mountain, Faiafun. But to steady them further I told Basil to remind them that they were already getting extra pay for working without full rations.

He smiled his wizened jockey's smile. "That will brighten them up. You don't know what a hard time I have had persuading them. They all been asking if I bring them here for punishment. They say they never known work like this, but I tell them they never known work at all! The thing is they are used to the savannah, they never been in the forest so long, or so far from home. But I have known real rough times prospecting and I try to show them it is not so bad."

From time to time during the morning he plunged out into the rain for short forays along the river-bank or into the nearby forest, and returned to where I was working carrying armfuls of beautiful orchids. Not only large, but tiny orchids grew in abundance on the trees. Above my hammock rope was a tuft, six inches high, with two flowers like violets.[1] Others, higher up the trunk, were like ferns or mosses, bearing small, curiously shaped and coloured flowers.

"I have never seen a place like this," said Basil. "Here is *Cattleya Lawrenceana*, and this is *Schomburgkii*. These are two of the most valuable orchids there are—I know because long ago I work for an orchid collector. I have brought a bulb of each for you."

"How kind of you," said I. "But you should keep them and sell them if they are valuable."

"Sir, there are plenty more about for me—it is just a matter of gathering them. But the difficulty will be to get them back alive."

Soon after midday the rain stopped and the sun appeared, casting a watery light. The river-banks were strewn with wreckage, and whole trees were being borne past on the flood. The water-level was still rising fast, and the island we had waded to the day before was now half its former size and separated from us by a wide, deep channel. Dragging the boat upstream, Kirifakka, Cyril and I paddled across to it. Leaning over the level terraces of reddish or grey rock were two beautiful small trees with gnarled and knobbly trunks: one, with sprays of bright green sequin-shaped leaves, and spikes of magenta flowers like those of a Judas tree, was *Securidaca rivinaefolia* var. *parvifolia*, usually found growing as a liane; the other, quite new to me, had twisted, sandpapery leaves, grey beneath, dark green above, with clusters of small chestnut-brown nutlets in their axils.[2]

Hopping from boulder to boulder, we crossed to another islet downstream, and then to two more. In the centre of each,

[1] *Stelis argentata.*   [2] *Dalbergia* sp.

away from the sun-warmed rock slabs and the leaning fringing trees, were little knots of dark, incredibly tangled woodland, through which the river raged for perhaps half the year. They grew on miniature chasmic landscapes of vertical-standing rocks, with precipices, grottoes, gorges, all clothed in dripping mosses, arums, and lianes. Elbowing branches pushed into our faces, leaf-mould lay knee-deep in the hollows, and trembling in the faint, dusky air were pendant pagodas of many-stamened pink-mauve flowers, belonging to a shrub of the rose family.[1]

We emerged opposite the big cataract, glittering under a blue sky. Here I collected what looked like a vegetable octopus[2] —a climbing arum with numerous stilt-like roots projecting from its stem, big leaves divided into finger-like segments, and small yellow and purple spathes—before turning my attention to the paku weeds.

As, calf-deep in the river, I cut away at their leathery hold-fasts, the speed and deafening noise of the water appalled me and made me dizzy—a slip would have meant death from battery against the rocks long before drowning. I began to appreciate why, despite their outward show of pink and white flowery fragility, it took five minutes of sawing instead of just a stroke of the penknife to sever the stipes of these plants.

Continuing down through the line of islands we stepped from the shade of the trees on to a balcony of rock overlooking a circular lake, blue-watered, dotted with rocks and islets, in a bowl of hills. On either side of us the two main branches of the river swept into it in vast creaming rushes.

It was a scene of such beauty that even the phlegmatic Indians were affected. Kirifakka leaped from rock to rock, as far out over the water as he could go, and then sat and gazed about him—a little red figure with a bowl of black hair and a long pigtail.

In front of us a gentle gurgle of dark water over red rocks led to shallows in which, like blown green clouds sprinkled with white roses, resting on the lake, water guavas grew on a yellow-glinting sandbank. Beyond them stood the ring of hills, 300 feet high, covered with that same richly variegated foliage I had noticed before, a mixture of greens and bronzes, golds,

[1] *Hirtella racemosa.*   [2] *Anthurium digitatum.*

and salmon pinks, with here and there a giant ichekele breaking above the general level, and splashes of mauve flowering
Jacaranda, yellow *Cassia*, or golden-green *Manilkara* leaves. This
forest, growing on a reddish soil derived from the crystalline
quartzes and granites of the hills and rapids, seemed of yet
another type new to me. What were its affinities?—with the
Acarai, the Irikoumé, the Amazon? Months more work would
be needed to discover.

Exploring further, climbing the hill behind the camp a little
way, I found a few *Clusia* flowers on the ground. They were
curiously globular, like those of various other genera of the
same family (Guttiferae), such as *Moronobea* or *Symphonia*, but
not at all typical of their own. They were four or five inches
across, of a waxy ox-blood crimson, paler buff on the undersides of the petals; and within (for they were all male flowers)
had a broad ring of reddish-fawn stamens, like an Elizabethan
ruff, surrounding a button of bright mustard-yellow gum—a
nectary, scented of honey.

The more I looked at them, the more unusual they seemed.
Clusias are mostly small bushes, or shrubby trees, up to about
thirty feet in height, and usually have a mass of stilt roots
springing from the base of their trunks. There were no stilt-
rooted trees around, so Kirifakka and I craned our necks backwards and looked into the tree-tops, for many are epiphytic,
living in the branches of other trees and sending moisture-
tapping roots to the ground.

Eventually we saw a few more flowers about sixty feet up, in
the crown of a tree with a straight, smooth, mottled trunk about
twelve inches in diameter. We walked all around, making sure
that this *was* the tree in which the *Clusia* was perched, and then
began to fell it: half an hour's work, for the wood was unusually
tough.

When at last it lay prostrate, the topmost twigs almost in the
river, my excitement ran higher than ever before, for the whole
tree was a *Clusia*—the largest *Clusia* ever seen![1]

Triumphant, laden with flowers, I returned to camp, after
searching all around for a female, or even another male tree,

[1] This remarkable tree has been named *Clusia guppyi* by Dr. Maguire of
the New York Botanical Garden.

without success. The river was still rising fast, though there
had been no more rain, and the current had grown so strong
that the men were making extra paddles to help the boat on its
way upriver the following morning.

By next day the islands we had walked on had disappeared,
showing only as a line of boulders and wave-tossed trees.
Another six inches, and the camp too would have been covered.
Soon the whole country-side would be transformed: the
Mapuera, in a month, would have risen perhaps twenty or
thirty feet above its present level; vast tracts of land, particularly in its lower reaches, would be submerged; and all the
inhabitants—animal, vegetable or human—of this part of
Amazonia would be leading their rainy season life—the totally
different other half of their strange double existence.

The current was now stronger but many of the rapids were
submerged, and this made our progress easier, if slower: where
rocks had shown, furious waves were dancing, slapping our
bow, pushing us sideways, drenching us with spray. Paddling
as hard as we could, with the little British-Seagull motor singing
like an aero-engine, slowly we made our way up the first two
steeply sloping miles to the more level waters above.

Overhead, a king vulture swung in wide circles, turning its
neck to watch us. Sometimes as it banked steeply I glimpsed its
white back, then it would pass in a long sweep, steadying itself
with broad tail and wings for a moment, and return on another
tack. Humming birds were frequent—little bright green fellows
with a white feather on each side of the tail—nipping out from
the riverside to scrutinize us, twinkling above our heads for a
minute, then flashing away.

The probing sunlight in which we had started disappeared;
the sky became foreboding. Soon rain was all around, hanging
in black banners from the clouds ahead, behind, on either side.
But till soon after midday none fell on us. Then it began,
lightly and steadily, as if it meant to go on for ever. The drops
were freezing, a bitter wind blew, and the world shrank to an
opaque oyster shell of misery. The sky was featureless, simply
rain; the river a sour yellow. Huddled down, stripped to the
waist, shuddering with cold, my mind dissolved. My horizon
was the dismal water at our bows.

3. Complex abstract basketwork design on a cassava sifter (a single sloth like that in 2 can be seen running diagonally from bottom left to top right).

2. Abstract painted design from back of a cassava grater. Compare with 3, from which it appears derivable.

1. Semi-naturalistic painted design in centre of a cassava grater (zigzags along either side represent running water; at the ends, palm leaves).

THE SLOTH DESIGN (MAWAYÁN)

FROM THE SUMMIT OF MT. FAIAFUN

"For many miles the country-side was flat, until in the farthest
distance it rose slowly to a low plateau" *(p. 315)* : view eastwards
over the Mapuera and Buna-wau floodplains to the Mud Hills,
Shiuru-palm hills, and the Serra Irikoumé

A few hours later, thawed, drying, fortified by a pink-fleshed fish called a cullet (to rhyme with pullet) that had been caught near the camp, one of Tanner's "bakes", and some farine, I laid a tarpaulin strip on the soggy leaf-strewn clay beneath my tent and sorted a few specimens that, even in the rain, I had plucked from the waterside. Then came an unpleasant discovery: my duffle-bag, stored by mischance near the bottom of the boat, had absorbed some of the water we had shipped in the rapids—my hammock and blankets were soaked. It was useless sleeping in them wearing anything dry, so wrapped in layers of wet pyjamas I passed the most wretched night of the expedition.

Morning came at last, with white skies and dense mist on the tree-tops. The river had risen another two feet, and it raged past, its yellow waves vicious as conger eels, leaping and jostling.

We found the small canoe we had left behind afloat, tugging at its moorings, nearly awash; and a few minutes later, with it in tow, drew level with the Buna-wau mouth. Most of the flood-waters came from it (its level had risen about eight feet), and like a torrent of bright yellow orange-juice they poured into the darker Mapuera. Already, after three days' rain, the land around the Mud Hills must be deeply inundated! We had escaped from the Frog Indian country just in time.

But the Mapuera also had risen by two or three feet: enough to enable us to haul the boat, without unloading, a little further up the big rapids which had given us so much trouble on our way down.

The going was excitingly rough for several miles above these, the water full of rocks throwing spray into the air; but the floods, rage though they might, were helping us, and we sailed forward through the lines of breakers without disembarking. The sun came out, gladdening us and drying our clothes.

The river was narrow now, intensely gloomy. We were back in the land of wallaba trees: on either side their long-stalked mobiles of counterpoised flowers and fruit hung above the water. In calmer stretches freshwater flying-fish were common, darting from the bows and skittering along the surface for many yards. I managed to observe them closely several times, enough to see that they were not the keel-breasted Hatchet fish[1] usually described as doing this, but slender minnows with exceptionally deep and high tail fins which they kept submerged and vibrated rapidly from side to side in their aerial runs.

At one turbulent place three men had to leap out. With a reedy shriek as his *camisha* was wetted for the first time in the day, Kirifakka flung himself overboard, and while Fonyuwé went ahead with a rope, stood with Mark shoulder deep beside the boat and drew us through the long striated rollings, past the packs of charging white foam-horses and the water-domed rocks. The engine raced, we paddled furiously, the boat edged forward . . . Then I noticed a thistledown, big as a grapefruit, floating in the air in a beam of sunlight. It scarcely moved: there was not a breath of wind, though a foot below it the waves were in torment. Infinitely slowly it sank; then touched—and in a flash was overwhelmed.

Fonyuwé suddenly pretended to be seriously ill. With knitted brows he showed me a minute scratch, perhaps an eighth of an inch long, and to indicate his agony gave a peculiar high-pitched whine:

"Meeshterguffin: Mmmmmmmmmmmmm!"

Then, with a heart-rending shake of the head went "Sniff! Sniff!"

In mid-afternoon rain clouds gathered in the east, above the southern slopes of the hidden Acarai, and soon their mauve amorphousness covered the whole of that half of the sky, while the sun still shone out of its cloudless hemisphere. Slowly they extended, from horizon to horizon. Chill darkness enveloped us. We became apprehensive, searching for a suitable camping-ground, and just as the cyclonic winds that prelude rain came dashing the branches of the trees, drew up at a high sloping bank tangled with roots. As I stepped ashore thunder rolled, and a minute later the rain came lashing down.

With deft downwards cutlass-strokes Fonyuwé and Kirifakka cut loose flaps of bark high up on the trunks of three trees close together, bound, as main roof beams, the stems of saplings behind them and to a post which they planted in the ground to make a fourth corner, laid a few stick-rafters across, then a

[1] *Gasteropelecus sternicla* and *Carnegiella strigata*.

thatching of large *Heliconia* leaves three or four deep from a clump near by, swept the floor, placed a handful of branches across a hollow in the ground as a rack for their few possessions, lit a fire, and slung their hammocks on either side. In ten minutes, half an hour before my own tarpaulin was up, their house for the night was complete.

Fonyuwé swung his arms exuberantly next day before we started:

"*Hawawa mé, hawawa mi, bifara wer, bifara wirow!*" he sang, pranced into the air, and leaped with a crash into the boat beside me.

Now that we were returning his restlessness was almost unendurable: he was like a colt newly let into a field, quivering with energy which somehow he had to release. He bounced, he jerked, he threw his arms about, mumbling and singing. Seizing a cane from the riverside, he split it into two strips and threaded one through the hole in his lower lip, one through his nasal septum, so that he wore an exaggerated mandarin's moustache and beard. Then he looked at us with wild, rolling eyes.

He had been very useful because of his knowledge of the various Indian names for plants, rivers, hills and rapids. In my efforts to elucidate the maps I always tried to get as many of these as possible, and now, disregarding his clownishness, I started to question him again. Below the Buna-wau mouth the Mapuera or Mapuer-wau (its Wapisiana name) was called the Comuo-photo or Comu-wo by the Wai-Wais, and the Musho-yoku by the Mawayáns, all these names meaning "Lu palm[1] river". I wanted now to see if there had been any change of name.

"*Atchi wau?*" I asked, pointing at the water—what's this river called?

But the infuriating creature would on no account tell me. Perhaps he thought I was being stupid? Instead he gazed at me with an enormous smile, like a Cheshire cat.

A little later I asked again, and this time he leaned forward, and in a confiding tone said:

"Meeshterguffin-*wau*."

[1] *Oenocarpus baccaba.*

There were chuckles all around, in which I could not help joining, and the great buffoon said not another word.

To give him something to do, I made him bowman. Bubbling and singing he stood up in the front, swishing the great paddle to and fro with gorilla-like antics, yet guiding the boat with sure judgment along the obstructed channel.

The river surface, turned to road, would have been a strain to ascend on a bicycle: the keel of the small canoe in front, paddled by Mark and Cyril, was well above our eyes.

Already, after only two and a half days—instead of the anticipated week—we were back in the upper reaches of the river. High water was still with us and we sailed smoothly over many formerly troublesome places; but the river was narrowing rapidly and before long we came to a series of small cataracts.

"*Camisha!*" would shout George, whenever Kirifakka, his merry face creased with smiles, leaped overboard and the waters closed over the little rows of white peccary teeth that hung on either red-brown hip.

In the open upper meander-plain, with its numerous bamboo clumps, every tree seemed to have burst forth into full flower. Then we returned to the hills and the enclosing forest tunnel. The river became a skein of torrents—in an hour we progressed perhaps three hundred yards. Then we were at the foot of the falls in which the boat had nearly been wrecked the day after her launching. It was most unexpected being here so soon. Manatá's village was only a mile away: the loads could be carried the rest of the distance. By a liane we tied our craft at the waterside.

A sudden sorrow seized me as I looked my last at her, unloaded, abandoned, for she was too big for the Indians to use. Her tin-patched sides were still intact, her two-inch bottom had survived many a battering. Inside she was green with mildew, powdery from the attacks of wood-borers. The first floods would carry her away and bury her downstream, and her hull would fill with sand and leaves. Yet in her I had made a journey that I should always remember.

19

Medicine Men

Apprehensive, I waited for the men; then together we walked towards the village. It felt curious, unreal, to be on that familiar leafy path beside the river. The small streams along the way had swollen, flooding their surroundings, and we had to detour through the forest. There was a sound of chopping, and we stepped into glaring sunlight—the jumbled, unfired wreckage of a field the Indians had just been beginning to clear when we had left.

"Yuhmé! Yuhmé! Yuhmé! Yuhmé! . . ."

Dropping his axe, with parrot-like insistence the old fellow called out his name as we approached—frightened perhaps that we might not remember him.

Then Sam came running to greet us, amidst the clamour of alarmed dogs. He was a sad sight, tears streaming down his face. He seized my hand: come, come, he begged, pulling me.

Outside the conical house, lying in a hammock under the shelter of a powis-tail and screened from the sun by a palm-leaf, was his wife. I could scarcely recognize her—the woman with the toothless, rather naughty smile I had known before. She looked 70, instead of about 35, dark greyish in colour, with a yellow, encrusted slime around her mouth, and a smell of sickness in the air around her. Her right knee and left hand were enormously swollen, as if poisoned, and she seemed almost unable to move.

"Please stay for a few days and cure her," begged Sam. "If she dies I will never come back here again. I will leave everything and come with you and go and live on the savannah."

While I took her temperature I asked him how long she had been ill.

"About seven days. It was Wayama who made her ill. He is

311

a sorcerer, and he blow [1] on her and speak words over her, and then he go away, back to the Essequebo. And ever since she has been ill."

Her temperature was 104°, and to judge from her looks she was very close to death. Her high temperature was horribly familiar—yet all the other symptoms, the swellings, the vomit on the ground, were new to me. The disease might have changed its form again, or they might be the result of the Indian methods of treatment.

I looked around: beneath a mournful-looking brown-speckled dog, sitting beside her in Sam's hammock, was a stool, with on it a fish-shaped strip of wickerwork some eight inches long, full of immense wriggling black ants, secured by the meshes with all their stings protruding on one side. It was an "ant-plaster", similar to, but much smaller than those used by many tribes of the region in initiation ordeals (of which the Maraké of the Oyana of French Guiana is the most famous). Such a plaster might be very effective as a remedy for rheumatism or muscular aches, but it was probably the cause of her swellings and present collapse.

I rubbed an embrocation on her hand and knee, and gave her four sulphathiazoles and two atebrines.

"Has anyone else been ill? What about old William?"

"No, everybody is well except she. They bring her out here so that her father, Manatá, who is a very great magician, can cure her. He is now out searching for medicines.[2] He is working hard on her, but Wayama's spell was a powerful and wicked one."

It was peculiarly unpleasant, horrifying in fact, to think of the gentle Wayama being blamed for something of which he was so innocent—for spreading an illness which had brought him, too, very low. Even if Sam's wife recovered he would henceforth be an enemy, and if she died his life would not be safe.

Judging that it would upset the sick woman less than if I

---

[1] Puffing air or tobacco smoke over someone, with or without the accompaniment of words, is the way in which in these parts sorcerers and others purport to cause or cure sickness.

[2] This probably meant more ants. The comparatively scarce, atrociously poisonous *Neoponera* ants, mentioned earlier, were the kind he used.

visited her again, I gave Sam four more sulphathiazoles and told him to make her swallow them when the sun was setting. Pathetically grateful, he promised me he would.

"Don't worry," I assured him. "She will be better in the morning."

Yapumo, Yeimiti, Ka'i, Manawanaro—the men we had relied upon to help us with our baggage—had gone ahead with Jonah two days before, said old Yuhmé. The sight of two of their wives, their behinds gaily painted with red stripes, bathing in the river when we went down to the camp-site, reassured us that they meant to return and not go straight on to the mission. But it might be a week before they did, and we could not afford to delay. Although everything we had left behind, including a little farine as a reserve for the recrossing of the Acarai, was safe, we were at the end of our resources. Much would depend on whether Manatá had any food to spare, and like the Mawayáns, he too might be beginning to run short.

In the morning while the last loads were fetched from the boat, and George and Cyril climbed Faiafun to open views at the summit, Basil and I went to see Sam's wife. She was already much stronger, sitting up and smiling wanly. But the whole atmosphere of the village had changed: Manatá had returned.

He was sitting on a log, looking very pink and white and well washed, but he did not rise, and he said not a word of greeting. He simply watched Sam silently.

With averted glance Sam crept up to me:

"Manatá has cured her with his magic," he said. "You must not give her any more pills. They are rubbish."

As he spoke he looked terrified and guilty. Both Basil, who had translated this, and I were severely shaken. We realized what had happened: Manatá regarded me as a rival sorcerer, and already by curing several people where he had failed I had detracted from his prestige. Now he was making a stand. The least false move would arouse his enmity. We were on very dangerous ground, for he was a powerful man.

I put my medicines in my pocket and said nothing. Sam's wife, I could see, was already past the crisis and would recover, if less quickly than with the help of more drugs; later, perhaps, I might find a way to treat her again.

Slowly we walked back to the camp. I was miserable, conscious that we were no longer welcome, that the sooner we left the better everyone would be pleased, that to stay too long might even be dangerous.

At the summit of Faiafun an immense panorama now spread before us to west and north-west. We jumped from crag to crag at the edge of the precipice, looking as far as we could in every direction. The air was cool and fragrant, and below us the domed tree crowns, their complicated arrangements of flowers, leaves and twigs sparkling in the sun, were like the jewelled interiors of immense watches. Some were as much as 150 feet across, shallow inverted saucers of foliage; others, smaller, were crowded with purple, yellow and white stars and trumpets.

Almost at our feet lay the Mapuera, its course marked by the spring green of the bamboo woodland along its banks. We could see the new field that Sam had cut, and a smudge of smoke where the village was hidden by trees. Beyond, easy-looking undulations led to the watershed where we had crossed the Acarai, while on either side was higher rolling country, peaked here and there, and glimmering a transcendent blue under the powder-puff sky.

Beyond the Acarai, a paler cobalt, were yet other peaks, the Kamo Mountains in British Guiana, 2,000 to 3,000 feet high, rising between the Kassikaityu and Kamo rivers. As I looked at them I saw a tiny blob of white appear beneath one of the highest points, then vanish. Then it came again, for a moment, appearing and disappearing at irregular intervals. It was hard to believe that it could be the smoke of a fire, visible from thirty or forty miles away, or even that a fire was likely in the middle of an almost inaccessible and totally uninhabited region. I strained and strained my eyes: still the irregular puffing occurred.

A little later, after I had been looking at other things, I glanced back—and now there was a long, thread-like vertical streak hanging down the mountain-side: a waterfall, perhaps a thousand feet high, but so slender that it might only be one of those ephemeral flows that occur after rain. The sun had shifted, and it was plain to see. None had ever been reported before from near there so it was certainly a discovery.

On the other, more sloping side of Faiafun, a long, narrow avenue of trees had been felled down which I could see almost due east over the glowing crown of a jacaranda.

For many miles the country-side was flat, until in the farthest distance it rose slowly to a low plateau—the Serra Irikoumé from which we had just come. Few men can have seen that view—perhaps the rare aviator and one or two Indians; but not many, for they live in their jungle darkness and care nothing for views. The highest point that I could see was perhaps that mountain from which Machira had descended; Shiuru-tirir lay half-way down the slopes, the Mud Hills nearer, with the Buna-wau invisible at their base. But what held me was the profile of the highest level land, for its clefts did not suggest hard rocks like the Pakaraima sandstones, but the rolling surfaces and steep gullies of white sand country. It seemed, if anything, to confirm my surmise that at the Mawayán capital we had been on the western edge of a large unknown area of White Sand Sea sands.

The next day Ka'i, Yapumo and Yeimiti returned, bearing a note from Jonah. Manawanaro had remained behind to name plants. Ka'i was smiling and pleased to see me, but neither of the other two would look me in the face. I soon discovered the reason.

"Jonah paid Ka'i, but gave us nothing," they affirmed solemnly as I opened the box of trade-goods to pay them. "You owe us for three days' work with him, and for paddling him upriver."

They did not understand what a letter was, and that already, from the note they had brought, I knew that they had been partly paid. It was a most awkward position. It was so unlike what I would have expected. And they had been such good friends, and had done so much for me in their own country that I could not for a moment consider accusing them outright of lying. I said nothing and paid them the balance that was due; then asked them if they would work for me again, to help carry our loads across the mountains.

Ka'i agreed to come at once, but the others could not now face Jonah, who would expose them, so they refused. Nothing would make them stir.

I needed their help badly—without it we might have to abandon some of our equipment. The position was serious: yet there was something so schoolboyish and naïve about them, they were so guilty-looking and obviously likeable despite their trick, that I could not help being amused.

As they began to realize that they were missing the chance of gaining much more than by their fraud (which, as it had been detected had in fact brought them nothing), they grew more and more miserable, while the virtuous Ka'i looked absurdly smug. They hung dejectedly round the camp watching me work on my specimens, so a little later I tried again to persuade them.

"I would *very* much like to work for you," said Yeimiti, "but I won't: you have paid me too badly."

Indeed, the little pile of oddments that had constituted the balance due to them, after I had deducted what Jonah had already paid, *had* looked somewhat small. I offered to raise my price.

"*No.* We are much too proud to work for a man who has cheated us."

"It looks like Manatá must have make them do it," commented Basil.

This put an altogether new and ugly complexion on the matter.

I frittered away my afternoon mending some pyjamas and helping Tanner stick canvas on a pair of shoes. Then I bathed: the river moved gently in its leafy, silty bed, the bamboos leaned dreaming over it. Tomorrow, whatever happened, we had to leave—or something would happen. Yet it was absurd that, because of a few fish-hooks and beads, we should be in difficulties. I could surely overcome Manatá's opposition with a little skill?

With Basil, Fonyuwé, Mark and Cyril, I went up to the village before sunset, intending to try new tactics—but it was useless: both Yapumo and Yeimiti were ill. They had begun to feel ill about two hours before. Manatá sat on his log, his eyes red and savage. His daughter was still very sick, he said, but he would not allow me to see her. I might go to the two men, however, if I wished. There was no sign of Sam, to whom I would have tried slipping a few tablets.

Rather timidly I went into the dark chaotic house interior, threading my way among the many suspended hammocks, the dimly seen bowls and stools and baskets on the floor. The hostility inside was like a kick in the stomach: the packs of snarling dogs along the walls were now barely restrained by their owners, the sneering dislike, as I took their temperatures, on the faces of the two men was as much as I could endure. Even the two Wapisianas with me were affected.

Both Yapumo and Yeimiti had pains in the chest and stomach—the latest manifestation of the epidemic, or perhaps a result of Manatá's treatments—and temperatures of 102°. Several criss-cross surface cuts had been made on their bodies, to let the pain, sickness, or evil spirits out from the places which hurt most. I gave them sulphathiazole and atebrine and came outside as quickly as I could.

Sickness seemed almost the only restraint on violence. I began to doubt whether we could get away without loss of equipment, though I was determined to save the collections. Fortunately, the blame for the illnesses had not been laid on me—at least, not yet. I was merely a rival medicine-man.

The morning brought confusion and discontent. We were almost out of food, except for a few reserve pounds of farine, and I had barely a dozen cartridges for the shotgun. None of the men seemed willing to take their usual loads. Nothing happened unless I went and stood over them. Periodically everyone disappeared, leaving me in the midst of the impedimenta. Ka'i and Yuhmé, the only two Mawayáns who had not yet specifically refused to come, were nowhere to be seen.

Manatá appeared, walking slowly, looking to see what was being left behind. With him was his second daughter, Manawanaro's wife, who gave me her usual come-hither smile. I presented them each with a safety-pin and a comb, but not a flicker of interest showed on Manatá's face. Instead, he pointed to various things on the ground, to indicate that he wanted them. What he wanted most were two kerosene tins: he could certainly have them when I had filled the lamps and a smaller container, so I nodded vigorously, shook them to show they were full, and waved to indicate that they would be left for him when we went.

At once his countenance changed. He scowled, turned, and stalked off, furiously kicking the fallen sticks out of his path. Perhaps he thought I was waving him away? I shall never know.

Five minutes later Basil came running up to say that Manatá had gone off fishing and had insisted upon taking Yuhmé with him. Now we were yet one more carrier short. But Manatá's motives were a little hard to fathom, for simultaneously he had done an apparently benevolent thing: an enormous load of cassava-bread and yams, packed in a palm-leaf warishi, now stood outside the village for us—food enough for our journey, although also an extra burden. It was doubtless designed to get rid of us quickly. With it we could go right across to the Chodikar without stopping to hunt or fish. Perhaps also he thought that, several men short and alarmed by him, we would not return and he could seize whatever we were forced to leave behind?

At this juncture the position seemed hopeless: scarcely anything was packed. The ground was littered with lanterns, boxes of specimens, trade-goods, unfolded tarpaulins, hammock bags, the bag of farine, the outboard motor—far more than we could ever carry.

Basil was in his most dismal frame of mind: "Sir, it is better if we leave all we can't manage and get away. We will have to make at least two journeys to carry everything, and if Sam's wife die it will mean bad trouble if we come back. We can't take a risk like that."

Then I saw that Ka'i was standing smilingly by, with his wife. They, at least, had not deserted us. She had an empty carrier on her back—she too could carry a load! I had forgotten that. I at once began to recover confidence.

Then the men reappeared, and soon, miraculously, everything was distributed except the outboard motor, a bag of tools, the empty jerry-can used for filling the motor (which we would need again at the Chodikar, where we had a reserve of fuel), the vasculum, and the load of cassava-bread and yams.

Where was Fonyuwé? He would have to take the motor.

"I shall take the cassava-bread," I said; and with Basil's help lifted the carrier on to my shoulders, tied the two bands of bark that stretched from top to bottom crosswise over my chest, slipped a third band over my forehead, and on top of all placed my haversack and the bag of tools—a total load of fifty or sixty pounds.

There was still no sign of Fonyuwé. A tiny, bright-eyed, apparently parentless Mawayán boy, aged about seven, called Bawaya, but nicknamed Haimara because of his closeness in size to a large specimen of that fish, stood watching.

"Haimara," said Basil, "would you like to earn a few beads? Could you carry these two?"—the jerry-can and the vasculum, about 14 lb.

He at once agreed, and cutting a few palm-leaves began to weave himself a warishi.

Fonyuwé now strolled up, in a very difficult mood, abstracted, his brows knitted. Perhaps he had been talking to his brother Yapumo, or perhaps Manatá had been trying to influence him? He was angry at having been left with the motor to carry, which though not particularly heavy, was angular and awkward. Very slowly he loaded it into his carrier, tied his bow and arrows together—then leaned them against a tree, and disappeared into the forest singing.

Leaving Basil to deal with him I set off after the other men into the muddy, creeper-netted swamp through which the path wound.

The weight was ill-distributed on my back, but alone I could do nothing much about it—the men always had to help each other adjust their loads. The whole warishi swung unsteadily from side to side, and the two upright spikes at the top kept catching in lianes and throwing me down. Sweat dripped from my face like a shower. I had become one of those painfully-moving beasts, queer, pitiful robots with bulky heads, whose processions I had accompanied in the past.

There came a wide knee-deep river, and clambering up the steep mud bank on the far side the beastly contrivance entangled itself in an overarching, springy root, flung me on my face and held me there. As I tried to get up I was forced sideways; then something gave, and on I went.

The sun threw my misshapen shadow ahead, showing me that I was going east—the right direction, even if I was uncertain, in the maze of paths made by the Indians, if I was on the right trail.

After an hour the path grew drier, and I tried taking the weight from my forehead by pulling with both hands on the band that went across it. Then I disengaged it altogether, and walked with arms swinging free, and the knobbly burden digging and chafing into my back and shoulders. In pain I put my arms behind me, hugging the warishi with fingers clasped; but this left me with no free hand for balancing or thrusting aside vines and branches.

I was walking fast, nevertheless, and at the Urana-wau overtook Ka'i, his wife, and Kirifakka. The river twisted serpentine between banked green liane masses and thickets of *Bactris* palms, whose fallen leaves, thickly beset with 3-inch spines, I had to step carefully to avoid as I waded along the bed. Then, as I clambered on to dry land the rotten canvas of my right shoe again gave way, and the heel swung loose. I had about twelve miles of rugged country ahead of me, and I wondered how I should traverse it if an unlucky slip tore the shoe further before I could find bark with which to mend it.

Ahead was the long, steep climb, of about 1,600 feet, to the general level of the crossing. I felt that I should never reach the top. My back was burning as if on fire—at least the ground was dry, affording a firm foothold. I was far from the other men, with no sound in the loneliness except the scuffling of dry leaves underfoot. I remembered the incident of the black jaguar, not far from here, and the men's warning never to walk alone.

A little further, turning me pale, a frightful groan reached my ears. Straining my banded neck around, I searched for its origin; then plodded on, and again heard it. It came from the tree-tops. Perhaps two branches were rubbing in the wind? Whatever the cause, it emphasized the despair that always lies in the shadows of the forests, and clutches at even those who know them best.

The distant barking of Ka'i's dogs and a far-away faint hail reassured me. Basil had probably reached the Urana-wau and discovered that I had walked ahead. I shouted loudly in reply.

Just when I thought the climb would finish me I reached the crest of the slope, and a little further descended a short way to a rivulet. Here I flung myself down, but hearing voices ahead, walked on a few yards and found George and the three Wapisianas preparing their lunch.

"Sir, this is very hard on you," said George, astounded by my burden.

"Nonsense! I've carried worse—whenever it's been necessary. But none of you have ever seen me do it."

"All the same, it is not easy."

When we got up to go he and the other three, with kindly attention, readjusted my load so that it sat more easily. The rest of the party had appeared, except Fonyuwé and Haimara, who had decided to walk together. In exasperation because Fonyuwé had spent so much time fiddling with his load, Basil had left him to walk on in his own time, and it was possible that little Haimara could not walk fast and was holding him back. On the other hand, it might be that, erratic, high-spirited creature as he was, he had decided to stay behind at the village for another day and then race after us. Or Manatá might have persuaded him to desert. There were several sinister possibilities —yet when all was said, I knew that I trusted him.

Two hours later, following Mark ahead of the others, I reached the broad Shururucanyi. All the way the hills had shown signs of continued dry weather, and here the water-level was falling fast: we were back in the Guiana weather system, with its two rainy seasons (the shorter still several weeks off) and two fairly dry ones. The Chodikar's level would be very low.

"Snake," said Mark.

I stepped aside. A spot of red showed between the leaves— a coral snake or coral snake mimic, a beautiful two-foot reptile of deep crimson-scarlet, black headed, with half-inch wide black bands bordered with white every four inches or so along its length.

Prodding it with a stick, Mark made it twist and lash.

"He no hurt. He only sting in tail," was his illuminating comment.

Climbing from the rocky, slippery, tortuous riverside we reached the upper levels again; a distant waterfall sounded; we plodded on and on . . . then came the long slow descent to the Taruini. A green square of tarpaulin showed among the leaves: Jonah was here.

Determined to let bygones be forgotten, I hailed loudly from across the river:

"Jonah! How are things with you?"

He came running forward to greet me.

20

Ka'i and Kabapböyö

For two more days we walked through the forests, my burden getting progressively lighter as we ate into it. Jonah and I were on good terms, though he was still very uncertain of me. I had been pleased with the work he had done on his own, and had said so, and he saw that I bore him no grudge. Yet it had shocked him deeply that I should have sent him away, and it had made him think about our relationship. His manner was now courteous, if anything over-respectful. It was a pleasant change from what it had been. But perhaps we should never return to our old easy footing: for both of us it meant starting again.

Fonyuwé and Haimara had arrived at the camp late the same night as the rest of us, laden with fish they had stopped to catch, very pleased with themselves, and bubbling with news.

"It is very lucky we had Fonyuwé with us," commented Basil the next day, as we walked along together. "It is purely because of him that Manatá sell us that food. And he say it *was* Manatá who made Yapumo and Yeimiti refuse to work, and try to cheat you. They didn't want to, but he poison their minds against you and tell them you was paying too little. But now it is hitting him, because they realize he is a bad man."

"Are they well again?"

"Yes, both is quite all right."

Their illness had been caught early—"But what about the sick woman?"

"When we leave she was up. But she cannot use her hand. It is still swell up and paralyse, like it is poisoned."

That was probably the result of Manatá's treatment; but I lamented inwardly. Nothing that he or any of the Indians had done had been as bad as that we, unwittingly, had brought sickness into their land. I thought of how I had left the Maw-ayáns, of Sam's wife, better though she was. When would the epidemic stop and what new and awful form might it take? What *was* it—the common cold, influenza, malaria, pneumonia?

I consoled myself by thinking that at least it had not caused any deaths. It was a mild, not a deadly virus. But it made me feel that, in the future, access to these wild Indians must some-how be controlled, allowed only to quarantine people, until there were doctors and nurses available to treat them. My feelings towards the missionaries softened: the future of the Indians was in their hands—and they had already brought a nurse with them. However much I disapproved of many of their policies, they would not encourage drink, fighting or prosti-tution, and they were as anxious as I to prevent the next epidemic from occurring—which might so easily destroy their entire flock.

At last one morning we embarked on the Chodikar. The large canoe in which we had ascended had either been swept away or taken by Indians, so we were forced to use a small, leaky dugout, which was all that we could find. It could not hold all of us, so, together with a quantity of equipment, Jonah, Gabriel and Manawanaro were left behind to continue their collecting until we sent back for them.

With the motor fixed to the side we crowded aboard, and baking in the airless tunnel of vegetation, irritated by insects and debris, lashed by branches, began the hacking and slashing, the dragging through and over and under fallen crowns and tree-trunks that marked all travel along this noisome channel. Yet there was a great difference between the fervour and steadiness of the homeward-bound crew and the bellowings of Andrew, the goadings and reluctant labourings of the outward voyage.

Beside me in the boat sat Ka'i's wife, Kabapböyö, a comfort-able-looking, rather Slavonic-featured woman, hugging and kissing a little puppy. Its mother, a large brown and white splashed bitch, howled and whimpered incessantly. In the heat and suffocation it was the most unendurable sound: it expressed so well the weariness and impatience we all felt. Every few minutes Madame Ka'i, conscious of how it was affecting us, would scowl at it and slap it firmly on the muzzle, and it would wrinkle its jowls and look abashed until some new incident of the voyage made it forget its punishment. Then a long sigh would escape from it, followed by the inevitable keening whine.

It was extraordinary to see, so unaffectedly portrayed by two almost naked "savages", the fondness and consideration that Ka'i and Kabapböyö showed for each other—so great indeed was their natural dignity that the rest of the men behaved with a circumspection that nothing had produced in them before. Whenever she embarked Ka'i would help his wife into the boat, and arrange her possessions—a fan, her hammock, a basket-work box containing her feather and bead jewellery—around her; and in the evenings he would bring her a bucket of water to wash in, or a folded leaf to drink from, and sling her hammock while she lit the fire and prepared the food.

At midday on the second day of our descent we discovered the missing canoe being paddled slowly downriver by three Wai-Wais. We had to think of the men left behind, so Tanner and George returned to fetch them, with the outboard motor, while the rest of us transferred ourselves to the larger boat and continued down the now rapidly broadening Chodikar. Ten pairs of muscular arms urged the craft along, and uncomfortable though my wooden seat was, I felt momentarily like a nabob being drawn, wallowing among silken cushions, on his pleasure barge.

We reached the Essequebo, its level now much fallen: yellow sandbanks lay in the wide ruffling sweeps of olive water, or pale beneath our keel. The day, which had started marble-skied, steadily improved. The sun declined, and its slanting beams illuminated in sculptured relief the rounded contours of the hills, the soft domed crowns and stately boles of the swamp acacias. Behind us we saw the blue-flowered slopes of the Serra Acarai, before a bend in the river hid them for the last time.

Basil and the Wapisianas wanted to stop early to fish, but I insisted on our going on till nearly dark, because I was growing increasingly worried: first Kabapböyö, then Ka'i had fell ill soon after we reached the Essequebo, and though I had given them sulphathiazole and atebrine tablets, by four o'clock in the afternoon they showed no signs of improvement—indeed, their temperatures had risen. Trembling, with glazed eyes, they lay in the boat, her temperature 103°, his only slightly less.

If sulphathiazole were having no effect, what could I do? I felt desperate—and I had now only fifteen tablets of it left. Two each at six o'clock, and four more each at eight would leave only three for the next day: we had to reach the mission and the nurse as fast as possible.

Ka'i's world, though he was so ill, consisted only of his wife. Late at night I awoke and saw him crouched beside her hammock, building up the fire he had lighted to keep her warm.

Neither was better in the morning, and judging Kabapböyö's need the greater, I gave her the last three tablets. Ka'i, whose strength had astonished us before, was now grey and feeble, but as always he took her arm when she got into the boat, and we made them as comfortable as we could. By their silence as they lay there we knew how deathly ill they felt.

The water was smooth and glossy, milky with a skin of mist on its surface. All around and above us the same indefinite mist hung, softening the blueness of the sky, making the riverside trees into looming, dripping monsters risen from the depths to survey us. Toucans called; the red, brown and black kingfishers rattled as they fled from our approach; an occasional cry of a monkey reached us. Silently and gently the river flowed, so different from the Mapuera, where the sound of tumultuous water was never out of our ears.

The sun rose, tinselling the waves, and seraphic breezes cooled our cheeks. Ka'i and his wife became delirious. The old spotted bitch rested its head on her shoulder and heaved one of its deep sighs. The only thing which seemed to soothe Kabapböyö was its puppy, and mumbling with fever, her brows contracted, she clutched and stroked and kissed it.

A shout from the bank, and a canoe shot forward with the pouting Chekemá in it. He came paddling over rapidly, talking all the while in a high-pitched screeching rush. He clung to our boat, gazed into our faces as if we were ghosts, and then pushed away with a wave.

"He was certain that we was all dead," said Basil. "He had a dream about it, and told everyone we had been killed by the

Fishkalienas. Now it turns out that it was a false dream, which is very unlucky."

Suddenly the bitch pricked its ears: listening, faintly we heard barking—the dogs of Mawiká, the chief's village.

An hour later we stopped there briefly—to let Fonyuwé and Kirifakka disembark—and in an instant were engulfed in a crowd of welcoming Wai-Wais. Fonyuwé, excited almost to the point of exploding, rushed up to his wife (who was also his aunt) and hugged her. Kirifakka, now a great traveller, was viewed with awe by the younger men; whilst among the seven-year-olds Haimara, sturdy, resolute as ever, engaged in dignified conversation.

Ka'i and Kabapböyö, both of whom had revived a little now that they felt they had reached a haven, wanted to stop here; but knowing how dangerously ill they were, I persuaded them to continue.

It seemed an age, though it was only two hours, before we reached the mission; but when at last soon after midday we turned the wide bend leading to it, an Indian saw the boat and went hurrying up the bank with the news.

"Thank the Lord you are safe and well," said Mr. Leavitt, clasping me by the hand as I stepped ashore.

A great feeling of relief swept over me as I greeted him, his wife, and the nurse. I was overjoyed to see them. All along, I now realized, their presence even far away had been an unconscious reassurance. They were friends: whatever the differences of our beliefs I knew them to be good people. And now the two sick Indians would be properly looked after.

"We were so worried about you," continued Mr. Leavitt. "We did not know what had happened—you stayed so long on the other side. We all prayed that you were safe. Then Chekemá told us he had heard you had been killed and I was just going to set out looking for you. None of us had ever been to the other side, but we knew that *He* would guide us."

"And we have had such troubles since you left," said Miss Riedle. "Everyone has been sick. We've spent our whole life treating people. Why, some of them nearly died—and it all started just with that cold of Yukumá's. I would never have believed it."

One of Mrs. Leavitt's wonderful meals awaited us, and when we sat down, after Ka'i and his wife had been attended to by the nurse, I felt carefree, even gay for the first time on the voyage. The strain of forcing the expedition along had been too much—I felt as if I had awakened from a long dream in which everything had been out of focus. Merely to be at a table, surrounded by china, curtains, pots and pans, listening to commonplaces, was marvellously restoring. It raised in me a sudden, deep, inexpressible yearning for familiar things.

Now we had to make our way out of the forests to the savannahs. For about 120 miles we should be travelling through completely deserted country: by canoe down the Essequebo and half-way up the Kassikaityu, then on foot along a broad bullock-trail through the forest cut and kept open by balata bleeders, until we reached the open plains, and, eventually, Lumid Pau airstrip. We had plenty of food now, and the men, keen on returning to their homes, would be working well. But time was short: the ninth of December, when we had to meet the plane, was only two weeks away.

I looked at our accumulated specimens and equipment—there were several hundred pounds of wood blocks alone. The heavier, less urgently needed things could wait for the next plane into Gunn's Strip, but much would still have to come with us, and there was far more than the men could carry.

We should have to have bullocks.

It would take them five days to get to the Kassikaityu river from the savannah, and five days to walk back again, laden. We had only three spare days in which, somehow, to get a message through asking for them to be sent from Karardanawa, close to Lumid Pau near the southern edge of the savannah—and Karardanawa was so isolated that messages from the coast ordinarily took a week or two to reach it.

There was only one hope: that night we radioed to B.G. Airways' headquarters in Georgetown and begged them to try to get a message by plane or radio to one of the ranches on the savannah, or to Lethem, the Government post near the western frontier with Brazil, asking for a man to be sent on foot or horseback to Karardanawa—fifty to a hundred miles away,

depending on who picked up the message—to find Indians
willing to go and meet us with bullocks.

There was only a very slim chance that our message would
arrive—but it was the only one.

The next three days were spent in taking the things we were
leaving behind to Gunn's Strip, in building shelters there to
protect them from sun and rain, in packing, issuing rations,
and paying the Wai-Wais and Mawayáns.

Ka'i and Kabapböyö (both much recovered—Miss Riedle
had continued my sulphathiazole treatment, giving them each
twelve tablets to start with) were overjoyed with the payments
they received—possessions which would make them the richest
living Mawayáns, though they would no doubt soon trade most
of them on to others.

Ka'i was full of excitement at the wonders of the mission.
While the other Indians at Shiuru-tirir had regarded us with
curiosity, he from the first had seen that there was much to be
learned from us, and had gone out of his way to help us, and
to show me all that he thought would interest me. His quick,
practical mind in civilization might have made him an engineer
or scientist, I thought; and as he told me how he had never
conceived of the existence of a settlement on such a scale as the
mission, or of houses built like those he had now seen, there was
no trace of a feeling of inferiority, only eagerness to learn new
things that he could take back to his own land.

"William" and Wayama appeared, both still wifeless; then
Fonyuwé and Kirifakka. To them for their great loyalty, their
hard work and good cheer, I owed so much that I thought that
I would try to give them what they most wanted in the world—
a shotgun each—though I could not help reflecting sadly, and a
little ironically, that in so doing I was hastening the processes
I deplored, and the coming of times when all that made these
Indians distinctive people would have vanished. But there was
no stopping such changes.

The missionary had authority to issue gun licences, and
readily granted my request. My two tangerine-coloured friends
rushed up to me when they heard the news.

"*Kiriwanhi!* Meeshterguffin," they said, bouncing with
delight—to which Kirifakka throatily added:

"Vairy . . . nice!"

The American Thanksgiving Day came, and I celebrated it happily in the company of the missionaries at a meal even more memorable than usual, watched by the customary cluster of astonished Indians, including Ka'i and Kabapböyö.

Then, on the last day of November, the day before I planned to leave, came unexpected, sorrowful news. Kabapböyö and Ka'i had left the mission the previous day and gone to the chief's village, where they could get the food to which they were used, and where they felt they would be happier, among their own kind—and within a few hours of arriving there Kabapböyö had died. She had already been buried.

Miss Riedle was shocked: how *could* she have died—and of what? There was only one likely explanation: the disease had weakened her, and had led to a sudden, overwhelming attack of pneumonia—perhaps itself the final manifestation of the germ.

I was appalled: I could not help thinking of her, large, gentle, uncomplaining in her sickness, with her puppy and her devoted Ka'i, nor remembering how she and Ka'i had stood by us at Manatá's village when we had been deserted by everyone else except little Haimara. Only a few years before, pneumonia had been unknown in this country; tuberculosis and venereal disease, both common on the savannah, had still to come: obliteration or transformation seemed the only fates possible for the Wai-Wais, Mawayáns, and all the other vague tribes of the forests southwards.

"It is most worrying," was the missionary's comment, "that she should have died just when the Indians are beginning to come across and live round the mission. They will think that an evil spirit is here which has killed her. It may seriously interfere with our work."

With the nurse and missionary (who wanted to place a cross on the grave), I set forth that afternoon for Mawiká.

Flutes were tootling, fires smoking, meals being cooked, headdresses adjusted, when we arrived: the village was packed with Indians from all the other settlements, for the largest of the Wai-Wai festivals, the harvest festival, was just beginning, and nights and days of music, dancing, drinking and love-making lay ahead.

Inside the conical house, hung up like so many overcoats, were the extraordinary costumes of the dance-leaders—the men who kept the rhythm with shack-shacks. They consisted of wickerwork frames, worn on the head like inverted top-hats, supporting immense double crowns of silvery-yellow egret plumes and shorter green, yellow and orange parrot feathers; while from the lower rims of these frames, completely sheathing the wearers (whose identities, for some reason, had to be concealed from women), hung shin-length curtains of dark bottle-green Ité palm leaf-strips, and a delicate waist-length mantle of pale yellow strips from the unopened buds of the same palm. The other men, whose faces women *might* see, contented themselves with extra-elaborate versions of their usual plumed and feathered festive outfits, in some cases with long spiky clusters of macaw feathers shooting up from their biceps bands, and dancing clubs or pendant swags of feathers at their wrists.

Making our way through all this confusion and gaiety, we came to where, alone and unnoticed in his hammock, Ka'i lay. He hardly seemed to understand what was happening, or to recognize our presence as we sat beside him.

I told him how sorry I was, Miss Riedle took his temperature, and Mr. Leavitt spoke to him—then sadly shook his head.

"How has he taken his wife's death?" I asked.

"He has accepted it well. His first worry was for her beads— that they might be stolen by the Wai-Wais—but I have reassured him. He is not going back to the Mapuera until after the next plane comes to Gunn's Strip. I told him about the Great Roaring Bird, and he is determined to see it. That is good, because then, when he goes back, he will describe all the wonders there are here."

The Indians accept death stoically; they are so familiar with it, and try to forget everything about a person once he has died. But Ka'i, it was obvious, had not yet accomplished that. He was still prostrated. As for the matter of the beads, if we translate each one into a shilling we may better be able to understand his feelings.

Fonyuwé came and sat beside us in the dusk, and on a long slender flute, held sideways, poured out a wonderful fluttering tune. It was as sweet as a blackbird's song. Entranced, I asked him to repeat it again and again, until he grew embarrassed.

One by one the various Indians I had known came and joined us, bringing things they thought I would like to buy, and in turn I distributed the last of my trade goods. The chief twinkled his eyes at me, and handed me a small piece of palm-leaf, folded and tied with string. Inside, when it was spread out, was an egret crown.

"My! You're lucky," said Miss Riedle.

"We've been trying to get one," said the missionary. "They don't like to sell those, because the feathers are hard to get."

The dance began, with men and women, weirdly clad, their dresses a-rattle with seeds, whirling and stamping round in a circle, shaking their shack-shacks and whistling eerily on little pan pipes of bamboo or bird quills. It was getting very dark, and I had to be away early, so laden with a basketful of new acquisitions, with a farewell handshake to Ka'i, Fonyuwé and Kirifakka, I embarked.

All night long the dance continued, and in the morning it was a very tired group of Wai-Wais who came to say a final goodbye. More shaking of hands, my warmest thanks to all the missionaries, a blessing from Mr. Leavitt, and we were off.

The clearing with its little group of thatched houses diminished behind us, at the end of the long, bubbling wake of the boat.

PART FOUR

Out of the Forest

21

Giant Snake River

Uninhabited, the Essequebo rolled ahead for two hundred miles, to the village of Apoteri, where the Rupununi joined it; but long before there we should be turning up its tributary the Kassikaityu—"River of the Dead", in the Taruma language. Not only the Tarumas, but the Daurais and Atorads had once, before the first epidemics of introduced diseases, peopled the country we should be traversing: there had probably been several thousands of them. Now there was no one. There was little to see or do as one sat in the boat, the sun burning into one's brain, while the banks, sombre and dark, slid by.

At Onoro mouth sheets of grey rock were now exposed, leaving a sill over which the water rolled, in a cleft little wider than the boat: should we lower with ropes? There was no time to spare if we were to catch the plane: we steered for the gap, hung for a moment above the drop, then swooped with a crashing swish, a soft, deep bounce.

The river slowly broadened, till it was about 250 yards across. Noon, and the trees flickered like green flames, tortured by the writhings of the atmosphere. Occasionally a solid, dark-bellied cloud blew across the sun—then a wind would spring up for a moment. Sandbanks were everywhere, curls of orange peel on the water. With bow and arrow Cyril shot one of many large fish gliding away at our approach through the shallows—a "tiger-fish", or cullet, a silvery catfish three feet long, with blue and black variegations and orange fins.

A two-toed sloth, like a tuft of hay, hung in a tree; electric eels, black toffee-sticks many feet long, floated just below the surface. We lunched sitting on rough granite rocks at the riverside and watched them rising from the depths to tip the surface with their noses, as if wanting to reassure themselves that the

335

upper world still existed, then sinking back until they were lost in the brown water.

Further, there were many small rocks in the channel, jumbles of surf, then wide shallow reaches, bordered by grey, battered yawarda palms, their dead thorny leaves everywhere, like discarded fly-whisks. A solitary blue mountain showed briefly ahead—one of the Amuku mountains near the Kassikaityu mouth—then was hidden. Extraordinary paku-weeds grew on the rocks, nine-inch high succulent red spikes tipped with a crescent of pink flowers, attached below water to a bronzy-red, crinkled cabbage leaf.[1]

By four-fifteen in the afternoon we had reached Sebur-teroan, the Howler-monkey rapids, where the river breaks into a rash of islets with a scatter of rocks in between, like teeth in a dentist's tray: not difficult to negotiate, though requiring caution. But Gabriel, less experienced in reading water-signs than George (who was resting), was bowman, and soon we were uncomfortably aware of heads of rock racing close by us: there were shouts of alarm, then we struck hard, rolled over, and water rushed in. The engine roared as the stern was lifted high, then stopped. For a moment it seemed as if we would sink, but we had been moving so fast that we slid off the rock, and settled deep, with half our goods afloat, borne downstream in the current. George and Gabriel leaped overboard and began drawing us into shallow water.

"She's holed!" lamented Basil. "We have to stop and mend her."

"Nonsense," I replied, for I had been watching to see if the level was rising, "all this water came over the side on to me!"

"De engine break," interposed Tanner. "De top knock off de carburettor, and de clutch gone carry away."

Bailing hard, we were at last beached and could draw breath.

"Every man into the water," I ordered. "We must find that carburettor top. If that is not found we have to paddle all the rest of the way. And then we'll have to carry everything, because the bullocks won't be able to stay in the forest without food."

In a fan we spread out, inch by inch, probing and scrutiniz-

[1] *Mourera fluviatilis.*

ing the bottom through the cold water, sometimes knee deep, sometimes up to our necks. The cap might easily have been carried a long distance, and after an hour, heavy-hearted, we gave up, drifted downriver, and camped on a grass-run beach, backed by a grove of red-barked myrtaceous trees.

There I began sorting, draining and drying all the things that had got wet, and set the men to work making paddles—though Tanner was full of hope.

"De clutch don' matter, sir. I scarcely uses it. George and me go try to make a new cap from sof' wood. De engine go work."

Rain clouds; and a light shower chilled the air. Above the falls the western sky was a sheet of pale blue, and night descended in darker, ferrocyanide curtains. Jonah and George camped apart, on a rocky islet, and I could see them crouched in silhouette beside their fire, from which columns of sparks blew upwards. Presently they lighted a lantern, and from it a long tassel of gold hung in the water. All night long the falls muttered, sending foam islands floating past below. The full moon rose, and veiled everything in pearly light.

At dawn the engine burst into loud song and we all awoke and crowded round the triumphant Tanner. An hour later he was wrestling with it again, for it refused to start a second time.

"Chief," said he, when at last we were away, "we got to keep her going, even when we stop for lunch."

Petrol leaked continuously, and had to be caught in a tin, and voluminous blue smoke poured from the exhaust.

A few miles more and the river curved through a wide gap between crunched, jagged masses of rock, its surface smooth, marked by tiny ripples. Here another disaster nearly overtook us. At great speed we were skimming along, when suddenly George pointed in alarm:

"Look *dat!*"

At the upstream end of one of these ripples, stationary, was a leaf: it was balanced on a needle of rock which just reached the surface. And we saw that all around, hardly visible in the murky liquid, were other slender pinnacles—a touch from any of which would rip us open.

But George was back at the bow; and two hours later, saved

by his skill, we reached Urana-pau, where there was an abandoned Wai-Wai village, a cone of ribs and rafters from which the thatch had fallen.

Here, while Tanner ran the engine, we dug yams, picked bananas, surveyed the three humps of the Amuku Mountains (showing above the trees on the far side of the river), and inspected a half-completed dwelling, in the style of the missionaries, that had been begun by our boat-builder, Charlie.

Watu-teroan—Parrot Falls—followed, a spacious baroque curve of red stone, rimmed with paku-weed, embellished with islands, and crowned with stately yawarda palms. The water looked deep, and conscious of the urgency with which we had to move, we manoeuvred towards the brink: buried in water, with two-foot high waves slapping our gunwales, we slid for three hundred yards, paddling, revving the engine to keep steering-control, and out into smooth water, with the river winding away towards a rock mass shaped like a beached whale surrounded by porpoises.

To the left stood another striking rock—a grey, horizontally banded horn thirty feet high, with beside it a dark, narrow opening—the Kassikaityu.

A duck rose from the surface and flapped low into its mouth. I raised my gun as we followed, engine straining, for the current was sweeping us down the Essequebo. Just a few yards up the river was a steep bank, and there—coiled on it, only a few feet away—was a colossal snake, an anaconda.

"Shoot, Chief!" yelled the men, and almost by reflex I pulled the trigger. A dark patch appeared on its head. The vast spotted body relaxed. To judge from one I had shot a few months before, seventeen feet long, this must be at least half that length again. That had been six inches in diameter, this was eight or ten.

"That the bigges' camoudi I yet see," said Jonah.

"It mus' be a good thirty feet from de size of de body an' head," ventured George.

As its head touched the water the most horrifying transformation I have ever witnessed took place: the whole monstrous creature convulsed like a spring gone mad. Writhing, lashing, it tumbled into the river and out of sight. It would have uprooted a tree, crushed us all if it had struck us. We were aghast. The boat swerved. The duck rose from just ahead and flapped away.

Revulsion swept over me at the thought that I might merely have wounded it, even if it was one of the most dreadful of existing creatures. It was impossible to say whether it had been killed, and it had certainly gone into very deep water.

"Can' stop, sir," said Tanner, "cause de moto' don' start."

That decided it. We continued up the sombre, narrow river. The water was black, edged with knobs of dark grey rock, walled with depressing dull green vegetation, ceilinged with a sky of hopeless white—exactly the colour-scheme of a municipal w.c.

Bush curry-curries—black ibis—were as common as on the Buna-wau, and snakebirds were abundant everywhere, crawling along logs, slipping into the water after fish, swimming with only their serpentine necks above the surface. Alarmed by our terrifying onrush they rose like flying pencils from the water and made flustered attempts to escape over the forest. Once aloft they looked like crosses hanging in the sky, so narrow were their wings and bodies; and despite this apparent lack of lifting surface, were successful soarers, sometimes continuing upwards in wide spirals, steering by inclining their odd, wedge-shaped tails. Already the vegetation appeared to indicate the drier zones ahead. It was as if the Kassikaityu mouth lay on the line of change.

We lunched on a slope of black rocks in the river-bed, under trees festooned to a height of twenty feet with the debris of the torrential floods of the rainy season. The stagnant, sun-soaked water was full of little fish: silver, fork-tailed minnows, with black and mother-of-pearl bands and magenta fins, or horizontally striped in silver and purple; and chubby cichlids with a black and silver V on their sides.

"Here a man get carry off by a camoudi time of de Boundary Commission," reminisced George. "He was killed before anybody could reach him. Not one of de Indians will bathe in this river, dey so 'fraid of them."

Every European traveller on the Kassikaityu and the nearby Kujuwini has seen giant snakes. The very first, Schomburgk, in 1837, wrote, "We also saw a large comuti snake (Boa), which, gorged with its prey, lay inactive in a swamp, emitting a very offensive smell. I wounded it with a ball, when it made a rush towards us, and obliged us to retreat. It appeared about 8 yards long, and was the largest I had ever seen."

In other places there are patches of territory where iguanas, or perai, or alligators, or other creatures abound, but in this region there are great numbers of immense anacondas—no one knows why, and no one has ever attempted to find out; even the anthropologist Farabee, in an article otherwise illustrated by photographs of Indians, shows pictures of two.

Because in their creation legend the ancestress of the Indians of this region was the daughter of an anaconda, no anaconda was ever harmed by a Taruma, but was regarded as a member of the tribe, addressed as "uncle", and avoided. This ancestress was fished up from a deep pool where she lived with her father, and according to Farabee some of the pools in this river were supposed by the Tarumas to be haunted still by enormous spirit-anacondas, with eyes as big as the full moon—spirits in their own right, not merely the ghosts of dead anacondas—which in former times swallowed many people—and in so doing conferred upon them a dubious kind of immortality, for unharmed they went on living inside them for ever.

But according to Basil it was "uncle" himself who, because he ate too many of them, finally made the Tarumas move completely away from the Kassikaityu (their first home in British Guiana), and go to live on the Essequebo.

Jonah laughed when he heard this. He was sitting near to me, so I turned to him.

"Well, Jonah, I hope things don't seem too bad now, and that at least you are enjoying the last part of the expedition."

Slowly I had been trying to restore and win back a little of his confidence, aware that he was an old man and that his pride had been wounded. Now, for the first time, he smiled with a trace of his old warmth.

"Sir, really it has been a wonderful trip, seeing so many strange things, but I shall be glad to get home. Now I feel I have travelled like the old-time Indians. You know, at one time no Indian thought anything of getting into his canoe with his wife and children, and going for a whole year or more visiting distant places. Wherever a man went he would find hospitality with people of his own clan. It was a thing you were born into. Some people might be of the Maipuri, or bush-cow clan, and others might be Hannaqua, and you could only marry a woman from that clan. There was no chief—the chief you obeyed was the headman of your village—but all the people in a clan were supposed to be related, even if they lived hundreds of miles apart. So wherever you went you searched them out, and they had to give you hospitality.

"But all those old ways are being forgotten. There are many Arawaks nowadays who don't even know what clan they belong to. But what I was really trying to tell you is why the Indians wandered as they did. They were looking for certain things, and the most important was the Great River that runs round the World."

"The sea, I suppose. Did you know that it was your tribe that first went to sea and lived in the West Indies, and that they got as far north as Cuba, and even Florida, I believe?"

"Yes, sir. And they used to come to and fro with Guiana. But you know, there was one thing all those travellers was afraid of—and that was what they called the Dead Sea. In it everything, even cotton, would sink. So whenever they came to water they fired special arrows made of very light grass ahead of them, to see if they would float."

As the day continued deep gulfs of blue appeared in the cloud above, and whenever the sun shone down the whole mood of the scene changed: the greens glowed, incandescent; the black water rippled and flashed, or lay quiet, filmed with an illuminated gauze of pollen-dust. We passed Karinab, where elephantine boulders, clustered round with piles of smaller cannon-balls, stood in murmuring water. Then there were long, straight, deep stretches, or gently curving bends. Even more than the Mapuera the Kassikaityu was a river of eerie dolmen-like rocks.

Slowly darkness fell, until we could no longer detect submerged snags. Then we turned into the side where a slope of sand, overgrown by knotty guavas, genipas and other small trees, rose steeply forty feet to a knife-edged ridge.

While I dined in an illuminated cavern among the tree-roots, an enormous moon floated over the wrinkled asphalt water. From my hammock, a little later, I watched the men throwing lines out and pulling in gigantic flapping haimaras, some of them four feet long. I could see their eyes glowing red in the water as they circled the pool of light cast by the midge-misted paraffin lamp.

Then I awoke with a jump, and it was full moonlight, with the sky overhead a silvery-blue bowl between the delicate leaf-sprays of the low trees. The wind shivered them, and the pattern changed. On the mosquito-net falling leaves had pressed their silhouettes close to my nose, and a tree frog sat with splayed toes above my tummy—a curious shape suspended in space.

Raising myself on an elbow, I gazed all around, at the chill radiance that lay in pools on the woodland floor and on the rocks in midstream. The river had become transparent: from my height of thirty feet above it I seemed able to look into the depths of the dark water, to see the contours of submerged sandbanks and rocks, a galaxy of islands lying beneath the surface. Perhaps it was the polarized light of the moon? Perhaps an illusion, a dream that lingered while I was half awake, before I lay back and went to sleep again.

By partly turning off the fuel, Tanner had made the motor run as well as usual and now it gave no trouble even to start. All morning we journeyed through low-lying country, with the river broad, curving between swamp-acacia bordered bays and lagoons. Then came a more rugged region, where it narrowed and took abrupt, angular bends whenever rock outcrops inter-rupted its path. Once or twice, at these places, we had to make short portages.

I burned with impatience at each delay. I felt I should hardly be able to endure it if we arrived too late for the plane—and already we were cutting it fine, trusting that our message asking for bullocks had got through.

What if when we reached the landing they were not there? I preferred not to think of that possibility.

I was overwrought: time, time, time had been pressing on me all through the expedition—and in my heart I wanted to be out of the forests. It was not that I did not love them or was not interested in them—years of work lay ahead of me from this expedition alone—but I had been in them too long, and I could not build my life in them or around them. I needed to get back to the centre of my civilization—not merely the West Indies, or Georgetown, but to Europe—to see my home again, to reassess myself, my purpose and direction.

Macaws flew overhead in pairs, heavy-headed, long-tailed, their stubby wings waving evenly up and down. Out of curiosity they turned aside and steered towards us, and then continued on their steadfast way. They set me dreaming, longing to wing away with them over the scalloped trees. I was transported, in my reverie, to places I had not seen for years: I saw the Alps, a line of white teeth on the horizon, from the top of a peak in the Jura; I heard the sound of boogie-woogie in a students' night-club in Paris, and smelt the smoke and the heated bodies. Then I was back on my river, standing on a gaunt prostrate tree-trunk while the boat was rocked over its barely covered spine.

We passed two stones covered with carvings, seemingly chosen at random from a jumble of rocks in a rapid. Shallow sunken lines, presumably made by stone implements struck against the stone, depicted in outline the figures of a man, and a four-legged creature that might have been a toad. Elsewhere there were scrawls and squiggles, meaningless to me.

"Who carved them?" I asked—"Tarumas?"

"No, before them," said Mark. "They say it was women who did it."

Timehri, as these carved rocks, or petroglyphs, are called, are common in the rapids in many of the Guiana rivers, and are occasionally found on dry land. A few seem recent, even modern, but no one knows or will tell what they mean, or who carved them. Most, however, appear very ancient, their designs quite unlike those of the present-day arts of the region, though sometimes showing men wearing feather headdresses similar to those still worn. Perhaps they are directional signs. It is the only "explanation" commonly put forward by anthropologists. They may have marked tribal boundaries, or intertribal meeting-places, been records of battles or hunts, or merely the idle work of passers-by. Or they may have had some deep magical, ritual, spiritual significance, of which we cannot guess. But whatever they meant the ancient ones are the sole relics telling of the former existence of peoples long disappeared.

Just before nightfall we reached the landing: a jumble of rocks on which was drawn up a boat, with low secondary forest rising behind.

"Charlie's boat!" pointed Mark—and at that minute Charlie appeared, panting, on the path.

He had run, he said, from his balata camp a mile away, when he had heard our motor. It was a pleasant reunion, and the men at once began telling of our adventures—but I was bursting with impatience.

Had the bullocks come?

What bullocks? No, there were no bullocks—what bullocks did I mean?

There were no bullocks . . .

I felt close to tears.

Now nothing I could do would be any use in helping to catch the plane. I could send a man out to the savannah with a message—for evidently mine had not arrived—but it would be eight or nine days before he returned, two weeks before we got to Lumid Pau—and the plane left in five days' time.

I was exhausted: I felt I had not the strength to work out some alternative plan. But Charlie and Basil were conferring together, and after a few minutes Basil turned to me with a smile.

"Charlie say he have his *own* bullocks coming in tomorrow, to take out his balata. His sons are bringing them. He will lend them to you, so it will be all right."

Luck, it seemed, was with me.

But when the next day came I waited with rising impatience, and there were no signs of bullocks. At first I was cheerful, and occupied myself examining the forest and doing accounts; but by mid-afternoon I was almost breathless. I could not sit still: I walked up and down, and climbed over the rocks in the river-bed. With Basil and Cyril I paddled downriver to have a closer look at the carved rocks, rubbing yam juice into the grooves to make the faint patterns stand out; then returned and began writing my journal.

Charlie's Wai-Wai wife appeared, a gay sight in her flowery scarlet, white and blue dress. Under it, rather as her sparse brown, green and yellow teeth obtruded beneath her sunny smile, there showed a much older, tattered, blackish-grey garment, long unwashed. She sat on a log about two feet from me and chattered briskly away. She was powerfully fishy, but her cheerful, incomprehensible flow of words somehow soothed me in my mood of blank desperation. The fact that she did not realize that I could not understand anything she said, or at least that it made no difference to her wanting to talk to me, rather pleased me.

Then she ambled down to the rocks, and took off first one, then the other dress: under them, to my horror, was a third yet more ancient. Wearing this, after a careful look around to see, perhaps, if there were any anacondas, she slipped into the water. Then she emerged, popped the other two on over the wet dress and came back to me. They now clung to her so closely that I could see, beneath them all, the outline of a bead apron. She must have been extremely hot beneath so many layers, and the wetting had greatly increased her pungency.

Desperate, as she squished down beside me and fixed me with a bright eye loaded with gossip, I slung a towel over my shoulder and in turn raced down to the rocks. A pinnacled cluster, large as a minor Gothic ruin, stood in the middle of the half-dry river-bed, and behind this, in a shallow scoop, I lay until she had gone; then returned refreshed, and dispatched Mark to see if any bullocks had arrived at Charlie's camp.

An hour later he came back and announced that there were none. If we were to catch the plane we could start no later than the morrow: furiously I set to work separating the bare minimum needed that we could carry, planning to walk to Lumid Pau, bullocks or no bullocks, and to send the rest back to the mission with the two men who, in any case, had to return the missionary's boat. My personal load came to sixty pounds. It would be gruelling going, especially when we reached the open, sun-scorched savannahs, but I was determined.

Almost as darkness fell Charlie appeared: the bullocks had come—they were at his balata camp now, and there his sons were resting. In the morning they would move to the riverside.

Joyfully I shook his hand.

"Charlie," I said, "you built our boat, and now you've got us bullocks. Without you, we could have done practically nothing! Thank you very much."

We began to load the boat. Certain things—the outboard motor, packed in its heavy wooden case, a few empty petrol drums, some wood blocks, collected on the way downriver— would have to go by plane. Gabriel and Mark were going to paddle back to the mission, from where, on the next plane from Gunn's Strip, I had arranged that they would be flown home to Lumid Pau. Meanwhile they could do odd jobs for the missionaries.

Perhaps Charlie would be going back to the mission too? No, said he. If he returned there he would probably have to stay and work. It would be hard to refuse. But he had more important things to do. He had been away from the savannahs too long, and it was time he went back and saw his other wife and house and field. But, he added, anytime *I* wanted him he would work for me, because I was a good boss.

I was still susceptible to flattery, so I beamed.

22

Savannah

As I was breakfasting, Charlie arrived; but with only one bullock.

"It is for your own use," translated Basil. "But none of his sons wants to work and all the other bullocks belong to them. All the same, they will come along soon." Which meant that they wanted big pay. In a rage I had everything packed and made ready beside the boat, as a warning that I would rather send it all back to the mission than submit to blackmail.

This may have had effect; in any case, when, an hour later, the sons appeared, there could not have been two more pleasant and amenable young men. By name Stanislaus (wearing a sort of Wehrmacht cap) and Robert, they were much alike, with broad, smiling faces, pointed chins, and dark eyebrows nearly meeting in the middle; and almost at once they struck a happy note by asking not merely a fair price for the hire of each bullock, but by charging only for the journey to the savannah —so that the total cost would actually be less than if those I had ordered had arrived. I felt now a little ashamed of my show of temper—though one could never tell: it might have contributed to the reasonableness of our agreement.

There were six bullocks—two black, two marmalade, one striped red and black, and one spotted black and white— fierce-looking creatures, standing shoulder-high to their drivers. They wore either ordinary riding saddles, ingeniously fastened with a wooden pin which allowed rapid unharnessing, or wooden baggage saddles with cross-shaped pommels fore and aft.

Gnawed by impatience, because we now had less than four days in which to make the journey, I sat on the river-bank while they were loaded, an exacting business which took till midday.

347

Weight had to be distributed evenly on either side, and care taken that nothing protruded so far that it would catch in the pathside trees, or dug into their flesh and irritated them. Again and again packages and bundles were transferred from one animal to another; then we started, and at once three rushed into the forest and tried to scrape their loads off against the trees.

"Whoa . . . ah! Whoa . . . ah!" cried Charlie's sons, in full pursuit.

Unwilling, the rebellious three allowed themselves to be led back, occasionally putting up a show of resistance, tugging at their halter-ropes with bulging eyes. Then placid, all six began to amble forward, but so slowly that soon the Wapisiana equivalent of gee-up—"Moo . . . ey! Moo . . . ey!"—resounded among the trees. Suddenly, a vast commotion. This time it was the tiger-coloured bullock: it pranced, kicked right and left, fled through the forest for fifty yards, and lay down.

Fortunately nothing was damaged, for it was only carrying kitbags of hammocks and clothing; and after this all went smoothly for a while.

In an hour we reached Charlie's balata camp, a clearing a hundred yards wide in the midst of tall forest. On one side was a rough palm-thatched shelter full of women and little girls— Charlie's sons' wives and their children—and slung with a dozen hammocks. A pack of hunting dogs, a macaw and a monkey completed the population.

All around were the strange implements of balata-bleeding: knives, climbing irons used in tapping the latex high up the tree-trunks, and shallow troughs, twelve feet long, raised on stilts, into which the liquid gum was poured. In these, protected by adjustable thatch screens from rain and overmuch sun (which affect the colour and quality), it slowly dries on the surface into a succession of skins which are lifted off when about a quarter of an inch thick, hung up to allow their undersides to dry, and folded or rolled for transport to the coast—from such remote forests come the waterproof sheathings of marine cables and the little soft bags of gum at the centre of every golf-ball.

Beyond Charlie's camp the trail was six or eight feet wide, smooth and firmly trodden, and kept well clear of projecting undergrowth branches by Charlie and his sons to allow the unimpeded passage of their bullocks. I walked fast so that I could look around undistracted, stopping from time to time to collect or examine plants.

Near the riverside the forest—evidently flooded much of the year—had been dry and scuffling, with small twisted trees. But here, and from just before the camp, on ground a few feet higher, we had entered what appeared to be the typical high forest of the region—tall, very much like the Acarai rain forests at first glance, but with slight differences which Jonah and I soon detected: the big trees were branchier, forming, a hundred feet overhead, a looser canopy which allowed more light to reach the ground, as a consequence of which there were more epiphytes lower down and a heavier undergrowth; and there were fewer species, and many more of them were familiar to us—though several, which we had not time to stop and collect, were completely strange. Balata trees, rare in the Acarai, were very common: rough, black-barked giants, with a fleshy-pink slash and flowing white milk. All were grooved by the bleeders to high up the trunk, sometimes to sixty feet, and many had been killed by over-bleeding—by cutting grooves all the way round the tree to get the maximum of latex at once.

The most important difference, however, between these forests and those of the Acarai, was one that we could only surmise, in the absence of knowledge, by analogy with other forests of similar appearance growing in the same sort of locality and containing many of the same species: that here such phenomena as flowering and fruiting, instead of taking place throughout the year (viewing the forest as a whole and not the individual species), would be more closely crowded into seasons—for which reason I classified them provisionally, not as Rain, but as Evergreen Seasonal Forests.

The tangled undergrowth was aswarm with ticks: large beasts as big as sixpences that waved from leaves, and others of pinhead size which in swarms took possession of patches of skin. Even worse were *bêtes rouges*, minute harvest-mites[1] scarcely visible to the eye, like little red spiders in shape. In thousands of millions they exist in dry forests, and here they

[1] Trombidiidae.

were at a zenith: nimble, unseen, they crawled over one's body, and wherever there was a constriction, such as beneath the belt, burrowed biting and stinging into the flesh. By mid-afternoon my waist was a band of fiery red inflammations, my whole body was mottled with a lighter rash, and try as I might I could not stop myself from scratching.

Beyond Aisher-wau, "the River of the *Lonochocarpus* Fish-poison Vine", a dismal, half-dry, rock-bedded branch of the Kassikaityu, the forest was full of patches of second growth, many years old, relics of the ancient population of Daurais and Atorads. In low-lying places there were dried-up *Euterpe* bogs, their leaves and peat crisp on the surface, mushy beneath; and at one of these, Yuru-lud ("Ité palm road"), where a vestigial pool of greenish water allowed us to drink but not bathe, we camped in the late afternoon. Burning, tickling, itching furiously, unable to do anything about my insects, I faced the night.

In little more than three hours, and about seven miles, our world had changed. We were on the move after a day of frustration, and from the black-watered Kassikaityu with its uncanny rock formations we were now deep in a peculiarly dark, dusty, and depressing forest—but a forest continually altering: almost before we knew it we should be in the open savannahs! After months of imprisonment it was an extraordinary thought.

Faint lights stirred in the abysmal blackness; then Tanner shook me and I got up and dressed. We set out in our long file as soon as we could see, the bullocks and men strange uneasy shapes among the leaves. The forest was full of bird sounds, flappings and flutterings; in a tree beside the path sat seven or eight toucans, clapping their bills together as they ate; close overhead—for we were now in second-growth only forty or fifty feet high—guans creaked from tree to tree; and within a few minutes Cyril had shot three fat black powis, which fell to earth, detaching themselves from the black silhouetted leaves and branches, with resounding thuds. (Above the right eye of one was a scarlet patch—a swarm of *bêtes rouges*.)

As dawn broke there was a wonderful feeling of life stirring, of a strange new country-side full of creatures, quite different from the forlorn Acarai.

350

In a few places the forest was still very tall and full of Brazil-nut trees—further west, said Basil, there were yet more, where flat land led into Brazil round the northern tip of the Acarai—and there were patches of pale brown sands, relics, I judged, of the White Sand Sea. Most of the rivers we crossed—we had to space our camping-grounds according to where we could find water—were dry; the largest, the Mabu-wau, or Honey River, reduced to a sandy bed with a series of clear pools in which fish were still active, while at the sides a frog or toad had laid its eggs, like jellied BB shot, in small, isolated, carefully scooped-out ponds.

By mid-afternoon Basil and I, far ahead of the bullocks, had walked about seventeen miles and reached our night's halt, the Ishkishi-wau, or Shrimp River, a dungeon-gloomy stream deep in a clay-sided channel. I bathed, soothing my pest-infested flesh. The sun came out briefly, making the mud golden, the dusty leaves of the overhanging trees glint green, and casting a reddish translucence into the water—revealing, hanging in it, until the light faded, two big torpedo-shaped striped fish.

Several men had been drained of blood by vampire bats at Shiuru-tirir, but here, approaching cattle country, they were especially common, and the previous night Basil, Cyril, and Stanislaus had all been bled. After my bath Basil helped me sling my hammock between two trees, and arranged the net so that there would be least chance of a toe or elbow touching it.

"We will keep a lamp alight tonight," he said, "though that doesn't always scare them when they are hungry."

At the foot of one of my hammock-trees I noticed a gently stirring greyish-green mass, a swarm of hundreds of small hairy caterpillars, which, as they were fairly quiescent, I did not worry about. At bedtime, though still not looking particularly active, they had moved about eight feet up the trunk, and at dawn were back at the base. Glancing up I saw that the tree, about thirty feet tall, which the previous day had been thickly bushy, covered with abundant foliage, was now bare. In its whole crown perhaps two complete leaves remained. By the time we started the innocent-seeming brood had moved about three feet along the ground, half-way to another tree.

Among the second-growth species in the numerous old fields

that we now passed were clumps of the South American species of traveller's-tree,[1] immense, weird-looking herbs, from the short thin stalks of which rose, twenty feet tall, a flat fan of imbricated leaves, with, among them, the colossal, erect flower-spikes, their purplish-red, orange-fringed bracts like garish pelicans' beaks. I stuck my penknife into the bases of the leaf-sheaths, but not a drop of water oozed out—the plants had either run dry or were less hospitable than their Madagascan relative. Alive, their leaves had none of the green translucence one would expect from their banana-like appearance; and dead, lay harsh and leathery on the ground, glaringly reflecting the light into our eyes.

The soil had changed to a pure white water-washed sand, the forest to low scrub except in the hollows, where there were small dried-up *Euterpe* bogs. An armadillo started up and ran away from us, plunging into its burrow—a damp, mouldy, mosquito-infested hole beneath a tree. A bushmaster, five feet long and very dark for its species, slid away from us. Cyril killed a small deadly-poisonous but beautiful tree viper,[2] dark green above, yellow below, with white rings round its eyes; then a herd of six peccaries appeared, which scattered, barking loudly like dogs. I saw several jaguar footprints, one very clear, in an old cowpat.

Then the soil became a powdery white silt, into which the path had sunk. A minute later we were in a tiny, lozenge-shaped patch of grassland: melastome shrublets clothed in claret-purple flowers,[3] bushes with golden-brown leaves, velvety on the undersides,[4] stood round the edges, and low overhead grey clouds were hurrying—but clear to see, unobscured by leaves or branches, telling of the open spaces ahead, and suffused with a wonderful glow from the sun behind them.

A little more forest, then came a much larger savannah with knee-high grass full of small bright flowers on wire-thin stalks: *Burmannia bicolor*, a herb seven inches tall, with orange-yellow petals showing above green calyces, on each sepal of which stood an enormous protruding keel of pale mauve—by far the most conspicuous part of the flower; *Eriocaulon tenuifolium*, like a pincushion stuck full of twelve-inch long hatpins, the heads

---

[1] *Ravenala guianensis.*
[2] *Bothrops bilineatus.*
[3] *Tococa nitens.*
[4] *Vochysia* sp.

of which were tight little knots of white flowers; a xyrid,[1] like a grass with the palest yellow miniature iris blossoms; wiry, pink-flowered *Turneras* and *Sipaneas* . . . and beside the path a little sprawling plant with chicory-blue petals.

I flung myself down full-length to examine these, and the sun broke through, baking me. George passed, a red and black Wai-Wai cassava-grater on his back, and disappeared over the swaying stalks into the tunnel a quarter of a mile away; then Cyril and Stanislaus, with three bullocks, which on coming into the open space raced with springy hoofs and flying tails before sharp cries halted them. Immediately they started cropping the grass, their first food for a week (for the Indians do not carry fodder for their animals, and make them work up to fifteen days in the forests without food), until driven on again.

It was December the seventh, Christmas was near, and as they walked the men were whistling carols—"Silent Night, Holy Night"—and "Jingle Bells".

A hundred yards into the forest the path turned sharply, and became a broad grassy avenue that led downhill for a few hundred yards to the Kujuwini: a broad, grey-green river, its waters dusty with pollen, crawling sluggishly over slabs of yellow rock between high mud walls.

A rotten-wooded canoe lay on the rocks under somnolent sprawling trees. We paddled across to a wide pavement and sat waiting while the cattle were swum over. From a tree above —a violet-flowered legume—bits of leaves fell in a steady flutter, cut by leaf-cutter ants, large red, musty-smelling insects which clung to the falling fragments, and as soon as they landed carried them off in procession to their nest high up on the river-bank. Watching, I saw that they used their jaws not like scissors, with both sides working equally, but with one held firm and the other slicing against it, cutting in a curve round themselves until the piece of leaf they were standing on was detached and parachuted them gently to the ground. Sometimes they fell into channels of stagnant water between the rocks, or into the river; and then, like bubbles rising in clear lentil soup, silvery fish would float up and nuzzle them, even taking them into their mouths, but always spitting them out again.

[1] *Xyris surinamensis.*

353

Beyond the river, a mile's walk through low woodland brought us into another stretch of grassland, the first of a group of small, mostly interconnected savannahs called the Parabara savannahs, after a fish living in the streams that cross them, and so beautiful that I have always wanted to return to them, perhaps even to live on them for a year or two.

With their forested rolling hills, their glades, woodlands, wide sweeping slopes dotted with magnificent trees, they were like an idealized English parkland, a product of skilled landscaping by a Brown or Repton—yet exotically jewelled by multitudes of tropical plants. Their whole country-side was in flower: orchids waved on the ground in purple clumps, or hung from the trees; there were groves of twisted *Byrsonima* trees, with red stems, honey-coloured leaves, and golden flowers; shrubberies of *Clusia nemorosa* with little apple-pink and white magnolia flowers set among dark leaves; *Vochysias*, laden with yellow sprays; and in marshy places lines of Ité palms raised their green explosions, dark below with bunches of fruit.

In the rainy season the dells would be full of water, and then one would travel from place to place by canoe. It was the sort of country-side that children love, full of unexpected, intimate, exciting things; and with a strange poetry given to it by its loneliness.

Fireflies were twinkling above the ground, the remnants of a spectacular sunset were fading in the sky ahead, when, some twenty-five miles from our start, we reached a long level of savannah where there had once been an airstrip. It had never been used. Like Gunn's Strip it had been made as a wartime emergency landing-place, and for a few more years kept open for possible use in flying produce out from the southern forests; then abandoned. On a low, stony hill there was a crude but strongly-made thatched shelter, and here we camped.

The cattle were turned loose to graze, the men went down to bathe in a creek that ran among a line of Ité palms, and I slung my hammock above a pile of empty tortoise-shells, relics of past feasts, before following them.

The night sky was ablaze with magnificent stars, a field of cloth of gold stretching clear overhead to the wide horizon all around. It was extraordinary to stand there, even in the darkness, and feel the sensation of freedom again—to feel a strong cold wind blowing low over the ground, full of scents from the forests we were leaving behind—to think of our many long days in their shadows, and of the wide savannahs that we should see on the morrow.

At four o'clock when we arose we could see heavy clouds driving close overhead. Fine drizzle and the chill wind had turned the country-side into a Scottish moorland, as, over springy turf between small bushes, we walked through the grey morning. Twice we crossed extensive patches of forest—a new type of forest (probably Semi-Evergreen Seasonal Forest), ankle-deep in crackling red leaves, of tall, slim, ridged-barked trees, many of them of species which lose all their leaves in the long dry seasons. The streams were clear-watered, with stony or sandy, root-tangled beds, the largest, the Kati-wau, or Sand River, being the last outlying arm of Amazonia—for according to Basil its waters flowed into the Amazon (via the Takutu, the Rio Branco and the Rio Negro) at Manáos, five hundred miles upriver from where the Trombetas empties the waters of the Mapuera into it. But, so interconnected in this region are the headwaters of Guiana and Amazonia, that only a mile or two later we came to a branch of the Rupununi, which pours, by way of the Essequebo, into the Atlantic 1,000 miles from the Amazon mouth.

In the rainy season much of this watershed region is flooded, and in exceptionally wet years it is possible for the creatures of each river system to swim across to the other—which accounts for the presence in some of the Guiana rivers of Amazonian species like fresh-water porpoises, sting-rays, and the giant arapaima fish (which has apparently only recently made the crossing, as records show that it is still slowly spreading down the Essequebo towards the sea).

Five hours from starting we emerged into a pleasant alley-way of grass between the trees, which, after a twist or two, widened and revealed before us the beginnings of the South Rupununi Savannah—part of that great forest-enclosed grass-land of the Guiana interior which, frequently changing its name, stretches on far into Brazil, to the Uraricoera River and the sandstone Pakaraimas.

A sparse scatter of Indian huts in the distance was the village of Karar-tun, an outpost of Karardanawa. Here some of the Wapisianas had their "farms", and lived when tending their crops, clearing new fields on the edge of the slowly-receding forest, or hunting. As we approached, people ran to their doors and gazed at us in wonder—men from the strange lands further south, from which few people ever came. Then they recognized their own kinsfolk among us, and hurried away to spread the news.

Cyril, in the lead, drove his bullock up to a house, disappeared inside, and came out carrying a bowl of purple yam-juice, which he proferred as we arrived. This was his family's house; and inside he introduced us to his mother and two young sisters, who were busily raking and stirring cassava meal in a heated bowl, making farine.

It was a square, one-roomed, wattle-sided, thatched house, with a partitioned-off kitchen, on the floor of which stood several big water-filled gourds. It represented an Indian way of life different from anything we had seen before on the expedition, one in which each family, ruled by its father, lived in its own separate house and cultivated its own fields. Inside there were five hammocks, and round about on the savannah were some twenty other houses: in this small area dwelt perhaps as many people as in all those thousands of square miles southwards.

Further, we crossed a jeep trail, two parallel tracks in the sand. Sometimes we saw more Indian houses, in groups of two or three, clustered far off on the hill-sides; and from each a path came snaking to join our own, till there was a broad web of interweaving trails all going in the general direction of the metropolis, Karardanawa, a mile beyond Lumid Pau.

"Shall we get there in time?" I asked Basil—the plane was due the following morning.

"Yes, we going to make it, but late this evening."

Soon, as we walked onwards into the loneliness of the savannah, there were no more houses. The tempering coldness and dullness had disappeared. Convoys of flat-bottomed cumuli rode across the sky, and the sun burnt down on our unaccustomed shoulders. Ahead and behind the landscape was now of stones and yellow grass, rising to low summits on which black rocks sweltered, the slopes tufted with occasional bushes: wild cashews, *Byrsonimas*, and frenzied sandpaper-trees,[1] their crinkled sandpaper-textured leaves glinting gold and green.

From a hill-top, crowned by an outcrop of white quartz crusted with red lichens, I surveyed the scorched, barren country-side. Behind, blue with distance, was the line of forest from which we had come, slowly ascending to the first aerial landmarks of the southern regions: Karawaimen-tau, Bat, and Maroudi mountains. Nearer at hand, and all around as far as the eye could reach to north, east and west, rocks, stones, rubble-piles carpeted the ground, bespeaking centuries of erosion. Only in the vales, where Ité palms followed the water-courses, was there any hint of coolness.

From all I could see there was little difference between soil and climate here and in the forests we had lately left that could not be accounted for by erosion following over-cultivation and repeated burning. It seemed likely that, just as the savannahs are certainly man-enlarged, so for the most part they were originally man-made, at a period when the populations were much larger.

I pulled out my maps, trying to locate myself, but even here they were useless.

Eighty miles to the north was the wall of the Kanuku Mountains, air-bloomed a delicate mauve; more westwards the crags of Mount Shiriri, the Kusad Mountains, and lower hills and mountains, all sacred to the Atorad and Wapisiana Indians as the scenes of incidents in their creation stories—and before them the dwelling-places of the unknown peoples who had carved the petroglyphs on the hill-sides and in the rivers. It was a landscape heavy with the nostalgia of vanished races, almost unchanged since remotest antiquity, and only now beginning to stir. On former journeys I had thought it inexpressibly remote and strange. Now it was like the edge of civilization.

The bullocks were slow, so I walked ahead, till I was far out of sight of them, sometimes leaving the path to examine a tree or gaze round at the view.

[1] *Curatella americana.*

357

I rested at a line of palms, in the shade cast by their great rustling fan-leaves, watching the slow-flowing crystalline water, the muddy hoof-marks at the ford; listening to the sweet plaintive song of a brown bird among the hanging swags of bronze fruit, thinking how much I would love to come back to this country, and to the remote Wai-Wai and Mawayán lands (now, in the openness of the savannah, almost unimaginable)— yet impatient to be gone. A wonderful somnolence was in the air . . . I got up and walked onwards fast.

A few hours, and the path was no longer as distinct as it had been. Each time it had branched I had kept along the broadest trail, and each trail had grown progressively fainter. Now the last branch of all died, dwindling away into the bare ground.

It was growing late. All around the swelling stony ground stretched to the level grey horizon, to the great distances where the clouds hung in profile. I was lost, I suddenly realized.

There was no Lumid Pau, no Karardanawa. The palms marched in their ranks along the moist places, the sandpaper trees writhed their branches on the slopes. Above the northern horizon the blue mountains reared like pale icebergs—eighty miles away. I was heading towards them, into the remotenesses of the savannah, as desolate as those of the forests.

The sun was almost setting, there was no time to lose. I fixed the faint relic of the path with my eye, so that I could pick it up again, and walked from it up a melancholy slope of stones covered with strange little plants like sea anemones,[1] with long cylindrical curved stalks lying flat on their sides, and a tuft of little arms at the tip. Their contorted shapes seemed to squiggle like worms on a sea-shore as I crunched them. At the hill-crest I saw far all around, and nothing to tell me where I was. Panic rose inside me like a balloon. I might find my way in the morning to the last houses, hours back—but I might miss the plane. It was absurd that I should have lost myself. I felt incoherent, helpless.

Returning to the path a sudden feeling of determination came over me. Instead of turning back and trying to pick up a more definite trail, I ran forward resolutely in the direction in

[1] *Bulbostylis capillaceus.*

which I had been going. Reason cried out that, with only about half an hour's daylight left, it was the stupidest thing possible to do—that my path (which anyway I had now left half a mile behind) might have curved away in a misleading direction—that now I *was* losing myself—

But I *could* not be so far wrong.

I cast my mind back to the last definite branching of the trail: the other path had continued westwards—I was certain. I turned, and ran up to the ridge of a smoothly rounded hill, already in a shadow—and there, a mile away, were the men and bullocks. Faintly I could hear the cries of "Mooey! Mooey!" as they urged the cattle forward.

Ahead the sun sank below the horizon.

In the dusk I rejoined them, sauntering nonchalantly, as if I had been merely strolling. It had been outright chance that they had been where I could see them when I reached the hill-top.

Following the white path in the deepening darkness, we reached the airstrip an hour later. There Basil had a strong earthen storeroom with padlocked doors, in which he kept his stores of balata awaiting shipment; and slinging our hammocks in this, we settled down to eat. On the hills all round gleamed solitary stars—fires in Indian houses; and further north, a whole constellation in the distance was Karardanawa.

My mind was far away, in Georgetown, among shops and cinemas, friends, white tablecloths, armchairs, future plans.

"What will you do when you get back?" I asked George, who was sitting beside me near the fire.

"Sir, I shall wait for another job. It was nearly a year since I get one before I hear you wanted somebody. I always goes to the Lands and Mines and waits there."

I pictured him, like so many other Indians and bushmen whom I scarcely glanced at whenever I visited the Government offices there, sitting on the pavement outside or leaning against the pillars. I would try to do something for him when we next met, for he had been a magnificent worker.

"Where do you live?"

"I doesn't have any special home, sir."

"Sir," said Basil, "if you wants to know, that is why I prefers

359

living in the savannah. In the coast it is hard to get a job and keep alive, but here I have my own house and a field I cut for myself. So that even if everything fails I have that to live on."

"You are wise."

"So when I work it is like something extra. It give me a little spare money to use. If it became bad here I really believe I would go into the forest, just like Foimo, and live with the Mawayáns. Anyway, I want to go back, because I have seen where we pass some sandstone, up by Yawarda village, and wherever that is, there may be diamonds. One thing, sir—if I gets some Brazil-nuts there, I will send you a can."

"Basil, that is very kind of you."

Yet already the men's personalities had dissolved; and in the morning, when I walked towards Karardanawa and then between the many mud-and-wattle houses (from which secretive children and people peered), they seemed merely shapes who smiled, whom I had paid wages to, and had shaken hands with, and who now waited for the plane to give me a final wave. I was in an odd suspended state, between one life and the next.

I remembered my last return from an expedition. It had taken me days to recover. My movements, used to the outdoors, had been disproportionately strong—I had blundered about in rooms; I had been rough and domineering, so accustomed had I grown to forcing my way against unwillingness. I had been a formidable creature for a civilized person to encounter. Then gradually the forest ways, the things that had seemed important, the strange ideas that loneliness and silence had bred, had faded away—but never completely. Something had happened. One was made isolated, fierce inside. One would bear the mark throughout one's life.

Swinging in a hammock, my eyes half-closed against the glare, I exchanged irrelevancies, through Basil, with the Captain of the village, who knew no English.

"Father! Father!" cried his little daughter, rushing up and clutching at my knee.

The Captain smiled. Evidently she mistook me for Father McKenna, the Jesuit priest, by reason of my beard.

"I shall have to shave it off," I thought.

Massive, curly, reaching to my chest, it seemed a shame to have to part with it. Perhaps I would trim it smaller and smaller, and then try various moustaches?

The morning wore on, the sky a burning, featureless blue. Irritation and impatience; and then the distant sound, and the plane touched earth at the far end of the airstrip. It trundled round in a half-circle, halted, and a perspex panel was pushed back high up in the nose. The goggled face of the Colonel peered forth:

"Clear that baboon off the runway!"

A moment later he was beside me:

"Nicky, we were getting worried. The papers said you were lost or eaten or something. I was hoping they'd send me down to look for you. You must have been stretching the rations a bit—you look a bit thin under all that grass. Can you eat through it? O.K.—We're expecting you. We want to learn all about it. Tonight about eight o'clock."

Into the fuselage went the bundles of dried plant specimens, of arrows, of feather ornaments, the rolls of hammocks and blankets, the stoves and presses and boxes of equipment. Then, my haversack over one shoulder, the little basket of orchid-bulbs given me by Basil in my hand, I climbed into the plane and strapped myself into one of the familiar metal bucket seats.

Index and Glossary

Abbreviations Used

At.	Atorad
Aw.	Arawak
C.	Creole
M.	Mawayán
Mt., Mts.	Mountain(s)
R.	River
T.	Taruma
Trib.	Tributary
Wap.	Wapisiana
Ww.	Wai-Wai

Index and Glossary

372